Mathematica®
THE STUDENT BOOK

Stephen Wolfram

Adapted by George Beck

W9-CCG-517

Mathematica®
THE STUDENT BOOK

Stephen Wolfram

Adapted by George Beck

 Addison-Wesley Publishing Company

Reading, Massachusetts • Menlo Park, California • New York •
Don Mills, Ontario • Wokingham, England • Amsterdam •
Bonn • Sydney • Singapore • Tokyo • Madrid • San Juan •
Milan • Paris

Library of Congress Cataloging–in–Publication Data

Wolfram, Stephen.
    Mathematica : the student book / Stephen Wolfram, with George Beck.
        p.   cm.
    Adaptation of: Mathematica. 1990.
    Includes bibliographical references and index.
    ISBN 0-201-55479-8
    1. Mathematica (Computer file) 2. Mathematics—Data processing.
  I. Wolfram, Stephen. Mathematica. II. Title.
  QA76.95.B43 1994
  510'.285'53—dc20
                                                           94–10963
                                                                 CIP

For information on *Mathematica*, contact:

Wolfram Research, Inc.
100 Trade Center Drive
Champaign, Illinois 61820-7237, USA
telephone: 217-398-0700
fax: 217-398-0747
email: info@wri.com

6 7 8 9 10-DOC-98979695

About the Author

Stephen Wolfram is president and founder of Wolfram Research, Inc., the company that developed *Mathematica*. Wolfram is the principal architect of the *Mathematica* system, and has been responsible for many parts of its implementation.

Born in London in 1959, Wolfram was educated at Eton, Oxford and Caltech. He received a Ph.D. in theoretical physics from Caltech in 1979. After two years on the faculty at Caltech and four years at the Institute for Advanced Study in Princeton, Wolfram moved to the University of Illinois, where until 1990 he was Director of the Center for Complex Systems Research, and Professor of Physics, Mathematics and Computer Science. Wolfram began the development of *Mathematica* in 1986, and founded Wolfram Research in 1987.

Wolfram's scientific contributions have spanned a number of areas. His early research (1976–1980) was primarily in high-energy physics, quantum field theory and cosmology. In 1980–1981, Wolfram led the development of the SMP computer algebra system, a forerunner of some elements of *Mathematica*. Wolfram received a MacArthur Prize Fellowship in 1981 for his work in physics and computer science.

In 1982, Wolfram started work on the major project of understanding the mechanisms by which complex behavior arises in a wide variety of natural and artificial systems. Wolfram pioneered the use of computational models known as cellular automata to study the origins of complexity in systems whose component parts are simple. His research has found applications in many areas, from physical and biological pattern formation, to chaos theory and massively parallel computation. In 1984, Wolfram invented a fast encryption scheme based on cellular automata, and in 1985, he was co-inventor of a new approach to computational fluid dynamics. Wolfram's work laid an important part of the groundwork for the burgeoning new field of complex systems research. In 1986, Wolfram founded *Complex Systems*, the primary journal in the field.

Wolfram continues his work on the development of *Mathematica*, as well as on the science of complex systems. (A collection of Wolfram's papers on complex systems is published by Addison-Wesley under the title *Cellular Automata and Complexity: Collected Papers*.)

About *Mathematica*

Mathematica is a general software system for technical computation. It is now used on a daily basis by scientists, engineers and analysts around the world, as well as by students at levels from high school to graduate school. The applications of *Mathematica* span all areas of science, technology and business.

Mathematica was first announced on June 23, 1988, and was immediately acclaimed as a major advance in the technology of mathematics, being ranked as one of the best new products of any kind in 1988 by *Business Week* magazine.

Mathematica is available for a wide range of computer systems, including PCs running MS-DOS and Microsoft Windows, Macintosh computers, SPARC workstations and other Unix workstations. *Mathematica* can be obtained directly from Wolfram Research as well as from its network of dealers and distributors worldwide.

This book describes Version 2 of *Mathematica*, first released in 1991. Updated versions of *Mathematica* remain compatible, but include many enhancements and new features. The latest information can be obtained at any time by contacting Wolfram Research.

About the Student Version

Mathematica for Students is a full-function version of *Mathematica*, and includes this book and a user manual written for high school and college students.

The leading tool for computer-based technical education as well as an indispensable aid in research, *Mathematica* is an important part of the curriculum at academic institutions around the world. Priced for the student budget, *Mathematica* for Students lets students take the power of *Mathematica* home with them.

Mathematica for Students is available directly from Wolfram Research, as well as from campus bookstores and software distributors worldwide.

Table of Contents

Interlude 2.

Part 3. The *Mathematica* Language

Interlude 3.

Part 4. Graphics and Sound

Appendix: Summary of *Mathematica*

What Is *Mathematica*?

Mathematica is a general computer software system and language intended for mathematical and other applications.

You can use *Mathematica* as:

- A **numerical** and **symbolic calculator** where you type in questions, and *Mathematica* prints out answers.

- A **visualization system** for functions and data.

- A high-level **programming language** in which you can create programs, large and small.

- A **modeling** and **data analysis** environment.

- A way to create **interactive documents** that mix text, animated graphics and sound with active formulas.

Mathematical computations can be divided into three main classes: **numerical**, **symbolic** and **graphical**. *Mathematica* handles these three classes in a unified way.

Mathematica uses symbolic expressions to provide a very general representation of mathematical and other structures. The generality of symbolic expressions allows *Mathematica* to cover a wide variety of applications with a fairly small number of methods from mathematics and computer science.

The simplest way to use *Mathematica* is like a calculator. You type in a calculation, and *Mathematica* prints back the answer. The range of calculations that you can do with *Mathematica* is however far greater than with a traditional electronic calculator, or, for that matter, with a traditional programming language such as Fortran or BASIC. Thus, for example, while a traditional system might support perhaps 30 mathematical operations, *Mathematica* has over 800 built in. In addition, while traditional systems handle only numerical computations, *Mathematica* also handles symbolic and graphical computations.

Here are some simple examples. Each one consists of a short "dialog" with *Mathematica*. The text on the lines labeled *In[n]* := is what you type in; the lines labeled *Out[n]*= are what *Mathematica* prints back. The "Tour of *Mathematica*" on page 1 gives more examples.

■ Numerical Computation

Whereas a traditional calculator or numerical computation system handles numbers only to fixed degree of precision, *Mathematica* can handle numbers of any precision. In addition, *Mathematica* includes a full range of higher mathematical functions.

Example: Find the numerical value of $\sqrt{3\pi}$.

Sqrt[3 Pi] is the *Mathematica*   `In[1]:= N[ Sqrt[ 3 Pi ] ]`
version of $\sqrt{3\pi}$. The N tells *Mathematica*
that you want a numerical result.   `Out[1]= 3.06998`

Here is $\sqrt{3\pi}$ to 40 decimal places.   `In[2]:= N[ Sqrt[ 3 Pi ], 40 ]`

       `Out[2]= 3.069980123839465465438654874667794582121`

Mathematica can do numerical computations not only with individual numbers, but also with objects such as matrices. It supports linear algebra operations such as matrix inversion and eigensystem computation. *Mathematica* can handle numerical data, allowing you to do statistical and other analysis, as well as performing operations such as Fourier transforms, interpolation and least-square fitting.

Mathematica can do numerical operations on functions, such as numerical integration, numerical minimization, and linear programming. It can also generate numerical solutions to both algebraic equations and ordinary differential equations.

■ Symbolic Computation

One major class of calculations made possible by *Mathematica*'s symbolic computation capabilities is those involving the manipulation of algebraic formulas. *Mathematica* can do many kinds of algebraic operations. It can expand, factor and simplify polynomials and rational expressions. It can find algebraic solutions to polynomial equations and systems of equations.

Example: Factor the polynomial $x^6 - y^6$.

This tells *Mathematica* to factor the   `In[3]:= Factor[x^6 - y^6]`
expression $x^6 - y^6$.

       `Out[3]= (-x + y) (x + y) (-x` ^{2} `+ x y - y` ^{2} `) (x` ^{2} `+ x y + y` ^{2} `)`

Mathematica can also do calculus. It can evaluate derivatives and integrals symbolically and find symbolic solutions to ordinary differential equations. It can derive and manipulate power series approximations, and find limits. Standard *Mathematica* packages cover areas such as vector analysis and Laplace transforms.

Example: Find a formula for the integral $\int x^4/(x^2-1)\, dx$.

Here is the expression $x^4/(x^2-1)$ in *Mathematica*.

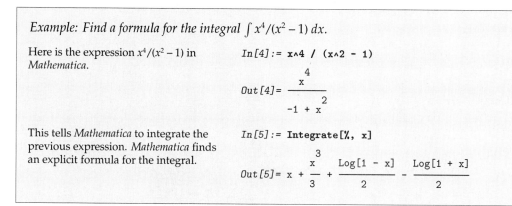

This tells *Mathematica* to integrate the previous expression. *Mathematica* finds an explicit formula for the integral.

■ Graphics

Mathematica produces both two- and three-dimensional graphics, as well as contour and density plots. You can plot both functions and lists of data. *Mathematica* provides many options for controlling the details of graphics output. In three dimensions, for example, you can control shading, color, lighting, surface shininess and other parameters. Most versions of *Mathematica* also support animated graphics.

Example: Plot the function $x(x+1)^2(x-2)^3$ for x between -3 and 3.

This generates a two-dimensional plot of $y = x(x+1)^2(x-2)^3$.
There are many options for controlling graphics in *Mathematica*.

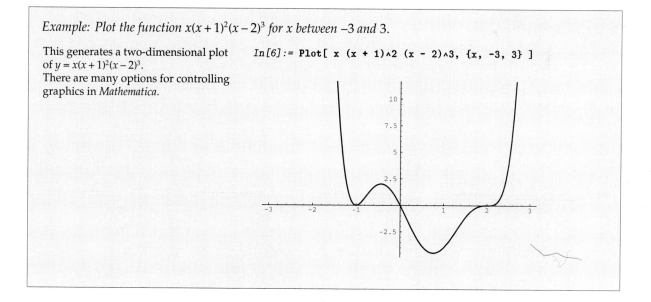

Mathematica incorporates a graphics language, in which you can give symbolic representations of geometrical objects using primitives such as polygons, then render the objects graphically. All graphics produced by *Mathematica* are in standard PostScript, and can be transferred to a wide variety of other programs.

Example: Plot the function sin(*xy*) *for x and y between* 0 *and* π.

This generates a three-dimensional plot of sin(*xy*) as a function of *x* and *y*.

In[7]:= **Plot3D[Sin[x y], {x, 0, Pi}, {y, 0, Pi}]**

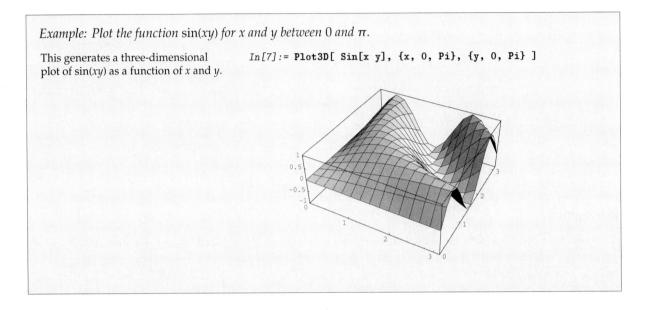

■ The *Mathematica* Language

In addition to having a large number of built-in functions, *Mathematica* also includes a full programming language, which allows you to add your own extensions to the system.

Mathematica is a high-level programming language, in which you can write programs, both large and small. The fact that *Mathematica* is an interactive system means that you can run your programs as soon as you have typed them in.

Example: Define a function to generate a list of primes.

This defines a function f which makes a list of the first *n* prime numbers.

In[8]:= **f[n_] := Table[Prime[i], {i, n}]**

You can immediately ask for the first dozen prime numbers.

In[9]:= **f[12]**

Out[9]= {2, 3, 5, 7, 11, 13, 17, 19, 23, 29, 31, 37}

Mathematica programs can make use of the symbolic aspects of *Mathematica*. They can create and manipulate arbitrary symbolic data structures. *Mathematica* programs themselves are also symbolic expressions, and can be combined and manipulated using standard *Mathematica* operations.

Mathematica supports several programming styles, including:

■ *Procedural programming*, with block structure, conditionals, iteration and recursion.

■ *Functional programming*, with pure functions, functional operators and program-structure operations.

■ *Rule-based programming*, with pattern matching and object orientation.

Fundamental to much of *Mathematica* is the notion of transformation rules, which specify how symbolic expressions of one form should be transformed into expressions of another form. Transformations are a very general and natural way to represent many kinds of information, particularly mathematical relations.

Using transformation rules you can, for example, transcribe almost directly into *Mathematica* the kind of material that appears in tables of mathematical formulas.

Example: Define your own logarithm function in Mathematica.

Mathematical form	Mathematica form
$\log(1) = 0$	`log[1] = 0`
$\log(e) = 1$	`log[E] = 1`
$\log(xy) = \log(x) + \log(y)$	`log[x_ y_] := log[x] + log[y]`
$\log(x^n) = n \log(x)$	`log[x_^n_] := n log[x]`

■ *Mathematica* Interfaces

Many *Mathematica* systems are divided into two parts: the kernel, which actually performs computations, and the front end, which handles interaction with the user. The kernel works the same on all computers that run *Mathematica*. The front end, on the other hand, is optimized for particular computers and graphical user interfaces.

On most computers, the front end for *Mathematica* supports sophisticated interactive documents called *notebooks*. These consist of text arranged in a hierarchical way, together with graphics that can be animated, and *Mathematica* expressions that can be used for actual *Mathematica* computations. With notebooks, you can create pedagogical and other material that both explains and performs computations.

About This Book

■ Features of *Mathematica* Not Described Here

This book is a shorter and simpler version of the book *Mathematica*: *A System for Doing Mathematics by Computer*, Second Edition. The descriptions of functions that are usually not relevant to students have been left out. However, almost all of these undescribed functions are listed in boxes like the one to the right, and you can get on-line help about them by using ? or ??, as discussed in Section 1.4.

■ The Parts of This Book

If at all possible, you should read this book in conjunction with using an actual *Mathematica* system. When you see examples in the book, you should try them out on your computer.

You can get a basic feeling of what *Mathematica* does by looking at the "Tour of *Mathematica*" on page 1. You may find it useful to try out examples from the Tour with your own copy of *Mathematica*.

Whatever your background, you should make sure to look at the first three chapters in Part 1 before you start to use *Mathematica* on your own. These sections describe the basics that you need to know in order to use *Mathematica* at any level.

Parts 1 and 2, Basic Mathematics and More Mathematics, show you how to do many different kinds of computations with *Mathematica*. If you are trying to do a specific calculation, you will often find it sufficient just to look at the sections that discuss the features of *Mathematica* you need to use. A good approach is to try and find examples in the book which are close to what you want to do.

The emphasis in the first two parts is on using the basic functions that are built into *Mathematica* to carry out various different kinds of mathematical computations at the high school and college level.

Part 3, The *Mathematica* Language, on the other hand, discusses the basic structure and principles that underlie all of *Mathematica*. Rather than describing a sequence of specific features, Part 3 takes a more global approach. If you want to learn how to create your own *Mathematica* functions, you should read Part 3.

Part 4, Graphics and Sound, amplifies the graphical capabilities of *Mathematica* and shows you how to produce sound. If you want to customize your graphics, this is where you can learn to control the plotting and drawing functions introduced in Parts 1 and 2.

The Interludes, which follow each of Parts 1, 2, and 3, describe important special topics: lists, packages, statistics, reading and writing files and data, and some others.

The main parts in this book are intended to be pedagogical, and can meaningfully be read in a sequential fashion. The Appendix, however, is intended solely for reference purposes. Once you are familiar with *Mathematica*, you will probably find the list of functions in the Appendix the best place to look up details you need.

◼ About the Examples in This Book

All the examples given in this book were generated by running an actual copy of *Mathematica* Version 2. If you have a copy of this version, you should be able to reproduce the examples on your computer as they appear in the book.

There are, however, a few points to watch:

- Until you are familiar with *Mathematica*, make sure to type the input *exactly* as it appears in the book. Do not change any of the capital letters or brackets. Later, you will learn what things you can change. When you start out, however, it is important that you do not make any changes; otherwise you may not get the same results as in the book.

- Never type the prompt `In[n]:=` that begins each input line. *Mathematica* will do that for you. Type only the text that follows this prompt.

- You will see that the lines in each dialog are numbered in sequence. Most subsections in the book contain separate dialogs. To make sure you get exactly what the book says, you should start a new *Mathematica* session each time the book does.

- Any examples that involve random numbers will generally give different results than in the book, since the sequence of random numbers produced by *Mathematica* is different in every session.

- Some examples that use machine-precision arithmetic may come out differently on different computer systems. This is a result of differences in floating-point hardware. If you use arbitrary-precision *Mathematica* numbers, you should not see differences.

- If the version of *Mathematica* is more recent than the one used to produce this book, then it is possible that some results you get may be different.

◼ Suggestions about Learning *Mathematica*

As with any other computer system, there are a few points that you need to get straight before you can even start using *Mathematica*. For example, you absolutely must know how to type your input to *Mathematica*. To find out these kinds of basic points, you should at least read Chapter 1, Running *Mathematica*, which follows the Tour.

Once you know the basics, you can begin to get a feeling for *Mathematica* by typing in some examples from this book. Always be sure that you type in exactly what appears in the book – do not change any capitalization, bracketing, etc.

After you have tried a few examples from the book, you should start experimenting for yourself. Change the examples slightly, and see what happens. You should look at each piece of output carefully, and try to understand why it came out as it did.

After you have run through some simple examples, you should be ready to take the next step: learning to go through what is needed to solve a complete problem with *Mathematica*.

You will probably find it best to start by picking a specific problem to work on. Pick a problem that you understand well – preferably one whose solution you could easily reproduce by hand. Then go through each step in solving the problem, learning what you need to know about *Mathematica* to do it. Always be ready to experiment with simple cases, and understand the results you get with these, before going back to your original problem.

In going through the steps to solve your problem, you will learn about various specific features of *Mathematica*, typically from parts of Parts 1 and 2. After you have done a few problems with *Mathematica*, you should get a feeling for many of the basic features of the system.

When you have built up a reasonable knowledge of the features of *Mathematica*, you should go back and learn about the overall structure of the *Mathematica* system. You can do this by systematically reading Part 3 of this book. What you will discover is that many of the features that seemed unrelated actually fit together into a coherent overall structure. Knowing this structure will make it much easier for you to understand and remember the specific features you have already learned.

You should not try to learn the overall structure of *Mathematica* too early. Unless you have had broad experience with advanced computer languages or pure mathematics, you will probably find Part 3 difficult to understand at first. You will find the structure and principles it describes difficult to remember, and you will always be wondering why particular aspects of them might be useful. However, if you first get some practical experience with *Mathematica*, you will find the overall structure much easier to grasp. You should realize that the principles on which *Mathematica* is built are very general, and it is usually difficult to understand such general principles before you have seen specific examples.

One of the most important aspects of *Mathematica* is that it applies a fairly small number of principles as widely as possible. This means that even though you have used a particular feature only in a specific situation, the principle on which that feature is based can probably be applied in many other situations. One reason it is so important to understand the underlying principles of *Mathematica* is that by doing so you can leverage your knowledge of specific features into a more general context. As an example, you may first learn about transformation rules in the context of algebraic expressions. But the basic principle of transformation rules applies to any symbolic expression. Thus you can also use such rules to modify the structure of, say, an expression that represents a *Mathematica* graphics object.

Learning to use *Mathematica* well involves changing the way you solve problems. The balance of what aspects of problem solving are difficult changes when you move from pencil and paper to *Mathematica*. With pencil and paper, you can often get by with a fairly imprecise initial formulation of your problem. Then when you actually do calculations in solving the problem, you can usually fix up the formulation as you go along. However, the calculations you do have to be fairly simple, and you cannot afford to try out many different cases.

When you use *Mathematica*, on the other hand, the initial formulation of your problem has to be quite precise. However, once you have the formulation, you can easily do many different calculations with it. This means that you can effectively carry out many mathematical experiments on your problem. By looking at the results you get, you can then refine the original formulation of your problem.

There are typically many different ways to formulate a given problem in *Mathematica*. In almost all cases, however, the most direct and simple formulations will be best. The more you can formulate your problem in *Mathematica* from the beginning, the better. Often, in fact, you will find that formulating your problem directly in *Mathematica* is better than first trying to set up a traditional mathematical formulation, say an algebraic one. The main point is that *Mathematica* allows you to express not only traditional mathematical operations, but also algorithmic and structural ones. This greater range of possibilities gives you a better chance of being able to find a direct way to represent your original problem.

For most of the more sophisticated problems that you want to solve with *Mathematica*, you will have to create *Mathematica* programs. *Mathematica* supports several types of programming, and you have to choose which one to use in each case. It turns out that no single type of programming suits all cases well. As a result, it is very important that you learn several different types of programming.

If you already know a traditional programming language such as BASIC, C, Fortran or Pascal, you will probably find it easiest to learn procedural programming in *Mathematica*, using Do, For and so on. But while almost any *Mathematica* program can, in principle, be written in a procedural way, this is rarely the best approach. In a symbolic system like *Mathematica*, functional and rule-based programming typically yield programs that are more efficient, and easier to understand.

If you find yourself using procedural programming a lot, you should make an active effort to convert at least some of your programs to other types. At first, you may find functional and rule-based programs difficult to understand. But after a while, you will find that their global structure is usually much easier to grasp than procedural programs. And as your experience with *Mathematica* grows over a period of months or years, you will probably find that you write more and more of your programs in non-procedural ways.

As you proceed in using and learning *Mathematica*, it is important to remember that *Mathematica* is a large system. Although after a while you should know all of its basic principles, you may never learn the details of all its features. As a result, even after you have had a great deal of experience with *Mathematica*, you will undoubtedly still find it useful to look through this book. When you do so, you are quite likely to notice features that you never noticed before, but that with your experience, you can now see how to use.

Tour of
Mathematica

Numerical Calculations

You can do arithmetic with *Mathematica* just as you would on a calculator. You type the input 5 + 7; *Mathematica* prints the result 12.

```
In[1]:= 5 + 7
Out[1]= 12
```

Unlike a calculator, however, *Mathematica* can give you *exact* results. Here is the exact result for 3^{100}. The ∧ is the *Mathematica* notation for raising to a power.

```
In[2]:= 3 ∧ 100
Out[2]= 515377520732011331036461129765621272702107522001
```

You can use the *Mathematica* function N to get *approximate* numerical results. The % stands for the last result. The answer is given in scientific notation.

```
In[3]:= N[%]
                 47
Out[3]= 5.15378 10
```

You can find numerical results to any degree of precision. This calculates $\sqrt{10}$ to 50 digits of precision.

```
In[4]:= N[ Sqrt[10], 50 ]
Out[4]= 3.1622776601683793319988935444327185337195551393252
```

Mathematica can evaluate all standard mathematical functions. Here is the value of the cosine function at 2.5.

```
In[5]:= Cos[2.5]
Out[5]= -0.801144
```

Here is a root of $\sin(2^x)$ near $x = 2$.

```
In[6]:= FindRoot[Sin[ 2∧x ], {x, 2}]
Out[6]= {x -> 1.6515}
```

You can calculate mathematical functions to any precision. This gives $\log_{10}(13)$ to 40 digits.

```
In[7]:= N[ Log[10, 13], 40 ]
Out[7]= 1.113943352306836769206505157942328430829  7
```

Mathematica can do many kinds of exact computations with integers. The integer 70612139395722186 factors as $2^1\, 3^2\, 43^5\, 26684839^1$.

```
In[8]:= FactorInteger[ 70612139395722186 ]
Out[8]= {{2, 1}, {3, 2}, {43, 5}, {26684839, 1}}
```

Mathematica can also handle complex numbers. Here is $(3+4i)^{10}$. In *Mathematica*, I stands for the imaginary number $\sqrt{-1}$.

```
In[9]:= (3 + 4 I) ∧ 10
Out[9]= -9653287 + 1476984 I
```

You can find a local minimum of $\sin(2^x)$ near $x = 2$. The function has a minimum, given by the first number, when x takes the value to the right of the arrow.

```
In[10]:= FindMinimum[Sin[ 2∧x ], {x, 2}]
Out[10]= {-1., {x -> 2.23646}}
```

You can do numerical integrals. Here is the numerical value of $\int_0^\pi \sin(\sin(x))dx$.

```
In[11]:= NIntegrate[ Sin[Sin[x]], {x, 0, Pi} ]
Out[11]= 1.78649
```

Graphics

Here is a plot of the function sin(2^x), with x ranging from 0 to π.

```
In[1]:= Plot[ Sin[ 2^x ], {x, 0, Pi} ]
```

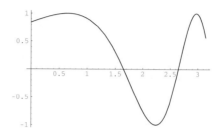

Mathematica provides many options that you can set to determine exactly how your plots will look.

```
In[2]:= Show[ %, Frame -> True,
              FrameLabel -> {"Time", "Signal"},
              GridLines -> Automatic ]
```

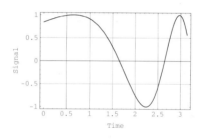

Here is a three-dimensional surface plot of a function of two variables.

```
In[3]:= Plot3D[ Sin[x + Sin[y]], {x, -3, 3}, {y, -3, 3} ]
```

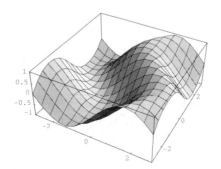

This generates a three-dimensional parametric surface. The x, y and z coordinates of points on the surface are specified as a function of the parameters t and u. The space in u Sin[t] denotes multiplication.

In[4]:= `ParametricPlot3D[ {u Sin[t], u Cos[t], t/3},`
`{t, 0, 15}, {u, -1, 1}, Ticks -> None ]`

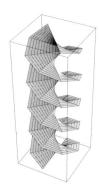

Here is a more complicated parametric surface.

In[5]:= `ParametricPlot3D[`
`{Sin[t], Sin[2t] Sin[u], Sin[2t] Cos[u]},`
`{t, -Pi/2, Pi/2}, {u, 0, 2 Pi}, Ticks -> None ]`

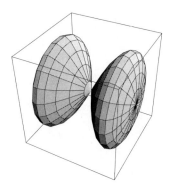

Mathematica allows you to combine different pieces of graphics together. The % stands for the last result; the %% for the result before that.

In[6]:= **Show[%, %%]**

Mathematica serves as a graphics language in which you can build up graphics from components. In this case, a three-dimensional graphic is built up from a collection of cubes placed at different points.

In[7]:= **Show[Graphics3D[**
     {Cuboid[{0, 0, 0}], Cuboid[{2, 2, 2}],
     Cuboid[{2, 1, 3}], Cuboid[{3, 2, 1}],
     Cuboid[{2, 1, 1}]}]]

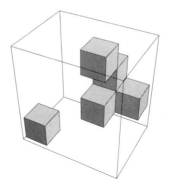

On computer systems with sound output, this generates an 8-second long sound with the specified amplitude as a function of time.

In[8]:= **Play[Sin[10000 / t], {t, -4, 4}]**

Out[8]= -Sound-

Algebra

Mathematica can work not only with numbers, but also with algebraic formulas.

$In[1]:=$ **(9 c x + 7 c y + 7 d x + 8 d y) + (6 c x + 5 c y + 3 d x)**

$Out[1]=$ 15 c x + 10 d x + 12 c y + 8 d y

Mathematica factors the expression as a product of linear terms.

$In[2]:=$ **Factor[%]**

$Out[2]=$ (3 c + 2 d) (5 x + 4 y)

Here is the formula $9(2+x)(x+y)+(x+y)^2$.

$In[3]:=$ **9 (2 + x) (x + y) + (x + y)^2**

$Out[3]=$ 9 (2 + x) (x + y) + (x + y)^2

This takes the previous expression, represented by %, raises it to the third power, and expands out products and powers. The result is fairly complicated.

$In[4]:=$ **Expand[%^3]**

$Out[4]=$ 5832 x^3 + 9720 x^4 + 5400 x^5 + 1000 x^6 + 17496 x^2 y +

30132 x^3 y + 17280 x^4 y + 3300 x^5 y + 17496 x y^2 +

32076 x^2 y^2 + 19494 x^3 y^2 + 3930 x^4 y^2 + 5832 y^3 +

12636 x y^3 + 8802 x^2 y^3 + 1991 x^3 y^3 + 972 y^4 + 1242 x y^4 +

393 x^2 y^4 + 54 y^5 + 33 x y^5 + y^6

Factoring this expression yields a much simpler form.

$In[5]:=$ **Factor[%]**

$Out[5]=$ (x + y)^3 (18 + 10 x + y)^3

This is a sum of rational functions.

$In[6]:=$ **2 x / 3 + 2 / (x - 1) - 1 / (x - 2)**

$Out[6]=$ $-(\dfrac{1}{-2 + x}) + \dfrac{2}{-1 + x} + \dfrac{2 x}{3}$

You can put them over a common denominator.

$In[7]:=$ **Together[%]**

$Out[7]=$ $\dfrac{-9 + 7 x - 6 x^2 + 2 x^3}{3 (-2 + x) (-1 + x)}$

Going the other way, you break up a rational function into a sum of fractions with simple denominators.

$In[8]:=$ **Apart[1 / (8 + 14 x + 7 x^2 + x^3)]**

$Out[8]=$ $\dfrac{1}{3 (1 + x)} - \dfrac{1}{2 (2 + x)} + \dfrac{1}{6 (4 + x)}$

Dividing $3x^3 - 5x^2 + 2x - 5$ by $x + 3$ gives this quotient and remainder.

$In[9]:=$ **PolynomialDivision[3 x^3 - 5 x^2 + 2 x - 5, x + 3, x]**

$Out[9]=$ {44 - 14 x + 3 x^2, -137}

Calculus

Mathematica can do calculus as well as algebra. Here is the derivative of tan(x^2).

$In[1]:=$ **D[Tan[x ^ 2], x]**

$Out[1]=$ 2 x Sec[x^2]^2

This is the second derivative.

$In[2]:=$ **D[Tan[x ^ 2], {x, 2}]**

$Out[2]=$ 2 Sec[x^2]^2 + 8 x^2 Sec[x^2]^2 Tan[x^2]

This shows the tangent at $x = 2$ to the curve $y = x^3$.

$In[3]:=$ **Plot[{x^3, 12 (x - 2) + 8}, {x,-4, 4}]**

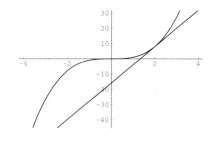

Mathematica can evaluate the limits of many functions.

$In[4]:=$ **Limit[(1 + 2 / n) ^ n, n -> Infinity]**

$Out[4]=$ E^2

Here is an easy integral.

$In[5]:=$ **Integrate[Tan[x], x]**

$Out[5]=$ -Log[Cos[x]]

The integral of $x^2 \sin(x)^2$ is a little harder.

$In[6]:=$ **Integrate[x^2 Sin[x]^2, x]**

$$Out[6]= \frac{4 x^3 - 6 x \cos[2 x] + 3 \sin[2 x] - 6 x^2 \sin[2 x]}{24}$$

Differentiating the result gives the original integrand, but in a somewhat different form.

$In[7]:=$ **D[%, x]**

$$Out[7]= \frac{12 x^2 - 12 x^2 \cos[2 x]}{24}$$

The *Mathematica* function Simplify uses algebraic and trigonometric identities to simplify the expression, in this case recovering the original form.

$In[8]:=$ **Simplify[%]**

$Out[8]=$ x^2 Sin[x]^2

This finds the power-series expansion of the previous result about the point $x = 0$.

$In[9]:=$ **Series[%, {x, 0, 14}]**

$$Out[9]= x^4 - \frac{x^6}{3} + \frac{2 x^8}{45} - \frac{x^{10}}{315} + \frac{2 x^{12}}{14175} - \frac{2 x^{14}}{467775} + O[x]^{15}$$

Solving Equations

Here is the quadratic equation $x^2 - 7x + 3a = 0$ in *Mathematica*.

```
In[1]:= x^2 - 7 x + 3 a == 0

                  2
Out[1]= 3 a - 7 x + x  == 0
```

This solves the equation on the previous line, represented by %. The two solutions are given in terms of the parameter *a*.

```
In[2]:= Solve[ %, x ]

              7 - Sqrt[49 - 12 a]            7 + Sqrt[49 - 12 a]
Out[2]= {{x ->  -------------------}, {x ->  -------------------}}
                        2                             2
```

Here is the solution to a simple set of simultaneous equations.

```
In[3]:= Solve[ { a x + b y == 0, x + y == c } , {x, y} ]

                   a c            a c
Out[3]= {{x -> c + -----, y -> -(-----)}}
                  -a + b         -a + b
```

NSolve finds numerically the 5 complex solutions to this fifth-order algebraic equation.

```
In[4]:= NSolve[ x^5 + 2 x + 1 == 0, x ]

Out[4]= {{x -> -0.701874 - 0.879697 I},

    {x -> -0.701874 + 0.879697 I}, {x -> -0.486389},

    {x -> 0.945068 - 0.854518 I}, {x -> 0.945068 + 0.854518 I}}
```

FindRoot allows you to solve transcendental equations numerically. This gives the solution to a pair of simultaneous equations near $x = 1, y = 0$.

```
In[5]:= FindRoot[ { Sin[x] == x - y, Cos[y] == x + y },
                                        {x, 1}, {y, 0} ]

Out[5]= {x -> 0.883401, y -> 0.1105}
```

Mathematica can also solve differential equations. Here is the closed-form solution for $y''(x) - ky(x) = 1$.

```
In[6]:= DSolve[y''[x] - k y[x] == 1, y[x], x]

                  1     C[1]        Sqrt[k] x
Out[6]= {{y[x] -> -(-) + --------- + E          C[2]}}
                  k     Sqrt[k] x
                       E
```

NDSolve finds numerical solutions to differential equations. This solves for the function *y* with *x* in the range 0 to 20.

```
In[7]:= NDSolve[ { y''[x] + Sin[x]^2 y'[x] + y[x] == Cos[x]^2 ,
                   y[0] == 1, y'[0] == 0 }, y, {x, 0, 20} ]

Out[7]= {{y -> InterpolatingFunction[{0., 20.}, <>]}}
```

This takes the solution found by NDSolve, and plots it as a function of *x*. The solution is given as an "interpolating function", which allows values of $y(x)$ to be found when specific values of *x* are supplied.

```
In[8]:= Plot[ Evaluate[ y[x] /. % ], {x, 0, 20} ]
```

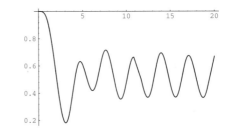

Lists

This makes a list of the first 15 factorials.

```
In[1]:= Table[ n!, {n, 1, 15} ]
Out[1]= {1, 2, 6, 24, 120, 720, 5040, 40320, 362880, 3628800,
         39916800, 479001600, 6227020800, 87178291200, 1307674368000}
```

This takes the logarithm of each entry in the list, and evaluates the result numerically. Functions like Log have the property of being "listable", so that they apply separately to each element in a list.

```
In[2]:= N[ Log[ % ] ]
Out[2]= {0, 0.693147, 1.79176, 3.17805, 4.78749, 6.57925,
         8.52516, 10.6046, 12.8018, 15.1044, 17.5023, 19.9872,
         22.5522, 25.1912, 27.8993}
```

Here is a plot of the entries in the list.

```
In[3]:= ListPlot[ % ]
```

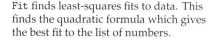

Fit finds least-squares fits to data. This finds the quadratic formula which gives the best fit to the list of numbers.

```
In[4]:= Fit[ %2, {1, x, x^2}, x ]
Out[4]= -1.48508 + 0.963131 x + 0.06766 x²
```

This creates a two-dimensional array in which the i, j element is 0 or 1 according to whether or not the greatest common divisor of i and j is equal to 1. Ending with a semicolon stops *Mathematica* from printing the rather large array.

```
In[5]:= coprimes = Table[ If[GCD[i, j] == 1, 1, 0],
                          {i, 30}, {j, 30} ] ;
```

This makes a plot of the array.

```
In[6]:= ListDensityPlot[coprimes]
```

Vectors and Matrices

Mathematica represents a vector as a list.

```
In[1]:= v = {a, b, c}
Out[1]= {a, b, c}
```

You can add two vectors together term by term.

```
In[2]:= v + {-1, 0, 1}
Out[2]= {-1 + a, b, 1 + c}
```

You can also multiply a vector by a number.

```
In[3]:= 10 v
Out[3]= {10 a, 10 b, 10 c}
```

This is the dot product of two vectors.

```
In[4]:= v . {x, y, z}
Out[4]= a x + b y + c z
```

This generates a matrix whose i, j^{th} element is $1/(i + j + 1)$. *Mathematica* represents the matrix as a list of lists.

```
In[5]:= m = Table[ 1 / (i + j + 1), {i, 3}, {j, 3} ]
```
$$Out[5]= \{\{\frac{1}{3}, \frac{1}{4}, \frac{1}{5}\}, \{\frac{1}{4}, \frac{1}{5}, \frac{1}{6}\}, \{\frac{1}{5}, \frac{1}{6}, \frac{1}{7}\}\}$$

The matrix can also be shown as a two-dimensional array.

```
In[6]:= MatrixForm[ % ]
```
$$Out[6]//MatrixForm= \begin{pmatrix} \frac{1}{3} & \frac{1}{4} & \frac{1}{5} \\ \frac{1}{4} & \frac{1}{5} & \frac{1}{6} \\ \frac{1}{5} & \frac{1}{6} & \frac{1}{7} \end{pmatrix}$$

This is the product of the matrix m and v, treated here as a column vector.

```
In[7]:= m . v
```
$$Out[7]= \{\frac{a}{3} + \frac{b}{4} + \frac{c}{5}, \frac{a}{4} + \frac{b}{5} + \frac{c}{6}, \frac{a}{5} + \frac{b}{6} + \frac{c}{7}\}$$

Here is the inverse of the matrix.

```
In[8]:= Inverse[ m ]
Out[8]= {{300, -900, 630}, {-900, 2880, -2100},
    {630, -2100, 1575}}
```

Multiplying the inverse by the original matrix gives the 3×3 identity matrix.

```
In[9]:= % . m
Out[9]= {{1, 0, 0}, {0, 1, 0}, {0, 0, 1}}
```

Mathematica can also manipulate symbolic matrices. This finds the eigenvectors of a matrix.

```
In[10]:= Eigenvectors[ {{a, b}, {-b, 2a}} ]
```
$$Out[10]= \{\{\frac{a + Sqrt[a^2 - 4 b^2]}{2 b}, 1\}, \{\frac{a - Sqrt[a^2 - 4 b^2]}{2 b}, 1\}\}$$

Transformation Rules and Definitions

The notation "/." tells *Mathematica* to use the rule x → 1 + a on the algebraic expression $1 + x^2 + 3x^3$.

```
In[1]:= 1 + x^2 + 3 x^3  /.  x -> 1 + a
                 2          3
Out[1]= 1 + (1 + a) + 3 (1 + a)
```

You can give transformation rules for any expression. This uses a rule for f[2].

```
In[2]:= {f[1], f[2], f[3]}  /.  f[2] -> b
Out[2]= {f[1], b, f[3]}
```

This replaces f[*anything*], where *anything* is named n, by n^2.

```
In[3]:= {f[1], f[2], f[3]}  /.  f[n_] -> n^2
Out[3]= {1, 4, 9}
```

Here is a *Mathematica* function definition. It specifies that f[*n*] is *always* to be transformed to *n*^2.

```
In[4]:= f[n_] := n^2
```

The definition for f is automatically used whenever it applies.

```
In[5]:= f[3] + f[a + b]
                     2
Out[5]= 9 + (a + b)
```

Here is the recursive rule for the factorial function.

```
In[6]:= fac[n_] := n fac[n-1]
```

This gives a rule for the end condition of the factorial function.

```
In[7]:= fac[1] := 1
```

Here are the two rules you have defined for fac.

```
In[8]:= ?fac
Global`fac
fac[1] := 1
fac[n_] := n*fac[n - 1]
```

Mathematica can now apply these rules to find values for factorials.

```
In[8]:= fac[20]
Out[8]= 2432902008176640000
```

Mathematica lets you give rules for transforming any expression. This defines ln of a product to be a sum of ln functions.

```
In[9]:= ln[x_ y_] := ln[x] + ln[y]
```

Mathematica uses the definition you have given to expand out this expression.

```
In[10]:= ln[a b c d]
Out[10]= ln[a] + ln[b] + ln[c] + ln[d]
```

You can add a rule for each property of the function.

```
In[11]:= ln[x_ ^ a_] := a ln[x]
```

Now the rules for ln apply to a greater variety of expressions.

```
In[12]:= ln[a^2 b^3]
Out[12]= 2 ln[a] + 3 ln[b]
```

Advanced Topic: Symbolic Computation

Here are the 6 possible ways of arranging the elements a, b and c in a row.

```
In[1]:= Permutations[{a, b, c}]
Out[1]= {{a, b, c}, {a, c, b}, {b, a, c}, {b, c, a}, {c, a, b},
   {c, b, a}}
```

Flatten "unravels" lists.

```
In[2]:= Flatten[ % ]
Out[2]= {a, b, c, a, c, b, b, a, c, b, c, a, c, a, b, c, b, a}
```

This gives the positions at which b appears in the list.

```
In[3]:= Position[ %, b ]
Out[3]= {{2}, {6}, {7}, {10}, {15}, {17}}
```

Here are cumulative products of the positions: $1, 1 \times 2, 1 \times 2 \times 6, \ldots$.

```
In[4]:= FoldList[Times, {1}, %]
Out[4]= {{1}, {2}, {12}, {84}, {840}, {12600}, {214200}}
```

This produces a list of successively nested cosine functions.

```
In[5]:= NestList[ Cos, x, 3 ]
Out[5]= {x, Cos[x], Cos[Cos[x]], Cos[Cos[Cos[x]]]}
```

Here are plots of the nested cosine functions. The curves meet at the point where $\cos(x) = x$.

```
In[6]:= Plot[ Evaluate[%], {x, 0, 1} ]
```

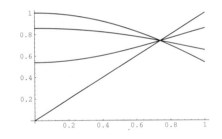

The Map operator allows you to "wrap" a function around each element in a list.

```
In[7]:= Map[f, {a, b, c, d}]
Out[7]= {f[a], f[b], f[c], f[d]}
```

Here is a matrix of a special form.

```
In[8]:= m = IdentityMatrix[6]; a m + b Map[Reverse, m] //
   MatrixForm
```

$$
Out[8]//MatrixForm=
\begin{matrix}
a & 0 & 0 & 0 & 0 & b \\
0 & a & 0 & 0 & b & 0 \\
0 & 0 & a & b & 0 & 0 \\
0 & 0 & b & a & 0 & 0 \\
0 & b & 0 & 0 & a & 0 \\
b & 0 & 0 & 0 & 0 & a
\end{matrix}
$$

This is its determinant.

```
In[9]:= Factor[Det[%]]
```

$$Out[9]= (a - b)^3 (a + b)^3$$

Programming

Here is a simple *Mathematica* program which generates an $n \times n$ Hilbert matrix.

```
Hilbert[n_] := Table[1/(i + j - 1), {i, n}, {j, n}]
```

This generates a circulant matrix. The entries in each row are the entries of the row before shifted right by one place; the last entry is moved to the beginning.

```
Circulant[v_List] := NestList[RotateRight, v, Length[v] - 1]
```

This program finds the characteristic polynomial for a matrix. The /; clause at the end checks that m is indeed a matrix.

```
CharPoly[m_, x_] :=
        Det[m - x IdentityMatrix[Length[m]]] /; MatrixQ[m]
```

Here is a procedural program in *Mathematica* for finding the next prime after a given integer. The pattern n_Integer matches only integers.

```
NextPrime[n_Integer] :=
        Module[{k = n}, While[!PrimeQ[k], k = k + 1]; k]
```

You can often avoid using loops in *Mathematica* by operating directly on complete lists. The resulting programs are usually more elegant and more efficient. Here are programs for computing the mean, variance and quantiles of a list.

```
Mean[list_List] := Apply[Plus, list] / Length[list]

Variance[list_List] := Mean[ (list - Mean[list])^2 ]

Quantile[list_List, q_] :=
    Part[ Sort[list], -Floor[-q Length[list]] ] /; 0 < q < 1
```

This function takes a list of random numbers in the interval from 0 to 1, and forms a succession of cumulative sums, thereby producing a sequence of points in a one-dimensional random walk.

```
RandomWalk[n_Integer] :=
        FoldList[Plus, 0, Table[Random[ ] - 1/2, {n}]]
```

Here is an elegant program, written in a functional programming style, which finds the first n terms in the continued fraction decomposition of a number x.

```
ContinuedFraction[x_Real, n_Integer] :=
 Floor[ NestList [ Function[{u}, 1/(u - Floor[u])], x, n - 1 ] ]
```

Mathematica programs can create graphics. This program makes polar plots.

```
PolarPlot[r_, {t_, tmin_, tmax_}] :=
        ParametricPlot[{r Cos[t], r Sin[t]}, {t, tmin, tmax},
                                  AspectRatio -> Automatic]
```

Here is a program which plots the solutions to a polynomial equation as points in the complex plane.

```
RootPlot[poly_, z_] :=
        ListPlot[{Re[z], Im[z]} /. NSolve[poly == 0, z]] /;
                                  PolynomialQ[poly, z]
```

Mathematica Packages

This loads a package that contains data on the chemical elements.

```
In[1]:= <<Miscellaneous`ChemicalElements`
```

This finds the atomic weight of tungsten from the data in the package.

```
In[2]:= AtomicWeight[Tungsten]
Out[2]= 183.85
```

If you ask for the atomic weight of an unstable element, *Mathematica* prints a warning message.

```
In[3]:= AtomicWeight[Plutonium]
AtomicWeight::unstable: No stable isotope of Plutonium exists.
Out[3]= 244
```

This switches off the warning message.

```
In[4]:= Off[AtomicWeight::unstable]
```

This plots the ratio of atomic weight to atomic number for all the elements.

```
In[5]:= ListPlot[ AtomicWeight[Elements] /
            AtomicNumber[Elements], PlotJoined -> True ]
```

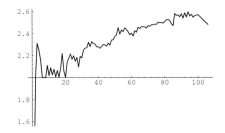

This loads a package which defines the geometry of various polyhedra.

```
In[6]:= <<Graphics`Polyhedra`
```

This generates a picture of the so-called "great icosahedron".

```
In[7]:= Show[ Polyhedron[GreatIcosahedron] ]
```

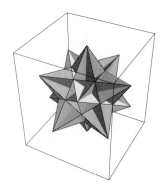

Front Ends and Notebooks

On most computer systems, there is a "front end" for *Mathematica* which allows you to take advantage of graphical user interface features.

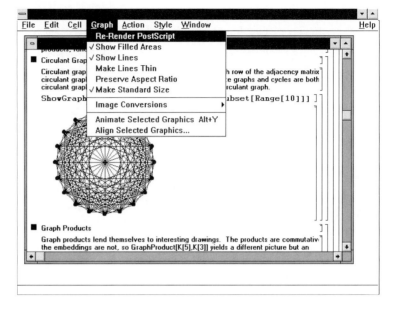

The *Mathematica* front end supports "notebooks", in which you can mix text, animated graphics, and actual *Mathematica* input.

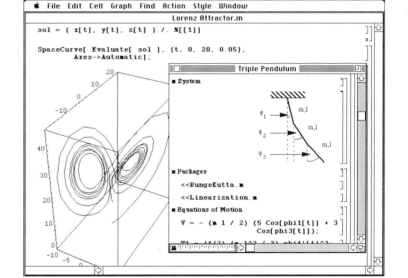

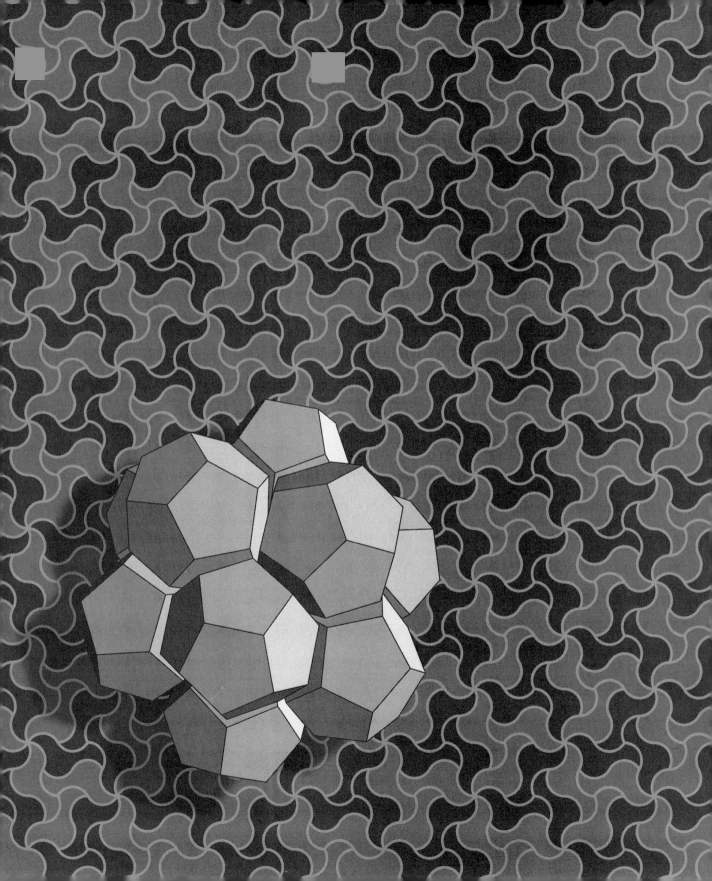

Part 1.   **Basic Calculations**

1. Running *Mathematica*

To find out how to install and run *Mathematica* you should read the documentation that came with your copy of *Mathematica*. The details differ from one computer system to another, and are affected by various kinds of customization that can be done on *Mathematica*.

Note that although the details of running *Mathematica* differ from one computer system to another, the structure of *Mathematica* calculations is the same in all cases. You enter input, then *Mathematica* processes it, and returns a result.

■ 1.1 Notebooks

Mathematica is built to be both exactly the same and yet quite different on different computer systems. It is exactly the same in the sense that the input you give and the output you get are the same. It is different in that the ways you give input and get output are typically customized to your particular kind of computer system.

On certain computers with graphical user interfaces, *Mathematica* supports a special "notebook" interface. Notebooks are interactive documents, into which you can insert *Mathematica* input as well as ordinary text and graphics. You typically interact with notebooks not only by typing text, but also by using a pointing device such as a mouse to indicate actions or choices graphically.

The fundamental computational part of *Mathematica* is called the *kernel*. Most of what is in this book is concerned with the operation of the kernel. The kernel is set up to work the same on all computers that run *Mathematica*. When you use *Mathematica* with a text-based interface, you are interacting almost directly with the kernel. But it is also possible to have a *front end* which lies between you and the *Mathematica* kernel. The front end is usually a separate program which handles various aspects of user interaction. Front ends typically allow you to prepare input in various ways, then send the input to the kernel, and then get results back for display. The notebook interface for *Mathematica* is an example of a *Mathematica* front end.

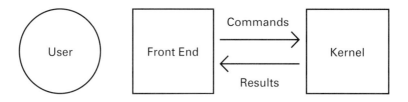

The notebook interface is currently a standard type of *Mathematica* front end, although it is by no means the only possible type. It is intended to provide easy and fairly direct access to all of the capabilities of the *Mathematica* kernel. There are other front ends for other purposes. Some front ends, for example, are active programs in their own right, which access *Mathematica* only for specific calculations, often in a way that is hidden from the user.

Notebooks consist of a hierarchy of cells. Each cell contains a particular kind of material: text, graphics, *Mathematica* input or output, and so on. Sequences of cells can be arranged in groups representing related material. A group of cells might, for example, correspond to a section or chapter in your document.

Notebooks consist of cells, which can be arranged hierarchically in groups. Notebook interfaces support many styles of text, allowing you to produce typographically complex documents.

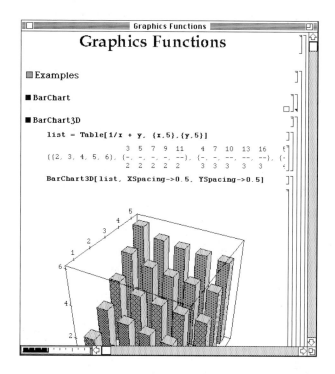

An important feature of notebook interfaces is that they allow you to manipulate your document at several levels. At the lowest level, you can modify text or other material within a single cell. At a higher level, you can do the same kinds of operations on a whole cell at a time. And beyond that, you can manipulate whole groups of cells.

Notebook interfaces can typically take advantage of the typographical capabilities of your computer system's graphical user interface. Thus, for example, cells containing text can have a variety of "styles". The styles can involve various fonts, sizes, and so on. In addition, even within a single cell, you can often mix several styles, allowing you to produce typographically complex text.

The extent of each cell in a notebook is typically indicated by a bracket to its right. When you have a group of cells, another bracket shows the extent of the group. By looking at these brackets, you can see how a particular notebook is organized.

When a group of cells corresponds to a section or chapter of your document, the first cell in the group typically gives some kind of heading for the section or chapter. Notebook interfaces allow you to "close" groups of cells so that only their first cells are visible. If the first cells contain headings, you can get an outline of your document in this way.

Double-clicking the bracket that spans a group of cells closes the group, leaving only the first cell visible.

```
┌──────────────────────── Untitled-1 ────────────────────┐
│ ■ Section Heading I                               ]  │
│                                                      │
│ ■ subsection A                                    ]  │
│                                                      │
│ □ sub-subsection 1                                ]  │
│                                                  ■ ] │
│ □ sub-subsection 2                                ]  │
│                                                      │
│ ■ subsection B                                    ]  │
│                                                      │
│ ■ subsection C                                    ]] │
│                                                      │
└──────────────────────────────────────────────────────┘
```

When a group is closed, the bracket for it has an arrow at the bottom. Double-clicking this arrow opens the group again.

```
┌──────────────────────── Untitled-1 ────────────────────┐
│ ■ Section Heading I                               ]  │
│                                                      │
│ ■ subsection A                                    ]  │
│                                                  ■ ] │
│ ■ subsection B                                    ]  │
│                                                      │
│ ■ subsection C                                    ]] │
│                                                      │
└──────────────────────────────────────────────────────┘
```

Notebook interfaces typically provide many options for displaying and importing graphics. One important feature is that you can take sequences of graphics cells, and "animate" them, treating each cell like a frame in a movie. The notebook interface typically allows you to set various parameters, such as speed and direction of your "movie".

■ 1.2 Starting and Quitting

double-click the *Mathematica* icon	the typical action for starting *Mathematica*
text SHIFT-RETURN	input for *Mathematica*
choose the **Quit** menu item	exiting *Mathematica*

Running *Mathematica* with a notebook interface.

To start *Mathematica* on a system with a"notebook" interface, you typically double-click the *Mathematica* icon.

When *Mathematica* starts up, it usually gives you a blank notebook. You enter *Mathematica* input into the notebook, then press SHIFT-RETURN (or certain other keys) to make *Mathematica* process your input. You can use the standard editing features of your graphical interface to prepare your input, which may go on for several lines. SHIFT-RETURN (or certain other keys) tells *Mathematica* that you have finished your input.

After you send input from your notebook to *Mathematica*, *Mathematica* will label your input with *In[n]:=*. It labels the corresponding output *Out[n]=*.

You type 2 + 2, then end your input with SHIFT-RETURN. *Mathematica* processes the input, then adds the input label *In[1]:=*, and gives the output.

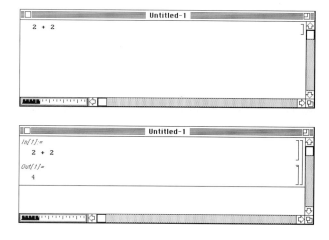

Throughout this book, "dialogs" with *Mathematica* are shown in the following way:

With a notebook interface, you just type in 2 + 2. *Mathematica* then adds the label *In[1]:=*, and prints the result.

In[1]:= 2 + 2

Out[1]= 4

Page xvii discusses some important details about reproducing the dialogs on your computer system. The following sections give more information on notebook interfaces to *Mathematica*.

You should realize that notebook interfaces are part of the "front end" for *Mathematica*. The kernel is not even started until you actually do a calculation with *Mathematica*.

To exit *Mathematica*, you typically choose the **Quit** menu item in the notebook interface.

■ 1.3 Entering Input

In a notebook interface, your *Mathematica* input and output appear as elements in the notebook document, potentially mixed with text and graphics. A complete notebook can look much like this book. It can contain specific pieces of *Mathematica* input and output, analogous to the dialogs in this book, together with explanatory text, graphics, and so on.

All the material in a notebook is organized into a sequence of *cells*. Each cell contains text or other material that is to be treated as some kind of unit. Thus, for example, each complete piece of *Mathematica* input occupies its own cell. When you evaluate the input, *Mathematica* automatically generates a new cell to be used for the output.

Within a particular cell, you can typically use any of the standard positioning and editing capabilities of the graphical user interface for your computer system. A piece of *Mathematica* input within a single cell may go on for several lines. Thus, for example, pressing the Return key when you are typing input into a particular cell simply goes to the next line in the cell. It does not tell the *Mathematica* front end that you have finished giving input in that cell.

In most notebook interfaces, you tell *Mathematica* that you have finished preparing input for it in a particular cell by pressing SHIFT-RETURN or ENTER. When you do this, all the text in your current cell is given as input to the *Mathematica* kernel.

■ Press SHIFT-RETURN or ENTER to send input to *Mathematica*.

Terminating your input with a notebook interface.

Mathematica requires that the input you give follow a definite syntax. Input like 4 +/ 5 does not follow the syntax, and cannot be processed by *Mathematica*. If you give input like this, *Mathematica* will reject it. Typically it will make your computer beep, then put you at the point in your current input cell where it first encountered a problem. You can then edit the material in the cell, and press SHIFT-RETURN or ENTER to resend it to *Mathematica*.

When you are first entering text in a particular notebook cell, the *Mathematica* front end does not yet know whether the text you give is intended to be actual *Mathematica* input. It is only when you press SHIFT-RETURN or ENTER that it can tell. As a result, it is only at this point that the front end labels your input with `In[n]:=`. In addition, if you ever go back and edit the cell, the label automatically disappears.

In general, notebook interfaces allow you to move around in, edit and annotate the "history" of your *Mathematica* session. As a result, the sequence of input and output lines that you gave to *Mathematica* may not appear in your notebook in the order in which they were given. In this case, only the `In[n]:=` and `Out[n]=` labels tell you the actual sequence that was used.

Notebook interfaces typically provide various features to reduce the amount of typing involved in entering *Mathematica* input. One standard feature is command completion. If you type part of a name known to *Mathematica*, you can ask your notebook interface to complete the name. If there is a unique completion, it is done. Otherwise, you get a menu of possible completions.

There are also various parameters, particularly graphical ones, that notebook interfaces typically allow you to choose using graphical tools. For example, many notebook interfaces allow you to choose the view point for a three-dimensional plot by interactively rotating a three-dimensional box. When you have found the view point you want, the front end generates the appropriate text to specify this view point in *Mathematica*.

By rotating the box, you can specify a view point, which is then fed to *Mathematica* in textual form.

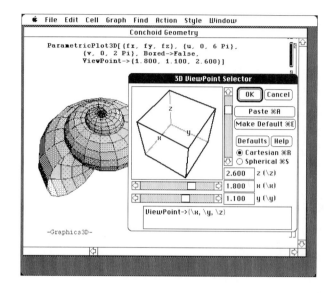

Another graphical feature common in notebook interfaces is the ability to read coordinates from graphs using a pointing device such as a mouse. You can also usually enter new points, whose coordinates you can get in textual form as *Mathematica* input.

Notebook interfaces typically allow you to find and specify coordinates graphically.

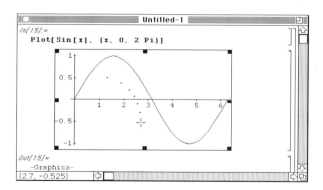

■ 1.4 Getting Information from *Mathematica*

Notebook interfaces typically provide various graphical mechanisms for getting help and information on *Mathematica* objects. These are based on the general mechanism for getting information which is built into the *Mathematica* kernel, and which is available on all versions of *Mathematica*.

?*Name*	show information on *Name*
??*Name*	show extra information on *Name*
?*Aaaa*∗	show information on all objects whose names begin with *Aaaa*

Ways to get information on *Mathematica* objects.

This gives information on the built-in function Log.	`In[1]:= ?Log`
	
	`Log[z] gives the natural logarithm of z (logarithm to base E).`
	`  Log[b, z] gives the logarithm to base b.`

You can ask for information about any object, whether it is built into *Mathematica*, has been read in from a *Mathematica* package, or has been introduced by you.

When you use ? to get information, you must make sure that the question mark appears as the first character in your input line. You need to do this so that *Mathematica* can tell when you are requesting information rather than giving ordinary input for evaluation.

You can get extra information with ??.	`In[1]:= ??Log`
	
	`Log[z] gives the natural logarithm of z (logarithm to base E).`
	`  Log[b, z] gives the logarithm to base b.`
	
	`Attributes[Log] = {Listable, Protected}`

This gives information on all *Mathematica* objects whose names begin with Plot. When there is more than one object, *Mathematica* just lists their names.	`In[1]:= ?Plot*`
	
	`Plot          PlotJoined   PlotRange    Plot3D`
	`PlotColor     PlotLabel    PlotRegion   Plot3Matrix`
	`PlotDivision  PlotPoints   PlotStyle`

?*Aaaa* will give you information on the particular object whose name you specify. Using the "metacharacter" ∗, however, you can get information on collections of objects with similar names. The rule is that ∗ is a "wild card" that can stand for any sequence of ordinary characters. So, for example, ?L∗ gets information on all objects whose names consist of the letter L, followed by any sequence of characters.

You can put a ∗ anywhere in the string you ask ? about. For example, ?*Expand would give you all objects whose names *end* with Expand. Similarly, ?x*0 would give you objects whose names start with x, and end with 0, and have any sequence of characters in between. (You may notice that the way you use ∗ to specify names in *Mathematica* is similar to the way you use ∗ in Unix and other operating systems to specify file names.)

You can ask for information on most of the special input forms that *Mathematica* uses. This asks for information about the := operator.

```
In[1]:= ?:=

lhs := rhs assigns rhs to be the delayed value of lhs. rhs is
    maintained in an unevaluated form. When lhs appears, it is
    replaced by rhs, evaluated afresh each time.
```

■ 1.5 Interrupting Calculations

There will probably be times when you want to stop *Mathematica* in the middle of a calculation. Perhaps you realize that you asked *Mathematica* to do the wrong thing. Or perhaps the calculation is just taking a long time, and you want to find out what is going on.

COMMAND-.	notebook interfaces

How to interrupt a calculation in *Mathematica*.

On some computer systems, it may take *Mathematica* some time to respond to your interrupt. When *Mathematica* does respond, it will typically give you a menu of possible things to do.

continue	continue the calculation
show	show what *Mathematica* is doing
inspect	inspect the current state of your calculation
abort	abort this particular calculation
exit	exit *Mathematica* completely

Some typical options available when you interrupt a calculation in *Mathematica*.

■ 1.6 Warnings and Messages

Mathematica usually goes about its work silently, giving output only when it has finished doing the calculations you asked for.

However, if it looks as if *Mathematica* is doing something you definitely did not intend, *Mathematica* will usually print a message to warn you. There is a list of standard *Mathematica* messages available as a Wolfram Research technical report, *Mathematica Warning Messages*.

The most common causes of "bugs" are spelling mistakes.

```
In[1]:= Pqrt[16]

General::spell:
    Possible spelling error: new symbol name "Pqrt"
      is similar to existing symbols {Part, Sqrt}.

Out[1]= Pqrt[16]
```

The square root function should have only one argument. *Mathematica* prints a message to warn you that you have given two arguments here.

In[2]:= **Sqrt[4, 5]**

Sqrt::argx: Sqrt called with 2
    arguments; 1 argument is expected.

Out[2]= Sqrt[4, 5]

Each message has a name. You can switch off messages using Off.

In[3]:= **Off[Sqrt::argx]**

The message Sqrt::argx has now been switched off, and will no longer appear.

In[4]:= **Sqrt[4, 5]**

Out[4]= Sqrt[4, 5]

This switches Sqrt::argx back on again.

In[5]:= **On[Sqrt::argx]**

Off[*Function*::*tag*]	switch off (suppress) a message
On[*Function*::*tag*]	switch on a message

Functions for controlling message output.

> Check ▪ Message ▪ $Language ▪ MessageName ▪ Messages ▪ MessageList ▪
> $MessageList ▪ $NewSymbol ▪ $NewMessage

Other *Mathematica* functions related to messages. (See page xvi.)

2. Numerical Calculations

■ 2.1 Arithmetic

You can do arithmetic with *Mathematica* just as you would on an electronic calculator.

This is the sum of two numbers.

In[1]:= **2.3 + 5.63**

Out[1]= 7.93

Here the ∧ stands for power. 10^3 means 10 times itself 3 times.

In[2]:= **10 ∧ 3**

Out[2]= 1000

Here the / stands for division. The power is done first.

In[3]:= **2.4 / 8.9 ∧ 2**

Out[3]= 0.0302992

Spaces denote multiplication in *Mathematica*. You can use a * for multiplication if you want to.

In[4]:= **2 3 4**

Out[4]= 24

You can type arithmetic expressions with parentheses.

In[5]:= **(3 + 4) ∧ 2 - 2 (3 + 1)**

Out[5]= 41

Spaces are not needed, though they often make your input easier to read.

In[6]:= **(3+4)∧2-2(3+1)**

Out[6]= 41

x∧y	power
$-x$	minus
x/y	divide
x y z or x*y*z	multiply
$x+y+z$	add

Arithmetic operations in *Mathematica*.

Arithmetic operations in *Mathematica* are grouped according to the standard mathematical conventions. As usual, 2 ∧ 3 + 4, for example, means (2 ∧ 3) + 4, and not 2 ∧ (3 + 4). You can always control grouping by explicitly using parentheses.

This result is given in scientific notation.

In[7]:= **2.4 ∧ 45**

Out[7]= $1.28678\ 10^{17}$

You can enter numbers in scientific notation like this.

In[8]:= **2.3 10 ∧ -70**

Out[8]= $2.3\ 10^{-70}$

■ 2.2 Exact and Approximate Results

A standard electronic calculator does all your calculations to a particular accuracy, say ten decimal digits. With *Mathematica*, however, you can often get *exact* results.

Mathematica gives an *exact* result for 2^{100}, even though it has 31 decimal digits.	`In[1]:= 2 ^ 100` `Out[1]= 1267650600228229401496703205376`

You can tell *Mathematica* to give you an approximate numerical result, just as a calculator would, by putting N[ ] around your input. The N stands for "numerical". It must be a capital letter.

This gives an approximate numerical result.	`In[2]:= N[ 2 ^ 100 ]` `Out[2]= 1.26765 10`^{30}
Mathematica can give results in terms of rational numbers.	`In[3]:= 1/3 + 2/7` `Out[3]= `$\frac{13}{21}$
N always gives the approximate numerical result.	`In[4]:= N[ 1/3 + 2/7 ]` `Out[4]= 0.619048`

N[*expr*]	give an approximate numerical value for *expr*

Getting numerical approximations.

When you type in an integer like 7, *Mathematica* assumes that it is exact. If you type in a number like 4.5, with an explicit decimal point, *Mathematica* assumes that it is accurate only to a fixed number of decimal places.

This is taken to be an exact rational number, and reduced to its lowest terms.	`In[5]:= 452/62` `Out[5]= `$\frac{226}{31}$
Whenever you give a number with an explicit decimal point, *Mathematica* produces an approximate numerical result.	`In[6]:= 452.3/62` `Out[6]= 7.29516`
Here again, the presence of the decimal point makes *Mathematica* give you an approximate numerical result.	`In[7]:= 452./62` `Out[7]= 7.29032`
When any number in an arithmetic expression is given with an explicit decimal point, you get an approximate numerical result for the whole expression.	`In[8]:= 1. + 452/62` `Out[8]= 8.29032`

■ 2.3 Some Mathematical Functions

Mathematica includes a very large collection of mathematical functions. Here are a few of the common ones.

Sqrt[x]	square root ($\sqrt{x}$)
Sin[x], Cos[x], Tan[x]	trigonometric functions (with arguments in radians)
n!	factorial (product of integers $1, 2, \ldots, n$)
Binomial[n, m]	binomial coefficient $\binom{n}{m} = \frac{n!}{m!(n-m)!}$
Round[x]	closest integer to x
Random[ ]	pseudorandom number between 0 and 1
Max[x, y, ...], Min[x, y, ...]	maximum, minimum of $x, y, \ldots$
Divisors[n]	positive integers dividing n
Log[b, x]	logarithm to base b ($\log_b x$)
Log[x]	natural logarithm ($\log_e x$)

Some common mathematical functions.

- The arguments of all *Mathematica* functions are enclosed in *square brackets*.
- The names of built-in *Mathematica* functions begin with *capital letters*.

Two important points about functions in *Mathematica*.

It is important to remember that all function arguments in *Mathematica* are enclosed in *square brackets*, not parentheses. Parentheses in *Mathematica* are used only to indicate the grouping of terms, and never to give function arguments.

This gives sin(8.4). Notice the capital letter for Sin, and the *square brackets* for the argument.

```
In[1]:= Sin[8.4]
Out[1]= 0.854599
```

Just as with arithmetic operations, *Mathematica* tries to give exact values for mathematical functions when you give it exact input.

This gives $\sqrt{16}$ as an exact integer.

```
In[2]:= Sqrt[16]
Out[2]= 4
```

This gives an approximate numerical result for $\sqrt{2}$.

```
In[3]:= N[ Sqrt[2] ]
Out[3]= 1.41421
```

The presence of an explicit decimal point tells *Mathematica* to give an approximate numerical result.

```
In[4]:= Sqrt[2.]
Out[4]= 1.41421
```

There is no exact result for $\sqrt{2}$, so *Mathematica* leaves the original form. This kind of "symbolic" result is discussed in Section 6.1.

```
In[5]:= Sqrt[2]
Out[5]= Sqrt[2]
```

Here is the exact integer result for $30 \times 29 \times \ldots \times 1$. Computing factorials like this can give you very large numbers. You should be able to calculate up to at least 1000! in a reasonable amount of time.

```
In[6]:= 30!
Out[6]= 265252859812191058636308480000000
```

This gives the approximate numerical value of the factorial. Large numbers are written in scientific notation.

```
In[7]:= N[30!]
            32
Out[7]= 2.65253 10
```

You can get scientific notation for smaller real numbers, too.

```
In[8]:= ScientificForm[123456.]
                               5
Out[8]//ScientificForm= 1.23456 10
```

Pi	$\pi \simeq 3.14159$
E	$e \simeq 2.71828$
Degree	$\pi/180$: degrees-to-radians conversion factor
GoldenRatio	$\phi = (1 + \sqrt{5})/2 \simeq 1.61803$
I	$i = \sqrt{-1}$
Infinity	∞
-Infinity	$-\infty$

Some common mathematical constants.

Notice that the names of these built-in constants all begin with capital letters.

This gives the numerical value of π^2.

```
In[9]:= N[Pi ^ 2]
Out[9]= 9.8696
```

This gives the exact result for $\sin(\pi/2)$. Notice that the arguments to trigonometric functions are always in radians.

```
In[10]:= Sin[Pi/2]
Out[10]= 1
```

This gives the numerical value of $\sin(20°)$. Multiplying by the constant **Degree** converts the argument to radians.

```
In[11]:= N[ Sin[20 Degree] ]
Out[11]= 0.34202
```

Log[x] gives logarithms to base e.

```
In[12]:= Log[E ^ 5]
Out[12]= 5
```

You can get logarithms in any base b using Log[b, x]. As in standard mathematical notation, the b is optional.

```
In[13]:= Log[10, 1000]
Out[13]= 3
```

■ 2.4 Arbitrary-Precision Calculations

When you use N to get a numerical result, *Mathematica* does what a standard calculator would do: it gives you a result to a fixed number of significant figures. You can also tell *Mathematica* exactly how many significant figures to keep in a particular calculation. This allows you to get numerical results in *Mathematica* to any degree of precision.

N[*expr*]	approximate numerical value of *expr*
N[*expr*, *n*]	numerical value of *expr* calculated with *n*-digit precision

Numerical evaluation functions.

This gives the numerical value of π to a fixed number of significant digits.

```
In[1]:= N[Pi]
Out[1]= 3.14159
```

This gives π to 40 digits.

```
In[2]:= N[Pi, 40]
Out[2]= 3.1415926535897932384626433832795028841972
```

Here is $\sqrt{7}$ to 30 digits.

```
In[3]:= N[Sqrt[7], 30]
Out[3]= 2.64575131106459059050161615753639
```

Doing any kind of numerical calculation can introduce small roundoff errors into your results. When you increase the numerical precision, these errors typically become correspondingly smaller. Making sure that you get the same answer when you increase numerical precision is often a good way to check your results.

This is close to 7.

```
In[4]:= 2.6457 ^ 2
Out[4]= 6.99973
```

The quantity $e^{\pi\sqrt{163}}$ turns out to be very close to an integer.

```
In[5]:= 262537412640768744 == N[ Exp[Pi Sqrt[163]] ]
Out[5]= True
```

To check that the result is not, in fact, an integer, you have to use sufficient numerical precision.

```
In[6]:= N[Exp[Pi Sqrt[163]], 50]
Out[6]= 2.6253741264076874399999999999992500725971981856689 10^17
```

■ 2.5 Getting Used to *Mathematica*

- Arguments of functions are given in *square brackets*.

- Names of built-in functions have their first letters capitalized.

- Multiplication can be represented by a space.

- Powers are denoted by ∧.

- Numbers in scientific notation are entered, for example, as 2.5 10∧-4.

Important points to remember in *Mathematica*.

You have now had a first glimpse of *Mathematica*. If you have used other computer systems before, you will probably have noticed some similarities and some differences. Often you will find the differences the most difficult parts to remember. It may help you, however, to understand a little about *why Mathematica* is set up the way it is, and why such differences exist.

One important feature of *Mathematica* that differs from other computer languages, and from conventional mathematical notation, is that function arguments are enclosed in square brackets, not parentheses. Parentheses in *Mathematica* are reserved specifically for indicating grouping of terms. There is obviously a conceptual distinction between giving arguments to a function and grouping terms together; the fact that the same notation has often been used for both is largely a consequence of typography and of early computer keyboards. In *Mathematica*, the concepts are distinguished by different notation.

This distinction has several advantages. In parenthesis notation, it is not clear whether $c(1+x)$ means c[1 + x] or c*(1 + x). Using square brackets for function arguments removes this ambiguity. It also allows multiplication to be indicated without an explicit * or other character. As a result, *Mathematica* can handle expressions like 2x and a x or a (1 + x), treating them just as in standard mathematical notation.

You will have seen that built-in *Mathematica* functions often have quite long names. You may wonder why, for example, the pseudorandom number function is called Random, rather than, say, Rand. The answer, which pervades much of the design of *Mathematica*, is consistency. There is a general convention in *Mathematica* that all function names are spelled out as full English words, unless there is a standard mathematical abbreviation for them. The great advantage of this scheme is that it is *predictable*. Once you know what a function does, you will usually be able to guess exactly what its name is. If the names were abbreviated, you would always have to remember which shortening of the standard English words was used.

Another feature of built-in *Mathematica* names is that they all start with capital letters. In later sections, you will see how to define variables and functions of your own. The capital letter convention makes it easy to distinguish built-in objects. If *Mathematica* used i to represent $\sqrt{-1}$, then you would never be able to use i as the name of one of your variables. In addition, when you read programs written in *Mathematica*, the capitalization of built-in names makes them easier to pick out.

3. One Thing after Another

■ 3.1 Defining Variables

When you do long calculations, it is often convenient to give *names* to your intermediate results. Just as in standard mathematics, or in other computer languages, you can do this by introducing named *variables*.

This sets the value of the *variable* x to be 5.	$In[1]:= \mathbf{x = 5}$ $Out[1]= 5$
Whenever x appears, *Mathematica* now replaces it with the value 5.	$In[2]:= \mathbf{x \wedge 2}$ $Out[2]= 25$
This assigns a new value to x.	$In[3]:= \mathbf{x = 7 + 4}$ $Out[3]= 11$
pi is set to be the numerical value of π to 40-digit accuracy.	$In[4]:= \mathbf{pi = N[Pi, 40]}$ $Out[4]= 3.141592653589793238462643383279502884197$
Here is the value you defined for pi.	$In[5]:= \mathbf{pi}$ $Out[5]= 3.141592653589793238462643383279502884197$
This gives the numerical value of π^2, to almost the same accuracy as pi.	$In[6]:= \mathbf{pi \wedge 2}$ $Out[6]= 9.869604401089358618834490999876151135314$

$x = value$	assign a value to the variable x
$x = y = value$	assign a value to both x and y
$x =.$ or $Clear[x]$	remove any value assigned to x

Assigning values to variables.

It is very important to realize that values you assign to variables are *permanent*. Once you have assigned a value to a particular variable, the value will be kept until you explicitly remove it. The value will, of course, disappear if you start a whole new *Mathematica* session.

Forgetting about definitions you made earlier is the single most common cause of mistakes when using *Mathematica*. If you set x = 5, *Mathematica* assumes that you *always* want x to have the value 5, until or unless you explicitly tell it otherwise. To avoid mistakes, you should remove values you have defined as soon as you have finished using them.

■ Remove values you assign to variables as soon as you finish using them.

A useful principle in using *Mathematica*.

The variables you define can have almost any names. There is no limit on the length of their names. One constraint, however, is that variable names can never *start* with numbers. For example, x2 could be a variable, but 2x means 2*x.

Mathematica uses both upper- and lower-case letters. There is a convention that built-in *Mathematica* objects always have names starting with upper-case (capital) letters. To avoid confusion, you should always choose names for your own variables that start with lower-case letters.

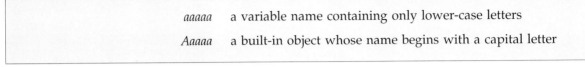

aaaaa	a variable name containing only lower-case letters
Aaaaa	a built-in object whose name begins with a capital letter

Naming conventions.

You can type formulas involving variables in *Mathematica* almost exactly as you would in mathematics. There are a few important points to watch, however.

■ x y means x times y.

■ xy with no space is the variable with name xy.

■ 5x means 5 times x.

■ x^2y means (x^2) y, not x^(2y).

Some points to watch when using variables in *Mathematica*.

■ 3.2 Using Previous Results

In doing calculations, you will often need to use previous results that you have got. In *Mathematica*, % always stands for your last result.

%	the last result generated
%%	the next-to-last result
%%... % (*k* times)	the *k*th previous result
%*n*	the result on output line Out[*n*] (to be used with care)

Ways to refer to your previous results.

Here is the first result.	*In[1]:=* **77 ^ 2**
	Out[1]= 5929
This adds 1 to the last result.	*In[2]:=* **% + 1**
	Out[2]= 5930
This uses both the last result, and the result before that.	*In[3]:=* **3 % + % ^ 2 + %%**
	Out[3]= 35188619

You will have noticed that all the input and output lines in *Mathematica* are numbered. You can use these numbers to refer to previous results.

This adds the results on lines 2 and 3 above.	*In[4]:=* **%2 + %3**
	Out[4]= 35194549

Successive input and output lines need not appear in order since you can for example "scroll back" and insert your next calculation wherever you want in the notebook. You should realize that % is always defined to be the last result that *Mathematica* generated. This may or may not be the result that appears immediately above your present position in the notebook. With a notebook interface, the only way to tell when a particular result was generated is to look at the Out[*n*] label that it has. Because you can insert and delete anywhere in a notebook, the textual ordering of results in a notebook need have no relation to the order in which the results were generated.

%*n* or Out[*n*]	the value of the *n*th output
In[*n*]	the *n*th input, for re-evaluation

Retrieving and re-evaluating previous input and output.

You can always use *Mathematica* to retrieve or re-evaluate previous input and output. In general, re-evaluating a particular piece of input or output may give you a different result than when you evaluated it in the first place. The reason is that in between you may have reset the values of variables that are used in that piece of input or output. If you ask for Out[*n*], then *Mathematica* will give you the final form of your *n*th output. On the other hand, if you ask for In[*n*], then *Mathematica* will take the *n*th input you gave, and re-evaluate it using whatever current assignments you have given for variables.

In a standard session, *Mathematica* stores *all* your input and output lines for the duration of the session. In a very long session, this may take up a large amount of computer memory. You can nevertheless get rid of the input and output lines by explicitly clearing the values of In and Out, using Unprotect[In, Out], followed by Clear[In, Out].

An alternative strategy is to reset the line number counter $Line, so that new lines are numbered so as to overwrite previous ones.

■ 3.3 Sequences of Operations

In doing a calculation with *Mathematica*, you usually go through a sequence of steps. If you want to, you can do each step on a separate line. Often, however, you will find it convenient to put several steps on the same line. You can do this simply by separating the pieces of input you want to give with semicolons.

$expr_1$; $expr_2$; $expr_3$	do several operations, giving the result of the last one
$expr_1$; $expr_2$;	do the operations, but print no output

Ways to do sequences of operations in *Mathematica*.

This does three operations on the same line. The result is the result from the last operation.

```
In[1]:= x = 4; y = 6; z = y + 6
Out[1]= 12
```

If you end your input with a semicolon, it is as if you are giving a sequence of operations, with an "empty" one at the end. This has the effect of making *Mathematica* perform the operations you specify, but display no output.

$expr$;	do an operation, but display no output

Inhibiting output.

Putting a semicolon at the end of the line tells *Mathematica* to produce no output.

```
In[2]:= x = 67 - 5 ;
```

You can still use % to get the output that would have been produced.

```
In[3]:= %
Out[3]= 62
```

■ 3.4 Making Lists of Objects

In doing calculations, it is often convenient to collect together several objects, and treat them as a single entity. *Lists* give you a way to make collections of objects in *Mathematica*. As you will see later, lists are very important and general structures in *Mathematica*.

A list such as {3, 5, 1} is a collection of three objects. But in many ways, you can treat the whole list as a single object. You can, for example, do arithmetic on the whole list at once, or assign the whole list to be the value of a variable.

Here is a list of three numbers.	*In[1]:=* **{3, 5, 1}**
	Out[1]= {3, 5, 1}
This squares each number in the list, and adds 1 to it.	*In[2]:=* **{3, 5, 1}^2 + 1**
	Out[2]= {10, 26, 2}
This takes differences between corresponding elements in the two lists. The lists must be the same length.	*In[3]:=* **{6, 7, 8} - {3.5, 4, 2.5}**
	Out[3]= {2.5, 3, 5.5}
The value of % is the whole list.	*In[4]:=* **%**
	Out[4]= {2.5, 3, 5.5}
You can apply any of the mathematical functions in Section 2.3 to whole lists.	*In[5]:=* **N[Sqrt[%]]**
	Out[5]= {1.58114, 1.73205, 2.34521}

Just as you can set variables to be numbers, so also you can set them to be lists.

This assigns v to be a list.	*In[6]:=* **v = {2, 4, 3.1}**
	Out[6]= {2, 4, 3.1}
Wherever v appears, it is replaced by the list.	*In[7]:=* **v / (v - 1)**
	Out[7]= $\{2, \frac{4}{3}, 1.47619\}$

■ 3.5 Manipulating Elements of Lists

Many of the most powerful list manipulation operations in *Mathematica* treat whole lists as single objects. Sometimes, however, you need to pick out or set individual elements in a list.

You can refer to an element of a *Mathematica* list by giving its "index". The elements are numbered in order, starting at 1.

$\{a, b, c\}$ a list

$list[[1]]$ the first element of *list*

$list[[i]]$ the ith element of *list*

$list[[\{i, j, \ldots\}]]$ a list of the ith, j^{th}, ... elements of *list*

Operations on list elements.

This extracts the second element of the list.	*In[1]:=* **{5, 8, 6, 9}[[2]]** *Out[1]=* 8
This extracts a list of elements.	*In[2]:=* **{5, 8, 6, 9}[[{3, 1, 3, 2, 4}]]** *Out[2]=* {6, 5, 6, 8, 9}
This assigns the value of v to be a list.	*In[3]:=* **v = {2, 4, 7}** *Out[3]=* {2, 4, 7}
You can extract elements of v.	*In[4]:=* **v[[2]]** *Out[4]=* 4

By assigning a variable to be a list, you can use *Mathematica* lists much like "arrays" in other computer languages. Thus, for example, you can reset an element of a list by assigning a value to $v[[i]]$.

$v[[i]]$ extract the ith element of a list

$v[[i]]$ = *value*   reset the ith element of a list

Array-like operations on lists.

Here is a list.	*In[5]:=* **v = {4, -1, 8, 7}** *Out[5]=* {4, -1, 8, 7}
This resets the third element of the list.	*In[6]:=* **v[[3]] = 0** *Out[6]=* 0
Now the list assigned to v has been modified.	*In[7]:=* **v** *Out[7]=* {4, -1, 0, 7}

The **Table** function generates lists from formulas.

This gives a list of the values of i^2, with i running from 1 to 6.	*In[8]:=* **Table[i^2, {i, 6}]** *Out[8]=* {1, 4, 9, 16, 25, 36}

You can also create lists of formulas.

$$In[9]:= \texttt{Table[x\^{}i, \{i, 5\}]}$$

$$Out[9]= \{x, x^2, x^3, x^4, x^5\}$$

■ 3.6 The Four Kinds of Bracketing in *Mathematica*

Over the course of the last few sections, we have introduced each of the four kinds of bracketing used in *Mathematica*. Each kind of bracketing has a very different meaning. It is important that you remember all of them.

(term)	parentheses for grouping
f[*x*]	square brackets for functions
{*a*, *b*, *c*}	curly braces for lists
v[[*i*]]	double brackets for indexing

The four kinds of bracketing in *Mathematica*.

When the expressions you type in are complicated, it is often a good idea to put extra space inside each set of brackets. This makes it somewhat easier for you to see matching pairs of brackets. *v*[[{*a*, *b*}]] is, for example, easier to recognize than *v*[[{*a*, *b*}]].

4. **Real and Complex Numbers**

■ 4.1 Types of Numbers

Four types of numbers are built into *Mathematica*.

`Integer`	arbitrary-length exact integer
`Rational`	*integer/integer* in lowest terms
`Real`	approximate real number, with any specified precision
`Complex`	complex number of the form *number* + *number* `I`

Intrinsic types of numbers in *Mathematica*.

Rational numbers always consist of a ratio of two integers, reduced to lowest terms.	`In[1]:= 12344/2222` $Out[1]= \dfrac{6172}{1111}$

Approximate real numbers are distinguished by the presence of an explicit decimal point.	`In[2]:= 5456.`
	
	`Out[2]= 5456.`

An approximate real number can have any number of digits.	`In[3]:= 4.5454352345454352345345234543`
	
	`Out[3]= 4.5454352345454352345345234543`

The number *i* times itself is −1, which is impossible for a real number.	`In[4]:= I I`
	
	`Out[4]= -1`

Complex numbers can be formed as arithmetic combinations of `I` with integers and rationals.	`In[5]:= 4 + 7/8 I` $Out[5]= 4 + \dfrac{7\ I}{8}$

They can also have approximate real number components.	`In[6]:= 4 + 5.6 I`
	
	`Out[6]= 4 + 5.6 I`

`123`	an exact integer
`123.`	an approximate real number
`123.0000000000000`	an approximate real number with a certain precision
`123. + 0. I`	a complex number with approximate real components

Several versions of the number 123.

■ 4.2 Numerical Functions

Round[x]	integer $\langle x \rangle$ closest to x
Floor[x]	greatest integer $\lfloor x \rfloor$ not larger than x
Ceiling[x]	least integer $\lceil x \rceil$ not smaller than x
Abs[x]	absolute value $|x|$ of x
Sign[x]	1 for $x > 0$, -1 for $x < 0$
Max[x_1, x_2, ...] or Max[{x_1, x_2, ... }, ...]	
	the maximum of $x_1, x_2, \ldots$
Min[x_1, x_2, ...] or Min[{x_1, x_2, ... }, ...]	
	the minimum of $x_1, x_2, \ldots$

Some numerical functions of real variables.

Round[x], Floor[x] and Ceiling[x] can all be considered to give versions of the integer part of x.

```
In[1]:= x = 2.3; {x, Round[x], Floor[x], Ceiling[x]}
Out[1]= {2.3, 2, 2, 3}
```

This gives the fractional parts of the numbers in the list w.

```
In[2]:= w = {3, 2.7, 4.2}; w - Floor[w]
Out[2]= {0, 0.7, 0.2}
```

This gives the least and the greatest numbers in w.

```
In[3]:= {Min[w], Max[w]}
Out[3]= {2.7, 4.2}
```

■ 4.3 Elementary Transcendental Functions

Mathematical functions in *Mathematica* are given names according to definite rules. As with most *Mathematica* functions, the names are usually complete English words, fully spelled out. For a few very common functions, *Mathematica* uses the traditional abbreviations. Thus the tangent function, for example, is Tan, not Tangent.

Sin[z], Cos[z], Tan[z], Csc[z], Sec[z], Cot[z]

trigonometric functions (with arguments in radians)

ArcSin[z], ArcCos[z], ArcTan[z], ArcCsc[z], ArcSec[z], ArcCot[z]

inverse trigonometric functions (giving results in radians)

Trigonometric functions.

The arguments of trigonometric functions are always given in radians.

$In[1]:=$ **Sin[Pi/2]**

$Out[1]=$ 1

You can convert from degrees by explicitly multiplying by the constant **Degree**.

$In[2]:=$ **N[Sin[30 Degree]]**

$Out[2]=$ 0.5

Log[b, z]   logarithm $\log_b(z)$ to base b

E^z or Exp[z]   exponential function e^z

Log[z]   logarithm $\log_e(z)$

Logarithms and exponential functions.

Mathematica gives exact results for logarithms whenever it can. Here is $\log_2 1024$.

$In[3]:=$ **Log[2, 1024]**

$Out[3]=$ 10

You can find the numerical values of mathematical functions to any precision.

$In[4]:=$ **N[Log[2], 40]**

$Out[4]=$ 0.6931471805599453094172321214581765680755

Sinh[z], Cosh[z], Tanh[z], Csch[z], Sech[z], Coth[z]

hyperbolic functions

ArcSinh[z], ArcCosh[z], ArcTanh[z], ArcCsch[z], ArcSech[z], ArcCoth[z]

inverse hyperbolic functions

Hyperbolic functions.

Here is a plot of the hyperbolic tangent function. It has a characteristic "sigmoidal" form.

$In[5]:=$ **Plot[Tanh[x], {x, -8, 8}]**

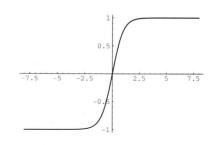

■ 4.4 Complex Numbers

You can enter complex numbers in *Mathematica* just by including the constant I, equal to $\sqrt{-1}$. Make sure that you type a capital I.

x + I y	the complex number $x + iy$
Re[z]	the real part $\mathrm{Re}\,z$
Im[z]	the imaginary part $\mathrm{Im}\,z$
Conjugate[z]	the complex conjugate z^* or $\bar{z}$
Abs[z]	the absolute value $|z|$
Arg[z]	the argument ϕ such that $z = |z|e^{i\phi}$

Numerical functions of complex variables.

This gives the imaginary number $2i$.

$In[1]:=$ **Sqrt[-4]**

$Out[1]=$ 2 I

This gives the product of two complex numbers.

$In[2]:=$ **(4 + 3 I) (2 - I)**

$Out[2]=$ 11 + 2 I

This gives their ratio.

$In[3]:=$ **w = (4 + 3 I) / (2 - I)**

$Out[3]=$ 1 + 2 I

These are the rectangular coordinates of w as a point in the complex plane.

$In[4]:=$ **{Re[w], Im[w]}**

$Out[4]=$ {1, 2}

Taking the conjugate of z reverses the sign of its imaginary part.

$In[5]:=$ **Conjugate[z = 3 - 4 I]**

$Out[5]=$ 3 + 4 I

The absolute value of a complex number $x + Iy$ is $\sqrt{x^2 + y^2}$.	$In[6]:= \textbf{Abs[z]}$ $Out[6]= 5$
This is an equivalent definition of the absolute value.	$In[7]:= \textbf{Sqrt[z Conjugate[z]]}$ $Out[7]= 5$
These are the polar coordinates (r, θ) of z.	$In[8]:= \textbf{\{Abs[z], Arg[z]\}}$ $Out[8]= \{5, -ArcTan[\frac{4}{3}]\}$
Here is the numerical value of a complex exponential.	$In[9]:= \textbf{N[Exp[2 + 9 I]]}$ $Out[9]= -6.73239 + 3.04517 I$
This gives a complex number result.	$In[10]:= \textbf{N[Log[-2]]}$ $Out[10]= 0.693147 + 3.14159 I$
Mathematica can evaluate logarithms with complex arguments.	$In[11]:= \textbf{N[Log[2 + 8 I]]}$ $Out[11]= 2.10975 + 1.32582 I$

■ 4.5 Defining *Mathematica* Functions

Mathematica contains hundreds of built-in mathematical functions like Round, Sqrt, and Sin, and these can be combined to form an endless number of possible expressions. These expressions can be simple like 1/x or more complicated like Abs[Abs[x] - 1]. The first step in *Mathematica* programming is to define a function to abbreviate such an expression. Part 3 describes *Mathematica*'s powerful programming language in detail.

This defines the function f. The _ ("blank") after the x means that the function's variable is x.	$In[1]:= \textbf{f[x\_] := 1 / (1 + x\^2)}$
You can evaluate f for any x you want, without having to retype the expression.	$In[2]:= \textbf{f[2]}$ $Out[2]= \frac{1}{5}$
Suppose you give x a value.	$In[3]:= \textbf{x = 10}$ $Out[3]= 10$
Evaluating the function doesn't affect the value of x.	$In[4]:= \textbf{\{f[2/3.], x\}}$ $Out[4]= \{0.692308, 10\}$
You can use any argument for f, and you can combine f with any other function, whether built-in or defined.	$In[5]:= \textbf{f[y + f[Sqrt[y]]]}$ $Out[5]= \dfrac{1}{1 + (y + \frac{1}{1 + y})^2}$

You can do anything with f that you can do with a built-in function like Sin or Sqrt. This plots the function over the range –3 to 3.

In[6]:= **Plot[f[x], {x, -3, 3}]**

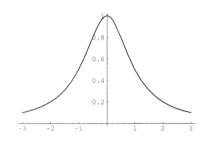

■ 4.6 The Problem of Inverse Functions

When you ask for the square root s of a number a, you are effectively asking for the solution to the equation $s^2 = a$. This equation, however, in general has two different solutions. Both $s = 2$ and $s = -2$ are, for example, solutions to the equation $s^2 = 4$. When you evaluate the "function" $\sqrt{4}$, however, you usually want to get a single number, and so you have to choose one of these two solutions. A standard choice is that $\sqrt{x}$ should be positive for $x > 0$. This is what the *Mathematica* function Sqrt[x] does.

The need to make one choice from two solutions means that Sqrt[x] cannot be a true *inverse function* for x^2. Taking a number, squaring it, and then taking the square root can give you a different number than you started with.

$\sqrt{4}$ gives +2, not –2.

In[1]:= **Sqrt[4]**

Out[1]= 2

Squaring and taking the square root does not necessarily give you the number you started with.

In[2]:= **Sqrt[(-2)^2]**

Out[2]= 2

When you evaluate $\sqrt{-2i}$, there are again two possible answers: $-1 + i$ and $1 - i$. In this case, however, it is less clear which one to choose.

The equation $s^3 = a$ always has a unique real solution if the number a is real. Therefore it is reasonable to expect that $\sqrt[3]{8} = 2$ and that $\sqrt[3]{-8} = -2$. However, the equation $s^3 = a$ has three solutions in all; the other two are complex. In taking this larger view, it turns out that it is more consistent to choose one of these complex solutions, rather than –2 for $\sqrt[3]{-8}$.

If we want to use complex numbers in a consistent way, we can no longer reasonably expect the seemingly natural fact that $(-8)^{\frac{1}{3}} = -2$.

In[3]:= **N[(-8)^(1/3)]**

Out[3]= 1. + 1.73205 I

However, we can define the real-valued function cuberoot.

In[4]:= **cuberoot[x_] := Sign[x] Abs[x] ^ (1/3)**

It works for both positive and negative numbers.

In[5]:= `cuberoot[{-8, 8}]`

Out[5]= `{-2, 2}`

We can use this function to plot cube roots.

In[6]:= `Plot[cuberoot[x], {x, -8, 8}]`

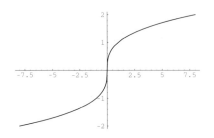

When you find an nth root using $z^{\frac{1}{n}}$, there are, in principle, n possible results. To get a single value, *Mathematica* has to choose a particular *principal root*. There is absolutely no guarantee that taking the nth root of an nth power will leave you with the same number.

This takes the tenth power of a complex number. The result is unique.

In[7]:= `(2.5 + I)^10`

Out[7]= `-15781.2 - 12335.8 I`

There are ten possible tenth roots. *Mathematica* chooses one of them. In this case it is not the number whose tenth power you took.

In[8]:= `%^(1/10)`

Out[8]= `2.61033 - 0.660446 I`

There are many mathematical functions which, like roots, essentially give solutions to equations. The logarithm function, and inverse trigonometric functions, are examples. In almost all cases, there are many possible solutions to the equations. Unique "principal" values nevertheless have to be chosen for the functions.

ArcSin is a multiple-valued function, so there is no guarantee that it always gives the "inverse" of Sin.

In[9]:= `ArcSin[Sin[4.5]]`

Out[9]= `-1.35841`

■ 4.7 Numerical Precision

As discussed in Section 2.2, *Mathematica* can handle approximate real numbers with any number of digits. In general, the *precision* of an approximate real number is the number of decimal digits in it which are treated as significant for computations. The *accuracy* of an approximate real number is the number of decimal digits which appear to the right of the decimal point. Precision is thus a measure of the relative error in a number, while accuracy is a measure of absolute error.

| Precision[x] | the total number of significant decimal digits in x |
| Accuracy[x] | the number of significant decimal digits to the right of the decimal point in x |

Precision and accuracy of real numbers.

Here is an approximate real number.

In[1]:= **xacc = 431.123145333555141444**

Out[1]= 431.123145333555141444

This gives the total number of digits entered to specify the real number.

In[2]:= **Precision[xacc]**

Out[2]= 21

This gives the number of digits that appear to the right of the decimal point.

In[3]:= **Accuracy[xacc]**

Out[3]= 18

When you use N[*expr*, *n*], *Mathematica* evaluates the expression *expr* starting with numbers that have *n* digits of precision. As discussed below, however, the fact that such numbers are used does not necessarily mean that the results you get will have *n* digits of precision. In most cases, your results will have at least slightly fewer digits of precision.

This evaluates Pi^25 using numbers with 30 digits of precision.

In[4]:= **N[Pi^25, 30]**

Out[4]= $2.68377941431776455490099281244 \; 10^{12}$

The result has 29 digits of precision.

In[5]:= **Precision[%]**

Out[5]= 29

In doing numerical computations, it is inevitable that you will sometimes end up with results that are less precise than you want. Particularly when you get numerical results that are very close to zero, you may well want to *assume* that the results should be exactly zero. The function Chop allows you to replace approximate real numbers that are close to zero by the exact integer 0.

| Chop[*expr*] | replace all approximate real numbers in *expr* with magnitude less than 10^{-10} by 0 |
| Chop[*expr*, *dx*] | replace numbers with magnitude less than *dx* by 0 |

Removing numbers close to zero.

Here is the numerical value of the square root of I in the first quadrant.

In[6]:= **N[Sqrt[I]]**

Out[6]= 0.707107 + 0.707107 I

This computation gives a small imaginary part.

In[7]:= **% ^ 2**

Out[7]= $1.5702 \; 10^{-16}$ + 1. I

You can get rid of the imaginary part using Chop.	*In[8]:=* **Chop[%]**
	Out[8]= 1. I

SetAccuracy ▪ SetPrecision ▪ $MaxPrecision ▪ $MinPrecision ▪ Interval ▪
IntervalMemberQ ▪ IntervalUnion ▪ IntervalIntersection ▪ MachineNumberQ ▪
$MachinePrecision ▪ $MachineEpsilon ▪ $MaxMachineNumber ▪ $MinMachineNumber ▪
$MaxNumber ▪ $MinNumber

Other *Mathematica* functions related to numerical precision. (See page xvi.)

■ 4.8 Advanced Topic: A Few Examples of Special Functions

Gamma[z]	Euler gamma function $\Gamma(z)$
Erf[z], Erfc[z]	error function erf(z) and complementary error function erfc(z)
BesselJ[n, z], BesselY[n, z]	Bessel functions $J_n(z)$ and $Y_n(z)$
Zeta[s]	Riemann zeta function $\zeta(s)$

Some special functions.

Gamma Function

For a positive integer n, $\Gamma(n) = (n-1)!$. $\Gamma(z)$ can be viewed as a generalization of the factorial function, valid for complex arguments z. The **Euler gamma function** Gamma[z] is defined by the integral $\Gamma(z) = \int_0^\infty t^{z-1} e^{-t} dt$.

Mathematica gives exact results for some values of special functions.	*In[1]:=* **Gamma[15/2]**
	Out[1]= $\dfrac{135135 \text{ Sqrt[Pi]}}{128}$
No exact result is known here.	*In[2]:=* **Gamma[15/7]**
	Out[2]= Gamma[$\dfrac{15}{7}$]
A numerical result, to arbitrary precision, can nevertheless be found.	*In[3]:=* **N[%, 40]**
	Out[3]= 1.069071500448624397994137689702693267367

You can give complex arguments to special functions.

In[4]:= **N[Gamma[3 + 4I]]**

Out[4]= 0.00522554 - 0.172547 I

Special functions automatically get applied to each element in a list.

In[5]:= **Gamma[{3/2, 5/2, 7/2}]**

$$Out[5]= \{\frac{Sqrt[Pi]}{2}, \frac{3\ Sqrt[Pi]}{4}, \frac{15\ Sqrt[Pi]}{8}\}$$

Here is a contour plot of the gamma function in the complex plane.

In[6]:= **ContourPlot[Abs[Gamma[x + I y]], {x, -3, 3},**
              {y, -2, 2}, PlotPoints -> 40]

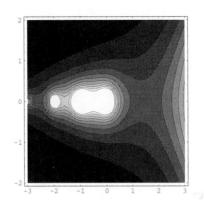

Error Function

The **error function** Erf[z] is related to the integral of the Gaussian distribution, given by erf(z) = $\frac{2}{\sqrt{\pi}}\int_0^z e^{-t^2}dt$. A common use of the error function is to evaluate the integral $\frac{2}{\sqrt{\pi}}\int_w^z e^{-t^2}dt$. This is given by Erf[w, z]. The **complementary error function** Erfc[z] is given simply by erfc(z) = 1 - erf(z).

Bessel Functions

The **Bessel functions** BesselJ[n, z] and BesselY[n, z] are linearly independent solutions to the differential equation $z^2\frac{d^2y}{dz^2} + z\frac{dy}{dz} + (z^2 - n^2)y = 0$.

Bessel functions arise in solving differential equations for systems with cylindrical symmetry.

$J_n(z)$ is often called the **Bessel function of the first kind**, or simply *the* Bessel function. $Y_n(z)$ is referred to as the **Bessel function of the second kind**, the **Weber function**, or the **Neumann function** (denoted $N_n(z)$).

You can use FindRoot to find roots of special functions.

In[7]:= **FindRoot[BesselJ[0, x], {x, 1}]**

Out[7]= {x -> 2.40483}

Zeta Function

The **Riemann zeta function** Zeta[s] is defined by the relation $\zeta(s) = \sum_{k=1}^{\infty} k^{-s}$ (for $s > 1$). Zeta functions with integer arguments arise in evaluating various sums and integrals. *Mathematica* gives exact results when possible for zeta functions with integer arguments.

It is possible to extend the definition of $\zeta(s)$ to arbitrary complex $s \neq 1$. The zeta function for complex arguments is central to number-theoretical studies of the distribution of primes. Of particular importance are the values about the critical line Re $s = \frac{1}{2}$.

Mathematica gives exact results for $\zeta(2n)$.	$In[8] := $ **Zeta[6]**

$$Out[8] = \frac{Pi^6}{945}$$

Here is a three-dimensional picture of the Riemann zeta function in the complex plane.

$In[9] := $ **Plot3D[Abs[Zeta[x + I y]], {x, -3, 3}, {y, 2, 35}, PlotPoints -> 30]**

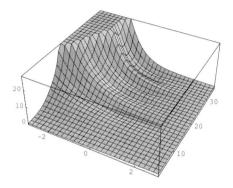

    Factorial2 ▪ Multinomial ▪ Pochhammer ▪ Beta ▪ LogGamma ▪ PolyGamma

Other *Mathematica* functions related to the factorial function. (See page xvi.)

    PolyLog ▪ LerchPhi ▪ RiemannSiegelTheta ▪ RiemannSiegelZ ▪ StieltjesGamma

Other *Mathematica* functions related to the zeta function. (See page xvi.)

AiryAi ▪ AiryAiPrime ▪ AiryBi ▪ AiryBiPrime ▪ BesselK ▪ BesselI ▪ Beta ▪
BetaRegularized ▪ ChebyshevT ▪ ChebyshevU ▪ EllipticK ▪ EllipticE ▪ Erf ▪
Erfc ▪ Erfi ▪ ExpIntegralE ▪ ExpIntegralEi ▪ FresnelS ▪ FresnelC ▪ Gamma ▪
GammaRegularized ▪ GegenbauerC ▪ HermiteH ▪ HypergeometricU ▪
Hypergeometric0F1 ▪ Hypergeometric1F1 ▪ Hypergeometric2F1 ▪
HypergeometricPFQ ▪ Hypergeometric0F1Regularized ▪
Hypergeometric1F1Regularized ▪ Hypergeometric2F1Regularized ▪
HypergeometricPFQRegularized ▪ JacobiP ▪ LaguerreL ▪ LegendreP ▪ LegendreQ ▪
SphericalHarmonicY ▪ LogIntegral ▪ SinIntegral ▪ CosIntegral ▪ SinhIntegral ▪
CoshIntegral

Other *Mathematica* special functions, related to the hypergeometric functions. (See page xvi.)

ChebyshevT ▪ ChebyshevU ▪ GegenbauerC ▪ HermiteH ▪ JacobiP ▪ LaguerreL ▪
LegendreP ▪ SphericalHarmonicY

Other *Mathematica* special functions, related to orthogonal polynomials. (See page xvi.)

EllipticE ▪ EllipticF ▪ EllipticK ▪ EllipticLog ▪ EllipticNomeQ ▪ EllipticPi ▪
JacobiZeta

Other *Mathematica* special functions, related to elliptic integrals. (See page xvi.)

JacobiAmplitude ▪ JacobiCD ▪ JacobiCN ▪ JacobiCS ▪ JacobiDC ▪ JacobiDN ▪
JacobiDS ▪ JacobiNC ▪ JacobiND ▪ JacobiNS ▪ JacobiSC ▪ JacobiSD ▪ JacobiSN ▪
InverseJacobiCD ▪ InverseJacobiCN ▪ InverseJacobiCS ▪ InverseJacobiDC ▪
InverseJacobiDN ▪ InverseJacobiDS ▪ InverseJacobiNC ▪ InverseJacobiND ▪
InverseJacobiNS ▪ InverseJacobiSC ▪ InverseJacobiSD ▪ InverseJacobiSN ▪
WeierstrassP ▪ WeierstrassPPrime ▪ InverseWeierstrassP ▪ EllipticTheta ▪
EllipticThetaPrime ▪ EllipticThetaS ▪ EllipticThetaC ▪ EllipticThetaN ▪
EllipticThetaD ▪ EllipticExp ▪ EllipticExpPrime

Other *Mathematica* special functions, related to elliptic functions. (See page xvi.)

5. Integers

■ 5.1 Digits and Number Bases

IntegerDigits[*n*]	a list of the decimal digits in the integer *n*
IntegerDigits[*n*, *b*]	the digits of *n* in base *b*

Extracting lists of digits.

With only one argument, IntegerDigits assumes the base is 10.

```
In[1]:= IntegerDigits[n = 1234135634]
Out[1]= {1, 2, 3, 4, 1, 3, 5, 6, 3, 4}
```

This is the list of base 100 digits for *n*.

```
In[2]:= IntegerDigits[n, 100]
Out[2]= {12, 34, 13, 56, 34}
```

Here is the list of base 16 digits for the same number.

```
In[3]:= IntegerDigits[n, 16]
Out[3]= {4, 9, 8, 15, 6, 10, 5, 2}
```

b^^*nnnn*	a number in base *b*
BaseForm[*x*, *b*]	print with *x* in base *b*

Numbers in other bases.

The number 100101_2 in base 2 is 37 in base 10, since $37 = 32 + 4 + 1$.

```
In[4]:= 2^^100101
Out[4]= 37
```

This prints 37 in base 2.

```
In[5]:= BaseForm[37, 2]
Out[5]//BaseForm= 100101_2
```

When the base is larger than 10, extra digits are represented by letters a–z.

Here is a number in base 16.

```
In[6]:= 16^^ffffaa00
Out[6]= 4294945280
```

You can do computations with numbers in base 16. Here the result is given in base 10.

```
In[7]:= 16^^fffaa2 + 16^^ff - 1
Out[7]= 16776096
```

This gives the result in base 16.

```
In[8]:= BaseForm[%, 16]
Out[8]//BaseForm= fffba0_16
```

You can give approximate real numbers, as well as integers, in other bases.

In[9]:= **2^^101.100101**

Out[9]= 5.58

Here is the beginning of the octal expansion of $\sqrt{2}$.

In[10]:= **BaseForm[N[Sqrt[2], 30], 8]**

Out[10]//BaseForm= 1.3240474631771674622042627661154678

RealDigits[*x*]	a list of the decimal digits in the approximate real number *x*, together with the number of digits to the left of the decimal point
RealDigits[*x*, *b*]	the digits of *x* in base *b*

Extracting lists of digits.

This gives a list of decimal digits, together with the number of digits that appear to the left of the decimal point.

In[11]:= **RealDigits[y = 123.4567891011121314151617181920]**

Out[11]= {{1, 2, 3, 4, 5, 6, 7, 8, 9, 1, 0, 1, 1, 1, 2, 1, 3, 1, 4, 1, 5, 1, 6, 1, 7, 1, 8, 1, 9, 2}, 3}

RealDigits is similar to IntegerDigits.

In[12]:= **RealDigits[y, 100]**

Out[12]= {{1, 23, 45, 67, 89, 10, 11, 12, 13, 14, 15, 16, 17, 18, 19}, 2}

MantissaExponent ▪ Rationalize ▪ Numerator ▪ Denominator

Other *Mathematica* functions related to number representation. (See page xvi.)

NumberForm ▪ EngineeringForm ▪ AccountingForm ▪ PaddedForm

Other *Mathematica* functions, related to number formatting. (See page xvi.)

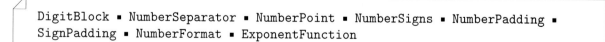

DigitBlock ▪ NumberSeparator ▪ NumberPoint ▪ NumberSigns ▪ NumberPadding ▪
SignPadding ▪ NumberFormat ▪ ExponentFunction

Mathematica options for number formatting. (See page xvi.)

■ 5.2 Division of Integers

EvenQ[*x*]	test whether *x* is an even integer
OddQ[*x*]	test whether *x* is an odd integer
Mod[*k*, *n*]	*k* modulo *n* (remainder from dividing *k* by *n*)
Quotient[*m*, *n*]	the quotient of *m* and *n* (integer part of *m*/*n*)

Division functions.

Range[*n*] gives the integers from 1 to *n*. Range is similar to Table.

```
In[1]:= r = Range[10]
Out[1]= {1, 2, 3, 4, 5, 6, 7, 8, 9, 10}
```

This is a fast way to get the even numbers up to 20.

```
In[2]:= 2 r
Out[2]= {2, 4, 6, 8, 10, 12, 14, 16, 18, 20}
```

Many functions work on whole lists.

```
In[3]:= EvenQ[r]
Out[3]= {False, True, False, True, False, True, False, True,
   False, True}
```

We can also get the odd numbers.

```
In[4]:= 2 r - 1
Out[4]= {1, 3, 5, 7, 9, 11, 13, 15, 17, 19}
```

The last three numbers are not odd integers.

```
In[5]:= OddQ[{2001, 2002, 3., 5 I}]
Out[5]= {True, False, False, False}
```

This is the remainder on dividing 17 by 3.

```
In[6]:= Mod[17, 3]
Out[6]= 2
```

This is the integer part of 17/3.

```
In[7]:= Quotient[17, 3]
Out[7]= 5
```

This gives the same thing.

```
In[8]:= Floor[17 / 3]
Out[8]= 5
```

Mod also works with real numbers.

```
In[9]:= Mod[5.6, 1.2]
Out[9]= 0.8
```

If the division is exact, we get the quotient with the remainder zero.

```
In[10]:= {Quotient[4.8, 1.2], Mod[4.8, 1.2]}
Out[10]= {4, 0.}
```

The result from Mod always has the same sign as the second argument.

```
In[11]:= Mod[-5.6, 1.2]
Out[11]= 0.4
```

For any integers *a* and *b*, it is always true that *b* * Quotient[*a*, *b*] + Mod[*a*, *b*] is equal to *a*.

■ 5.3 Factoring Integers

Divisors[*n*]	a list of the integers that divide *n*
GCD[n_1, n_2, ...]	the greatest common divisor of n_1, n_2, ...
LCM[n_1, n_2, ...]	the least common multiple of n_1, n_2, ...

Functions to do with division.

The integer 24 has 8 divisors.

```
In[1]:= Divisors[24]
Out[1]= {1, 2, 3, 4, 6, 8, 12, 24}
```

These are the divisors of 15.

```
In[2]:= Divisors[15]
Out[2]= {1, 3, 5, 15}
```

The **greatest common divisor** function GCD[n_1, n_2, ...] gives the largest integer that divides all the n_i exactly. When you enter a ratio of two integers, *Mathematica* effectively uses GCD to cancel out common factors, and give a rational number in lowest terms.

The **least common multiple** function LCM[n_1, n_2, ...] gives the smallest integer that contains all the factors of each of the n_i.

The largest integer that divides both 24 and 15 is 3.

```
In[3]:= GCD[24, 15]
Out[3]= 3
```

The smallest integer divisible by both 24 and 15 is 120.

```
In[4]:= LCM[24, 15]
Out[4]= 120
```

The product of the gcd and lcm is always equal to the product of the numbers.

```
In[5]:= {GCD[24, 15] LCM[24, 15] , 24 15}
Out[5]= {360, 360}
```

Prime[*k*]	the kth prime number
FactorInteger[*n*]	a list of the prime factors of *n*, and their exponents
PrimeQ[*n*]	give True if *n* is a prime, and False otherwise

Integer factoring and related functions.

A prime is an integer with exactly two positive divisors.

```
In[6]:= Divisors[23]
Out[6]= {1, 23}
```

There are 25 primes up to 100.

```
In[7]:= Prime[ Range[25] ]
Out[7]= {2, 3, 5, 7, 11, 13, 17, 19, 23, 29, 31, 37, 41, 43,
         47, 53, 59, 61, 67, 71, 73, 79, 83, 89, 97}
```

Here is a plot of the first 100 primes.

In[8]:= **ListPlot[Prime[Range[100]]]**

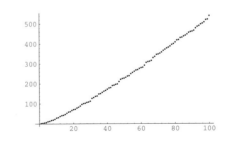

This gives the factors of 24 as 2^3, 3^1. The first element in each list is the factor; the second is its exponent.

In[9]:= **FactorInteger[24]**

Out[9]= {{2, 3}, {3, 1}}

The factors of 360 are 2^3, 3^2, 5^1. Every integer factors as a product of primes.

In[10]:= **FactorInteger[360]**

Out[10]= {{2, 3}, {3, 2}, {5, 1}}

Here are the factors of a larger integer.

In[11]:= **FactorInteger[111111111111111111]**

Out[11]= {{3, 2}, {7, 1}, {11, 1}, {13, 1}, {19, 1}, {37, 1},
{52579, 1}, {333667, 1}}

You should realize that according to current mathematical thinking, integer factoring is a fundamentally difficult computational problem. As a result, you can easily type in an integer that *Mathematica* will not be able to factor in anything short of an astronomical length of time. As long as the integers you give are less than about 20 digits long, FactorInteger should have no trouble. Only in special cases, however, will it be able to deal with much longer integers. (You can make some factoring problems go faster by setting the option FactorComplete -> False, so that FactorInteger[*n*] tries to pull out only one factor from *n*.)

Here is a rather special long integer, the product of the integers from 1 to 30.

In[12]:= **30!**

Out[12]= 265252859812191058636308480000000

Mathematica can easily factor this special integer.

In[13]:= **FactorInteger[%]**

Out[13]= {{2, 26}, {3, 14}, {5, 7}, {7, 4}, {11, 2}, {13, 2},
{17, 1}, {19, 1}, {23, 1}, {29, 1}}

Although *Mathematica* may not be able to factor a large integer, it can often still test whether or not the integer is a prime. In addition, *Mathematica* has a fast way of finding the kth prime number.

It is often much faster to test whether a number is prime than to factor it.

In[14]:= **PrimeQ[234242423]**

Out[14]= False

This is the millionth prime.

In[15]:= **Prime[1000000]**

Out[15]= 15485863

PowerMod ▪ PrimePi ▪ EulerPhi ▪ MoebiusMu ▪ DivisorSigma ▪ JacobiSymbol ▪ ExtendedGCD ▪ ArithmeticGeometricMean ▪ LatticeReduce ▪ GaussianIntegers

Other *Mathematica* functions related to number theory. (See page xvi.)

BernoulliB ▪ EulerE ▪ StirlingS1 ▪ StirlingS2 ▪ PartitionsP ▪ PartitionsQ ▪ Signature ▪ ClebschGordan ▪ ThreeJSymbol ▪ SixJSymbol

Other *Mathematica* functions, related to combinatorics. (See page xvi.)

6. Algebra

■ 6.1 Symbolic Computation

One of the most important features of *Mathematica* is that it can do *symbolic*, as well as *numerical* calculations. This means that it can handle algebraic formulas as well as numbers.

Here is a typical numerical computation.

In[1]:= **3 + 62 - 1**

Out[1]= 64

This is a symbolic computation.

In[2]:= **3x - x + 2**

Out[2]= 2 + 2 x

numerical computation	3 + 62 - 1 ⟶ 64
symbolic computation	3x - x + 2 ⟶ 2 + 2 x

Numerical and symbolic computations.

You can type any algebraic expression into *Mathematica*. The expression is printed out in an approximation to standard mathematical notation.

In[3]:= **-1 + 2x + x∧3**

Out[3]= -1 + 2 x + x^3

Mathematica automatically carries out standard algebraic simplifications. Here it combines x^2 and $-4x^2$ to get $-3x^2$.

In[4]:= **x∧2 + x - 4 x∧2**

Out[4]= x - 3 x^2

You can type in any algebraic expression, using the operators listed on page 27. You can use spaces to denote multiplication. Be careful not to forget the space in x y. If you type in xy with no space, *Mathematica* will interpret this as a single symbol, with the name xy, not as a product of the two symbols x and y.

Mathematica rearranges and combines terms using the standard rules of algebra.

In[5]:= **x y + 2 x∧2 y + y∧2 x∧2 - 2 y x**

Out[5]= -(x y) + 2 x^2 y + x^2 y^2

Here is another algebraic expression.

In[6]:= **(x + 2y + 1)(x - 2)∧2**

Out[6]= (-2 + x)^2 (1 + x + 2 y)

The function Expand multiplies out products and powers.

In[7]:= **Expand[%]**

Out[7]= 4 - 3 x^2 + x^3 + 8 y - 8 x y + 2 x^2 y

Factor does essentially the inverse of Expand.

In[8]:= **Factor[%]**

Out[8]= (-2 + x)^2 (1 + x + 2 y)

When you type in more complicated expressions, it is important that you put parentheses in the right places. Thus, for example, you have to give the expression x^{4y} in the form $x\wedge(4y)$. If you leave out the parentheses, you get x^4y instead. It never hurts to put in too many parentheses, but to find out exactly when you need to use parentheses, look at Section A2.

Here is a more complicated formula, requiring several parentheses.

```
In[9]:= Sqrt[8]/9801 (4n)! (1103 + 26390 n) /
                         (n!∧4 396∧(4n))
```

$$Out[9]= \frac{2 \text{ Sqrt}[2] \ (1103 + 26390 \text{ n}) \ (4 \text{ n})!}{9801 \ 396^{4 \text{ n}} \ \text{n}!^4}$$

When you type in an expression, *Mathematica* automatically applies its large repertoire of rules for transforming expressions. These rules include the standard rules of algebra, such as $x - x = 0$, together with much more sophisticated rules involving higher mathematical functions.

Mathematica uses standard rules of algebra to replace $(\sqrt{1+x})^4$ by $(1+x)^2$.

```
In[10]:= Sqrt[1 + x]∧4
```

$$Out[10]= (1 + x)^2$$

Mathematica knows no rules for this expression, so it leaves the expression in the original form you gave.

```
In[11]:= Sqrt[1 + Cos[x]]

Out[11]= Sqrt[1 + Cos[x]]
```

The notion of transformation rules is a very general one. In fact, you can think of the whole of *Mathematica* as simply a system for applying a collection of transformation rules to many different kinds of expressions.

The general principle that *Mathematica* follows is simple to state. It takes any expression you input, and gets results by applying a succession of transformation rules, stopping when it knows no more transformation rules that can be applied.

> ■ Take any expression, and apply transformation rules until the result no longer changes.

The fundamental principle of *Mathematica*.

■ 6.2 Using Symbols for Units

There are many ways to use symbols in *Mathematica*. So far, we have concentrated on using symbols to store values and to represent mathematical variables. This subsection describes another way to use symbols in *Mathematica*.

The idea is to use symbols as "tags" for different types of objects.

Working with physical units gives one simple example. When you specify the length of an object, you want to give not only a number, but also the units in which the length is measured. In standard notation, you might write a length as 12 meters.

You can imitate this notation almost directly in *Mathematica*. You can for example simply use a symbol `meters` to indicate the units of our measurement.

The symbol `meters` here acts as a tag, which indicates the units used.

```
In[1]:= 12 meters
Out[1]= 12 meters
```

You can add lengths like this.

```
In[2]:= % + 5.3 meters
Out[2]= 17.3 meters
```

This gives a speed.

```
In[3]:= % / (25 seconds)
```

$$Out[3]= \frac{0.692\ meters}{seconds}$$

This converts to a speed in feet per second.

```
In[4]:= % /. meters -> 3.28084 feet
```

$$Out[4]= \frac{2.27034\ feet}{seconds}$$

There is in fact a standard *Mathematica* package that allows you to work with units. The package defines many symbols that represent standard types of units. Packages are discussed in Chapter 22.

Load the *Mathematica* package for handling units.

```
In[5]:= <<Miscellaneous`Units`
```

The package uses standardized names for units.

```
In[6]:= 12 Meter/Second
```

$$Out[6]= \frac{12\ Meter}{Second}$$

The function `Convert[expr, units]` converts to the specified units.

```
In[7]:= Convert[ %, Mile/Hour ]
```

$$Out[7]= \frac{26.8432\ Mile}{Hour}$$

You generally have to give prefixes for units as separate words, but the standard units `Kilogram` and `Centimeter` are exceptions; they may be given as `Kilogram` and `Centimeter`, as well as `Kilo Gram` and `Centi Meter`.

```
In[8]:= Convert[ 3 Kilo Meter / Hour, Inch / Minute ]
```

$$Out[8]= \frac{1968.5\ Inch}{Minute}$$

■ 6.3 Values for Symbols

When *Mathematica* transforms an expression such as x + x into 2x, it is treating the variable x in a purely symbolic or formal fashion. In such cases, x is a symbol which can stand for any expression.

Often, however, you need to replace a symbol like x with a definite "value". Sometimes this value will be a number; often it will be another expression.

To take an expression such as 1 + 2x and replace the symbol x that appears in it with a definite value, you can create a *Mathematica* transformation rule, and then apply this rule to the expression. To replace x with the value 3, you would create the transformation rule x -> 3. You must type -> as a pair of characters, with no space in between. You can think of x -> 3 as being a rule in which "x goes to 3".

To apply a transformation rule to a particular *Mathematica* expression, you type *expr* /. *rule*. The "replacement operator" /. is typed as a pair of characters, with no space in between.

This uses the transformation rule x -> 3 in the expression 1 + 2x.	*In[1]:=* **1 + 2x /. x -> 3** *Out[1]=* 7
You can replace x with any expression. Here every occurrence of x is replaced by 2 - y.	*In[2]:=* **1 + x + x^2 /. x -> 2 - y** *Out[2]=* $3 + (2 - y)^2 - y$
Here is a transformation rule. *Mathematica* treats it like any other symbolic expression.	*In[3]:=* **x -> 3 + y** *Out[3]=* x -> 3 + y
This applies the transformation rule on the previous line to the expression x^2 - 9.	*In[4]:=* **x^2 - 9 /. %** *Out[4]=* $-9 + (3 + y)^2$

expr /. *x* -> *value*	replace *x* by *value* in the expression *expr*
expr /. {*x* -> *xval*, *y* -> *yval*}	perform several replacements

Replacing symbols by values in expressions.

You can apply rules together by putting the rules in a list.	*In[5]:=* **(x + y) (x - y)^2 /. {x -> 3, y -> 1 - a}** *Out[5]=* $(4 - a) (2 + a)^2$

The replacement operator /. allows you to apply transformation rules to a particular expression. Sometimes, however, you will want to define transformation rules that should *always* be applied. For example, you might want to replace x with 3 whenever x occurs.

As discussed in Section 3.1, you can do this by *assigning* the value 3 to x using x = 3. Once you have made the assignment x = 3, x will always be replaced by 3, whenever it appears.

This assigns the value 3 to x.	*In[6]:=* **x = 3** *Out[6]=* 3
Now x will automatically be replaced by 3 wherever it appears.	*In[7]:=* **x^2 - 1** *Out[7]=* 8
This assigns the expression 1 + a to be the value of x.	*In[8]:=* **x = 1 + a** *Out[8]=* 1 + a

Now x is replaced by 1 + a.

```
In[9]:= x^2 - 1
                        2
Out[9]= -1 + (1 + a)
```

You can define the value of a symbol to be any expression, not just a number. You should realize that once you have given such a definition, the definition will continue to be used whenever the symbol appears, until you explicitly change or remove the definition. For most people, forgetting to remove values you have assigned to symbols is the single most common source of mistakes in using *Mathematica*.

$x = value$	define a value for x which will always be used
$x =.$	remove any value defined for x

Assigning values to symbols.

The symbol x still has the value you assigned to it above.

```
In[10]:= x + 5 - 2x
Out[10]= 6 + a - 2 (1 + a)
```

This removes the value you assigned to x.

```
In[11]:= x =.
```

Now x has no value defined, so it can be used as a purely symbolic variable.

```
In[12]:= x + 5 - 2x
Out[12]= 5 - x
```

A symbol such as x can serve many different purposes in *Mathematica*, and in fact, much of the flexibility of *Mathematica* comes from being able to mix these purposes at will. However, you need to keep some of the different uses of x straight in order to avoid making mistakes. The most important distinction is between the use of x as a name for another expression, and as a symbolic variable that stands only for itself.

Traditional programming languages that do not support symbolic computation allow variables to be used only as names for objects, typically numbers, that have been assigned as values for them. In *Mathematica*, however, x can also be treated as a purely formal variable, to which various transformation rules can be applied. Of course, if you explicitly give a definition, such as x = 3, then x will always be replaced by 3, and can no longer serve as a formal variable.

You should understand that explicit definitions such as x = 3 have a global effect. On the other hand, a replacement such as *expr* /. x -> 3 affects only the specific expression *expr*. It is usually much easier to keep things straight if you avoid using explicit definitions except when absolutely necessary.

You can always mix replacements with assignments. With assignments, you can give names to expressions in which you want to do replacements, or to rules that you want to use to do the replacements.

This assigns a value to the symbol t.

```
In[13]:= t = 1 + x^2
                2
Out[13]= 1 + x
```

This finds the value of t, and then replaces x by 2 in it.

```
In[14]:= t /. x -> 2
Out[14]= 5
```

This finds the value of t for a different value of x.

```
In[15]:= t /. x -> 5a
               2
Out[15]= 1 + 25 a
```

This finds the value of t when x is replaced by Pi, and then evaluates the result numerically.

```
In[16]:= N[ t /. x -> Pi ]
Out[16]= 10.8696
```

■ 6.4 Transforming Algebraic Expressions

There are often many different ways to write the same algebraic expression. As one example, the expression $(1 + x)^2$ can be written as $1 + 2x + x^2$. *Mathematica* provides a large collection of functions for converting between different forms of algebraic expressions.

Expand[*expr*]	multiply out products and powers, writing the result as a sum of terms
Factor[*expr*]	write *expr* as a minimal product of factors

Two common functions for transforming algebraic expressions.

Expand gives the "expanded form", with products and powers multiplied out.

```
In[1]:= Expand[ (1 + x)^2 ]
                     2
Out[1]= 1 + 2 x + x
```

Factor recovers the original form.

```
In[2]:= Factor[ % ]
                   2
Out[2]= (1 + x)
```

It is easy to generate complicated expressions with Expand.

```
In[3]:= Expand[ (1 + x + 3 y)^4 ]
                       2      3    4                           2
Out[3]= 1 + 4 x + 6 x  + 4 x  + x  + 12 y + 36 x y + 36 x  y +

             3         2          2        2 2        3         3
        12 x  y + 54 y  + 108 x y  + 54 x  y  + 108 y  + 108 x y  +

            4
        81 y
```

Factor often gives you simpler expressions.

```
In[4]:= Factor[ % ]
                       4
Out[4]= (1 + x + 3 y)
```

There are some cases, though, where Factor can give you more complicated expressions.

In[5]:= **Factor[x^10 - 1]**

$$Out[5]= (-1 + x) (1 + x) (1 - x + x^2 - x^3 + x^4)$$
$$(1 + x + x^2 + x^3 + x^4)$$

In this case, Expand gives the "simpler" form.

In[6]:= **Expand[%]**

$$Out[6]= -1 + x^{10}$$

■ 6.5 Simplifying Algebraic Expressions

There are many situations where you want to write a particular algebraic expression in the simplest possible form. Although it is difficult to know exactly what one means in all cases by the "simplest form", a worthwhile practical procedure is to look at many different forms of an expression, and pick out the one that involves the smallest number of parts.

Simplify[*expr*]	try to find the form of *expr* with the smallest number of parts, by applying a variety of algebraic transformations

Simplifying algebraic expressions.

Simplify writes $x^2 + 2x + 1$ in factored form.

In[1]:= **Simplify[x^2 + 2x + 1]**

$$Out[1]= (1 + x)^2$$

Simplify leaves $x^{10} - 1$ in expanded form, since for this expression, the factored form is larger.

In[2]:= **Simplify[x^10 - 1]**

$$Out[2]= -1 + x^{10}$$

You can often use Simplify to "clean up" complicated expressions.

In[3]:= **1 / (1 + x) + 1 / (1 - x) + 2 / (1 + x^2)**

$$Out[3]= \frac{1}{1 - x} + \frac{1}{1 + x} + \frac{2}{1 + x^2}$$

Simplify succeeds in getting a simpler form of the expression.

In[4]:= **Simplify[%]**

$$Out[4]= \frac{4}{1 - x^4}$$

For many simple algebraic calculations, you may find it convenient to use Simplify routinely on your results.

In more complicated calculations, however, you often need to exercise more control over the exact form of answer that you get. In addition, when your expressions are complicated, Simplify may spend a long time testing a large number of possible forms in its attempt to find the simplest one.

<table>
<tr><td>PowerExpand[expr]</td><td>expand out $(ab)^c$ and $(a^b)^c$ in expr</td></tr>
</table>

Expanding powers.

Mathematica does not automatically expand out expressions of the form $(a\ b)\wedge c$ except when c is an integer. In general it is only correct to do this expansion if a and b are positive reals. Nevertheless, the function PowerExpand does the expansion, effectively assuming that a and b are indeed positive reals.

Mathematica does not automatically expand out this expression.	`In[5]:= (x y)^r` $Out[5]= (x\ y)^r$
PowerExpand does the expansion, effectively assuming that x and y are either zero or positive reals.	`In[6]:= PowerExpand[%]` $Out[6]= x^r\ y^r$

Mathematica does not automatically expand this out either.	`In[7]:= Sqrt[x y]`
	
	`Out[7]= Sqrt[x y]`

PowerExpand forces the expansion.	`In[8]:= PowerExpand[%]`
	
	`Out[8]= Sqrt[x] Sqrt[y]`

The expansion is guaranteed to be correct only if x and y are both non-negative.	`In[9]:= {Sqrt[x y], Sqrt[x] Sqrt[y]} /. {x -> -1, y -> -1}`
	
	`Out[9]= {1, -1}`

ComplexExpand ▪ Collect ▪ Coefficient ▪ Exponent ▪ Numerator ▪ Denominator

Other *Mathematica* functions related to formula manipulation. (See page xvi.)

■ 6.6 Sums and Products

This constructs the sum $\sum_{i=1}^{7} \frac{x^i}{i}$.	`In[1]:= Sum[x^i/i, {i, 1, 7}]` $Out[1]= x + \frac{x^2}{2} + \frac{x^3}{3} + \frac{x^4}{4} + \frac{x^5}{5} + \frac{x^6}{6} + \frac{x^7}{7}$
You can leave out the lower limit if it is equal to 1.	`In[2]:= Sum[x^i/i, {i, 7}]` $Out[2]= x + \frac{x^2}{2} + \frac{x^3}{3} + \frac{x^4}{4} + \frac{x^5}{5} + \frac{x^6}{6} + \frac{x^7}{7}$

This makes *i* increase in steps of 2, so that only odd-numbered values are included.

```
In[3]:= Sum[x^i/i, {i, 1, 5, 2}]
```

$$Out[3]= x + \frac{x^3}{3} + \frac{x^5}{5}$$

Products work just like sums.

```
In[4]:= Product[x + i, {i, 1, 4}]
```

$$Out[4]= (1 + x) (2 + x) (3 + x) (4 + x)$$

Sum[*f*, {*i*, *imin*, *imax*}]	the sum $\sum_{i=imin}^{imax} f$
Sum[*f*, {*i*, *imin*, *imax*, *di*}]	the sum with *i* increasing in steps of *di*
Product[*f*, {*i*, *imin*, *imax*}]	the product $\prod_{i=imin}^{imax} f$

Sums and products.

Mathematica gives an exact result for this sum.

```
In[5]:= Sum[1/i^3, {i, 1, 20}]
```

$$Out[5]= \frac{336658814638864376538323}{280346265322438720204800}$$

Here is the numerical value.

```
In[6]:= N[ % ]
```

```
Out[6]= 1.20087
```

Mathematica cannot give you an exact result for this infinite sum.

```
In[7]:= Sum[1/i^3, {i, 1, Infinity}]
```

$$Out[7]= Sum[i^{-3}, \{i, 1, Infinity\}]$$

You can still get a numerical result.

```
In[8]:= N[ % ]
```

```
Out[8]= 1.20206
```

Numerical summation will be discussed in Section 14.7. *Mathematica* also has a notation for multiple sums and products. Sum[*f*, {*i*, *imin*, *imax*}, {*j*, *jmin*, *jmax*}] represents a sum over *i* and *j*, which would be written in standard mathematical notation as $\sum_{i=imin}^{imax} \sum_{j=jmin}^{jmax} f$. Notice that in *Mathematica* notation, as in standard mathematical notation, the range of the *outermost* variable is given *first*.

This is the multiple sum $\sum_{i=1}^{3} \sum_{j=1}^{i} x^i y^j$. Notice that the outermost sum over *i* is given first, just as in the mathematical notation.

```
In[9]:= Sum[x^i y^j, {i, 1, 3}, {j, 1, i}]
```

$$Out[9]= x y + x^2 y + x^2 y^2 + x^3 y + x^3 y^2 + x^3 y^3$$

The way the ranges of variables are specified in Sum and Product is an example of the rather general *iterator notation* that *Mathematica* uses. You will see this notation when we discuss generating tables and lists using Table (Section 11.2), and you will see it again when we describe Do loops (Section 28.6).

{*imax*}	iterate *imax* times, without incrementing any variables
{*i*, *imax*}	*i* goes from 1 to *imax* in steps of 1
{*i*, *imin*, *imax*}	*i* goes from *imin* to *imax* in steps of 1
{*i*, *imin*, *imax*, *di*}	*i* goes from *imin* to *imax* in steps of *di*
{*i*, *imin*, *imax*}, {*j*, *jmin*, *jmax*}, ...	*i* goes from *imin* to *imax*, and for each value of *i*, *j* goes from *jmin* to *jmax*, etc.

Mathematica iterator notation.

■ 6.7 Advanced Topic: Putting Expressions into Different Forms

Complicated algebraic expressions can usually be written in many different ways. *Mathematica* provides a variety of functions for converting expressions from one form to another.

In most applications, the commonest of these functions are Expand, Factor and Simplify. However, particularly when you have rational expressions that contain quotients, you may need to use other functions.

ExpandNumerator[*expr*]	expand numerators only
ExpandDenominator[*expr*]	expand denominators only
Expand[*expr*]	multiply out products and powers
ExpandAll[*expr*]	apply Expand everywhere
Factor[*expr*]	reduce to a product of factors
Together[*expr*]	put all terms over a common denominator
Apart[*expr*]	separate into terms with simple denominators
Cancel[*expr*]	cancel common factors between numerators and denominators

Functions for transforming algebraic expressions.

Here is a rational expression that can be written in many different forms.

```
In[1]:= e = (x - 1)^2 (2 + x) / ((1 + x) (x - 3)^2)
```

$$Out[1]= \frac{(-1 + x)^2 (2 + x)}{(-3 + x)^2 (1 + x)}$$

ExpandDenominator expands out the denominator.

$In[2]:=$ **ExpandDenominator[e]**

$$Out[2]= \frac{(-1 + x)^2 (2 + x)}{9 + 3 x - 5 x^2 + x^3}$$

ExpandNumerator writes the numerator in expanded form.

$In[3]:=$ **ExpandNumerator[e]**

$$Out[3]= \frac{2 - 3 x + x^3}{(-3 + x)^2 (1 + x)}$$

Expand expands out the numerator, but leaves the denominator in factored form.

$In[4]:=$ **Expand[e]**

$$Out[4]= \frac{2}{(-3 + x)^2 (1 + x)} - \frac{3 x}{(-3 + x)^2 (1 + x)} + \frac{x^3}{(-3 + x)^2 (1 + x)}$$

ExpandAll expands out everything, including the denominator.

$In[5]:=$ **ExpandAll[e]**

$$Out[5]= \frac{2}{9 + 3 x - 5 x^2 + x^3} - \frac{3 x}{9 + 3 x - 5 x^2 + x^3} + \frac{x^3}{9 + 3 x - 5 x^2 + x^3}$$

Together collects all the terms together over a common denominator.

$In[6]:=$ **Together[%]**

$$Out[6]= \frac{2 - 3 x + x^3}{9 + 3 x - 5 x^2 + x^3}$$

Apart breaks the expression apart into terms with simple denominators. In mathematical terms, Apart decomposes a rational expression into "partial fractions".

$In[7]:=$ **Apart[%]**

$$Out[7]= 1 + \frac{5}{(-3 + x)^2} + \frac{19}{4 (-3 + x)} + \frac{1}{4 (1 + x)}$$

Factor factors everything, in this case reproducing the original form.

$In[8]:=$ **Factor[%]**

$$Out[8]= \frac{(-1 + x)^2 (2 + x)}{(-3 + x)^2 (1 + x)}$$

Getting expressions into the form you want is something of an art. In most cases, it is best simply to experiment, trying different transformations until you get what you want.

PolynomialQ ▪ Variables ▪ CoefficientList ▪ PolynomialMod ▪
PolynomialQuotient ▪ PolynomialRemainder ▪ PolynomialGCD ▪ PolynomialLCM ▪
PolynomialDivision ▪ Resultant ▪ FactorSquareFree ▪ FactorSquareFreeList ▪
FactorTerms ▪ FactorTermsList ▪ FactorList ▪ Cyclotomic ▪ Decompose ▪
InterpolatingPolynomial ▪ GroebnerBasis ▪ AlgebraicRules ▪ Modulus ▪
GaussianIntegers

Other *Mathematica* functions related to polynomials. (See page xvi.)

■ 6.8 Advanced Topic: Transforming Trigonometric Expressions

As we have seen, even when you restrict yourself to polynomials and rational expressions, there are many different ways to write any particular expression. If you consider more complicated expressions, involving, for example, higher mathematical functions, the variety of possible forms becomes still greater. As a result, it is totally infeasible to have a specific function built into *Mathematica* to produce each possible form. Rather, *Mathematica* allows you to construct arbitrary sets of transformation rules for converting between different forms. Many *Mathematica* packages include such rules; the details of how to construct them for yourself are given in Chapter 27.

There are nevertheless a few additional built-in *Mathematica* functions for transforming expressions.

Without Trig -> True, Expand leaves trigonometric functions unchanged.	$In[1]:=$ **Expand[Sin[x]^2 + Sin[2x]^2]** $Out[1]=$ $\text{Sin[x]}^2 + \text{Sin[2 x]}^2$
With Trig -> True, Expand transforms trigonometric functions.	$In[2]:=$ **Expand[%, Trig -> True]** $Out[2]=$ $1 - \dfrac{\text{Cos[2 x]}}{2} - \dfrac{\text{Cos[4 x]}}{2}$
This generates a multiple angle form for the trigonometric expression.	$In[3]:=$ **Expand[Cos[x]^3 Sin[x]^2, Trig -> True]** $Out[3]=$ $\dfrac{\text{Cos[x]}}{8} - \dfrac{\text{Cos[3 x]}}{16} - \dfrac{\text{Cos[5 x]}}{16}$
This gets back the original form.	$In[4]:=$ **Factor[%, Trig -> True]** $Out[4]=$ $\text{Cos[x]}^3 \text{Sin[x]}^2$

Expand[*expr*, Trig -> True]	write $\sin(x)^2$ in terms of $\sin(2x)$, etc.
Factor[*expr*, Trig -> True]	write $\sin(2x)$ in terms of $\sin(x)^2$, etc.

Expanding and factoring trigonometric expressions.

Expand writes products and powers of trigonometric functions in terms of trigonometric functions with combined arguments.

In[5]:= **Expand[Sin[a x] Cos[b x]∧2, Trig -> True]**

Out[5]= $\dfrac{\text{Sin[a x]}}{2} + \dfrac{\text{Sin[a x - 2 b x]}}{4} + \dfrac{\text{Sin[a x + 2 b x]}}{4}$

Factor writes trigonometric functions in terms of products and powers of trigonometric functions with simpler arguments.

In[6]:= **Factor[%, Trig -> True]**

Out[6]= $\text{Cos[b x]}^2 \text{ Sin[a x]}$

7. Solving Equations

■ 7.1 Equations

Section 3.1 discussed *assignments* such as $x = y$ which *set* x equal to y. This section discusses *equations*, which *test* equality. The equation $x == y$ tests whether x is equal to y.

This *tests* whether 2 + 2 and 4 are equal. The result is the symbol `True`.

```
In[1]:= 2 + 2 == 4
Out[1]= True
```

It is very important that you do not confuse $x = y$ with $x == y$. While $x = y$ is an *imperative* statement that actually causes an assignment to be done, $x == y$ merely *tests* whether x and y are equal, and causes no explicit action.

$x = y$	assigns x to have value y
$x == y$	tests whether x and y are equal

Assignments and tests.

This *assigns* x to have value 4.

```
In[2]:= x = 4
Out[2]= 4
```

If you ask for x, you now get 4.

```
In[3]:= x
Out[3]= 4
```

This *tests* whether x is equal to 4. In this case, it is.

```
In[4]:= x == 4
Out[4]= True
```

x is equal to 4, not 6.

```
In[5]:= x == 6
Out[5]= False
```

This removes the value assigned to x.

```
In[6]:= x =.
```

The tests we have used so far involve only numbers, and always give a definite answer, either `True` or `False`. You can also do tests on symbolic expressions.

Mathematica cannot get a definite result for this test unless you give x a specific numerical value.

```
In[7]:= x == 5
Out[7]= x == 5
```

If you replace x by the specific numerical value 4, the test gives `False`.

```
In[8]:= % /. x -> 4
Out[8]= False
```

Even when you do tests on symbolic expressions, there are some cases where you can get definite results. An important one is when you test the equality of two expressions that are *identical*. Whatever the numerical values of the variables in these expressions may be, *Mathematica* knows that the expressions must always be equal.

The two expressions are *identical*, so the result is True, whatever the value of x may be.	$In[9] := $ **2 x + x^2 == 2 x + x^2** $Out[9] = $ True

Mathematica does not try to tell whether these expressions are equal. In this case, using Expand would make them have the same form.

$In[10] := $ **2 x + x^2 == x (2 + x)**

$Out[10] = $ 2 x + x^2 == x (2 + x)

Expressions like x == 4 represent *equations* in *Mathematica*. There are many functions in *Mathematica* for manipulating and solving equations.

This is an *equation* in *Mathematica*.

$In[11] := $ **x^2 + 2 x - 7 == 0**

$Out[11] = $ -7 + 2 x + x^2 == 0

You can assign a name to the equation.

$In[12] := $ **eqn = %**

$Out[12] = $ -7 + 2 x + x^2 == 0

If you ask for eqn, you now get the equation.

$In[13] := $ **eqn**

$Out[13] = $ -7 + 2 x + x^2 == 0

■ 7.2 Solving Algebraic Equations

An expression like x^2 + 2 x - 7 == 0 represents an *equation* in *Mathematica*. You will often need to *solve* equations like this, to find out for what values of x they are true.

It is easy to solve a linear equation in x.

$In[1] := $ **Solve[a x + b == c, x]**

$Out[1] = $ $\{\{x \rightarrow -(\frac{b - c}{a})\}\}$

This is how to get the solution by itself.

$In[2] := $ **x /. Solve[a x + b == c, x][[1]]**

$Out[2] = $ $-(\frac{b - c}{a})$

This gives the two solutions to the quadratic equation $x^2 + 2x - 7 = 0$. The solutions are given as replacements for x.

$In[3] := $ **Solve[x^2 + 2x - 7 == 0, x]**

$Out[3] = $ $\{\{x \rightarrow \frac{-2 - 4\ \text{Sqrt}[2]}{2}\}, \{x \rightarrow \frac{-2 + 4\ \text{Sqrt}[2]}{2}\}\}$

Here are the numerical values of the solutions.

$In[4] := $ **N[%]**

$Out[4] = $ {{x -> -3.82843}, {x -> 1.82843}}

You can get a list of the actual solutions for x by applying the rules using the replacement operator.

In[5]:= **x /. %**

Out[5]= {-3.82843, 1.82843}

You can equally well apply the rules to any other expression involving x.

In[6]:= **x^2 + 3 x /. %%**

Out[6]= {3.17157, 8.82843}

Solve[*lhs* == *rhs*, *x*]	solve an equation, giving a list of rules for *x*
x /. *solution*	use the list of rules to get values for *x*
expr /. *solution*	use the list of rules to get values for an expression

Finding and using solutions to equations.

Solve always tries to give you explicit *formulas* for the solutions to equations. However, it is a basic mathematical result that, for sufficiently complicated equations, explicit algebraic formulas cannot be given. If you have an algebraic equation in one variable, and the highest power of the variable is at most four, then *Mathematica* can always give you formulas for the solutions. However, if the highest power is five or more, it may be mathematically impossible to give explicit algebraic formulas for all the solutions.

Mathematica solves quadratic equations by applying a simple formula.

In[7]:= **Solve[x^2 + a x + 2 == 0 , x]**

$$Out[7]= \left\{\left\{x \to \frac{-a - \sqrt{-8 + a^2}}{2}\right\}, \left\{x \to \frac{-a + \sqrt{-8 + a^2}}{2}\right\}\right\}$$

Mathematica can also find the exact solution to an arbitrary cubic equation. The results are however often very complicated. Here is the first solution to a comparatively simple cubic equation.

In[8]:= **Solve[x^3 + 34 x + 1 == 0 , x] [[1]]**

$$Out[8]= \left\{x \to \frac{-34 \cdot 2^{1/3}}{(-27 + 3\sqrt{471729})^{1/3}} + \frac{(-27 + 3\sqrt{471729})^{1/3}}{3 \cdot 2^{1/3}}\right\}$$

It can solve some equations that involve higher powers.

In[9]:= **Solve[x^6 == 1, x]**

$$Out[9]= \{\{x \to -1\}, \{x \to 1\}, \{x \to -(-1)^{1/3}\}, \{x \to (-1)^{1/3}\},$$
$$\{x \to -(-1)^{2/3}\}, \{x \to (-1)^{2/3}\}\}$$

There are some equations, however, for which it is mathematically impossible to find explicit formulas for the solutions. *Mathematica* uses the function Roots to represent the solutions in this case.

In[10]:= **Solve[2 - 4 x + x^5 == 0, x]**

$$Out[10]= \{\text{ToRules}[\text{Roots}[-4 x + x^5 == -2, x]]\}$$

Even though you cannot get explicit formulas, you can still find the solutions numerically.

$In[11]:=$ **N[%]**

$Out[11]=$ {{x -> -1.51851}, {x -> -0.116792 - 1.43845 I},

{x -> -0.116792 + 1.43845 I}, {x -> 0.508499}, {x -> 1.2436}}

When *Mathematica* can find solutions to an nth-degree polynomial equation, it always gives exactly n solutions. The number of times that each root of the polynomial appears is equal to its multiplicity.

Solve gives two identical solutions to this equation.

$In[12]:=$ **Solve[(x-1)^2 == 0, x]**

$Out[12]=$ {{x -> 1}, {x -> 1}}

■ 7.3 Solving Simultaneous Equations

> Solve[{*lhs₁*==*rhs₁*, *lhs₂*==*rhs₂*, ... }, {*x, y,* ... }]
>
> solve a set of simultaneous equations for *x, y, ...*
>
> Solve[*eqns*]   try to solve *eqns* for all the objects that appear in them

Solving sets of simultaneous equations.

You can also use *Mathematica* to solve sets of simultaneous equations. You simply give the list of equations, and specify the list of variables to solve for.

Here is a list of two simultaneous equations, to be solved for the variables *x* and *y*.

$In[1]:=$ **Solve[{a x + y == 0, 2 x + (1 - a) y == 1}, {x, y}]**

$Out[1]=$ $\{\{x \rightarrow -(\dfrac{1}{-2 + (1 - a) \, a}), \, y \rightarrow \dfrac{a}{-2 + (1 - a) \, a}\}\}$

Here is another example.

$In[2]:=$ **Solve[{a x + b y == 1, x - y == 2}, {x, y}]**

$Out[2]=$ $\{\{x \rightarrow 2 - \dfrac{-1 + 2 \, a}{a + b}, \, y \rightarrow -(\dfrac{-1 + 2 \, a}{a + b})\}\}$

If you do not explicitly specify objects to solve for, Solve will try to solve for all the variables.

$In[3]:=$ **Solve[{ x + y == 1, x - 3 y == 2 }]**

$Out[3]=$ $\{\{x \rightarrow \dfrac{5}{4}, \, y \rightarrow -(\dfrac{1}{4})\}\}$

Mathematica can solve any set of simultaneous *linear* equations. *Mathematica* can also solve a large class of simultaneous polynomial equations. Even when it does not manage to solve the equations explicitly, *Mathematica* will still usually reduce them to a much simpler form.

Here are some more complicated simultaneous equations. The two solutions are given as two lists of replacements for x and y.

$In[4]:=$ **Solve[{x^2 + y^2 == 1, x + 3 y == 0}, {x, y}]**

$Out[4]=$ $\{\{x \rightarrow \dfrac{-3}{Sqrt[10]}, y \rightarrow \dfrac{1}{Sqrt[10]}\},$

$\{x \rightarrow \dfrac{3}{Sqrt[10]}, y \rightarrow -(\dfrac{1}{Sqrt[10]})\}\}$

Here are the two pairs of solutions.

$In[5]:=$ **{x, y} /. %**

$Out[5]=$ $\{\{\dfrac{-3}{Sqrt[10]}, \dfrac{1}{Sqrt[10]}\}, \{\dfrac{3}{Sqrt[10]}, -(\dfrac{1}{Sqrt[10]})\}\}$

This uses the solutions to evaluate the expression x + y. There are two possibilities.

$In[6]:=$ **x + y /. %%**

$Out[6]=$ $\{-Sqrt[\dfrac{2}{5}], Sqrt[\dfrac{2}{5}]\}$

■ 7.4 Numerical Solution of Polynomial Equations

When Solve cannot find explicit solutions to polynomial equations, it returns a symbolic form of the result.

$In[1]:=$ **Solve[x^5 + 7x + 1 == 0, x]**

$Out[1]=$ $\{ToRules[Roots[7 x + x^5 == -1, x]]\}$

You can get numerical solutions by applying N.

$In[2]:=$ **N[%]**

$Out[2]=$ $\{\{x \rightarrow -1.11308 - 1.15173 I\},$

$\{x \rightarrow -1.11308 + 1.15173 I\}, \{x \rightarrow -0.142849\},$

$\{x \rightarrow 1.1845 - 1.15139 I\}, \{x \rightarrow 1.1845 + 1.15139 I\}\}$

This gives the first numerical solution to 20-digit precision.

$In[3]:=$ **N[%%, 20] [[1]]**

$Out[3]=$ $\{x \rightarrow -1.1130779765477107356 - 1.1517343621516743 0505 I\}$

You can use NSolve to get numerical solutions to polynomial equations directly, without first trying to find exact results.

$In[4]:=$ **NSolve[x^7 + x + 1 == 0, x]**

$Out[4]=$ $\{\{x \rightarrow -0.796544\}, \{x \rightarrow -0.705298 - 0.637624 I\},$

$\{x \rightarrow -0.705298 + 0.637624 I\}, \{x \rightarrow 0.123762 - 1.05665 I\},$

$\{x \rightarrow 0.123762 + 1.05665 I\}, \{x \rightarrow 0.979808 - 0.516677 I\},$

$\{x \rightarrow 0.979808 + 0.516677 I\}\}$

NSolve[*poly*==0, *x*]	get approximate numerical solutions to a polynomial equation
NSolve[*poly*==0, *x*, *n*]	get solutions to *n*-digit precision

Numerical solution of polynomial equations.

NSolve will always give you the complete set of numerical solutions to any polynomial equation in one variable.

You can also use NSolve to solve sets of simultaneous equations numerically.

```
In[5]:= NSolve[{x + y == 2, x - 3 y + z == 3, x - y + z == 0},
              {x, y, z}]

Out[5]= {{z -> -5., x -> 3.5, y -> -1.5}}
```

■ 7.5 Solving Non-Algebraic Equations

The main equations that Solve and related *Mathematica* functions deal with are *polynomial equations*. In addition to being able to solve purely algebraic equations, *Mathematica* can also solve some equations involving other functions.

After printing a warning, *Mathematica* returns one solution to this equation.

```
In[1]:= Solve[ Sin[x] == a, x ]

Solve::ifun:
     Warning: Inverse functions are being used by Solve, so some
        solutions may not be found.

Out[1]= {{x -> ArcSin[a]}}
```

It is important to realize that an equation such as $\sin(x) = a$ actually has an infinite number of possible solutions, in this case differing by multiples of 2π. However, Solve by default returns just one solution, but prints a message telling you that other solutions may exist.

There is no explicit "closed form" solution for a transcendental equation like this.

```
In[2]:= Solve[ Cos[x] == x, x ]

Solve::tdep:
     The equations appear to involve transcendental functions of
        the variables in an essentially non-algebraic way.

Out[2]= Solve[Cos[x] == x, x]
```

There seems to be a root near 1.

```
In[3]:= Plot[{Cos[x], x}, {x, -5, 5}]
```

You can find an approximate numerical solution using FindRoot, and giving a starting value for x.

```
In[4]:= FindRoot[ Cos[x] == x, {x, 1} ]

Out[4]= {x -> 0.739085}
```

FindRoot will be discussed in more detail in Section 13.1.

Solve can also handle equations involving symbolic functions. In such cases, it again prints a warning, then gives results in terms of formal inverse functions.

Mathematica returns a result in terms of
the formal inverse function of f.

```
In[5]:= Solve[ f[x^2] == a, x ]
```
```
Solve::ifun:
    Warning: inverse functions are being used by Solve, so some
    solutions may not be found.
```
$$Out[5]= \{\{x \to Sqrt[f^{(-1)}[a]]\}, \{x \to -Sqrt[f^{(-1)}[a]]\}\}$$

■ 7.6 Eliminating Variables

When you are working with sets of equations in several variables, it is often convenient to reorganize the equations by eliminating some variables between them.

This eliminates y between the two
equations, giving a single equation for x.

```
In[1]:= Eliminate[{a x + y == 0, 2 x + (1-a) y == 1}, y]
```
$$Out[1]= (2 - a + a^2) \ x == 1$$

When you write down a set of simultaneous equations in *Mathematica*, you are specifying a collection of constraints between variables. When you use Solve, you are finding values for some of the variables in terms of others, subject to the constraints represented by the equations.

Solve[*eqns*, *vars*, *elims*]	find solutions for *vars*, eliminating the variables *elims*
Eliminate[*eqns*, *elims*]	rearrange equations to eliminate the variables *elims*

Eliminating variables.

Here are two equations involving x, y
and the "parameter" a.

```
In[2]:= eqn = {x == 1 + 2 a, y == 9 + 2 x}
```
$$Out[2]= \{x == 1 + 2 \ a, \ y == 9 + 2 \ x\}$$

If you solve for both x and y, you get
results in terms of a.

```
In[3]:= Solve[eqn, {x, y}]
```
$$Out[3]= \{\{y \to 9 - 2 \ (-1 - 2 \ a), \ x \to 1 + 2 \ a\}\}$$

Similarly, if you solve for x and a, you
get results in terms of y.

```
In[4]:= Solve[eqn, {x, a}]
```
$$Out[4]= \{\{a \to -(\frac{1}{2}) + \frac{-9 + y}{4}, \ x \to \frac{-9 + y}{2}\}\}$$

If you only want to solve for x, however,
you have to specify whether you want
to eliminate y or a. This eliminates y,
and so gives the result in terms of a.

```
In[5]:= Solve[eqn, x, y]
```
$$Out[5]= \{\{x \to 1 + 2 \ a\}\}$$

If you eliminate a, then you get a result in terms of y.

In[6]:= **Solve[eqn, x, a]**

$$Out[6]= \{\{x \to \frac{-9 + y}{2}\}\}$$

In some cases, you may want to construct explicitly equations in which variables have been eliminated. You can do this using `Eliminate`.

This combines the two equations in the list eqn, by eliminating the variable a.

In[7]:= **Eliminate[eqn, a]**

Out[7]= y == 9 + 2 x

This is what you get if you eliminate y instead of a.

In[8]:= **Eliminate[eqn, y]**

$$Out[8]= a == -(\frac{1}{2}) + \frac{x}{2}$$

As a more sophisticated example of `Eliminate`, consider the problem of writing $x^5 + y^5$ in terms of the "symmetric polynomials" $x+y$ and xy.

To solve the problem, we simply have to write f in terms of a and b, eliminating the original variables x and y.

In[9]:= **Eliminate[{f == x^5 + y^5, a == x + y, b == x y},**
                              {x, y}]

$$Out[9]= a^5 - 5 a^3 b + 5 a b^2 == f$$

SolveAlways ▪ Reduce ▪ Mode ▪ Modular ▪ Modulus ▪ AlgebraicRules

Other *Mathematica* functions related to solving equations. (See page xvi.)

8. Plotting Curves

■ 8.1 Plotting Functions

$\texttt{Plot}[f, \{x, xmin, xmax\}]$ plot f as a function of x from $xmin$ to $xmax$

$\texttt{Plot}[\{f_1, f_2, \dots\}, \{x, xmin, xmax\}]$

   plot several functions together

Basic plotting functions.

This plots a graph of sin(x) as a function of x from 0 to 2π.

$In[1]:= \texttt{Plot[Sin[x], \{x, 0, 2Pi\}]}$

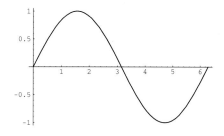

You can plot functions that have singularities. *Mathematica* will try to choose appropriate scales.

$In[2]:= \texttt{Plot[Tan[x], \{x, -3, 3\}]}$

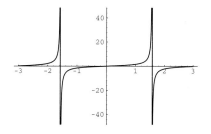

■ 8.2 Parametric Plots

Section 8.1 described how to plot curves in *Mathematica* in which you give the y coordinate of each point as a function of the x coordinate. You can also use *Mathematica* to make *parametric* plots. In a parametric plot, you give both the x and y coordinates of each point as a function of a third parameter, say t.

> ParametricPlot[{f_x, f_y}, {t, $tmin$, $tmax$}]
>
>   make a parametric plot
>
> ParametricPlot[{f_x, f_y}, {t, $tmin$, $tmax$}, AspectRatio -> Automatic]
>
>   attempt to preserve the shapes of curves

Functions for generating parametric plots.

Here is the curve made by taking the *x* coordinate of each point to be Sin[t] and the *y* coordinate to be Sin[2t].

In[1]:= **ParametricPlot[{Sin[t], Sin[2t]}, {t, 0, 2Pi}]**

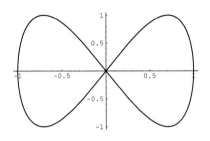

The "shape" of the curve produced depends on the ratio of height to width for the whole plot.

In[2]:= **ParametricPlot[{Sin[t], Cos[t]}, {t, 0, 2Pi}]**

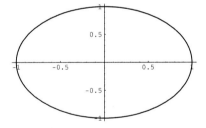

Setting the option AspectRatio to Automatic makes *Mathematica* preserve the "true shape" of the curve, as defined by the actual coordinate values it involves.

In[3]:= **Show[%, AspectRatio -> Automatic]**

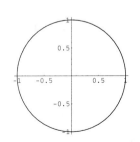

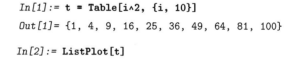

■ 8.3 Plotting Lists of Data

So far, we have discussed how you can use *Mathematica* to make plots of *functions*. You give *Mathematica* a function, and it builds up a curve by evaluating the function at many different points.

This section describes how you can make plots from lists of data, instead of functions. The *Mathematica* commands for plotting lists of data are direct analogs of the ones discussed in Section 8.1 for plotting functions.

`ListPlot[{`y_1`, `y_2`, ... }]`	plot $y_1, y_2, ...$ at x values 1, 2, ...
`ListPlot[{{`x_1`, `y_1`}, {`x_2`, `y_2`}, ... }]`	
	plot points $(x_1, y_1), ...$
`ListPlot[`*list*`, PlotJoined -> True]`	
	join the points with lines

Functions for plotting lists of data.

Here is a list of values.

In[1]:= **t = Table[i^2, {i, 10}]**

Out[1]= {1, 4, 9, 16, 25, 36, 49, 64, 81, 100}

This plots the values.

In[2]:= **ListPlot[t]**

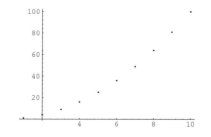

This joins the points with lines.

In[3]:= **ListPlot[t, PlotJoined -> True]**

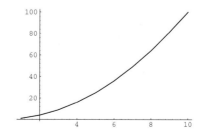

This gives a list of *x, y* pairs.	*In[4]:=* **Table[{i∧3, i + 4 i∧2}, {i, 10}]**
	Out[4]= {{1, 5}, {8, 18}, {27, 39}, {64, 68}, {125, 105},
	{216, 150}, {343, 203}, {512, 264}, {729, 333}, {1000, 410}}
This plots the points.	*In[5]:=* **ListPlot[%]**

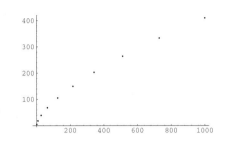

■ 8.4 Options for Plot

When *Mathematica* plots a graph for you, it has to make many choices. It has to work out what the scales should be, where the function should be sampled, how the axes should be drawn, and so on. Most of the time, *Mathematica* will probably make pretty good choices. However, if you want to get the very best possible pictures for your particular purposes, you may have to help *Mathematica* in making some of its choices.

There is a general mechanism for specifying "options" in *Mathematica* functions. Each option has a definite name. As the last arguments to a function like Plot, you can include a sequence of rules of the form *name* -> *value*, to specify the values for various options. Any option for which you do not give an explicit rule is taken to have its "default" value.

Plot[*f*, {*x*, *xmin*, *xmax*}, *option* -> *value*]

                         make a plot, specifying a particular value for an option

---

Choosing an option for a plot.

A function like Plot has many options that you can set. Usually you will need to use at most a few of them at a time. If you want to optimize a particular plot, you will probably do best to experiment, trying a sequence of different settings for various options.

Each time you produce a plot, you can specify options for it. Section 30.1 will also discuss how you can change some of the options, even after you have produced the plot.

option name	default value	
AspectRatio	1/GoldenRatio	the height-to-width ratio for the plot; Automatic sets it from the absolute x and y coordinates
Axes	Automatic	whether to include axes
AxesLabel	None	labels to be put on the axes: *ylabel* specifies a label for the y axis, {*xlabel*, *ylabel*} for both axes
AxesOrigin	Automatic	the point at which axes cross
DefaultFont	$DefaultFont	the default font to use for text in the plot
DisplayFunction	$DisplayFunction	how to display graphics; Identity causes no display
Frame	False	whether to draw a frame around the plot
FrameLabel	None	labels to be put around the frame; give a list in clockwise order starting with the lower x axis
FrameTicks	Automatic	what tick marks to draw if there is a frame; None gives no tick marks
GridLines	None	what grid lines to include: Automatic includes a grid line for every major tick mark
PlotLabel	None	an expression to be printed as a label for the plot
PlotRange	Automatic	the range of coordinates to include in the plot: All includes all points
Ticks	Automatic	what tick marks to draw if there are axes; None gives no tick marks

Some of the options for Plot. These can also be used in Show.

Here is a plot with all options having their default values.

In[1]:= **Plot[Sin[x^2], {x, 0, 3}]**

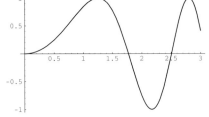

This draws axes on a frame around the plot.

In[2]:= **Plot[Sin[x^2], {x, 0, 3}, Frame -> True]**

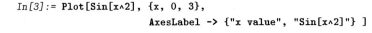

This specifies labels for the *x* and *y* axes. The expressions you give as labels are printed just as they would be if they appeared as *Mathematica* output. You can give any piece of text by putting it inside a pair of double quotes.

In[3]:= **Plot[Sin[x^2], {x, 0, 3},**
AxesLabel -> {"x value", "Sin[x^2]"}]

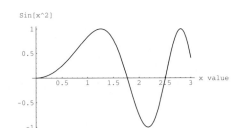

You can give several options at the same time, in any order.

In[4]:= **Plot[Sin[x^2], {x, 0, 3}, Frame -> True,**
                    GridLines -> Automatic]

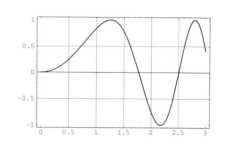

Setting the AspectRatio option changes the whole shape of your plot. AspectRatio gives the ratio of width to height. Its default value is the inverse of the Golden Ratio – supposedly the most pleasing shape for a rectangle.

In[5]:= **Plot[Sin[x^2], {x, 0, 3}, AspectRatio -> 1]**

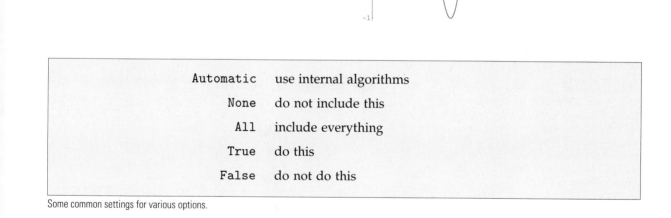

Automatic	use internal algorithms
None	do not include this
All	include everything
True	do this
False	do not do this

Some common settings for various options.

When *Mathematica* makes a plot, it tries to set the x and y scales to include only the "interesting" parts of the plot. If your function increases very rapidly, or has singularities, the parts where it gets too large will be cut off. By specifying the option PlotRange, you can control exactly what ranges of x and y coordinates are included in your plot.

`Automatic`	show at least a large fraction of the points, including the "interesting" region (the default setting)
`All`	show all points
{*ymin*, *ymax*}	show a specific range of *y* values
{*xrange*, *yrange*}	show the specified ranges of *x* and *y* values

Settings for the option `PlotRange`.

The setting for the option PlotRange gives explicit *y* limits for the graph. With the *y* limits specified here, the bottom of the curve is cut off.

In[6]:= `Plot[Sin[x^2], {x, 0, 3}, PlotRange -> {0, 1.2}]`

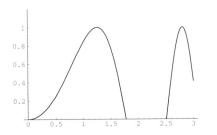

Mathematica always tries to plot functions as smooth curves. As a result, in places where your function wiggles a lot, *Mathematica* will use more points. In general, *Mathematica* tries to *adapt* its sampling of your function to the form of the function. There is, however, a limit, which you can set, to how finely *Mathematica* will ever sample a function.

The function $\sin(\frac{1}{x})$ wiggles infinitely often when $x \approx 0$. *Mathematica* tries to sample more points in the region where the function wiggles a lot, but it can never sample the infinite number that you would need to reproduce the function exactly. As a result, there are slight glitches in the plot.

In[7]:= `Plot[Sin[1/x], {x, -1, 1}]`

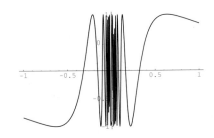

option name	default value	
PlotStyle	Automatic	a list of lists of graphics primitives to use for each curve
PlotPoints	25	the minimum number of points at which to sample the function
MaxBend	10.	the maximum kink angle between successive segments of a curve
PlotDivision	20.	the maximum factor by which to subdivide in sampling the function

More options for `Plot`. These cannot be used in `Show`.

It is important to realize that since *Mathematica* can only sample your function at a limited number of points, it can always miss features of the function. By increasing `PlotPoints`, you can make *Mathematica* sample your function at a larger number of points. Of course, the larger you set `PlotPoints` to be, the longer it will take *Mathematica* to plot *any* function, even a smooth one.

Since `Plot` needs to evaluate your function many times, it is important to make each evaluation as quickly as possible. As a result, *Mathematica* usually *compiles* your function into a low-level pseudocode that can be executed very efficiently. Note that *Mathematica* can only compile "in-line code"; it cannot for example compile functions that you have defined. As a result, you should, when possible, use `Evaluate` as described on page 88 to evaluate any such definitions and get a form that the *Mathematica* compiler can handle.

■ 8.5 Plotting Lists of Functions

Plot[{f_1, f_2, ... }, {x, $xmin$, $xmax$}]

plot several functions together

ParametricPlot[{{f_x, f_y}, {g_x, g_y}, ... }, {t, $tmin$, $tmax$}]

plot several parametric curves together

Plotting more than one function.

You can give a list of functions to plot.   *In[1]:=* `Plot[{Sin[x], Sin[2x], Sin[3x]}, {x, 0, 2Pi}]`

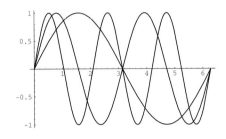

To get smooth curves, *Mathematica* has to evaluate functions you plot at a large number of points. As a result, it is important that you set things up so that each function evaluation is as quick as possible.

When you ask *Mathematica* to plot an object, say *f*, as a function of *x*, there are two possible approaches it can take. One approach is first to try and evaluate *f*, presumably getting a symbolic expression in terms of *x*, and then subsequently evaluate this expression numerically for the specific values of *x* needed in the plot. The second approach is first to work out what values of *x* are needed, and only subsequently to evaluate *f* with those values of *x*.

If you type `Plot[f, {x, xmin, xmax}]` it is the second of these approaches that is used. This has the advantage that *Mathematica* only tries to evaluate *f* for specific numerical values of *x*; it does not matter whether sensible values are defined for *f* when *x* is symbolic.

There are, however, some cases in which it is much better to have *Mathematica* evaluate *f* before it starts to make the plot. A typical case is when *f* is actually a command that generates a table of functions. You want to have *Mathematica* first produce the table, and then evaluate the functions, rather than trying to produce the table afresh for each value of *x*. You can do this by typing `Plot[Evaluate[f], {x, xmin, xmax}]`.

The `Evaluate` tells *Mathematica first* to make the table of functions, and only *then* to evaluate them for particular values of the variable **x**.   *In[2]:=* `Plot[Evaluate[Table[Sin[n x^2], {n, 4}]], {x, 0, 2}]`

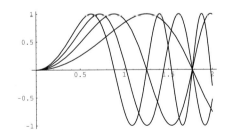

9. Two-Dimensional Graphics

■ 9.1 Two-Dimensional Graphics Elements

Point[{*x*, *y*}]	point at position *x, y*
Line[{{*x₁*, *y₁*}, {*x₂*, *y₂*}, ... }]	
	line through the points {*x₁*, *y₁*}, {*x₂*, *y₂*}, ...
Rectangle[{*xmin*, *ymin*}, {*xmax*, *ymax*}]	
	filled rectangle
Polygon[{{*x₁*, *y₁*}, {*x₂*, *y₂*}, ... }]	
	filled polygon with the specified list of corners
Circle[{*x*, *y*}, *r*]	circle with radius *r* centered at *x, y*
Disk[{*x*, *y*}, *r*]	filled disk with radius *r* centered at *x, y*
Raster[{{*a₁₁*, *a₁₂*, ... }, {*a₂₁*, ... }, ... }]	
	rectangular array of gray levels between 0 and 1
Text[*expr*, {*x*, *y*}]	the text of *expr*, centered at *x, y* (see Section 36.2)

Basic two-dimensional graphics elements.

Here is a line primitive.

```
In[1]:= sawline = Line[Table[{n, (-1)^n}, {n, 6}]]
Out[1]= Line[{{1, -1}, {2, 1}, {3, -1}, {4, 1}, {5, -1},
   {6, 1}}]
```

This shows the line as a two-dimensional graphics object.

```
In[2]:= sawgraph = Show[ Graphics[sawline] ]
```

This redisplays the line, with axes added.

In[3]:= **Show[%, Axes -> True]**

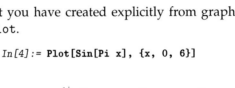

You can combine graphics objects that you have created explicitly from graphics primitives with ones that are produced by functions like Plot.

This produces an ordinary *Mathematica* plot.

In[4]:= **Plot[Sin[Pi x], {x, 0, 6}]**

This combines the plot with the sawtooth picture made above.

In[5]:= **Show[%, sawgraph]**

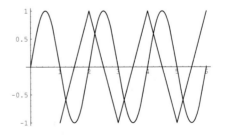

You can combine different graphical elements simply by giving them in a list. In two-dimensional graphics, *Mathematica* will render the elements in exactly the order you give them. Later elements are therefore effectively drawn on top of earlier ones.

Here is a list of two Rectangle graphics elements.

In[6]:= **{Rectangle[{1, -1}, {2, -0.6}],**
                    Rectangle[{4, .3}, {5, .8}]};

This draws the rectangles on top of the line that was defined above.

`In[7]:= Show[ Graphics[ {sawline, %} ]]`

The `Polygon` graphics primitive takes a list of x, y coordinates, corresponding to the corners of a polygon. *Mathematica* joins the last corner with the first one, and then fills the resulting area.

Here are the coordinates of the corners of a regular pentagon.

`In[8]:= pentagon = Table[{Sin[2 Pi n/5], Cos[2 Pi n/5]}, {n, 5}]`

$Out[8]= \{\{Sin[\dfrac{2\ Pi}{5}],\ Cos[\dfrac{2\ Pi}{5}]\},\ \{Sin[\dfrac{4\ Pi}{5}],\ Cos[\dfrac{4\ Pi}{5}]\},$

$\{Sin[\dfrac{6\ Pi}{5}],\ Cos[\dfrac{6\ Pi}{5}]\},\ \{Sin[\dfrac{8\ Pi}{5}],\ Cos[\dfrac{8\ Pi}{5}]\},\ \{0,\ 1\}\}$

This displays the pentagon. With the default choice of aspect ratio, the pentagon looks somewhat squashed.

`In[9]:= Show[ Graphics[ Polygon[pentagon] ] ]`

This chooses the aspect ratio so that the shape of the pentagon is preserved.

`In[10]:= Show[%, AspectRatio -> Automatic]`

Circle[{x, y}, r]	a circle with radius r centered at the point {x, y}
Circle[{x, y}, {r_x, r_y}]	an ellipse with semi-axes r_x and r_y
Circle[{x, y}, r, {$theta_1$, $theta_2$}]	
	a circular arc
Circle[{x, y}, {r_x, r_y}, {$theta_1$, $theta_2$}]	
	an elliptical arc
Disk[{x, y}, r], etc.	filled disks

Circles and disks.

This shows two circles with radius 2. Setting the option AspectRatio -> Automatic makes the circles come out with their natural aspect ratio.

```
In[11]:= Show[ Graphics[
              {Circle[{0, 0}, 2], Circle[{1, 1}, 2]} ],
                       AspectRatio -> Automatic ]
```

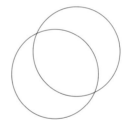

This shows a sequence of disks with progressively larger semi-axes in the x direction, and progressively smaller ones in the y direction.

```
In[12]:= Show[ Graphics[
              Table[Disk[{3n, 0}, {n/4, 2-n/4}], {n, 4}] ],
                       AspectRatio -> Automatic ]
```

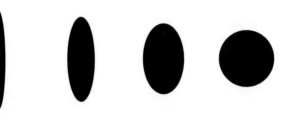

Mathematica allows you to generate arcs of circles, and segments of ellipses. In both cases, the objects are specified by starting and finishing angles. The angles are measured counterclockwise in radians with zero corresponding to the positive *x* direction. For segments of ellipses, the angles are measured as on a circle that is then transformed by scaling into an ellipse.

This draws a 140° wedge centered at the origin.

In[13]:= **Show[Graphics[Disk[{0, 0}, 1, {0, 140 Degree}]],**
AspectRatio -> Automatic]

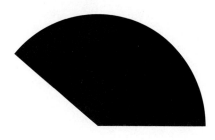

`Raster[{{`a_{11}`, `a_{12}`, ... }, {`a_{21}`, ... }, ... }]`	
	array of gray levels between 0 and 1
`Raster[`*array*`, {{`*xmin*`, `*ymin*`}, {`*xmax*`, `*ymax*`}}, {`*zmin*`, `*zmax*`}]`	
	array of gray levels between *zmin* and *zmax* drawn in the rectangle defined by {*xmin*, *ymin*} and {*xmax*, *ymax*}
`RasterArray[{{`g_{11}`, `g_{12}`, ... }, {`g_{21}`, ... }, ... }]`	
	rectangular array of cells colored according to the graphics directives g_{ij}

Raster-based graphics elements.

Here is a 4×4 array of values between 0 and 1.

In[14]:= **modtab = Table[Mod[i, j] / 3., {i, 4}, {j, 4}]**

Out[14]= {{0, 0.333333, 0.333333, 0.333333},

{0, 0, 0.666667, 0.666667}, {0, 0.333333, 0, 1.},

{0, 0, 0.333333, 0}}

This uses the array of values as gray levels in a raster.

In[15]:= **Show[Graphics[Raster[%]]]**

This shows two overlapping copies of the raster.

In[16]:= **Show[Graphics[{Raster[modtab, {{0, 0}, {2, 2}}],**
Raster[modtab, {{1.5, 1.5}, {3, 2}}]}]]

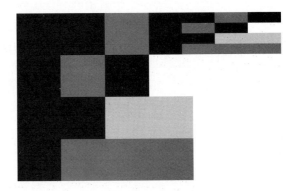

In the default case, Raster always generates an array of gray cells. As described on page 194, you can use the option ColorFunction to apply a "coloring function" to all the cells.

You can also use the graphics primitive RasterArray. While Raster takes an array of *values*, RasterArray takes an array of *Mathematica graphics directives*. The directives associated with each cell are taken to determine the color of that cell. Typically the directives are chosen from the set GrayLevel, RGBColor or Hue. By using RGBColor and Hue directives, you can create color rasters using RasterArray.

■ 9.2 Graphics Directives and Options

When you set up a graphics object in *Mathematica*, you typically give a list of graphical elements. You can include in that list *graphics directives* which specify how subsequent elements in the list should be rendered.

In general, the graphical elements in a particular graphics object can be given in a collection of nested lists. When you insert graphics directives in this kind of structure, the rule is that a particular graphics directive affects all subsequent elements of the list it is in, together with all elements of sublists that may occur. The graphics directive does not, however, have any effect outside the list it is in.

The first sublist contains the graphics directive GrayLevel.	*In[1]:=* **{{GrayLevel[0.5], Rectangle[{0, 0}, {1, 1}]}, Rectangle[{1, 1}, {2, 2}]}**
	Out[1]= {{GrayLevel[0.5], Rectangle[{0, 0}, {1, 1}]}, Rectangle[{1, 1}, {2, 2}]}
Only the rectangle in the first sublist is affected by the GrayLevel directive.	*In[2]:=* **Show[Graphics[%]]**

Mathematica provides various kinds of graphics directives. One important set is those for specifying the colors of graphical elements. Even if you have a black-and-white display device, you can still give color graphics directives. The colors you specify will be converted to gray levels at the last step in the graphics rendering process. Note that you can get black-and-white display even on a color device by setting the option ColorOutput -> GrayLevel.

GrayLevel[*i*]	gray level between 0 (black) and 1 (white)
RGBColor[*r*, *g*, *b*]	color with specified red, green and blue components, each between 0 and 1
Hue[*h*]	color with hue *h* between 0 and 1
Hue[*h*, *s*, *b*]	color with specified hue, saturation and brightness, each between 0 and 1

Basic *Mathematica* color specifications.

On a color display, the two curves would be shown in color. Here they are shown in gray.

```
In[3]:= Plot[{x^2, x^3}, {x, 1, 3},
          PlotStyle ->
            {{RGBColor[1, 0, 0]}, {RGBColor[0, 1, 0]}}]
```

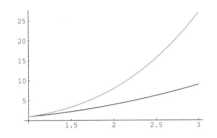

The function Hue[h] provides a convenient way to specify a range of colors using just one parameter. As h varies from 0 to 1, Hue[h] runs through red, yellow, green, cyan, blue, magenta, and back to red again. Hue[h, s, b] allows you to specify not only the "hue", but also the "saturation" and "brightness" of a color. Taking the saturation to be equal to one gives the deepest colors; decreasing the saturation towards zero leads to progressively more "washed out" colors.

For most purposes, you will be able to specify the colors you need simply by giving appropriate RGBColor or Hue directives.

When you give a graphics directive such as RGBColor, it affects *all* subsequent graphical elements that appear in a particular list. *Mathematica* also supports various graphics directives which affect only specific types of graphical elements.

The graphics directive PointSize[d] specifies that all Point elements which appear in a graphics object should be drawn as circles with a diameter d. In PointSize, the diameter d is measured as a fraction of the width of your whole plot.

Mathematica also provides the graphics directive AbsolutePointSize[d], which allows you to specify the "absolute" diameter of points, measured in fixed units. The units are approximately printer's points, equal to 1/72 of an inch.

PointSize[d]	give all points a diameter d as a fraction of the width of the whole plot
AbsolutePointSize[d]	give all points a diameter d measured in absolute units

Graphics directives for points.

Here is a list of points.

```
In[4]:= Table[Point[{n, Prime[n]}], {n, 6}]
Out[4]= {Point[{1, 2}], Point[{2, 3}], Point[{3, 5}],
          Point[{4, 7}], Point[{5, 11}], Point[{6, 13}]}
```

This makes each point have a diameter equal to one-tenth of the width of the plot.

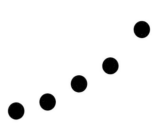

Here each point has size 3 in absolute units.

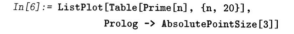

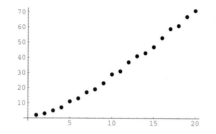

`Thickness[r]`	give all lines a thickness *r* as a fraction of the width of the whole plot
`AbsoluteThickness[d]`	give all lines a thickness *d* measured in absolute units
`Dashing[{r₁, r₂, ... }]`	show all lines as a sequence of dashed segments, with lengths $r_1, r_2, ...$
`AbsoluteDashing[{d₁, d₂, ... }]`	
	use absolute units to measure dashed segments

Graphics directives for lines.

This generates a list of lines with different absolute thicknesses.

```
In[7]:= Table[
            {AbsoluteThickness[n], Line[{{0, 0}, {n, 1}}]}, {n, 4}]
Out[7]= {{AbsoluteThickness[1], Line[{{0, 0}, {1, 1}}]},
    {AbsoluteThickness[2], Line[{{0, 0}, {2, 1}}]},
    {AbsoluteThickness[3], Line[{{0, 0}, {3, 1}}]},
    {AbsoluteThickness[4], Line[{{0, 0}, {4, 1}}]}}
```

Here is a picture of the lines.

In[8]:= **Show[Graphics[%]]**

The **Dashing** graphics directive allows you to create lines with various kinds of dashing. The basic idea is to break lines into segments which are alternately drawn and omitted. By changing the lengths of the segments, you can get different line styles. Dashing allows you to specify a sequence of segment lengths. This sequence is repeated as many times as necessary in drawing the whole line.

This gives a dashed line and a dot-dashed line.

In[9]:= **Show[Graphics[{**
    Dashing[{0.05, 0.05}],
    Line[{{-1, -1}, {1, 1}}],
    Dashing[{0.01, 0.05, 0.05, 0.05}],
    Line[{{-1, 1}, {1, -1}}]
    }]]

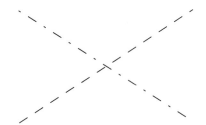

10. Three-Dimensional Graphics

■ 10.1 Three-Dimensional Graphics Primitives

One of the most powerful aspects of graphics in *Mathematica* is the availability of three-dimensional as well as two-dimensional graphics primitives. By combining three-dimensional graphics primitives, you can represent and render three-dimensional objects in *Mathematica*.

Point[{x, y, z}]	point with coordinates x, y, z
Line[{{x_1, y_1, z_1}, {x_2, y_2, z_2}, ... }]	
	line through the points {x_1, y_1, z_1}, {x_2, y_2, z_2}, ...
Polygon[{{x_1, y_1, z_1}, {x_2, y_2, z_2}, ... }]	
	filled polygon with the specified list of corners
Cuboid[{$xmin$, $ymin$, $zmin$}, {$xmax$, $ymax$, $zmax$}]	
	cuboid
Text[*expr*, {x, y, z}]	text at position {x, y, z} (see Section 36.2)

Three-dimensional graphics elements.

Every time you evaluate rcoord, it generates a random coordinate in three dimensions.

```
In[1]:= rcoord := {Random[ ], Random[ ], Random[ ]}
```

This generates a list of 20 random points in three-dimensional space.

```
In[2]:= pts = Table[Point[rcoord], {20}] ;
```

Here is a plot of the points.

```
In[3]:= Show[ Graphics3D[ pts ] ]
```

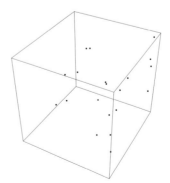

This gives a plot showing a line through 10 random points in three dimensions.

In[4]:= **Show[Graphics3D[Line[Table[rcoord, {10}]]]]**

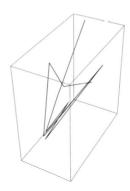

If you give a list of graphics elements in two dimensions, *Mathematica* simply draws each element in turn, with later elements obscuring earlier ones. In three dimensions, however, *Mathematica* collects together all the graphics elements you specify, then displays them as three-dimensional objects, with the ones in front in three-dimensional space obscuring those behind.

Every time you evaluate rantri, it generates a random triangle in three-dimensional space.

In[5]:= **rantri := Polygon[Table[rcoord, {3}]]**

This draws a single random triangle.

In[6]:= **Show[Graphics3D[rantri]]**

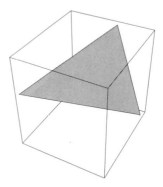

This draws a collection of five random triangles. The triangles in front obscure those behind.

`In[7]:= Show[ Graphics3D[ Table[rantri, {5}] ] ]`

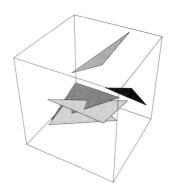

By creating an appropriate list of polygons, you can build up any three-dimensional object in *Mathematica*. Thus, for example, all the surfaces produced by `ParametricPlot3D` are represented simply as lists of polygons.

The package `Graphics`Polyhedra`` contains examples of lists of polygons which correspond to polyhedra in three dimensions.

This loads a package which defines various polyhedra.

`In[8]:= <<Graphics`Polyhedra`;`

Here is the list of the four polygons corresponding to a tetrahedron centered at the origin.

```
In[9]:= Tetrahedron[ ]
Out[9]= {Polygon[{{0., 0., 1.73205}, {0., 1.63299, -0.57735},
    {-1.41421, -0.816497, -0.57735}}],
  Polygon[{{0., 0., 1.73205}, {-1.41421, -0.816497, -0.57735},
    {1.41421, -0.816497, -0.57735}}],
  Polygon[{{0., 0., 1.73205}, {1.41421, -0.816497, -0.57735},
    {0., 1.63299, -0.57735}}],
  Polygon[{{0., 1.63299, -0.57735},
    {1.41421, -0.816497, -0.57735},
    {-1.41421, -0.816497, -0.57735}}]}
```

This displays the tetrahedron as a
three-dimensional object.

In[10]:= **Show[Graphics3D[%]]**

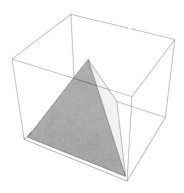

Dodecahedron[ ] is another
three-dimensional object defined in the
polyhedra package.

In[11]:= **Show[Graphics3D[Dodecahedron[ ]]]**

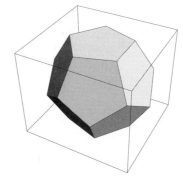

This shows four intersecting
dodecahedra.

In[12]:= **Show[Graphics3D[**
      Table[Dodecahedron[0.8 {k, k, k}], {k, 0, 3}]]]

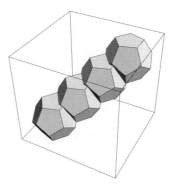

Mathematica allows polygons in three dimensions to have any number of vertices. However, these vertices should lie in a plane, and should form a convex figure. If they do not, then *Mathematica* will break the polygon into triangles, which are planar by definition, before rendering it.

Cuboid[{x, y, z}]	a unit cube with opposite corners having coordinates {x, y, z} and {x+1, y+1, z+1}
Cuboid[{$xmin$, $ymin$, $zmin$}, {$xmax$, $ymax$, $zmax$}]	a cuboid (rectangular parallelepiped) with opposite corners having the specified coordinates

Cuboid graphics elements.

This draws 20 random unit cubes in three-dimensional space.

In[13]:= **Show[Graphics3D[Table[Cuboid[10 rcoord], {20}]]]**

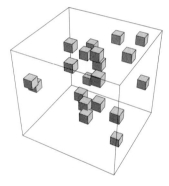

■ 10.2 Three-Dimensional Graphics Directives

In three dimensions, just as in two dimensions, you can give various graphics directives to specify how the different elements in a graphics object should be rendered.

All the graphics directives for two dimensions also work in three dimensions. There are however some additional directives in three dimensions.

Just as in two dimensions, you can use the directives PointSize, Thickness and Dashing to tell *Mathematica* how to render Point and Line elements. Note that in three dimensions, the lengths that appear in these directives are measured as fractions of the total width of the display area for your plot.

This generates a list of 20 random points in three dimensions.

In[1]:= **pts = Table[Point[Table[Random[ ], {3}]], {20}];**

This displays the points, with each one being a circle whose diameter is 5% of the display area width.

`In[2]:= Show[Graphics3D[ { PointSize[0.05], pts } ]]`

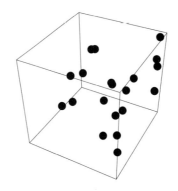

As in two dimensions, you can use `AbsolutePointSize`, `AbsoluteThickness` and `AbsoluteDashing` if you want to measure length in absolute units.

This generates a line through 10 random points in three dimensions.

`In[3]:= line = Line[Table[Random[ ], {10}, {3}]] ;`

This shows the line dashed, with a thickness of 2 printer's points.

`In[4]:= Show[Graphics3D[ { AbsoluteThickness[2],`
`                           AbsoluteDashing[{5, 5}], line } ]]`

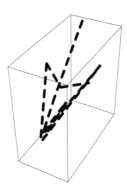

For `Point` and `Line` objects, the color specification directives also work the same in three dimensions as in two dimensions. For `Polygon` objects, however, they can work differently.

In two dimensions, polygons are always assumed to have an intrinsic color, specified directly by graphics directives such as `RGBColor`. In three dimensions, however, *Mathematica* also provides the option of generating colors for polygons using a more physical approach based on simulated illumination. With the default option setting `Lighting -> True` for `Graphics3D` objects, *Mathematica* ignores explicit colors specified for polygons, and instead determines all polygon colors using the simulated illumination model. Even in this case, however, explicit colors are used for points and lines.

Lighting -> False	intrinsic colors
Lighting -> True	colors based on simulated illumination (default)

The two schemes for coloring polygons in three dimensions.

This loads a package which defines various polyhedra.

In[5]:= <<Graphics`Polyhedra` ;

This draws an icosahedron, using the same gray level for all faces.

In[6]:= Show[Graphics3D[{GrayLevel[0.7], Icosahedron[ ]}],
                                    Lighting -> False]

With the default setting
Lighting -> True, the colors of polygons are determined by the simulated illumination model, and explicit color specifications are ignored.

In[7]:= Show[%, Lighting -> True]

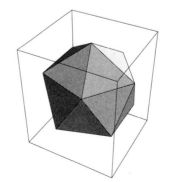

Explicit color directives are, however, always followed for points and lines.

```
In[8]:= Show[{%, Graphics3D[{GrayLevel[0.5], Thickness[0.05],
            Line[{{0, 0, -2}, {0, 0, 2}}]}]}]
```

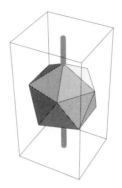

| EdgeForm[ ] | draw no lines at the edges of polygons |
| EdgeForm[g] | draw edges using the graphics directives g |

Giving graphics directives for the edges of polygons.

When you render a three-dimensional graphics object in *Mathematica*, there are two kinds of lines that can appear. The first kind are lines from explicit Line primitives that you included in the graphics object. The second kind are lines that were generated as the edges of polygons.

You can tell *Mathematica* how to render lines of the second kind by giving a list of graphics directives inside EdgeForm.

This renders a dodecahedron with its edges shown as thick gray lines.

```
In[9]:= Show[Graphics3D[
            {EdgeForm[{GrayLevel[0.5], Thickness[0.02]}],
            Dodecahedron[ ]}]]
```

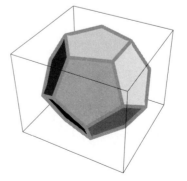

FaceForm[*gfront*, *gback*]	use *gfront* graphics directives for the front face of each polygon, and *gback* for the back

Rendering the fronts and backs of polygons differently.

An important aspect of polygons in three dimensions is that they have both front and back faces. *Mathematica* uses the following convention to define the "front face" of a polygon: if you look at a polygon from the front, then the corners of the polygon will appear counter-clockwise, when taken in the order that you specified them.

This defines a dodecahedron with one face removed.

In[10]:= **d = Drop[Dodecahedron[ ], {6}] ;**

You can now see inside the dodecahedron.

In[11]:= **Show[Graphics3D[d]]**

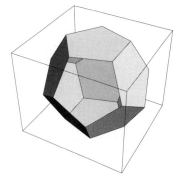

This makes the front (outside) face of each polygon light gray, and the back (inside) face dark gray.

In[12]:= **Show[Graphics3D[**
  {FaceForm[GrayLevel[0.8], GrayLevel[0.3]], d},
  Lighting -> False]

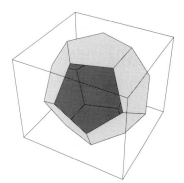

Interlude 1.   **Lists**

11. Lists

■ 11.1 Collecting Objects Together

We first encountered lists in Section 3.4 as a way of collecting numbers together. In this chapter, we shall see many different ways to use lists. You will find that lists are some of the most flexible and powerful objects in *Mathematica*. You will see that lists in *Mathematica* represent generalizations of several standard concepts in mathematics and computer science.

At a basic level, what a *Mathematica* list essentially does is to provide a way for you to collect together several expressions of any kind.

Here is a list of numbers.	`In[1]:= v = {2, 3, 4}` `Out[1]= {2, 3, 4}`
This doubles each element.	`In[2]:= 2 v` `Out[2]= {4, 6, 8}`
This adds two lists.	`In[3]:= v + {0, 3, 5}` `Out[3]= {2, 6, 9}`
This divides through by 3.	`In[4]:= % / 3` `Out[4]= {`$\frac{2}{3}$`, 2, 3}`
This gives a list of symbolic expressions.	`In[5]:= x^v - 1` `Out[5]= {-1 + x`^{2}`, -1 + x`^{3}`, -1 + x`^{4}`}`
You can differentiate these expressions.	`In[6]:= D[%, x]` `Out[6]= {2 x, 3 x`^{2}`, 4 x`^{3}`}`
Or you can find their values when x is replaced with 3.	`In[7]:= %% /. x -> 3` `Out[7]= {8, 26, 80}`

The mathematical functions that are built into *Mathematica* are mostly set up so that they act separately on each element of a list. This is, however, not true of all functions in *Mathematica*. Unless you set it up specially, a new function f that you introduce will treat lists just as single objects. Section 25.4 will describe how you can use Map to apply a function like this separately to each element in a list.

■ 11.2 Making Tables of Values

You can use lists as tables of values. You can generate the tables, for example, by evaluating an expression for a sequence of different parameter values.

This gives a table of the values of i^3, with i running from 1 to 5.

```
In[1]:= Table[i^3, {i, 5}]
Out[1]= {1, 8, 27, 64, 125}
```

You can also make tables of formulas.

```
In[2]:= Table[x^i + 2i, {i, 4}]
                       2       3       4
Out[2]= {2 + x, 4 + x , 6 + x , 8 + x }
```

Here is a table of $\sin(n\pi/5)$ for n running from 0 to 4.

```
In[3]:= Table[Sin[n Pi/5], {n, 0, 4}]
                  Pi        2 Pi        3 Pi        4 Pi
Out[3]= {0, Sin[--], Sin[----], Sin[----], Sin[----]}
                  5           5           5           5
```

This gives the numerical values.

```
In[4]:= N[%]
Out[4]= {0, 0.587785, 0.951057, 0.951057, 0.587785}
```

This makes a table with values of x running from 0 to 1 in steps of 0.25.

```
In[5]:= Table[Sqrt[x], {x, 0, 1, 0.25}]
Out[5]= {0, 0.5, 0.707107, 0.866025, 1.}
```

You can perform other operations on the lists you get from Table.

```
In[6]:= %^2 + 3
Out[6]= {3, 3.25, 3.5, 3.75, 4.}
```

TableForm displays lists in a "tabular" format. Notice that both words in the name TableForm begin with capital letters.

```
In[7]:= TableForm[ % ]
Out[7]//TableForm= 3
                   3.25
                   3.5
                   3.75
                   4.
```

Sometimes you may want to generate a table by evaluating a particular expression many times, without incrementing any variables.

This creates a list containing four copies of the symbol x.

```
In[8]:= Table[x, {4}]
Out[8]= {x, x, x, x}
```

This gives a list of four pseudorandom numbers. Table re-evaluates Random[ ] for each element in the list, so that you get a different pseudorandom number.

```
In[9]:= Table[Random[ ], {4}]
Out[9]= {0.0560708, 0.6303, 0.359894, 0.871377}
```

All the examples so far have been of tables obtained by varying a single parameter. You can also make tables that involve several parameters. These multidimensional tables are specified using the standard *Mathematica* iterator notation, discussed in Section 6.6.

This is the multiplication table up to 10 times 6.

$In[10]:=$ **TableForm[Table[i j, {i, 10}, {j, 6}]]**

$Out[10]//TableForm=$

1	2	3	4	5	6
2	4	6	8	10	12
3	6	9	12	15	18
4	8	12	16	20	24
5	10	15	20	25	30
6	12	18	24	30	36
7	14	21	28	35	42
8	16	24	32	40	48
9	18	27	36	45	54
10	20	30	40	50	60

This makes a table of $x^i + y^j$ with i running from 1 to 3 and j running from 1 to 2.

$In[11]:=$ **Table[x^i + y^j, {i, 3}, {j, 2}]**

$Out[11]=$ $\{\{x + y, x + y^2\}, \{x^2 + y, x^2 + y^2\}, \{x^3 + y, x^3 + y^2\}\}$

The table in this example is a *list of lists*. The three elements of the outer list correspond to successive values of i. The pairs of elements of each inner list correspond to successive values of j, with i fixed.

Table[f, {$imax$}]	give a list of $imax$ values of f
Table[f, {i, $imax$}]	give a list of the values of f as i runs from 1 to $imax$
Table[f, {i, $imin$, $imax$}]	give a list of values with i running from $imin$ to $imax$
Table[f, {i, $imin$, $imax$, di}]	use steps of di
Table[f, {i, $imin$, $imax$}, {j, $jmin$, $jmax$}, ...]	generate a multidimensional table
TableForm[$list$]	display a list in tabular form

Functions for generating tables.

■ 11.3 Getting Pieces of Lists

First [*list*]	the first element in *list*
Last [*list*]	the last element
Rest [*list*]	*list* with its first element dropped
list [[*n*]]	the nth element
list [[-*n*]]	the nth element from the end
list [[{n_1, n_2, ... }]]	the list of elements at the places $n_1, n_2, ...$

Picking out elements of lists.

We will use this list for the examples.

```
In[1]:= t = {a,b,c,d,e,f,g}
Out[1]= {a, b, c, d, e, f, g}
```

Here is the last element of t.

```
In[2]:= Last[t]
Out[2]= g
```

This gives t with the first element dropped.

```
In[3]:= Rest[t]
Out[3]= {b, c, d, e, f, g}
```

This gives the third element.

```
In[4]:= t[[3]]
Out[4]= c
```

This gives a list of the first and fourth elements.

```
In[5]:= t[[ {1, 4} ]]
Out[5]= {a, d}
```

Take [*list*, *n*]	the first *n* elements in *list*
Take [*list*, -*n*]	the last *n* elements
Take [*list*, {*m*, *n*}]	elements *m* through *n* (inclusive)
Drop [*list*, *n*]	*list* with its first *n* elements dropped
Drop [*list*, -*n*]	*list* with its last *n* elements dropped
Drop [*list*, {*m*, *n*}]	*list* with elements *m* through *n* dropped

Picking out sequences in lists.

This gives the first three elements of the list t defined above.

```
In[6]:= Take[t, 3]
Out[6]= {a, b, c}
```

This gives the last three elements.	*In[7]:=* **Take[t, -3]**
	Out[7]= {e, f, g}
This gives elements 2 through 5 inclusive.	*In[8]:=* **Take[t, {2, 5}]**
	Out[8]= {b, c, d, e}
This gives t with its first three elements dropped.	*In[9]:=* **Drop[t, 3]**
	Out[9]= {d, e, f, g}
This gives t with its last three elements dropped.	*In[10]:=* **Drop[t, -3]**
	Out[10]= {a, b, c, d}
This gives t with only its third element dropped.	*In[11]:=* **Drop[t, {3, 3}]**
	Out[11]= {a, b, d, e, f, g}

list[[*i, j, ...*]]	the element *list*[[*i*]][[*j*]]...

Extracting parts of nested lists.

Here is a list of lists.	*In[12]:=* **t = {{a, b, c}, {d, e, f}}**
	Out[12]= {{a, b, c}, {d, e, f}}
This picks out the first sublist.	*In[13]:=* **t[[1]]**
	Out[13]= {a, b, c}
This picks out the second sublist.	*In[14]:=* **t[[2]]**
	Out[14]= {d, e, f}
This picks out the second element in the first sublist.	*In[15]:=* **t[[1, 2]]**
	Out[15]= b
This picks out the first element in the second sublist.	*In[16]:=* **t[[2, 1]]**
	Out[16]= d
This is equivalent to t[[1, 2]], but is clumsier to write.	*In[17]:=* **t[[1]][[2]]**
	Out[17]= b
This gives a list containing two copies of the second part of t, followed by one copy of the first part.	*In[18]:=* **t[[{2, 2, 1}]]**
	Out[18]= {{d, e, f}, {d, e, f}, {a, b, c}}

The functions in this section allow you to pick out pieces that occur at particular positions in lists. Section 26.2 will show how you can use functions like Select and Cases to pick out elements of lists based not on their positions, but instead on their properties.

■ 11.4 Testing and Searching List Elements

`Position[`*list*`, `*form*`]`	the positions at which *form* occurs in *list*
`Count[`*list*`, `*form*`]`	the number of times *form* appears as an element of *list*
`MemberQ[`*list*`, `*form*`]`	test whether *form* is an element of *list*
`FreeQ[`*list*`, `*form*`]`	test whether *form* occurs nowhere in *list*

Testing and searching for elements of lists.

The previous section discussed how to extract pieces of lists based on their positions or indices. *Mathematica* also has functions that search and test for elements of lists, based on the values of those elements.

This gives a list of the positions at which a appears in the list.

```
In[1]:= Position[{a, b, c, a, b}, a]
Out[1]= {{1}, {4}}
```

Count counts the number of occurrences of a.

```
In[2]:= Count[{a, b, c, a, b}, a]
Out[2]= 2
```

This shows that a is an element of {a, b, c}.

```
In[3]:= MemberQ[{a, b, c}, a]
Out[3]= True
```

On the other hand, d is not.

```
In[4]:= MemberQ[{a, b, c}, d]
Out[4]= False
```

This assigns m to be the 3×3 identity matrix, a list of lists.

```
In[5]:= m = IdentityMatrix[3]
Out[5]= {{1, 0, 0}, {0, 1, 0}, {0, 0, 1}}
```

The sublist {0, 1, 0} is an element of m.

```
In[6]:= MemberQ[m, {0, 1, 0}]
Out[6]= True
```

But 0 is not an element of m.

```
In[7]:= MemberQ[m, 0]
Out[7]= False
```

This shows that 0 does occur *somewhere* in m.

```
In[8]:= FreeQ[m, 0]
Out[8]= False
```

This gives a list of the three positions at which 1 occurs in m.

```
In[9]:= Position[m, 1]
Out[9]= {{1, 1}, {2, 2}, {3, 3}}
```

The functions `Count` and `Position`, as well as `MemberQ` and `FreeQ`, can be used not only to search for *particular* list elements, but also to search for classes of elements which match specific "patterns". This is discussed in Section 26.2.

■ 11.5 Adding, Removing and Modifying List Elements

Prepend[*list*, *element*]	add *element* at the beginning of *list*
Append[*list*, *element*]	add *element* at the end of *list*
Insert[*list*, *element*, *i*]	insert *element* at position *i* in *list*
Insert[*list*, *element*, *-i*]	insert at position *i* counting from the end of *list*
Delete[*list*, *i*]	delete the element at position *i* in *list*

Functions for adding and deleting elements in lists.

This gives a list with x prepended.

```
In[1]:= Prepend[{a, b, c}, x]
Out[1]= {x, a, b, c}
```

This adds x at the end.

```
In[2]:= Append[{a, b, c}, x]
Out[2]= {a, b, c, x}
```

This inserts x so that it becomes element number 2.

```
In[3]:= Insert[{a, b, c}, x, 2]
Out[3]= {a, x, b, c}
```

Negative numbers count from the end of the list.

```
In[4]:= Insert[{a, b, c}, x, -2]
Out[4]= {a, b, x, c}
```

Delete removes an element from the list.

```
In[5]:= Delete[{a, b, c, d}, 3]
Out[5]= {a, b, d}
```

■ 11.6 Combining Lists

Join[*list₁*, *list₂*, ...]	concatenate lists together
Union[*list₁*, *list₂*, ...]	combine lists, removing repeated elements and sorting the result

Functions for combining lists.

Join concatenates any number of lists together.

```
In[1]:= Join[{a, b, c}, {x, y}, {c, {d, e}, a}]
Out[1]= {a, b, c, x, y, c, {d, e}, a}
```

Union combines lists, keeping only distinct elements and sorting them.

```
In[2]:= Union[{a, b, c}, {c, a, d}, {a, d}]
Out[2]= {a, b, c, d}
```

■ 11.7 Lists as Sets

Mathematica usually keeps the elements of a list in exactly the order you originally entered them. If you want to treat a *Mathematica* list like a mathematical *set*, however, you may want to ignore the order of elements in the list.

Union[*list$_1$*, *list$_2$*, ...]	give a list of the distinct elements in the *list$_i$*
Intersection[*list$_1$*, *list$_2$*, ...]	give a list of the elements that are common to all the *list$_i$*
Complement[*universal*, *list$_1$*, ...]	give a list of the elements that are in *universal*, but not in any of the *list$_i$*

Set theoretical functions.

Union gives the elements that occur in *any* of the lists.

```
In[1]:= Union[{c, a, b}, {d, a, c}, {a, e}]
Out[1]= {a, b, c, d, e}
```

You can use Union to remove duplicates from a single list.

```
In[2]:= Union[{a, b, a, b, c, a}]
Out[2]= {a, b, c}
```

Intersection gives only elements that occur in *all* the lists.

```
In[3]:= Intersection[{a, c, b}, {b, a, d, a}]
Out[3]= {a, b}
```

Complement gives elements that occur in the first list, but not in any of the others.

```
In[4]:= Complement[{a, b, c, d}, {a, d, e}]
Out[4]= {b, c}
```

■ 11.8 Rearranging Lists

Sort[*list*]	sort the elements of *list* into a standard order
Reverse[*list*]	reverse the order of elements in *list*
RotateLeft[*list*, *n*]	rotate the elements of *list* *n* places to the left
RotateRight[*list*, *n*]	rotate *n* places to the right
RotateLeft[*list*]	rotate right by one position
RotateRight[*list*]	rotate left by one position
Permutations[*list*]	give all possible orderings of *list*

Functions for rearranging lists.

This sorts the elements of a list into a standard order. In simple cases like this, the order is alphabetical or numerical.

```
In[1]:= Sort[{b, a, c, a, b}]
Out[1]= {a, a, b, b, c}
```

This reverses the list.

```
In[2]:= Reverse[{a, b, c, d}]
Out[2]= {d, c, b, a}
```

This rotates ("shifts") the elements in the list two places to the left.

```
In[3]:= RotateLeft[{a, b, c, d, e}, 2]
Out[3]= {c, d, e, a, b}
```

You can rotate to the right by giving a negative displacement, or by using RotateRight.

```
In[4]:= RotateLeft[{a, b, c, d, e}, -2]
Out[4]= {d, e, a, b, c}
```

You can leave out the last argument to rotate by one position.

```
In[5]:= RotateLeft[{a, b, c, d, e}]
Out[5]= {b, c, d, e, a}
```

The factorial function $n!$ gives the number of ways of ordering n objects. The function Permutations allows you to *generate* these orderings as lists.

This gives the 3! = 6 possible permutations of three elements.

```
In[6]:= TableForm[ Permutations[{a, b, c}] ]
Out[6]//TableForm=  a   b   c
                    a   c   b
                    b   a   c
                    b   c   a
                    c   a   b
                    c   b   a
```

■ 11.9 Grouping and Ungrouping Elements of Lists

Partition[*list*, *n*]	partition *list* into *n* element pieces
Partition[*list*, *n*, *d*]	use offset *d* for successive pieces
Flatten[*list*]	flatten out all levels in *list*
Flatten[*list*, *n*]	flatten out the top *n* levels in *list*

Functions for grouping and ungrouping elements of lists.

Here is a list.

```
In[1]:= t = {a, b, c, d, e, f, g};
```

This groups the elements of the list in pairs, and in this case throws away the single element which is left at the end.

```
In[2]:= Partition[t, 2]
Out[2]= {{a, b}, {c, d}, {e, f}}
```

This groups elements in triples. There is no overlap between the triples.	In[3]:= **Partition[t, 3]**
	Out[3]= {{a, b, c}, {d, e, f}}

This makes triples of elements, with each successive triple offset by just one element.

In[4]:= **Partition[t, 3, 1]**

Out[4]= {{a, b, c}, {b, c, d}, {c, d, e}, {d, e, f}, {e, f, g}}

Here is a triply nested 2×2×2 array.

In[5]:= **u = {{{a, b}, {c, d}}, {{e, f}, {g, h}}};**

This "flattens out" sublists. You can think of it as effectively removing the inner sets of braces.

In[6]:= **Flatten[u]**

Out[6]= {a, b, c, d, e, f, g, h}

This flattens only the first level of sublists.

In[7]:= **Flatten[u, 1]**

Out[7]= {{a, b}, {c, d}, {e, f}, {g, h}}

This flattens each sublist on the first level.

In[8]:= **Map[Flatten, u]**

Out[8]= {{a, b, c, d}, {e, f, g, h}}

You should realize that because of the way *Mathematica* stores lists, it is usually less efficient to add a sequence of elements to a particular list than to create a nested structure that consists, for example, of lists of length 2 at each level. When you have built up such a structure, you can always reduce it to a single list using Flatten.

This sets up a nested list structure for w.

In[9]:= **w = {0}; Do[w = {w, k^2}, {k, 1, 4}]; w**

Out[9]= {{{{{0}, 1}, 4}, 9}, 16}

You can use Flatten to unravel the structure.

In[10]:= **Flatten[w]**

Out[10]= {0, 1, 4, 9, 16}

VectorQ ▪ MatrixQ ▪ TensorRank ▪ Depth ▪ FlattenAt ▪ ReplacePart ▪ Thread ▪
Outer ▪ Inner ▪ Level ▪ OrderedQ ▪ Signature

Other *Mathematica* functions related to lists. (See page xvi.)

Part 2.   **More Mathematics**

12. Differentiation and Limits

■ 12.1 Differentiation

$D[f, x]$	derivative of f with respect to x
$D[f, \{x, n\}]$	n^{th} derivative of f with respect to x
$D[f, x_1, x_2, \ldots]$	multiple derivative of f, first with respect to x_1, then $x_2, \ldots$

Partial differentiation operations.

Here is the derivative of x^n with respect to x.

```
In[1]:= D[ x^n, x ]
                -1 + n
Out[1]= n x
```

This uses the product rule.

```
In[2]:= D[x Sin[x], x]
Out[2]= x Cos[x] + Sin[x]
```

Mathematica knows the derivatives of all the standard mathematical functions.

```
In[3]:= D[ArcTan[x], x]
                1
Out[3]= --------
                 2
           1 + x
```

Mathematica knows the chain rule.

```
In[4]:= D[f[g[x]], x]
Out[4]= f'[g[x]] g'[x]
```

You can mix derivatives of known and unknown functions.

```
In[5]:= D[f[x] Sin[x], x]
Out[5]= Cos[x] f[x] + Sin[x] f'[x]
```

This gives the third derivative.

```
In[6]:= D[x^n, {x, 3}]
                                   -3 + n
Out[6]= (-2 + n) (-1 + n) n x
```

You can differentiate with respect to any expression.

```
In[7]:= D[ x[1]^2 + x[2]^2, x[1] ]
Out[7]= 2 x[1]
```

D does *partial differentiation*. It assumes here that y is independent of x.

```
In[8]:= D[x^2 + y^2, x]
Out[8]= 2 x
```

If y does in fact depend on x, you can use the explicit functional form y[x].

```
In[9]:= D[x^2 + y[x]^2, x]
Out[9]= 2 x + 2 y[x] y'[x]
```

This differentiates first with respect to x, with y held constant, and then with respect to y, with x held constant.

```
In[10]:= D[x y^2, x, y]
Out[10]= 2 y
```

■ 12.2 Total Derivatives

Dt[*f*]	total differential *df*
Dt[*f*, *x*]	total derivative
Dt[*f*, x_1, x_2, ...]	multiple total derivative
y/: Dt[*y*, *x*] = 0	set $\frac{dy}{dx} = 0$

Total differentiation operations.

When you find the derivative of some expression *f* with respect to *x*, you are effectively finding out how fast *f* changes as you vary *x*. Often *f* will depend not only on *x*, but also on other variables, say *y* and *z*. The results that you get then depend on how you assume that *y* and *z* vary as you change *x*.

There are two common cases. Either *y* and *z* are assumed to stay fixed when *x* changes, or they are allowed to vary with *x*. In a standard *partial derivative* $\frac{\partial f}{\partial x}$, all variables other than *x* are assumed fixed. On the other hand, in the *total derivative* $\frac{df}{dx}$, all variables are allowed to change with *x*.

In *Mathematica*, D[*f*, *x*] gives a partial derivative, with all other variables assumed independent of *x*. Dt[*f*, *x*] gives a total derivative, in which all variables are assumed to depend on *x*. In both cases, you can add an argument to give more information on dependencies.

This gives the *partial derivative* $\frac{\partial}{\partial x}(x^2 + y^2)$. *y* is assumed to be independent of *x*.

```
In[1]:= D[x^2 + y^2, x]
Out[1]= 2 x
```

This gives the *total derivative* $\frac{d}{dx}(x^2 + y^2)$. Now *y* is assumed to depend on *x*.

```
In[2]:= Dt[x^2 + y^2, x]
Out[2]= 2 x + 2 y Dt[y, x]
```

You can make a replacement for $\frac{dy}{dx}$.

```
In[3]:= % /. Dt[y, x] -> yx
Out[3]= 2 x + 2 y yx
```

This differentiates first with respect to *x* and then with respect to *y*, without holding either constant.

```
In[4]:= Dt[x y^2, x, y]
Out[4]= 2 y + 2 x Dt[y, x] + 2 y Dt[x, y] Dt[y, x]
```

■ 12.3 Derivatives of Unknown Functions

Differentiating a known function gives an explicit result.

```
In[1]:= D[Log[x]^2, x]
Out[1]= 2 Log[x]
         ────────
            x
```

Differentiating an unknown function f gives a result in terms of f'.

```
In[2]:= D[f[x], x]
Out[2]= f'[x]
```

Mathematica applies the chain rule for differentiation, and leaves the result in terms of f'.

```
In[3]:= D[x f[x^2], x]

Out[3]= f[x ] + 2 x  f'[x ]
          2        2    2
```

Differentiating again gives a result in terms of f, f' and f''.

```
In[4]:= D[%, x]

Out[4]= 6 x f'[x ] + 4 x  f''[x ]
                 2        3      2
```

When a function has more than one argument, superscripts are used to indicate how many times each argument is being differentiated.

```
In[5]:= D[g[x^2, y^2], x]
                (1,0)  2   2
Out[5]= 2 x g       [x , y ]
```

This represents $\frac{\partial}{\partial x} \frac{\partial}{\partial x} \frac{\partial}{\partial y} g(x,y)$. *Mathematica* assumes that the order in which derivatives are taken with respect to different variables is irrelevant.

```
In[6]:= D[g[x, y], x, x, y]
            (2,1)
Out[6]= g       [x, y]
```

You can find the value of the derivative when $x = 0$ by replacing x with 0.

```
In[7]:= % /. x -> 0
            (2,1)
Out[7]= g       [0, y]
```

$f'[x]$	first derivative of a function of one variable	
$f^{(n)}[x]$	nth derivative of a function of one variable	
$f^{(n_1, n_2, \ldots)}[x]$	derivative of a function of several variables, n_i times with respect to variable i	

Output forms for derivatives of unknown functions.

■ 12.4 Advanced Topic: Indeterminate and Infinite Results

If you type in an expression like 0/0, *Mathematica* prints a message, and returns the result Indeterminate.

```
In[1]:= 0/0
                                       1
Power::infy: Infinite expression - encountered.
                                       0

Infinity::indet:
    Indeterminate expression 0 ComplexInfinity encountered.

Out[1]= Indeterminate
```

An expression like 0/0 is an example of an *indeterminate numerical result*. If you type in 0/0, there is no way for *Mathematica* to know what answer you want. If you got 0/0 by taking the limit of x/x as $x \to 0$, then you might want the answer 1. On the other hand, if you got 0/0 instead as the limit of $2x/x$, then you probably want the answer 2. The expression 0/0 on its own does not contain enough information to choose between these and other cases. As a result, its value must be considered indeterminate.

·Whenever an indeterminate result is produced in an arithmetic computation, *Mathematica* prints a warning message, and then returns Indeterminate as the result of the computation. If you ever try to use Indeterminate in an arithmetic computation, you always get the result Indeterminate. A single indeterminate expression effectively "poisons" any arithmetic computation. (The symbol Indeterminate plays a role in *Mathematica* similar to the "not a number" object in the IEEE Floating Point Standard.)

The usual laws of arithmetic simplification are suspended in the case of Indeterminate.

```
In[2]:= Indeterminate - Indeterminate

Out[2]= Indeterminate
```

Indeterminate "poisons" any arithmetic computation, and leads to an indeterminate result.

```
In[3]:= 2 Indeterminate - 7

Out[3]= Indeterminate
```

Indeterminate	an indeterminate numerical result
Infinity	a positive infinite quantity
-Infinity	a negative infinite quantity (DirectedInfinity[-1])
DirectedInfinity[*r*]	an infinite quantity with complex direction *r*
ComplexInfinity	an infinite quantity with an undetermined direction
DirectedInfinity[ ]	equivalent to ComplexInfinity

Indeterminate and infinite quantities.

There are many situations where it is convenient to be able to do calculations with infinite quantities. The symbol Infinity in *Mathematica* represents a positive infinite quantity. You can use it to specify such things as limits of sums and integrals. You can also do some arithmetic calculations with it.

Here is an integral with an infinite limit.

```
In[4]:= Integrate[1/x^3, {x, 1, Infinity}]

          1
Out[4]=  -
          2
```

Mathematica knows that $1/\infty = 0$.

```
In[5]:= 1/Infinity

Out[5]= 0
```

If you try to find the difference between two infinite quantities, you get an indeterminate result.

```
In[6]:= Infinity - Infinity

Infinity::indet:
    Indeterminate expression -Infinity + Infinity encountered.

Out[6]= Indeterminate
```

1/0 gives an undirected form of infinity. There is no way to tell if it should be $+\infty$ or $-\infty$.

```
In[7]:= 1/0
                    1
Power::infy: Infinite expression - encountered.
                    0
Out[7]= ComplexInfinity
```

■ 12.5 Finding Limits

In doing many kinds of calculations, you need to evaluate expressions when variables take on particular values. In many cases, you can do this simply by applying transformation rules for the variables using the /. operator.

You can get the value of $\cos(x^2)$ at 0 just by explicitly replacing x with 0, and then evaluating the result.

```
In[1]:= Cos[x^2] /. x -> 0
Out[1]= 1
```

In some cases, however, you have to be more careful.

Here is the expression $\sin(x)/x$.

```
In[2]:= t = Sin[x]/x
          Sin[x]
Out[2]= -------
            x
```

If you replace x by 0, the expression becomes 0/0, and you get an indeterminate result.

```
In[3]:= t /. x -> 0
                    1
Power::infy: Infinite expression - encountered.
                    0
Infinity::indet:
    Indeterminate expression 0 ComplexInfinity encountered.
Out[3]= Indeterminate
```

If you find the numerical value of $\sin(x)/x$ for x close to 0, however, you get a result that is close to 1.

```
In[4]:= t /. x -> 0.01
Out[4]= 0.999983
```

This finds the *limit* of $\sin(x)/x$ as x approaches 0. The result is indeed 1.

```
In[5]:= Limit[t, x -> 0]
Out[5]= 1
```

Limit[*expr*, x -> x_0]	the limit of *expr* as x approaches x_0

Limits.

No finite limit exists in this case.

```
In[6]:= Limit[ Sin[x]/x^2, x -> 0 ]
Out[6]= Infinity
```

Limit can find this limit, even though you cannot get an ordinary power series for $x\log(x)$ at $x = 0$.

```
In[7]:= Limit[ x Log[x], x -> 0 ]
Out[7]= 0
```

The same is true here.

$In[8]:=$ **Limit[(1 + 2 x) ^ (1/x), x -> 0]**

$Out[8]=$ E^2

Not all functions have definite limits at particular points. For example, the function sin(1/x) oscillates infinitely often near $x = 0$, so it has no definite limit there. Nevertheless, at least so long as x remains real, the values of the function near $x = 0$ always lie between –1 and 1. Limit represents such values using Interval objects. In general, Interval[{*xmin*, *xmax*}] represents an uncertain value which lies somewhere in the interval *xmin* to *xmax*.

Limit returns an Interval object, representing the range of possible values of sin(1/x) near its essential singularity at $x = 0$.

$In[9]:=$ **Limit[Sin[1/x], x -> 0]**

$Out[9]=$ Interval[{-1, 1}]

Mathematica can do arithmetic with Interval objects.

$In[10]:=$ **(1 + %)^3**

$Out[10]=$ Interval[{0, 8}]

Mathematica represents this limit symbolically in terms of an Interval object.

$In[11]:=$ **Limit[Exp[a Sin[x]], x -> Infinity]**

$Out[11]=$ E$^{a\ Interval[\{-1,\ 1\}]}$

Some functions may have different limits at particular points, depending on the direction from which you approach those points. You can use the Direction option for Limit to specify the direction you want.

Limit[*expr*, x -> x_0, Direction -> 1]

  find the limit as x approaches x_0 from below

Limit[*expr*, x -> x_0, Direction -> -1]

  find the limit as x approaches x_0 from above

Directional limits.

The function 1/x has a different limiting value at $x = 0$, depending on whether you approach from above or below.

$In[12]:=$ **Plot[1/x, {x, -1, 1}]**

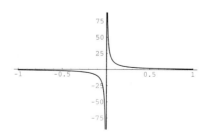

Approaching from below gives a limiting value of −∞.

In[13]:= **Limit[1/x, x -> 0, Direction -> 1]**

Out[13]= -Infinity

Approaching from above gives a limiting value of ∞.

In[14]:= **Limit[1/x, x -> 0, Direction -> -1]**

Out[14]= Infinity

Limit makes no assumptions about functions like f[x] about which it does not have definite knowledge. As a result, Limit remains unevaluated in most cases involving symbolic functions.

Limit has no definite knowledge about f, so it leaves this limit unevaluated.

In[15]:= **Limit[x f[x], x -> 0]**

Out[15]= Limit[x f[x], x -> 0]

13. Roots and Minimization

■ 13.1 Numerical Root Finding

If your equations involve only linear functions or polynomials, then you can use NSolve to get numerical approximations to all the solutions (see Section 7.4). However, when your equations involve more complicated functions, there is in general no systematic procedure for finding all solutions, even numerically. In such cases, you can use FindRoot to search for solutions. You have to give FindRoot a place to start its search.

This searches for a numerical solution, starting at $x = 1$.

In[1]:= **FindRoot[3 Cos[x] == Log[x], {x, 1}]**

Out[1]= {x -> 1.44726}

The equation has seven solutions.

In[2]:= **Plot[{3 Cos[x], Log[x]}, {x, .01, 30}]**

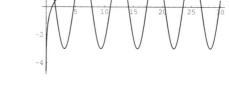

If you start at a different x, FindRoot may return a different solution.

In[3]:= **FindRoot[3 Cos[x] == Log[x], {x, 10}]**

Out[3]= {x -> 13.1064}

FindRoot [*lhs*==*rhs*, {*x*, x_0}]	search for a numerical solution to the equation *lhs*==*rhs*, starting with *x*=x_0
FindRoot [*eqn*, {*x*, {x_0, x_1}}]	search for a solution using x_0 and x_1 as the first two values of *x* (this form must be used if symbolic derivatives of the equation cannot be found)
FindRoot [*eqn*, {*x*, *xstart*, *xmin*, *xmax*}]	search for a solution, stopping the search if *x* ever gets outside the range *xmin* to *xmax*
FindRoot [{eqn_1, eqn_2, ... }, {*x*, x_0}, {*y*, y_0}, ...]	search for a numerical solution to the simultaneous equations

Numerical root finding.

This is a plot of the absolute value of the Riemann zeta function on the critical line $\mathrm{Re}\,z = \frac{1}{2}$. You can see the first few zeros of the zeta function.

In[15]:= **Plot[Abs[Zeta[1/2 + I y]], {y, 0, 40}]**

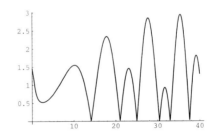

If *Mathematica* cannot get an explicit formula for the function that appears in your equation, you *have to* specify the first two values to try. Here FindRoot finds a zero of the Riemann zeta function.

In[16]:= **FindRoot[Zeta[1/2 + I t] == 0, {t, {12, 13}}]**

Out[16]= {t -> 14.1347 - 4.42626 10^{-7} I}

If you are finding a root of a function of one variable, and the first two points you tell FindRoot to try give values of the function with opposite signs, then FindRoot is guaranteed to find a root. (This is true so long as your function is real and satisfies some basic continuity conditions.)

■ 13.2 Numerical Minimization

FindRoot gives you a way to find points at which a particular function is equal to zero. It is also often important to be able to find points at which a function has its minimum value. In principle, you could do this by applying FindRoot to the derivative of the function. In practice, however, there are much more efficient approaches.

FindMinimum gives you a way to find a minimum value for a function. As in FindRoot, you specify the first one or two points to try, and then FindMinimum tries to get progressively more accurate approximations to a minimum. If FindMinimum returns a definite result, then the result is guaranteed to correspond to at least a local minimum of your function. However, it is important to understand that the result may not be the global minimum point.

You can understand something about how FindMinimum works by thinking of the values of your function as defining the height of a surface. What FindMinimum does is essentially to start at the points you specify, then follow the path of steepest descent on the surface. Except in pathological cases, this path always leads to at least a local minimum on the surface. In many cases, however, the minimum will not be a global one. As a simple analogy which illustrates this point, consider a physical mountain. Any water that falls on the mountain takes the path of steepest descent down the side of the mountain. Yet not all the water ends up at the bottom of the valleys; much of it gets stuck in mountain lakes which correspond to local minima of the mountain height function.

You should also realize that because FindMinimum does not take truly infinitesimal steps, it is still possible for it to overshoot even a local minimum.

This finds the value of x which minimizes $\Gamma(x)$, starting from $x = 2$.

```
In[1]:= FindMinimum[Gamma[x], {x, 2}]
Out[1]= {0.885603, {x -> 1.46163}}
```

Here is a function with many local minima.

```
In[2]:= Plot[Sin[x] + x/5, {x, -10, 10}]
```

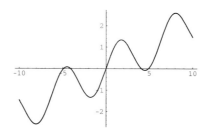

FindMinimum finds the local minimum closest to $x = 1$. This is not the global minimum for the function.

```
In[3]:= FindMinimum[Sin[x] + x/5, {x, 1}]
Out[3]= {-1.33423, {x -> -1.77215}}
```

With a different starting point, you may reach a different local minimum.

```
In[4]:= FindMinimum[Sin[x] + x/5, {x, 5}]
Out[4]= {-0.0775897, {x -> 4.51103}}
```

This finds the local minimum of a function of two variables.

```
In[5]:= FindMinimum[Sin[x y], {x, 2}, {y, 2}]
Out[5]= {-1., {x -> 2.1708, y -> 2.1708}}
```

As in FindRoot, it is a good idea to choose starting values that are not too "special".

```
In[6]:= FindMinimum[x^4 + 3 x^2 y + 5 y^2 + x + y,
                      {x, 0.1}, {y, 0.2}]
Out[6]= {-0.832579, {x -> -0.886326, y -> -0.335672}}
```

FindMinimum$[f, \{x, x_0\}]$	search for a local minimum in the function f, starting from the point $x=x_0$
FindMinimum$[f, \{x, \{x_0, x_1\}\}]$	search for a local minimum using x_0 and x_1 as the first two values of x (this form must be used if symbolic derivatives of f cannot be found)
FindMinimum$[f, \{x, xstart, xmin, xmax\}]$	
	search for a local minimum, stopping the search if x ever gets outside the range *xmin* to *xmax*
FindMinimum$[f, \{x, x_0\}, \{y, y_0\}, ...]$	
	search for a local minimum in a function of several variables

Numerical minimization.

■ 13.3 Linear Programming

`FindMinimum` can find local minima for arbitrary functions. In solving optimization problems, it is however often important to be able to find *global* maxima and minima.

Linear programming provides a way to do this for linear functions. In general, linear programming allows you to find the global minimum or maximum of any linear function subject to a set of constraints defined by linear inequalities.

For a function of n variables, the constraints effectively define a region in n-dimensional space. Each linear inequality gives a plane in n-dimensional space which forms one of the sides of the region.

`ConstrainedMax[f, {`*inequalities*`}, {x, y, ... }]`
> find the global maximum of f in the region specified by the inequalities

`ConstrainedMin[f, {`*inequalities*`}, {x, y, ... }]`
> find the global minimum of f in the region specified by the inequalities

---

Solving linear optimization problems.

The functions `ConstrainedMax` and `ConstrainedMin` allow you to specify an "objective function" to maximize or minimize, together with a set of linear constraints on variables. *Mathematica* assumes in all cases that the variables are constrained to have non-negative values.

The maximum value of $x + y$ in this case is attained when $x = 1$ and $y = 2$.

```
In[1]:= ConstrainedMax[x + y, {x < 1, y < 2}, {x, y}]

Out[1]= {3, {x -> 1, y -> 2}}
```

Mathematica assumes that x and y are constrained to be non-negative.

```
In[2]:= ConstrainedMin[x + y, {x < 1, y < 2}, {x, y}]

Out[2]= {0, {x -> 0, y -> 0}}
```

Here is a slightly more complicated linear programming problem.

```
In[3]:= ConstrainedMax[17x - 20y + 18z,
               {x - y + z < 10, x < 5, x + z > 20}, {x, y, z}]

Out[3]= {160, {x -> 0, y -> 10, z -> 20}}
```

You can give both exact and approximate numbers as coefficients in linear programming problems. When the numbers you give are exact, *Mathematica* will always generate results in terms of exact rational numbers.

If the coefficients in your input are exact, *Mathematica* will give exact rational numbers in the output.

```
In[4]:= ConstrainedMin[x + 3 y + 7 z,
               {x - 3 y < 7, 2 x + 3 z >= 5, x + y + z < 10},
                                            {x, y, z}]
```

$$Out[4]= \{\frac{5}{2}, \{x \to \frac{5}{2}, y \to 0, z \to 0\}\}$$

Mathematica allows you to use both strict inequalities of the form $a < b$ and non-strict inequalities of the form $a <= b$ in specifying linear programming problems. If you work with approximate numbers, then these types of inequalities cannot be distinguished. However, if you work with exact numbers, then these types of inequalities could in principle yield different results.

In most practical linear optimization problems, the region corresponding to the constraints you specify is finite in all directions. It is however possible to give inequalities which specify infinite regions. In such cases, there may be no bound on the objective function, and *Mathematica* will return infinite or indeterminate results.

The region specified in this case is unbounded.

```
In[5]:= ConstrainedMax[x, {x > 1}, {x}]

ConstrainedMax::nbdd: Specified domain appears unbounded.

Out[5]= {Infinity, {x -> Indeterminate}}
```

In `ConstrainedMax` and `ConstrainedMin` the objective functions and constraints are specified in symbolic form. Sometimes, however, it is more convenient to handle linear programming problems simply by setting up vectors and matrices which represent the appropriate coefficients of the linear functions that appear. You can do this using `LinearProgramming`.

LinearProgramming[c, m, b]	find the vector x which minimizes c.x subject to the constraints m.x $\geq$ b and x ≥ 0

Linear programming in matrix form.

Here is a linear programming problem given in symbolic form.

```
In[6]:= ConstrainedMin[2x - 3y,
                    {x + y < 10, x - y > 2, x > 1}, {x, y}]
Out[6]= {0, {x -> 6, y -> 4}}
```

Here is the same problem given in matrix form.

```
In[7]:= LinearProgramming[{2, -3},
                    {{-1, -1}, {1, -1}, {1, 0}}, {-10, 2, 1}]
Out[7]= {6, 4}
```

14. Integration and Sums

■ 14.1 Indefinite Integrals

Integrate[f, x]   the indefinite integral $\int f\, dx$ of the expression f

---

Indefinite integration.

The *Mathematica* function Integrate[f, x] gives you the *indefinite integral* $\int f\, dx$. You can think of the process of indefinite integration as like an inverse of differentiation. If you take the result from Integrate[f, x], and then differentiate it, you always get a result that is mathematically equal to the original expression f.

In general, however, there is a whole family of results which have the property that their derivative is f. Integrate[f, x] gives you *an* expression whose derivative is f. You can get other expressions by adding an arbitrary constant of integration.

When you fill in explicit limits for your integral, any such constants of integration must cancel out. Even though the indefinite integral contains arbitrary constants, it is still often very convenient to manipulate it before filling in the limits.

Mathematica applies standard rules to find indefinite integrals.	*In[1]:=* **Integrate[x^2, x]**
	$Out[1]= \dfrac{x^3}{3}$
You can add an arbitrary constant to the indefinite integral, and still get the same derivative. Integrate simply gives you *an* expression with the required derivative.	*In[2]:=* **D[% + c , x]**
	$Out[2]= x^2$
This gives the indefinite integral $\int \frac{dx}{x^2-1}$.	*In[3]:=* **Integrate[1/(x^2 - 1), x]**
	$Out[3]= \dfrac{\text{Log}[1 - x]}{2} - \dfrac{\text{Log}[1 + x]}{2}$
Differentiating should give the original function back again.	*In[4]:=* **D[%, x]**
	$Out[4]= \dfrac{-1}{2\,(1 - x)} - \dfrac{1}{2\,(1 + x)}$
You need to manipulate it to get it back into the original form.	*In[5]:=* **Simplify[%]**
	$Out[5]= \dfrac{1}{-1 + x^2}$

The `Integrate` function assumes that any object that does not explicitly contain the integration variable is independent of it, and can be treated as a constant. As a result, `Integrate` is like an inverse of the *partial differentiation* function D.

The variable a is assumed to be independent of x.

$$In[6]:= \texttt{Integrate[a x\^{}2, x]}$$

$$Out[6]= \frac{a\ x^3}{3}$$

The integration variable can be any expression.

$$In[7]:= \texttt{Integrate[x b[x]\^{}2, b[x]]}$$

$$Out[7]= \frac{x\ b[x]^3}{3}$$

Another assumption that `Integrate` implicitly makes is that all the symbolic quantities in your integrand have "generic" values. Thus, for example, *Mathematica* will tell you that $\int x^n\,dx$ is $\frac{x^{n+1}}{n+1}$ even though this is not true in the special case $n = -1$.

Mathematica gives the standard result for this integral, implicitly assuming that n is not equal to –1.

$$In[8]:= \texttt{Integrate[x\^{}n, x]}$$

$$Out[8]= \frac{x^{1+n}}{1+n}$$

If you specifically give an exponent of –1, *Mathematica* produces a different result.

$$In[9]:= \texttt{Integrate[x\^{}-1, x]}$$

$$Out[9]= \texttt{Log[x]}$$

■ 14.2 Integrals That *Mathematica* Can and Cannot Do

Evaluating integrals is much more difficult than evaluating derivatives. For derivatives, there is a systematic procedure involving the chain and product rules that allows one to work out any derivative. For integrals, however, there is no such systematic procedure. There are some general principles, but there are many integrals that cannot be done using these principles.

Mathematica knows how to do many kinds of integrals. It can integrate any rational expression (ratio of polynomials), at least as long as the denominator does not involve too high a power of x. *Mathematica* can also integrate expressions that include exponential, logarithmic and trigonometric functions, as long as the resulting integrals can be given in terms of this same set of functions.

There are however many integrals for which no explicit formulas can be given, at least in terms of standard mathematical functions. Even a seemingly innocuous integral like $\int \frac{\log(1+2x)}{x}\,dx$ can only be evaluated in terms of the dilogarithm function. And an integral like $\int \sin(\sin(x))\,dx$ simply cannot be done in terms of any of the functions that are defined in standard mathematical handbooks.

Before going any further, one must address the important question of exactly what it means to "do" an integral. As an operational matter, the important issue is usually whether one can write down a definite formula for the integral, which one can then easily manipulate or evaluate. The most useful formulas are typically ones that involve only rather simple functions, such as logarithms and exponentials.

The class of integrals that can be done in terms of "simple functions" is an important one, albeit in many respects not a particularly large one. One of the main capabilities of the built-in *Mathematica* `Integrate` function is being able to take essentially any integrand that involves only a particular set of "simple functions", and find the integral if it can be expressed in terms of the same set of simple functions. The relevant set of "simple functions" includes rational functions, exponentials and logarithms, as well as trigonometric and inverse trigonometric functions.

Integrals of rational functions are usually quite easy to evaluate. The answers come out in terms of rational functions, together with logarithms and inverse trigonometric functions.

$$In[1]:= \text{Integrate}[x/((x - 1)(x + 2)), x]$$

$$Out[1]= \frac{\text{Log}[1 - x]}{3} + \frac{2 \text{ Log}[2 + x]}{3}$$

If *Mathematica* cannot get explicit formulas for the roots of the denominator polynomial, however, it cannot give you an explicit formula for the integral.

$$In[2]:= \text{Integrate}[1/(1 + 3x + x^5), x]$$

$$Out[2]= \text{Integrate}\left[\frac{1}{1 + 3 x + x^5}, x\right]$$

Integrals involving logarithms and powers can be done in terms of logarithms and powers.

$$In[3]:= \text{Integrate}[x^4 \text{ Log}[x]^2, x]$$

$$Out[3]= \frac{2 x^5}{125} - \frac{2 x^5 \text{ Log}[x]}{25} + \frac{x^5 \text{ Log}[x]^2}{5}$$

Integrals of trigonometric functions usually come out in terms of other trigonometric functions.

$$In[4]:= \text{Integrate}[\text{Sin}[x]^3 \text{ Cos}[x]^2, x]$$

$$Out[4]= \frac{-30 \text{ Cos}[x] - 5 \text{ Cos}[3 x] + 3 \text{ Cos}[5 x]}{240}$$

When you combine "simple functions", you sometimes get integrals that can be done.

$$In[5]:= \text{Integrate}[\text{Sin}[\text{Log}[x]], x]$$

$$Out[5]= \frac{-(x \text{ Cos}[\text{Log}[x]]) + x \text{ Sin}[\text{Log}[x]]}{2}$$

Often, however, you get integrals that cannot be done in terms of simple functions.

$$In[6]:= \text{Integrate}[\text{Sin}[\text{Sin}[x]], x]$$

$$Out[6]= \text{Integrate}[\text{Sin}[\text{Sin}[x]], x]$$

It is remarkable what simple integrands can lead to integrals that cannot be done, say in terms of "simple functions". In fact, if you were randomly to combine simple functions together, most of the integrals you would get could probably not be done in terms of simple functions.

■ 14.3 Definite Integrals

> Integrate[f, {x, xmin, xmax}]
>
> the definite integral $\int_{xmin}^{xmax} f \, dx$
>
> Integrate[f, {x, xmin, xmax}, {y, ymin, ymax}]
>
> the multiple integral $\int_{xmin}^{xmax} dx \int_{ymin}^{ymax} dy \, f$

Definite integration.

Here is the integral $\int_{a}^{b} x^2 \, dx$.

```
In[1]:= Integrate[x^2, {x, a, b}]
```

$$Out[1]= \frac{-a^3}{3} + \frac{b^3}{3}$$

Either of the limits of integration can be infinite.

```
In[2]:= Integrate[2 E ^ x Sin[x], {x, -Infinity, t}]
```

$$Out[2]= -(E^t \, (Cos[t] - Sin[t]))$$

This gives the multiple integral $\int_{0}^{a} dx \int_{0}^{b} dy \, (x^2 + y^2)$.

```
In[3]:= Integrate[x^2 + y^2, {x, 0, a}, {y, 0, b}]
```

$$Out[3]= \frac{a^3 b}{3} + \frac{a b^3}{3}$$

The y integral is done first. Its limits can depend on the value of x. This ordering is the same as is used in functions like Sum and Table.

```
In[4]:= Integrate[x^2 + y^2, {x, 0, a}, {y, 0, x}]
```

$$Out[4]= \frac{a^4}{3}$$

You can often do a definite integral by first finding the indefinite one, and then explicitly substituting in the limits. You have to be careful, however, when the integration region contains a singularity. The integral $\int_{-1}^{1} x^{-2} \, dx$, for example, has an indefinite form which is finite at each end point. Nevertheless, the integrand has a double pole at $x = 0$, and the true integral is infinite.

■ 14.4 Numerical Mathematics in *Mathematica*

One of the most important features of *Mathematica* is its ability to give you exact, symbolic, results for computations. There are, however, computations where it is just mathematically impossible to get exact "closed form" results. In such cases, you can still often get approximate numerical results.

There is no "closed form" result for $\int_{0}^{1} \sin(\sin(x)) \, dx$. *Mathematica* returns the integral in its original symbolic form.

```
In[1]:= Integrate[Sin[Sin[x]], {x, 0, 1}]
Out[1]= Integrate[Sin[Sin[x]], {x, 0, 1}]
```

If, however, you ask for the integral from −1000 to 1000, NIntegrate will miss the peak near $x = 0$, and give the wrong answer.

```
In[3]:= NIntegrate[Exp[-x^2], {x, -1000, 1000}]

NIntegrate::ploss:
    Numerical integration stopping due to loss of precision.
        Achieved neither the requested PrecisionGoal nor
        AccuracyGoal; suspect one of the following: highly
        oscillatory integrand or the true value of the integral is
        0.

Out[3]= 1.34946 10
```
$$Out[3]= 1.34946 \times 10^{-26}$$

Although `NIntegrate` follows the principle of looking only at the numerical values of your integrand, it nevertheless tries to make the best possible use of the information that it can get. Thus, for example, if `NIntegrate` notices that the estimated error in the integral in a particular region is large, it will take more samples in that region. In this way, `NIntegrate` tries to "adapt" its operation to the particular integrand you have given.

The kind of adaptive procedure that `NIntegrate` uses is similar, at least in spirit, to what `Plot` does in trying to draw smooth curves for functions. In both cases, *Mathematica* tries to go on taking more samples in a particular region until it has effectively found a smooth approximation to the function in that region.

The kinds of problems that can appear in numerical integration can also arise in doing other numerical operations on functions.

When you try to find a numerical approximation to the minimum of a function, *Mathematica* samples only a finite number of values, then effectively assumes that the actual function interpolates smoothly between these values. If in fact the function has a sharp dip in a particular region, then *Mathematica* may miss this dip, and you may get the wrong answer for the minimum.

If you work only with numerical values of functions, there is simply no way to avoid the kinds of problems we have been discussing. Exact symbolic computation, of course, allows you to get around these problems.

In many calculations, it is therefore worthwhile to go as far as you can symbolically, and then resort to numerical methods only at the very end. This gives you the best chance of avoiding the problems that can arise in purely numerical computations.

■ 14.6 Numerical Integration

N[Integrate[*expr*, {*x*, *xmin*, *xmax*}]]

      try to perform an integral exactly, then find numerical approximations to the parts that remain

NIntegrate[*expr*, {*x*, *xmin*, *xmax*}]

      find a numerical approximation to an integral

NIntegrate[*expr*, {*x*, *xmin*, *xmax*}, {*y*, *ymin*, *ymax*}, ...]

      multidimensional numerical integral $\int_{xmin}^{xmax} dx \int_{ymin}^{ymax} dy \, ... \, expr$

Numerical integration functions.

This finds a numerical approximation to the integral $\int_0^\infty e^{-x^3} \, dx$.

```
In[1]:= NIntegrate[Exp[-x^3], {x, 0, Infinity}]
Out[1]= 0.89298
```

Here is the numerical value of the double integral $\int_{-1}^{1} dx \int_{-1}^{1} dy \, (x^2 + y^2)$.

```
In[2]:= NIntegrate[x^2 + y^2, {x, -1, 1}, {y, -1, 1}]
Out[2]= 2.66667
```

An important feature of NIntegrate is its ability to deal with functions that "blow up" at known points. NIntegrate automatically checks for such problems at the end points of the integration region.

The function $1/\sqrt{x}$ blows up at $x = 0$, but NIntegrate still succeeds in getting the correct value for the integral.

```
In[3]:= NIntegrate[1/Sqrt[x], {x, 0, 1}]
Out[3]= 2.
```

Mathematica can find the integral of $1/\sqrt{x}$ exactly.

```
In[4]:= Integrate[1/Sqrt[x], {x, 0, 1}]
Out[4]= 2
```

NIntegrate detects that the singularity in $\frac{1}{x}$ at $x = 0$ is not integrable.

```
In[5]:= NIntegrate[1/x, {x, 0, 1}]

NIntegrate::slwcon:
    Numerical integration converging too slowly; suspect one of
      the following: singularity, oscillatory integrand, or
      insufficient WorkingPrecision.

NIntegrate::ncvb:
    NIntegrate failed to converge to prescribed accuracy after 7
                                                   -57
      recursive bisections in x near x = 4.36999 10   .

Out[5]= 23953.1
```

Here is a double integral over a triangular domain. Note the order in which the variables are given.

```
In[6]:= NIntegrate[ Sin[x y], {x, 0, 1}, {y, 0, x} ]
Out[6]= 0.119906
```

■ 14.7 Numerical Evaluation of Sums and Products

`NSum[f, {i, imin, imax}]`	find a numerical approximation to the sum $\sum_{i=imin}^{imax} f$
`NSum[f, {i, imin, imax, di}]`	use step di in the sum
`NProduct[f, {i, imin, imax}]`	find a numerical approximation to the product $\prod_{i=imin}^{imax} f$

Numerical sums and products.

This gives a numerical approximation to $\sum_{i=1}^{\infty} \frac{(-1)^{i+1}}{i}$.

```
In[1]:= NSum[(-1)^(i+1) 1/i, {i, 1, Infinity}]
Out[1]= 0.693147
```

Mathematica does not know the exact result for this sum, so leaves it in symbolic form.

```
In[2]:= Sum[(-1)^(i+1) 1/i, {i, 1, Infinity}]
                1 + i
               (-1)
Out[2]= Sum[─────────, {i, 1, Infinity}]
                 i
```

You can apply N explicitly to get a numerical result.

```
In[3]:= N[%]
Out[3]= 0.693147
```

The way NSum works is to include a certain number of terms explicitly, and then to try and estimate the contribution of the remaining ones.

The most common place to use NSum is in evaluating sums with infinite limits. You can, however, also use it for sums with finite limits. By making implicit assumptions about the objects you are evaluating, NSum can often avoid doing as many function evaluations as an explicit Sum computation would require.

This finds the numerical value of $\sum_{n=0}^{100} e^{-n}$ by extrapolation techniques.

```
In[4]:= NSum[Exp[-n], {n, 0, 100}]
Out[4]= 1.58198
```

You can also get the result, although much less efficiently, by constructing the symbolic form of the sum, then evaluating it numerically.

```
In[5]:= N[ Sum[Exp[-n], {n, 0, 100}] ]
Out[5]= 1.58198
```

NProduct works in essentially the same way as NSum.

15. Power Series

■ 15.1 Overview

Series[*expr*, {*x*, x_0, *n*}]	find the power series expansion of *expr* about the point $x = x_0$ to order at most $(x - x_0)^n$
Normal[*series*]	truncate a power series to give an ordinary expression

Functions for creating power series.

The mathematical operations we have discussed so far are *exact*. Given precise input, their results are exact formulas.

In many situations, however, you do not need an exact result. It may be quite sufficient, for example, to find an *approximate* formula that is valid, say, when the quantity x is small.

This gives a power series approximation to $1/(1-x)$ for x close to 0, up to terms of order x^6.

$$In[1]:= \text{Series}[1 \ / \ (1 \ - \ x), \ \{x, \ 0, \ 6\}]$$

$$Out[1]= 1 + x + x^2 + x^3 + x^4 + x^5 + x^6 + O[x]^7$$

Mathematica knows the power series expansions for many mathematical functions.

$$In[2]:= \text{Series}[\text{ArcTan}[t], \ \{t, \ 0, \ 10\}]$$

$$Out[2]= t - \frac{t^3}{3} + \frac{t^5}{5} - \frac{t^7}{7} + \frac{t^9}{9} + O[t]^{11}$$

If you give it a function that it does not know, Series writes out the power series in terms of derivatives.

$$In[3]:= \text{Series}[\text{f}[x], \ \{x, \ 0, \ 3\}]$$

$$Out[3]= f[0] + f'[0] \ x + \frac{f''[0] \ x^2}{2} + \frac{f^{(3)}[0] \ x^3}{6} + O[x]^4$$

Power series are approximate formulas that play much the same role with respect to algebraic expressions as approximate numbers play with respect to numerical expressions. *Mathematica* allows you to perform operations on power series, in all cases maintaining the appropriate order or "degree of precision" for the resulting power series.

You can recognize a power series that is printed out in standard output form by the presence of an O[x] term. This term mimics the standard mathematical notation $O(x)$, and represents omitted terms of order x. For various reasons of consistency, *Mathematica* uses the notation O[x]^n for omitted terms of order x^n, corresponding to the mathematical notation $O(x)^n$, rather than the equivalent form $O(x^n)$.

You can think of the O[x] term as if it meant "and so on".

Here is a simple power series, accurate to order x^5.

$$In[4]:= \text{s} = \text{Series}[\text{Exp}[x], \ \{x, \ 0, \ 5\}]$$

$$Out[4]= 1 + x + \frac{x^2}{2} + \frac{x^3}{6} + \frac{x^4}{24} + \frac{x^5}{120} + O[x]^6$$

When you do operations on a power series, the result is computed only to the appropriate order in x.

$In[5]:=$ **s^2 (1 + s)**

$$Out[5]= 2 + 5\ x + \frac{13\ x^2}{2} + \frac{35\ x^3}{6} + \frac{97\ x^4}{24} + \frac{55\ x^5}{24} + O[x]^6$$

This turns the last power series into an ordinary expression.

$In[6]:=$ **Normal[%]**

$$Out[6]= 2 + 5\ x + \frac{13\ x^2}{2} + \frac{35\ x^3}{6} + \frac{97\ x^4}{24} + \frac{55\ x^5}{24}$$

Now the square is computed *exactly.*

$In[7]:=$ **%^2**

$$Out[7]= (2 + 5\ x + \frac{13\ x^2}{2} + \frac{35\ x^3}{6} + \frac{97\ x^4}{24} + \frac{55\ x^5}{24})^2$$

Applying Expand gives a result with ten terms.

$In[8]:=$ **Expand[%]**

$$Out[8]= 4 + 20\ x + 51\ x^2 + \frac{265\ x^3}{3} + \frac{467\ x^4}{4} + \frac{1505\ x^5}{12} +$$

$$\frac{7883\ x^6}{72} + \frac{1385\ x^7}{18} + \frac{24809\ x^8}{576} + \frac{5335\ x^9}{288} + \frac{3025\ x^{10}}{576}$$

To evaluate a power series you should use Normal.

$In[9]:=$ **Normal[Series[Exp[x], {x, 0, 4}]] /. x -> 1**

$$Out[9]= \frac{65}{24}$$

This defines a function which will give the first *n* terms of the Taylor series of sin(x).

$In[10]:=$ **f[n_] := Normal[Series[Sin[x], {x, 0, n}]]**

This plots sin(x) together with its Taylor series taken to three terms.

$In[11]:=$ **Plot[Evaluate[{Sin[x], f[3]}], {x, -7, 7}]**

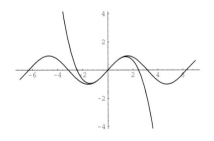

Taking 11 terms gives a much better approximation.

$In[12]:=$ **Plot[Evaluate[{Sin[x], f[11]}], {x, -7, 7}]**

■ 15.2 Operations on Power Series

Mathematica allows you to perform many operations on power series. In all cases, *Mathematica* gives results only to as many terms as can be justified from the accuracy of your input.

Assuming that x is real justifies simplifying with PowerExpand.

$In[1]:=$ **PowerExpand[Log[E ∧ (2 x)]]**

$Out[1]=$ 2 x

Here is a power series accurate to fourth order in x.

$In[2]:=$ **Series[Exp[x], {x, 0, 4}]**

$$Out[2]= 1 + x + \frac{x^2}{2} + \frac{x^3}{6} + \frac{x^4}{24} + O[x]^5$$

When you square the power series, you get another power series, also accurate to fourth order.

$In[3]:=$ **%^2**

$$Out[3]= 1 + 2 x + 2 x^2 + \frac{4 x^3}{3} + \frac{2 x^4}{3} + O[x]^5$$

Taking the logarithm gives you the result 2x, but only to order x^4.

$In[4]:=$ **Log[%]**

$$Out[4]= 2 x + O[x]^5$$

Mathematica keeps track of the orders of power series in much the same way as it keeps track of the precision of approximate real numbers. Just as with numerical calculations, there are operations on power series which can increase, or decrease, the precision (or order) of your results.

Here is a power series good to order x^4.

$In[5]:=$ **Series[Exp[x], {x, 0, 4}]**

$$Out[5]= 1 + x + \frac{x^2}{2} + \frac{x^3}{6} + \frac{x^4}{24} + O[x]^5$$

This gives a power series that is accurate only to order x^2.

$In[6]:=$ **1 / (1 - %)**

$$Out[6]= -(\frac{1}{x}) + \frac{1}{2} - \frac{x}{12} + O[x]^3$$

Mathematica also allows you to do calculus with power series.

Here is a power series for cos(x).

$In[7]:=$ **Series[Cos[x], {x, 0, 6}]**

$$Out[7]= 1 - \frac{x^2}{2} + \frac{x^4}{24} - \frac{x^6}{720} + O[x]^7$$

Here is its derivative with respect to x.

$$In[8] := \textbf{D[\%, x]}$$

$$Out[8] = -x + \frac{x^3}{6} - \frac{x^5}{120} + O[x]^6$$

Integrating with respect to x gives back a power series with the same dependence on x as the original one, but with a different constant of integration.

$$In[9] := \textbf{Integrate[\%, x]}$$

$$Out[9] = \frac{-x^2}{2} + \frac{x^4}{24} - \frac{x^6}{720} + O[x]^7$$

When you perform an operation that involves both a normal expression and a power series, *Mathematica* absorbs the normal expression into the power series whenever possible.

The 1 is automatically absorbed into the power series.

$$In[10] := \textbf{1 + Series[Exp[x], \{x, 0, 4\}]}$$

$$Out[10] = 2 + x + \frac{x^2}{2} + \frac{x^3}{6} + \frac{x^4}{24} + O[x]^5$$

The x^2 is also absorbed into the power series.

$$In[11] := \textbf{\% + x\textasciicircum 2}$$

$$Out[11] = 2 + x + \frac{3 x^2}{2} + \frac{x^3}{6} + \frac{x^4}{24} + O[x]^5$$

If you add Sin[x], *Mathematica* generates the appropriate power series for Sin[x], and combines it with the power series you have.

$$In[12] := \textbf{\% + Sin[x]}$$

$$Out[12] = 2 + 2 x + \frac{3 x^2}{2} + \frac{x^4}{24} + O[x]^5$$

Mathematica also absorbs expressions that multiply power series. The symbol a is assumed to be independent of x.

$$In[13] := \textbf{(a + x) \%\textasciicircum 2}$$

$$Out[13] = 4 a + (4 + 8 a) x + (8 + 10 a) x^2 + (10 + 6 a) x^3 +$$

$$(6 + \frac{29 a}{12}) x^4 + O[x]^5$$

Mathematica knows how to apply a wide variety of functions to power series. However, if you apply an arbitrary function to a power series, it is impossible for *Mathematica* to give you anything but a symbolic result.

Mathematica does not apply the function f to a power series, so it just leaves the symbolic result.

$$In[14] := \textbf{f[Series[Exp[x], \{x, 0, 3\}]]}$$

$$Out[14] = f[1 + x + \frac{x^2}{2} + \frac{x^3}{6} + O[x]^4]$$

Residue ▪ SeriesCoefficient ▪ InverseSeries ▪ ComposeSeries

Other *Mathematica* functions related to series. (See page xvi.)

16. Vectors and Matrices

■ 16.1 Vectors

Vectors and matrices in *Mathematica* are simply represented by lists and by lists of lists, respectively.

$\{a, \ b, \ c\}$ vector (a, b, c)

$\{\{a, \ b\}, \ \{c, \ d\}\}$ matrix $\begin{pmatrix} a & b \\ c & d \end{pmatrix}$

The representation of vectors and matrices by lists.

Most mathematical functions in *Mathematica* are set up to apply themselves separately to each element in a list. A consequence is that most mathematical functions are applied element by element to matrices and vectors.

The Log applies itself separately to each element in the vector.

```
In[1]:= Log[ {a, b, c} ]
Out[1]= {Log[a], Log[b], Log[c]}
```

The differentiation function D also applies separately to each element in a list.

```
In[2]:= D[ {x, x^2, x^3}, x ]
                          2
Out[2]= {1, 2 x, 3 x }
```

The sum of two vectors is carried out element by element.

```
In[3]:= {a, b} + {ap, bp}
Out[3]= {a + ap, b + bp}
```

If you try to add two vectors with different lengths, you get an error.

```
In[4]:= {a, b, c} + {ap, bp}
Thread::tdlen:
    Objects of unequal length in {a, b, c} + {ap, bp}
        cannot be combined.
Out[4]= {ap, bp} + {a, b, c}
```

This adds the scalar 1 to each element of the vector.

```
In[5]:= 1 + {a, b}
Out[5]= {1 + a, 1 + b}
```

Any object that is not manifestly a list is treated as a scalar. Here c is treated as a scalar, and added separately to each element in the vector.

```
In[6]:= {a, b} + c
Out[6]= {a + c, b + c}
```

This multiplies each element in the vector by the scalar k.

```
In[7]:= k {a, b}
Out[7]= {a k, b k}
```

This takes the dot ("scalar") product of two vectors.

```
In[8]:= {x, y} . {xp, yp}
Out[8]= x xp + y yp
```

It is important to realize that *Mathematica* treats an object as a vector in a particular operation only if the object is explicitly a list at the time when the operation is done. If the object is not explicitly a list, *Mathematica* always treats it as a scalar. This means that you can get different results, depending on whether you assign a particular object to be a list before or after you do a particular operation.

The object p is treated as a scalar, and added separately to each element in the vector.	`In[9]:= {a, .b} + p`
	
	`Out[9]= {a + p, b + p}`

This is what happens if you now replace p by the list {c, d}.	`In[10]:= % /. p -> {c, d}`
	
	`Out[10]= {{a + c, a + d}, {b + c, b + d}}`

You would have got a different result if you had replaced p by {c, d} before you did the first operation.	`In[11]:= {a, b} + {c, d}`
	
	`Out[11]= {a + c, b + d}`

Table[*f*, {*i*, *n*}]	build a length-*n* vector by evaluating *f* with *i*=1, *i*=2, ... , *i*=*n*
Array[*a*, *n*]	build a length-*n* vector of the form {*a*[1], *a*[2], ... }
Range[*n*]	create the list {1, 2, 3, ... , *n*}
Range[*n₁*, *n₂*]	create the list {n_1, n_1+1, ... , n_2}
Range[*n₁*, *n₂*, *dn*]	create the list {n_1, n_1+*dn*, ... , n_2}
list[[*i*]]	give the *i*th element in the vector *list*
Length[*list*]	give the number of elements in *list*
ColumnForm[*list*]	display the elements of *list* in a column

Functions for vectors.

This gives a vector of alternating plus and minus ones.	`In[12]:= Table[(-1)^i, {i, 8}]`
	
	`Out[12]= {-1, 1, -1, 1, -1, 1, -1, 1}`

This gives a vector with symbolic elements. You can use this in deriving general formulas that are valid with any choice of vector components.	`In[13]:= Array[a, 4]`
	
	`Out[13]= {a[1], a[2], a[3], a[4]}`

Range gives arithmetic progressions.	`In[14]:= v = Range[10, 14, .5]`
	
	`Out[14]= {10, 10.5, 11., 11.5, 12., 12.5, 13., 13.5, 14.}`

This is how to get the number of components in a list or vector.	`In[15]:= Length[v]`
	
	`Out[15]= 9`

This is the third component of the vector.	`In[16]:= v[[3]]`
	
	`Out[16]= 11.`

You can show the vector vertically as a column.	*In[17]:=* **ColumnForm[v]**
	Out[17]= 10 10.5 11. 11.5 12. 12.5 13. 13.5 14.

■ 16.2 Matrices

Table[*f*, {*i*, *m*}, {*j*, *n*}]	build an $m \times n$ matrix where *f* is a function of *i* and *j* that gives the value of i,j^{th} entry
MatrixForm[*list*]	display *list* in matrix form
Array[*f*, {*m*, *n*}]	build an $m \times n$ matrix whose i,j^{th} entry is *f*[*i*, *j*]
Dimensions[*list*]	give the dimensions of a matrix represented by *list*
Transpose[*m*]	transpose
DiagonalMatrix[*list*]	generate a matrix with the elements of *list* on the diagonal
IdentityMatrix[*n*]	generate an $n \times n$ identity matrix

Functions for matrices.

A matrix is a list of vectors of the same length.	*In[1]:=* **m = {{a, b}, {c, d}}** *Out[1]=* {{a, b}, {c, d}}
As with vectors, mathematical functions applied to a matrix get applied to each of the entries.	*In[2]:=* **Log[m]** *Out[2]=* {{Log[a], Log[b]}, {Log[c], Log[d]}}
This builds a 3×3 matrix *s* with elements $s_{ij} = i + j$.	*In[3]:=* **s = Table[i+j, {i, 3}, {j, 3}]** *Out[3]=* {{2, 3, 4}, {3, 4, 5}, {4, 5, 6}}

This displays s in standard two-dimensional matrix format.	*In[4]:=* **MatrixForm[s]**
	Out[4]//MatrixForm= 2 3 4
	          3 4 5
	          4 5 6

This multiplies each of the entries of s by the scalar *c*.	*In[5]:=* **c s** *Out[5]=* {{2 c, 3 c, 4 c}, {3 c, 4 c, 5 c}, {4 c, 5 c, 6 c}}

This gives a 3×2 matrix with symbolic elements in matrix format.

```
In[6]:= Array[p, {3, 2}]
Out[6]= {{p[1, 1], p[1, 2]}, {p[2, 1], p[2, 2]},
   {p[3, 1], p[3, 2]}}
```

Here are the dimensions of the matrix on the previous line.

```
In[7]:= Dimensions[%]
Out[7]= {3, 2}
```

Transposing a matrix interchanges the rows and columns in the matrix. If you transpose an $m \times n$ matrix, you get an $n \times m$ matrix as the result.

Transposing a 2×3 matrix gives a 3×2 result.

```
In[8]:= Transpose[ {{a, b, c}, {ap, bp, cp}} ]
Out[8]= {{a, ap}, {b, bp}, {c, cp}}
```

DiagonalMatrix makes a matrix with zeros everywhere except on the leading diagonal.

```
In[9]:= DiagonalMatrix[{a, b, c}]
Out[9]= {{a, 0, 0}, {0, b, 0}, {0, 0, c}}
```

IdentityMatrix[n] produces an $n \times n$ identity matrix.

```
In[10]:= IdentityMatrix[3]
Out[10]= {{1, 0, 0}, {0, 1, 0}, {0, 0, 1}}
```

Of the functions for constructing matrices mentioned above, Table is the most general. You can use Table to produce many kinds of matrices.

Table[0, {m}, {n}]	a zero matrix
Table[Random[ ], {m}, {n}]	a matrix with pseudorandom numerical entries

Some special types of matrices.

Table evaluates Random[ ] separately for each element, to give a different pseudorandom number in each case.

```
In[11]:= Table[Random[ ], {2}, {2}]
Out[11]= {{0.0560708, 0.6303}, {0.359894, 0.871377}}
```

This gives an upper-triangular matrix.

```
In[12]:= MatrixForm[ Table[If[i <= j, 1, 0], {i, 3}, {j, 3}] ]
Out[12]//MatrixForm= 1   1   1
                     0   1   1
                     0   0   1
```

■ 16.3 Getting Pieces of Matrices

$m[[i, j]]$	the i,j^{th} entry
$m[[i]]$	the ith row
$\text{Transpose}[m][[i]]$	the ith column

$m[[\text{Range}[i_0, i_1], \text{Range}[j_0, j_1]]]$

a submatrix with elements having row and column indices respectively in the ranges i_0 through i_1 and j_0 through j_1

$m[[\{i_1, \ldots, i_r\}, \{j_1, \ldots, j_s\}]]$

the $r \times s$ submatrix of m with elements having row indices i_k and column indices j_k

Ways to get pieces of matrices.

Matrices in *Mathematica* are represented as lists of lists. You can use all the standard *Mathematica* list-manipulation operations on matrices.

Here is a sample 3×3 matrix.

```
In[1]:= MatrixForm[t = Array[a, {3, 3}] ]
Out[1]//MatrixForm= a[1, 1]   a[1, 2]   a[1, 3]
                    a[2, 1]   a[2, 2]   a[2, 3]
                    a[3, 1]   a[3, 2]   a[3, 3]
```

This picks out the second row of the matrix.

```
In[2]:= t[[2]]
Out[2]= {a[2, 1], a[2, 2], a[2, 3]}
```

Here is the second column of the matrix.

```
In[3]:= Transpose[t][[2]]
Out[3]= {a[1, 2], a[2, 2], a[3, 2]}
```

This way of picking out a submatrix is convenient when you deal with bigger matrices.

```
In[4]:= MatrixForm[ t[[ Range[1,2], Range[2,3] ]] ]
Out[4]//MatrixForm= a[1, 2]   a[1, 3]
                    a[2, 2]   a[2, 3]
```

This picks out the four corners of the matrix.

```
In[5]:= MatrixForm[ t[[ {1, 3}, {1, 3} ]] ]
Out[5]//MatrixForm= a[1, 1]   a[1, 3]
                    a[3, 1]   a[3, 3]
```

■ 16.4 Multiplying Vectors and Matrices

c v, *c m*, etc.	multiply each element by a scalar
v.v, *v.m*, *m.v*, *m.m*, etc.	vector and matrix multiplication

Different kinds of vector and matrix multiplication.

This multiplies each element of the vector by the scalar k.

```
In[1]:= k {a, b, c}
Out[1]= {a k, b k, c k}
```

The "dot" operator gives the scalar product of two vectors.

```
In[2]:= {a, b, c} . {ap, bp, cp}
Out[2]= a ap + b bp + c cp
```

You can also use dot to multiply a matrix by a vector.

```
In[3]:= {{a, b}, {c, d}} . {x, y}
Out[3]= {a x + b y, c x + d y}
```

Dot is also the notation for matrix multiplication in *Mathematica*.

```
In[4]:= {{a, b}, {c, d}} . {{1, 2}, {3, 4}}
Out[4]= {{a + 3 b, 2 a + 4 b}, {c + 3 d, 2 c + 4 d}}
```

It is important to realize that you can use "dot" for both left- and right-multiplication of vectors by matrices. *Mathematica* makes no distinction between "row" and "column" vectors. Dot carries out whatever operation is possible. The multiplication of matrices always results in a matrix; the multiplication of a matrix and a vector results in a vector; the multiplication of vectors results in a scalar.

Here are definitions for a matrix m and a vector v.

```
In[5]:= m = {{a, b}, {c, d}} ;  v = {x, y}
Out[5]= {x, y}
```

This left-multiplies the vector v by m. The object v is effectively treated as a column vector in this case.

```
In[6]:= m . v
Out[6]= {a x + b y, c x + d y}
```

You can also use dot to right-multiply v by m. Now v is effectively treated as a row vector.

```
In[7]:= v . m
Out[7]= {a x + c y, b x + d y}
```

You can multiply m by v on both sides, to get a scalar.

```
In[8]:= v . m . v
Out[8]= x (a x + c y) + y (b x + d y)
```

■ 16.5 Matrix Inversion

Inverse[*m*]	find the inverse of a square matrix

Matrix inversion.

Here is a simple 2×2 matrix.

```
In[1]:= m = {{a, b}, {c, d}}
Out[1]= {{a, b}, {c, d}}
```

This gives the inverse of m. In producing this formula, *Mathematica* implicitly assumes that the determinant a d − b c is non-zero.

$$In[2]:= \textbf{Inverse[m]}$$
$$Out[2]= \{\{\frac{d}{-(b\ c)\ +\ a\ d},\ -(\frac{b}{-(b\ c)\ +\ a\ d})\},$$
$$\{-(\frac{c}{-(b\ c)\ +\ a\ d}),\ \frac{a}{-(b\ c)\ +\ a\ d}\}\}$$

Multiplying the inverse by the original matrix should give the identity matrix.

$$In[3]:= \textbf{\% . m}$$
$$Out[3]= \{\{-(\frac{b\ c}{-(b\ c)\ +\ a\ d})\ +\ \frac{a\ d}{-(b\ c)\ +\ a\ d},\ 0\},$$
$$\{0,\ -(\frac{b\ c}{-(b\ c)\ +\ a\ d})\ +\ \frac{a\ d}{-(b\ c)\ +\ a\ d}\}\}$$

You have to use Together to clear the denominators, and get back a standard identity matrix.

```
In[4]:= Together[ % ]
Out[4]= {{1, 0}, {0, 1}}
```

Here is a matrix of rational numbers.

$$In[5]:= \textbf{hb = Table[1/(i + j), \{i, 4\}, \{j, 4\}]}$$
$$Out[5]= \{\{\frac{1}{2},\ \frac{1}{3},\ \frac{1}{4},\ \frac{1}{5}\},\ \{\frac{1}{3},\ \frac{1}{4},\ \frac{1}{5},\ \frac{1}{6}\},\ \{\frac{1}{4},\ \frac{1}{5},\ \frac{1}{6},\ \frac{1}{7}\},\ \{\frac{1}{5},\ \frac{1}{6},\ \frac{1}{7},\ \frac{1}{8}\}\}$$

Mathematica finds the exact inverse of the matrix.

```
In[6]:= Inverse[hb]
Out[6]= {{200, -1200, 2100, -1120},
    {-1200, 8100, -15120, 8400}, {2100, -15120, 29400, -16800},
    {-1120, 8400, -16800, 9800}}
```

Multiplying by the original matrix gives the identity matrix.

```
In[7]:= % . hb
Out[7]= {{1, 0, 0, 0}, {0, 1, 0, 0}, {0, 0, 1, 0}, {0, 0, 0, 1}}
```

If you try to invert a singular matrix, *Mathematica* prints a warning message, and returns the inverse undone.

```
In[8]:= Inverse[ {{1, 2}, {1, 2}} ]
LinearSolve::nosol:
    Linear equation encountered which has no solution.
Out[8]= Inverse[{{1, 2}, {1, 2}}]
```

If you give a matrix with exact symbolic or numerical entries, *Mathematica* gives the exact inverse. If, on the other hand, some of the entries in your matrix are approximate real numbers, then *Mathematica* finds an approximate numerical result.

Here is a matrix containing approximate real numbers.	*In[9]:=* **m = {{1.2, 5.7}, {4.2, 5.6}}**
	Out[9]= {{1.2, 5.7}, {4.2, 5.6}}
This finds the numerical inverse.	*In[10]:=* **Inverse[%]**
	Out[10]= {{-0.325203, 0.33101}, {0.243902, -0.0696864}}

Multiplying by the original matrix gives you an identity matrix with small numerical errors.

In[11]:= **% . m**

Out[11]= {{1., 1.91036×10^{-16}}, {1.00831×10^{-17}, 1.}}

You can get rid of the small off-diagonal terms using Chop.

In[12]:= **Chop[%]**

Out[12]= {{1., 0}, {0, 1.}}

When you try to invert a matrix with exact numerical entries, *Mathematica* can always tell whether or not the matrix is singular. When you invert an approximate numerical matrix, *Mathematica* can never tell for certain whether or not the matrix is singular: all it can tell is for example that the determinant is small compared to the entries of the matrix. When *Mathematica* suspects that you are trying to invert a singular numerical matrix, it prints a warning.

Mathematica prints a warning if you invert a numerical matrix that it suspects is singular.

In[13]:= **Inverse[{{1., 2.}, {1., 2.}}]**

Inverse::sing: Matrix {{1., 2.}, {1., 2.}} is singular.

Out[13]= Inverse[{{1., 2.}, {1., 2.}}]

If you work with high-precision approximate numbers, *Mathematica* will keep track of the precision of matrix inverses that you generate.

This generates a 6×6 numerical matrix with entries of 50-digit precision.

In[14]:= **m = N [Table[Exp[i j], {i, 6}, {j, 6}], 50] ;**

This takes the matrix, multiplies it by its inverse, and shows the first row of the result.

In[15]:= **(m . Inverse[m]) [[1]]**

Out[15]= {1., $0. 10^{-54}$, $0. 10^{-56}$, $0. 10^{-58}$, $0. 10^{-58}$, $0. 10^{-63}$}

This gives the accuracy of the result. It is close to 50 digits.

In[16]:= **Accuracy[%]**

Out[16]= 46

This generates a 50-digit numerical approximation to a 6×6 Hilbert matrix. Hilbert matrices are notoriously hard to invert numerically.

In[17]:= **m = N[Table[1/(i + j - 1), {i, 6}, {j, 6}], 50] ;**

The actual numbers given are again correct.

In[18]:= **(m . Inverse[m]) [[1]]**

Out[18]= {1., $0. 10^{-49}$, $0. 10^{-48}$, $0. 10^{-48}$, $0. 10^{-48}$, $0. 10^{-48}$}

The accuracy of the result, however, is lower.

In[19]:= **Accuracy[%]**

Out[19]= 38

■ 16.6 Basic Matrix Operations

Det[*m*]	determinant
Minors[*m*, *k*]	a matrix of the $k \times k$ minors of *m*
Sum[*m*[[*i*, *i*]], {*i*, n}]	trace of m if $n \times n$

Some basic matrix operations.

Det[*m*] gives the determinant of a square matrix *m*. Minors[*m*, *k*] gives a matrix of the determinants of all the $k \times k$ submatrices of *m*. You can apply Minors to rectangular, as well as square, matrices.

Here is the determinant of a simple 2×2 matrix.

```
In[1]:= Det[ {{a, b}, {c, d}} ]
Out[1]= -(b c) + a d
```

This generates a 3×3 matrix, whose i,j^{th} entry is a[*i*, *j*].

```
In[2]:= MatrixForm[ m = Array[a, {3, 3}] ]
Out[2]//MatrixForm= a[1, 1]   a[1, 2]   a[1, 3]
                    a[2, 1]   a[2, 2]   a[2, 3]
                    a[3, 1]   a[3, 2]   a[3, 3]
```

Here is the determinant of m.

```
In[3]:= Det[ m ]
Out[3]= -(a[1, 3] a[2, 2] a[3, 1]) + a[1, 2] a[2, 3] a[3, 1] +
    a[1, 3] a[2, 1] a[3, 2] - a[1, 1] a[2, 3] a[3, 2] -
    a[1, 2] a[2, 1] a[3, 3] + a[1, 1] a[2, 2] a[3, 3]
```

This is the matrix of all 2×2 minors of m.

```
In[4]:= Minors[m, 2]
Out[4]= {{-(a[1, 2] a[2, 1]) + a[1, 1] a[2, 2],
    -(a[1, 3] a[2, 1]) + a[1, 1] a[2, 3],
    -(a[1, 3] a[2, 2]) + a[1, 2] a[2, 3]},
   {-(a[1, 2] a[3, 1]) + a[1, 1] a[3, 2],
    -(a[1, 3] a[3, 1]) + a[1, 1] a[3, 3],
    -(a[1, 3] a[3, 2]) + a[1, 2] a[3, 3]},
   {-(a[2, 2] a[3, 1]) + a[2, 1] a[3, 2],
    -(a[2, 3] a[3, 1]) + a[2, 1] a[3, 3],
    -(a[2, 3] a[3, 2]) + a[2, 2] a[3, 3]}}
```

You can use Det to find the characteristic polynomial for a matrix. Section 17.2 discusses ways to find eigenvalues and eigenvectors directly.

Here is a 3×3 matrix.

```
In[5]:= m = Table[ 1/(i + j), {i, 3}, {j, 3} ]
Out[5]= {{1/2, 1/3, 1/4}, {1/3, 1/4, 1/5}, {1/4, 1/5, 1/6}}
```

Following precisely the standard mathematical definition, this gives the characteristic polynomial for m.

$In[6]:=$ **Det[m - x IdentityMatrix[3]]**

$$Out[6]= \frac{1}{43200} - \frac{131\ x}{3600} + \frac{11\ x^2}{12} - x^3$$

There are many other operations on matrices that can be built up from standard *Mathematica* functions. One example is the *trace* or *spur* of a matrix, given by the sum of the terms on the leading diagonal.

Here is a simple 2×2 matrix.

$In[7]:=$ **m = {{a, b}, {c, d}}**

$Out[7]=$ {{a, b}, {c, d}}

You can get the trace of the matrix by explicitly constructing a sum of the elements on its leading diagonal.

$In[8]:=$ **Sum[m[[i, i]], {i, 2}]**

$Out[8]=$ a + d

MatrixPower[m, n]	n^{th} matrix power
MatrixExp[m]	matrix exponential

Powers and exponentials of matrices.

Here is a 2×2 matrix.

$In[9]:=$ **m = {{0.4, 0.6}, {0.525, 0.475}}**

$Out[9]=$ {{0.4, 0.6}, {0.525, 0.475}}

This gives the third matrix power of m.

$In[10]:=$ **MatrixPower[m, 3]**

$Out[10]=$ {{0.465625, 0.534375}, {0.467578, 0.532422}}

It is equivalent to multiplying three copies of the matrix.

$In[11]:=$ **m . m . m**

$Out[11]=$ {{0.465625, 0.534375}, {0.467578, 0.532422}}

Here is the millionth matrix power.

$In[12]:=$ **MatrixPower[m, 10^6]**

$Out[12]=$ {{0.466667, 0.533333}, {0.466667, 0.533333}}

This gives the matrix exponential of m.

$In[13]:=$ **MatrixExp[m]**

$Out[13]=$ {{1.7392, 0.979085}, {0.8567, 1.86158}}

Here is an approximation to the exponential of m, based on a power series approximation.

$In[14]:=$ **Sum[MatrixPower[m, i]/i!, {i, 0, 5}]**

$Out[14]=$ {{1.73844, 0.978224}, {0.855946, 1.86072}}

17. Linear Algebra

■ 17.1 Solving Linear Systems

Many calculations involve solving systems of linear equations. In many cases, you will find it convenient to write down the equations explicitly, and then solve them using `Solve`.

In some cases, however, you may prefer to convert the system of linear equations into a matrix equation, and then apply matrix manipulation operations to solve it. This approach is often useful when the system of equations arises as part of a general algorithm, and you do not know in advance how many variables will be involved.

A system of linear equations can be stated in matrix form as **m.x = b**, where **x** is the vector of variables.

`LinearSolve[m, b]`	give a vector x which solves the matrix equation $m.x == b$
`NullSpace[m]`	a list of basis vectors whose linear combinations satisfy the matrix equation $m.x == 0$
`RowReduce[m]`	a simplified form of m obtained by making linear combinations of rows

Functions for solving linear systems.

Here is a 2×2 matrix.

```
In[1]:= m = {{1, 5}, {2, 1}}
Out[1]= {{1, 5}, {2, 1}}
```

This gives two linear equations.

```
In[2]:= m . {x, y} == {a, b}
Out[2]= {x + 5 y, 2 x + y} == {a, b}
```

You can use `Solve` directly to solve these equations.

```
In[3]:= Solve[ %, {x, y} ]
```
$$Out[3]= \{\{x \to \frac{b}{2} + \frac{-2\,a + b}{18}, \ y \to \frac{2\,a - b}{9}\}\}$$

You can also get the vector of solutions by calling `LinearSolve`. The result is equivalent to the one you get from `Solve`.

```
In[4]:= LinearSolve[m, {a, b}]
```
$$Out[4]= \{a - \frac{5\,(2\,a - b)}{9}, \ \frac{2\,a - b}{9}\}$$

Another way to solve the equations is to invert the matrix m, and then multiply {a, b} by the inverse. This is not as efficient as using `LinearSolve`.

```
In[5]:= Inverse[m] . {a, b}
```
$$Out[5]= \{\frac{-a}{9} + \frac{5\,b}{9}, \ \frac{2\,a}{9} - \frac{b}{9}\}$$

■ 17.2 Eigenvalues and Eigenvectors

Eigenvalues[m]	a list of the eigenvalues of m
Eigenvectors[m]	a list of the eigenvectors of m
Eigensystem[m]	a list of the form {*eigenvalues*, *eigenvectors*}
Eigenvalues[N[m]], etc.	numerical eigenvalues
Eigenvalues[N[m, k]], etc.	numerical eigenvalues, starting with k-digit precision
CharacteristicPolynomial[m, x]	
	the characteristic polynomial of m in the variable x

Eigenvalues and eigenvectors.

The eigenvalues of a matrix **m** are the values λ_i for which one can find non-zero vectors $\mathbf{x}_i$ such that $\mathbf{m}.\mathbf{x}_i = \lambda_i\mathbf{x}_i$. The eigenvectors are the vectors $\mathbf{x}_i$.

Finding the eigenvalues of an $n \times n$ matrix in principle involves solving an nth degree polynomial equation. Since for $n \geq 5$ explicit algebraic solutions cannot in general be found, it is impossible to give explicit algebraic results for the eigenvalues and eigenvectors of all but the simplest or sparsest matrices.

Even for a matrix as simple as this, the explicit form of the eigenvalues is quite complicated.

```
In[1]:= Eigenvalues[ {{a, b}, {-b, 2a}} ]
```

$$Out[1]= \{\frac{3\ a\ -\ Sqrt[9\ a^2\ -\ 4\ (2\ a^2\ +\ b^2)]}{2},$$

$$\frac{3\ a\ +\ Sqrt[9\ a^2\ -\ 4\ (2\ a^2\ +\ b^2)]}{2}\}$$

If you give a matrix of approximate real numbers, *Mathematica* will find the approximate numerical eigenvalues and eigenvectors.

Here is a 2×2 numerical matrix.

```
In[2]:= m = {{2.3, 4.5}, {6.7, -1.2}}
Out[2]= {{2.3, 4.5}, {6.7, -1.2}}
```

The matrix has two eigenvalues, in this case both real.

```
In[3]:= Eigenvalues[ m ]
Out[3]= {6.31303, -5.21303}
```

Here are the two eigenvectors of m.

```
In[4]:= Eigenvectors[ m ]
Out[4]= {{0.746335, 0.66557}, {-0.513839, 0.857886}}
```

Eigensystem computes the eigenvalues and eigenvectors at the same time. The assignment sets vals to the list of eigenvalues, and vecs to the list of eigenvectors.

```
In[5]:= {vals, vecs} = Eigensystem[m]
Out[5]= {{6.31303, -5.21303},
        {{0.746335, 0.66557}, {-0.513839, 0.857886}}}
```

This verifies that the first eigenvalue and eigenvector satisfy the appropriate condition.

```
In[6]:= m . vecs[[1]] == vals[[1]] vecs[[1]]

Out[6]= True
```

This matrix represents a rotation.

```
In[7]:= a = Pi/3; r = {{Cos[a], Sin[a]}, {-Sin[a], Cos[a]}}

            1   Sqrt[3]      -Sqrt[3]   1
Out[7]= {{-, ───────}, {────────, -}}
            2      2            2       2
```

This finds its eigenvalues. For non-symmetric matrices, the eigenvalues can have imaginary parts.

```
In[8]:= Eigenvalues[r]

            1 - I Sqrt[3]   1 + I Sqrt[3]
Out[8]= {─────────────, ─────────────}
                2               2
```

The function `Eigenvalues` always gives you a list of n eigenvalues for an $n \times n$ matrix. The eigenvalues correspond to the roots of the characteristic polynomial for the matrix, and may not necessarily be distinct. `Eigenvectors`, on the other hand, gives a list of eigenvectors which are guaranteed to be independent. If the number of such eigenvectors is less than n, then `Eigenvectors` appends zero vectors to the list it returns, so that the total length of the list is always n.

Here is a 3×3 matrix.

```
In[9]:= mz = {{0, 1, 0}, {0, 0, 1}, {0, 0, 0}}

Out[9]= {{0, 1, 0}, {0, 0, 1}, {0, 0, 0}}
```

The matrix has three eigenvalues, all equal to zero.

```
In[10]:= Eigenvalues[mz]

Out[10]= {0, 0, 0}
```

The eigenvalues are the roots of the characteristic polynomial.

```
In[11]:= CharacteristicPolynomial[mz, x]

                3
Out[11]= -x
```

There is, however, only one independent eigenvector for the matrix. `Eigenvectors` appends two zero vectors to give a total of three vectors in this case.

```
In[12]:= Eigenvectors[mz]

Out[12]= {{1, 0, 0}, {0, 0, 0}, {0, 0, 0}}
```

Outer ▪ CharacteristicPolynomial ▪ SingularValues ▪ PseudoInverse ▪
QRDecomposition ▪ SchurDecomposition ▪ LUDecomposition ▪ LUBackSubstitution ▪
HermiteNormalForm ▪ JordanDecomposition ▪ LinearProgramming ▪ LatticeReduce

Other *Mathematica* functions related to linear algebra. (See page xvi.)

ZeroTest ▪ Modulus ▪ Tolerance ▪ Pivoting ▪ Method

Mathematica options for some linear algebra functions. (See page xvi.)

18. Approximating Functions

■ 18.1 Curve Fitting

Built into *Mathematica* are various facilities for finding least-squares fits to data. The basic idea of the fits is to take a list of functions that you specify, and try to find a linear combination of them which approximates your data as well as possible. The goodness of fit is measured by the quantity $\chi^2 = \sum_i |F_i - f_i|^2$, where F_i is the value of your i^{th} data point, and f_i is the value obtained from the fit. The best fit is the one which minimizes χ^2.

Fit[*data*, *funs*, *vars*]	fit a list of data points using the functions *funs* of variables *vars*

The basic form of the **Fit** function.

Fit[{f_1, f_2, ... }, {1, x}, x]	linear fit
Fit[{f_1, f_2, ... }, {1, x, x^2}, x]	quadratic fit
Fit[*data*, Table[x^i, {i, 0, n}], x]	n^{th}-degree polynomial fit

Some fits to lists of data.

Here is a table of the first 20 primes.

```
In[1]:= fp = Table[Prime[x], {x, 20}]

Out[1]= {2, 3, 5, 7, 11, 13, 17, 19, 23, 29, 31, 37, 41, 43,
         47, 53, 59, 61, 67, 71}
```

Here is a plot of this "data".

```
In[2]:= gp = ListPlot[ fp ]
```

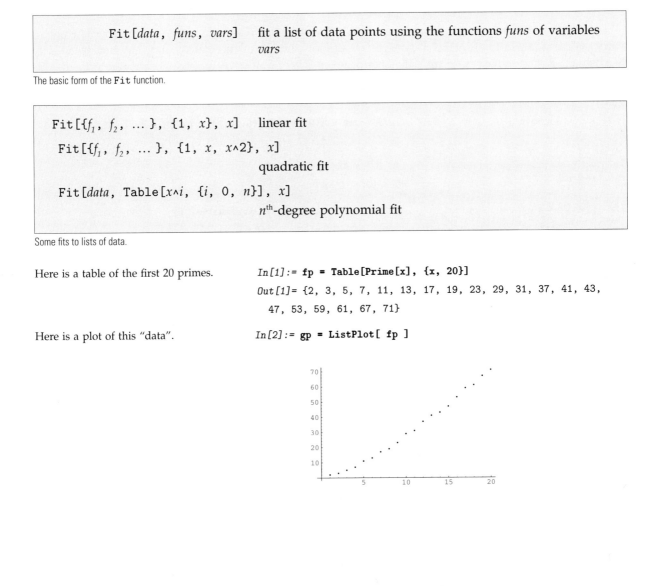

This gives a linear fit to the list of primes. The result is the best linear combination of the functions 1 and x.

In[3]:= **Fit[fp, {1, x}, x]**

Out[3]= -7.67368 + 3.77368 x

Here is a plot of the fit.

In[4]:= **Plot[%, {x, 0, 20}]**

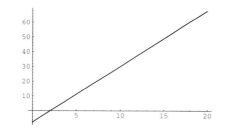

Here is the fit superimposed on the original data.

In[5]:= **Show[%, gp]**

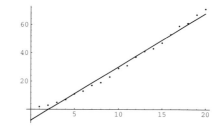

This gives a quadratic fit to the data.

In[6]:= **Fit[fp, {1, x, x^2}, x]**

Out[6]= $-1.92368 + 2.2055 x + 0.0746753 x^2$

Here is a plot of the quadratic fit.

In[7]:= **Plot[%, {x, 0, 20}]**

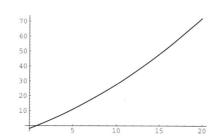

This shows the fit superimposed on the original data. The quadratic fit is better than the linear one.

In[8]:= **Show[%, gp]**

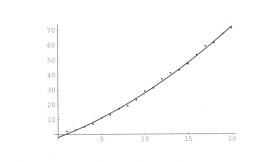

Polynomial fits are the most common kind to use. However, if you have a reason to believe that your data follows some other functional form, you can include the appropriate functions in the list you give to Fit.

This gives a table of the values of $1 + 2e^{-x/3}$ for x from 1 to 10 in steps of 1.

In[9]:= **ft = Table[N[1 + 2 Exp[-x/3]] , {x, 10}]**

Out[9]= {2.43306, 2.02683, 1.73576, 1.52719, 1.37775, 1.27067,

    1.19394, 1.13897, 1.09957, 1.07135}

This fit recovers the original functional form.

In[10]:= **Fit[ft, {1, Exp[-x/3]}, x]**

$$Out[10]= 1. + \frac{2.}{E^{x/3}}$$

If you include other functions in the list, Fit determines that they occur with small coefficients.

In[11]:= **Fit[ft, {1, Sin[x], Exp[-x/3], Exp[-x]}, x]**

$$Out[11]= 1. + \frac{2.38633 \; 10^{-15}}{E^{x}} + \frac{2.}{E^{x/3}} - 1.46882 \; 10^{-16} \; Sin[x]$$

You can use Chop to get rid of the terms with small coefficients.

In[12]:= **Chop[%]**

$$Out[12]= 1. + \frac{2.}{E^{x/3}}$$

There are several common reasons for doing fits. If you have a particular model for some data, you can do a fit to try and determine the parameters of the model. Another common use of fits is in finding approximate formulas to describe a particular set of data. You can use the form you get from a Fit as a summary of your actual data.

In the examples of Fit so far, the data points you give are assumed to correspond to the results of evaluating a function of one variable when the variable successively takes on values 1, 2, ... You can also specify data that depends on several variables, each given an arbitrary sequence of values, not necessarily arranged in any kind of regular array.

> $\{f_1, f_2, \dots\}$ data points obtained when a single coordinate takes on values 1, 2, …
>
> $\{\{x_1, y_1, \dots, f_1\}, \{x_2, y_2, \dots, f_2\}, \dots\}$
>
>   data points obtained with values $x_i, y_i, \dots$ of a sequence of coordinates

Ways of specifying data in `Fit`.

This gives a table of the values of x, y and $1 + 5x - xy$. You need to use `Flatten` to get it in the right form for `Fit`.

```
In[13]:= Flatten[ Table[ {x, y, 1 + 5x - x y},
                 {x, 0, 1, 0.4}, {y, 0, 1, 0.4} ], 1]
Out[13]= {{0, 0, 1}, {0, 0.4, 1}, {0, 0.8, 1}, {0.4, 0, 3.},
         {0.4, 0.4, 2.84}, {0.4, 0.8, 2.68}, {0.8, 0, 5.},
         {0.8, 0.4, 4.68}, {0.8, 0.8, 4.36}}
```

This produces a fit to a function of two variables.

```
In[14]:= Fit[ % , {1, x, y, x y}, {x, y} ]

Out[14]= 1. + 5. x - 2.30935 10^-17 y - 1. x y
```

`Fit` takes the list of functions you give, and finds the best fit to your data, according to the least-squares criterion, using these functions. There is absolutely no guarantee that the fit you get will in fact accurately reproduce your data. To find out whether it can, you should use statistical testing functions, such as those in the statistics section of the *Mathematica* library.

■ 18.2 Approximate Functions and Interpolation

In many kinds of numerical computations, it is convenient to introduce *approximate functions*. Approximate functions can be thought of as generalizations of ordinary approximate real numbers. While an approximate real number gives the value to a certain precision of a single numerical quantity, an approximate function gives the value to a certain precision of a quantity which depends on one or more parameters. *Mathematica* uses approximate functions, for example, to represent numerical solutions to differential equations obtained with `NDSolve`, as will be discussed in Section 19.2.

Approximate functions in *Mathematica* are represented by `InterpolatingFunction` objects. The basic idea is that when given a particular argument, an `InterpolatingFunction` object finds the approximate function value that corresponds to that argument.

The `InterpolatingFunction` object contains a representation of the approximate function based on interpolation. Typically it contains values and possibly derivatives at a sequence of points. It effectively assumes that the function varies smoothly between these points. As a result, when you ask for the value of the function with a particular argument, the `InterpolatingFunction` object can interpolate to find an approximation to the value you want.

Interpolation[{f_1, f_2, ... }]	construct an approximate function with values f_i at successive integers
Interpolation[{{x_1, f_1}, {x_2, f_2}, ... }]	
	construct an approximate function with values f_i at points x_i

Constructing approximate functions.

Here is a table of the values of the sine function.

```
In[1]:= Table[{x, Sin[x]}, {x, 0, 2, 0.25}]
Out[1]= {{0, 0}, {0.25, 0.247404}, {0.5, 0.479426},
   {0.75, 0.681639}, {1., 0.841471}, {1.25, 0.948985},
   {1.5, 0.997495}, {1.75, 0.983986}, {2., 0.909297}}
```

This constructs an approximate function which represents these values.

```
In[2]:= sin = Interpolation[%]
Out[2]= InterpolatingFunction[{0, 2.}, <>]
```

The approximate function reproduces each of the values in the original table.

```
In[3]:= sin[0.25]
Out[3]= 0.247404
```

It also allows you to get approximate values at other points.

```
In[4]:= sin[0.3]
Out[4]= 0.2955
```

In this case the interpolation is a fairly good approximation to the true sine function.

```
In[5]:= Sin[0.3]
Out[5]= 0.29552
```

You can work with approximate functions much as you would with any other *Mathematica* functions. You can plot approximate functions, or perform numerical operations such as integration or root finding.

If you give a non-numerical argument, the approximate function is left in symbolic form.

```
In[6]:= sin[x]
Out[6]= InterpolatingFunction[{0, 2.}, <>][x]
```

Here is a numerical integral of the approximate function.

```
In[7]:= NIntegrate[sin[x]^2, {x, 0, Pi/2}]
Out[7]= 0.78531
```

Here is the same numerical integral for the true sine function.

```
In[8]:= NIntegrate[Sin[x]^2, {x, 0, Pi/2}]
Out[8]= 0.785398
```

A plot of the approximate function is essentially indistinguishable from the true sine function.

`In[9]:= Plot[sin[x], {x, 0, 2}]`

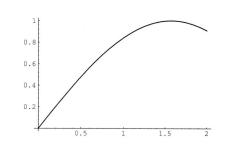

`InterpolatingFunction` objects contain all the information that *Mathematica* needs about approximate functions. In standard *Mathematica* output format, however, only the first element of each `InterpolationFunction` object is printed explicitly. This element gives the range of arguments for which values of the approximate function can be found. The later elements of the `InterpolatingFunction` object give actual values of the approximate function, its derivatives, and so on.

In standard output format, only the first element of `InterpolatingFunction` objects is printed explicitly.

`In[10]:= sin`

`Out[10]= InterpolatingFunction[{0, 2.}, <>]`

Mathematica will not compute values for approximate functions outside the range of arguments specified by the first element.

`In[11]:= sin[3]`

```
InterpolatingFunction::dmval:
    Input value lies outside domain of the interpolating
        function.
```

`Out[11]= InterpolatingFunction[{0, 2.}, <>][3]`

■ 18.3 Fourier Transforms

A common operation in analyzing various kinds of data is to find the Fourier transform, or spectrum, of a list of values. The idea is typically to pick out components of the data with particular frequencies, or ranges of frequencies.

`Fourier[{`a_0`, `a_1`, ... }]`	Fourier transform
`InverseFourier[{`b_0`, `b_1`, ... }]`	inverse Fourier transform

Fourier transforms.

There are several conventions that can be used in defining Fourier transforms. In *Mathematica*, the Fourier transform b_s of a list a_r of length n is taken to be $\frac{1}{\sqrt{n}} \sum_{r=1}^{n} a_r e^{2\pi i (r-1)(s-1)/n}$. Notice that the zero frequency term appears at position 1 in the resulting list.

Note that the convention for defining the Fourier transform used in *Mathematica* is the one common in the physical sciences. In electrical engineering, the sign of the exponent is typically reversed, leading to a list of values which is reversed.

The Fourier transform takes you from a time series of data to the frequency components of the data. You can use the inverse Fourier transform to get back to the time series. The inverse Fourier transform a_r of a list b_s of length n is defined to be $\frac{1}{\sqrt{n}} \sum_{s=1}^{n} b_s e^{-2\pi i (r-1)(s-1)/n}$.

Here is some data, corresponding to a square pulse.	`In[1]:= N[{-1, -1, -1, -1, 1, 1, 1, 1}]` `Out[1]= {-1., -1., -1., -1., 1., 1., 1., 1.}`

Here is the Fourier transform of the data. It involves complex numbers.

```
In[2]:= Fourier[%]
Out[2]= {0. + 0. I, -0.707107 - 1.70711 I, 0. + 0. I,
   -0.707107 - 0.292893 I, 0. + 0. I, -0.707107 + 0.292893 I,
   0. + 0. I, -0.707107 + 1.70711 I}
```

Here is the inverse Fourier transform.

```
In[3]:= InverseFourier[%]
                              -17                -16
Out[3]= {-1. + 7.85046 10    I, -1. - 1.1101 10     I,

               -16                -16
  -1. + 2.7477 10    I, -1. + 1.43555 10    I,

             -17              -16
  1. - 7.85046 10   I, 1. + 1.1101 10    I,

            -16              -16
  1. - 2.7477 10   I, 1. - 1.43555 10   I}
```

After using Chop, this gives back exactly your original data.

```
In[4]:= Chop[%]
Out[4]= {-1., -1., -1., -1., 1., 1., 1., 1.}
```

Fourier works whether or not your list of data has a length which is a power of two. It is, however, significantly more efficient when the length is a power of two.

```
In[5]:= Fourier[ N[{1, -1, 1}] ]
Out[5]= {0.57735 + 0. I, 0.57735 - 1. I, 0.57735 + 1. I}
```

This generates a length-256 list containing a periodic signal with random noise added.

```
In[6]:= data = Table[ N[Sin[30 2 Pi n/256] + (Random[ ] - 1/2)],
                {n, 256} ] ;
```

The data looks fairly random if you plot it directly.

```
In[7]:= ListPlot[ data, PlotJoined -> True ]
```

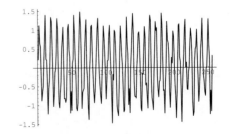

The Fourier transform, however, shows a very strong peak at 30, the frequency of the original periodic signal. There is a second peak at $256 - 30$, which is essentially a consequence of symmetry.

```
In[8]:= ListPlot[ Abs[Fourier[data]], PlotJoined -> True,
                 PlotRange -> All ]
```

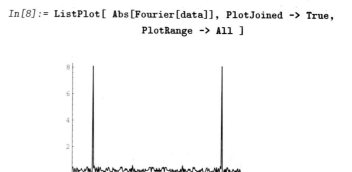

A common and important application of Fourier transforms is doing *convolutions*. The basic idea is that integrals of the form $\bar{f}(x) = \int f(y)k(y-x)dy$ can be evaluated simply by multiplying the Fourier transforms of f and k. Convolutions are used extensively, for example, in smoothing data.

This generates some "data".

```
In[9]:= data = Table[ N[BesselJ[1, 10 n/256] +
                    0.2 (Random[ ] - 1/2)], {n, 256} ] ;
```

Here is a plot of the data.

```
In[10]:= ListPlot[data]
```

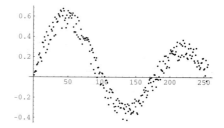

This generates a typical convolution kernel suitable for smoothing data.

```
In[11]:= kern = Table[ N[Exp[-200 (n/256)^2]], {n, 256} ] ;
```

Here is a plot of the convolution kernel.

```
In[12]:= ListPlot[kern, PlotRange -> All]
```

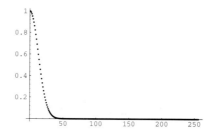

The convolution is done by multiplying the Fourier transform of the data by the Fourier transform of the kernel, then taking the inverse Fourier transform of the result.

In[13]:= `conv = InverseFourier[ Fourier[data] Fourier[kern] ] ;`

This plots the result. The `Chop` removes small imaginary parts that are generated in the Fourier transforms. The final plot is a smoothed version of the original data.

In[14]:= `ListPlot[ Chop[conv] ]`

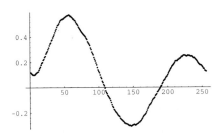

`Fourier[{{a00, a01, ... }, {a10, a11, ... }, ... }]`
two-dimensional Fourier transform

Two-dimensional Fourier transform.

Mathematica can find Fourier transforms for data in any number of dimensions. In n dimensions, the data is specified by a list nested n levels deep. Two-dimensional Fourier transforms are often used in image processing.

19. Differential Equations

■ 19.1 Symbolic Solution of Differential Equations

DSolve[*eqn*, y[x], x]	solve a differential equation for y[x]
DSolve[*eqn*, y, x]	solve a differential equation for the function y

Solving an ordinary differential equation.

Here is the solution to the differential equation $y'(x) = ay(x)$. C[1] is a coefficient which must be determined from boundary conditions.

In[1]:= **DSolve[y'[x] == a y[x], y[x], x]**

Out[1]= {{y[x] -> E$^{a\ x}$ C[1]}}

If you include appropriate boundary conditions, there are no undetermined coefficients in the solution.

In[2]:= **DSolve[{y'[x] == a y[x], y[0] == 1}, y[x], x]**

Out[2]= {{y[x] -> E$^{a\ x}$}}

Whereas algebraic equations such as $x^2 + x = 1$ are equations for *variables*, differential equations such as $y''(x) + y'(x) = y(x)$ are equations for *functions*. In *Mathematica*, you must always give differential equations explicitly in terms of functions such as y[x], and you must specify the variables such as x on which the functions depend. As a result, you must write an equation such as $y''(x) + y'(x) = y(x)$ in the form y''[x] + y'[x] == y[x]. You cannot write it as y'' + y' == y.

Mathematica can solve both linear and non-linear ordinary differential equations, as well as lists of simultaneous equations. In many cases, the solutions you get will involve undetermined coefficients. Each time you use DSolve, it names the undetermined coefficients C[1], C[2], etc.

Here is a pair of simultaneous differential equations. The solution you get involves two undetermined coefficients.

In[3]:= **DSolve[{x'[t] == y[t], y'[t] == x[t]},**
{x[t], y[t]}, t]

$$Out[3]= \{\{x[t] \rightarrow (\frac{1}{2\ E^t} + \frac{E^t}{2})\ C[1] + (\frac{-1}{2\ E^t} + \frac{E^t}{2})\ C[2],$$

$$y[t] \rightarrow (\frac{-1}{2\ E^t} + \frac{E^t}{2})\ C[1] + (\frac{1}{2\ E^t} + \frac{E^t}{2})\ C[2]\}\}$$

Solving a differential equation consists essentially in finding the form of an unknown function. In *Mathematica*, unknown functions are represented by expressions like y[x]. The derivatives of such functions are represented by y'[x], y''[x] and so on.

The *Mathematica* function DSolve returns as its result a list of rules for functions. There is a question of how these functions are represented. If you ask DSolve to solve for y[x], then DSolve will indeed return a rule for y[x]. In some cases, this rule may be all you need. But this rule, on its own, does not give values for y'[x] or even y[0]. In many cases, therefore, it is better to ask DSolve to solve not for y[x], but instead for y itself. In this case, what DSolve will return is a rule which gives y as a pure function, in the sense discussed in more detail in Section 25.5.

Suppose that you define the function sq with sq[x_] := x ∧ 2. You can now apply the function sq to the argument 3 by entering the expression sq[3], which will evaluate to 9. The built-in *Mathematica* function Function allows you to condense these two steps into one, without having to name the function explicitly. In our example, the expression Function[x, x ∧ 2] plays the role of sq. The first argument, x, is the variable, and the second argument is a formula involving x which defines what the function does.

To use a pure function, you use an argument enclosed in square brackets, just as with a built-in function.	*In[4]:=* **Function[x, x ∧ 2][3]** *Out[4]=* 9
You can give the pure function an explicit name.	*In[5]:=* **sq = Function[x, x ∧ 2]** *Out[5]=* Function[x, x^2]
Now you can use this name to work with the function.	*In[6]:=* **sq[5]** *Out[6]=* 25
If you ask DSolve to solve for y[x], it will give a rule specifically for y[x].	*In[7]:=* **DSolve[y'[x] + y[x] == 1, y[x], x]** *Out[7]=* {{y[x] -> 1 + $\frac{C[1]}{E^x}$}}
The rule applies only to y[x] itself, and not, for example, to objects like y[0] or y'[x].	*In[8]:=* **y[x] + 2y'[x] + y[0] /. %** *Out[8]=* {1 + $\frac{C[1]}{E^x}$ + y[0] + 2 y'[x]}
If you ask DSolve to solve for y, it gives a rule for the object y on its own as a pure function.	*In[9]:=* **DSolve[y'[x] + y[x] == 1, y, x]** *Out[9]=* {{y -> Function[x, 1 + $\frac{C[1]}{E^x}$]}}
This rule applies to all occurrences of y.	*In[10]:=* **y[x] + 2y'[x] + y[0] /. %** *Out[10]=* {2 + C[1] - $\frac{C[1]}{E^x}$}

In standard mathematical notation, one typically represents solutions to differential equations by explicitly introducing "dummy variables" to represent the arguments of the functions that appear. If all you need is a symbolic form for the solution, then introducing such dummy variables may be convenient. However, if you actually intend to use the solution in a variety of other computations, then you will usually find it better to get the solution in pure-function form, without dummy variables. Notice that this form, while easy to represent in *Mathematica*, has no direct analog in standard mathematical notation.

> DSolve[{*eqn$_1$*, *eqn$_2$*, ... }, {*y$_1$*, *y$_2$*, ... }, x]
>
> solve a list of differential equations

Solving simultaneous differential equations.

This solves two simultaneous differential equations.

In[11]:= **DSolve[{y[x] == -z'[x], z[x] == -y'[x]}, {y, z}, x]**

Out[11]= {{y ->

$$\text{Function}[x, (\frac{1}{2 E^x} + \frac{E^x}{2}) C[1] + (\frac{1}{2 E^x} - \frac{E^x}{2}) C[2]],$$

$$z \to \text{Function}[x, (\frac{1}{2 E^x} - \frac{E^x}{2}) C[1] + (\frac{1}{2 E^x} + \frac{E^x}{2}) C[2]]\}\}$$

Mathematica returns two distinct solutions for y in this case.

In[12]:= **DSolve[y[x] y'[x] == 1, y, x]**

Out[12]= {{y -> Function[x, -Sqrt[2 x + C[1]]]},

{y -> Function[x, Sqrt[2 x + C[1]]]}}

You can add constraints and boundary conditions for differential equations by explicitly giving additional equations such as y[0] == 0.

This asks for a solution which satisfies the condition y[0] == 1.

In[13]:= **DSolve[{y'[x] == a y[x], y[0] == 1}, y[x], x]**

Out[13]= {{y[x] -> E$^{a x}$}}

Without sufficient constraints or boundary conditions, a particular differential equation typically has a whole family of possible solutions. These solutions typically differ in the values of certain undetermined "constants of integration". When necessary, *Mathematica* automatically generates objects to represent undetermined constants that occur in the solutions of differential equations.

■ 19.2 Numerical Solution of Differential Equations

The function NDSolve allows you to find numerical solutions to differential equations. NDSolve handles both single differential equations, and sets of simultaneous differential equations. It has the restriction, however, that all the differential equations must be *ordinary differential equations*, not *partial differential equations*. This means that while the differential equations you give can involve any number of unknown functions y_i, all of these functions must depend on a single "independent variable" x, which is the same for each function.

NDSolve[{*eqn$_1$*, *eqn$_2$*, ... }, *y*, {*x*, *xmin*, *xmax*}]

find a numerical solution for the function *y* with *x* in the range *xmin* to *xmax*

NDSolve[{*eqn$_1$*, *eqn$_2$*, ... }, {*y$_1$*, *y$_2$*, ... }, {*x*, *xmin*, *xmax*}]

find numerical solutions for several functions *y$_i$*

Finding numerical solutions to differential equations.

NDSolve represents solutions for the functions y_i as InterpolatingFunction objects. The InterpolatingFunction objects provide approximations to the y_i over the range of values *xmin* to *xmax* for the independent variable *x*.

NDSolve starts at a particular value of *x*, then takes a sequence of steps, trying eventually to cover the whole range *xmin* to *xmax*.

In order to get started, NDSolve has to be given appropriate "initial conditions" for the y_i and their derivatives. Initial conditions specify values for $y_i[x]$, and perhaps derivatives $y_i'[x]$, at particular values of *x*. In general, the initial conditions you give can be at any value of *x*: NDSolve will automatically start stepping from that value to cover the range *xmin* to *xmax*.

This finds a solution for y with x in the range 0 to 2, using an initial condition for y[0].

```
In[1]:= NDSolve[{y'[x] == y[x], y[0] == 1}, y, {x, 0, 2}]
Out[1]= {{y -> InterpolatingFunction[{0., 2.}, <>]}}
```

This still finds a solution with x in the range 0 to 2, but now the initial condition is for y[3].

```
In[2]:= NDSolve[{y'[x] == y[x], y[3] == 1}, y, {x, 0, 2}]
Out[2]= {{y -> InterpolatingFunction[{0., 3.}, <>]}}
```

When you use NDSolve, the initial conditions you give must be sufficient to determine the solutions for the y_i completely. When you use DSolve to find symbolic solutions to differential equations, you can get away with specifying fewer initial conditions. The reason is that DSolve automatically inserts arbitrary constants C[*i*] to represent degrees of freedom associated with initial conditions that you have not specified explicitly. Since NDSolve must give a numerical solution, it cannot represent these kinds of additional degrees of freedom. As a result, you must explicitly give all the initial conditions that are needed to determine the solution.

In a typical case, if you have differential equations with up to n^{th} derivatives, then you need to specify initial conditions for up to $(n-1)^{th}$ derivatives.

With a third-order equation, you need to give initial conditions for up to second derivatives.

```
In[3]:= NDSolve[
            { y'''[x] + 8 y''[x] + 17 y'[x] + 10 y[x] == 0,
              y[0] == 6, y'[0] == -20, y''[0] == 84},
                  y, {x, 0, 1} ]
Out[3]= {{y -> InterpolatingFunction[{0., 1.}, <>]}}
```

This plots the solution obtained.

In[4]:= **Plot[Evaluate[y[x] /. %], {x, 0, 1}]**

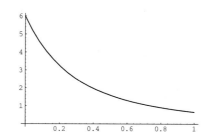

In most cases, all the initial conditions you give must involve the same value of x, say x_0. As a result, you can avoid giving both *xmin* and *xmax* explicitly. If you specify your range of x as $\{x, x_1\}$, then *Mathematica* will automatically generate a solution over the range x_0 to x_1.

This generates a solution over the range 0 to 2.

In[5]:= **NDSolve[{y'[x] == y[x], y[0] == 1}, y, {x, 2}]**

Out[5]= **{{y -> InterpolatingFunction[{0., 2.}, <>]}}**

You can give initial conditions as equations of any kind. In some cases, these equations may have multiple solutions. In such cases, NDSolve will correspondingly generate multiple solutions.

The initial conditions in this case lead to multiple solutions.

In[6]:= **NDSolve[{y'[x]^2 - y[x]^2 == 0, y[0]^2 == 4},**
y[x], {x, 1}]

Out[6]= **{{y[x] -> InterpolatingFunction[{0., 1.}, <>][x]},**
{y[x] -> InterpolatingFunction[{0., 1.}, <>][x]},
{y[x] -> InterpolatingFunction[{0., 1.}, <>][x]},
{y[x] -> InterpolatingFunction[{0., 1.}, <>][x]}}

Here is a plot of all the solutions.

In[7]:= **Plot[Evaluate[y[x] /. %], {x, 0, 1}]**

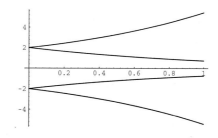

You can use `NDSolve` to solve systems of coupled differential equations.

This finds a numerical solution to a pair of coupled equations.

```
In[8]:= sol = NDSolve[
            {x'[t] == -y[t] - x[t]^2, y'[t] == 2 x[t] - y[t],
             x[0] == y[0] == 1}, {x, y}, {t, 10}]
Out[8]= {{x -> InterpolatingFunction[{0., 10.}, <>],
           y -> InterpolatingFunction[{0., 10.}, <>]}}
```

This plots the solution for y from these equations.

```
In[9]:= Plot[Evaluate[y[t] /. sol], {t, 0, 10}]
```

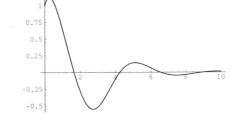

This generates a parametric plot using both x and y.

```
In[10]:= ParametricPlot[Evaluate[{x[t], y[t]} /. sol],
             {t, 0, 10}, PlotRange -> All]
```

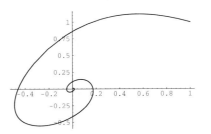

`NDSolve` follows the general procedure of reducing step size until it tracks solutions accurately. There is a problem, however, when the true solution has a singularity. In this case, `NDSolve` might go on reducing the step size forever, and never terminate. To avoid this problem, the option `MaxSteps` specifies the maximum number of steps that `NDSolve` will ever take in attempting to find a solution. The default setting is `MaxSteps -> 500`.

The default setting `MaxSteps -> 500` should be sufficient for most equations with smooth solutions. When solutions have a complicated structure, however, you may sometimes have to choose larger settings for `MaxSteps`. With the setting `MaxSteps -> Infinity` there is no upper limit on the number of steps used.

To reproduce the full structure of the solution to the Lorenz equations, you need to give a larger setting for MaxSteps.

```
In[11]:= NDSolve[ {x'[t] == -3 (x[t] - y[t]),
              y'[t] == -x[t] z[t] + 26.5 x[t] - y[t],
              z'[t] == x[t] y[t] - z[t],
              x[0] == z[0] == 0, y[0] == 1},
             {x, y, z}, {t, 0, 20}, MaxSteps -> 3000 ];
```

Here is a parametric plot of the solution in three dimensions.

```
In[12]:= ParametricPlot3D[Evaluate[{x[t], y[t], z[t]} /. %],
                {t, 0, 20}, PlotPoints -> 1000]
```

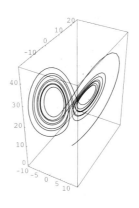

20. Surfaces and Space Curves

■ 20.1 Three-Dimensional Surface Plots

Plot3D[*f*, {*x*, *xmin*, *xmax*}, {*y*, *ymin*, *ymax*}]

      make a three-dimensional plot of *f* as a function of the variables *x* and *y*

Basic 3D plotting function.

This makes a three-dimensional plot of the function sin(*xy*).	*In[1]:=* **Plot3D[Sin[x y], {x, 0, 3}, {y, 0, 3}]**

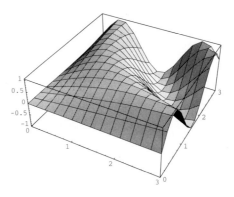

This redraws the plot, with options changed. With this setting for PlotRange, only the part of the surface in the range $-0.5 \le z \le 0.5$ is shown.	*In[2]:=* **Show[%, PlotRange -> {-0.5, 0.5}]**

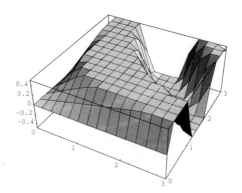

There are many options for three-dimensional plots in *Mathematica*. Some will be discussed in this section; others will be described in more detail in Part 4. The first set of options for three-dimensional plots largely is analogous to those for the two-dimensional case.

option name	default value	
PlotRange	Automatic	the range of coordinates to include in the plot: you can specify All, {*zmin*, *zmax*} or {{*xmin*,*xmax*},{*ymin*,*ymax*},{*zmin*,*zmax*}}
Axes	True	whether to include axes
AxesLabel	None	labels to be put on the axes: *zlabel* specifies a label for the *z* axis, {*xlabel*, *ylabel*, *zlabel*} for all axes
Boxed	True	whether to draw a three-dimensional box around the surface
DefaultFont	$DefaultFont	the default font to use for text in the plot
DisplayFunction	$DisplayFunction	how to display graphics; Identity causes no display
FaceGrids	None	how to draw grids on faces of the bounding box; All draws a grid on every face
HiddenSurface	True	whether to draw the surface as solid
Lighting	True	whether to color the surface using simulated lighting
Mesh	True	whether an *xy* mesh should be drawn on the surface
Shading	True	whether the surface should be shaded or left white
ColorFunction	Automatic	what colors to use for shading; Hue uses a sequence of hues
ViewPoint	{1.3, -2.4, 2}	the point in space from which to look at the surface
PlotPoints	15	the number of points in each direction at which to sample the function; {n_x, n_y} specifies different numbers in the *x* and *y* directions

Some options for `Plot3D`. All but the last one can be used in `Show`.

Probably the single most important issue in plotting a three-dimensional surface is specifying where you want to look at the surface from. The `ViewPoint` option for `Plot3D` and `Show` allows you to specify the point {*x*, *y*, *z*} in space from which you view a surface. The details of how the coordinates for this point are defined will be discussed in Section 33.2. In many versions of *Mathematica*, there are ways to choose three-dimensional view points interactively, then get the coordinates to give as settings for the `ViewPoint` option.

Here is a surface, viewed from the default view point {1.3, −2.4, 2}. This view point is chosen to be "generic", so that visually confusing coincidental alignments between different parts of your object are unlikely.

In[3]:= `Plot3D[Sin[x y], {x, 0, 3}, {y, 0, 3}]`

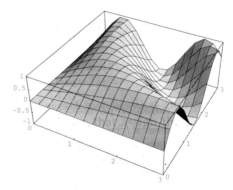

This redraws the picture, with the view point directly in front. Notice the perspective effect that makes the back of the box look much smaller than the front.

In[4]:= `Show[%, ViewPoint -> {0, -2, 0}]`

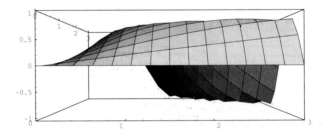

The human visual system is not particularly good at understanding complicated mathematical surfaces. As a result, you need to generate pictures that contain as many clues as possible about the form of the surface.

View points slightly above the surface usually work best. It is generally a good idea to keep the view point close enough to the surface that there is some perspective effect. Having a box explicitly drawn around the surface is helpful in recognizing the orientation of the surface.

{1.3, -2.4, 2}	default view point
{0, -2, 0}	directly in front
{0, -2, 2}	in front and up
{0, -2, -2}	in front and down
{-2, -2, 0}	left-hand corner
{2, -2, 0}	right-hand corner
{0, 0, 2}	directly above

Typical choices for the `ViewPoint` option.

When you make the original plot, you can choose to sample more points. You will need to do this to get good pictures of functions that wiggle a lot.

In[5]:= **Plot3D[10 Sin[x + Sin[y]], {x, -10, 10}, {y, -10, 10},**
PlotPoints -> 40]

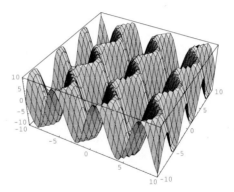

Here is the same plot, with labels for the axes, and grids added to each face.

In[6]:= **Show[%, AxesLabel -> {"Time", "Depth", "Value"},**
FaceGrids -> All]

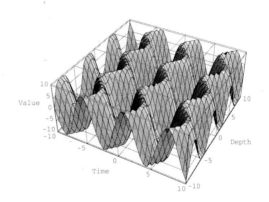

Here is a plot with the default settings for surface rendering options.

$In[7]:=$ **g = Plot3D[Exp[-(x^2+y^2)], {x, -2, 2}, {y, -2, 2}]**

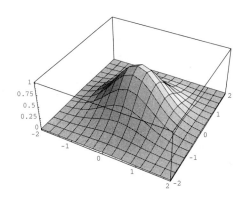

This shows the surface without the mesh drawn. It is usually much harder to see the form of the surface if the mesh is not there.

$In[8]:=$ **Show[g, Mesh -> False]**

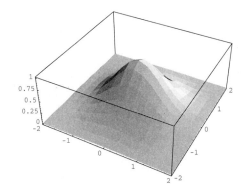

This shows the surface with no shading. Some display devices may not be able to show shading.

$In[9]:=$ **Show[g, Shading -> False]**

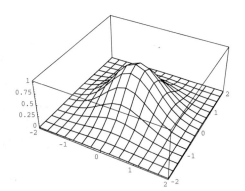

Plot3D usually colors surfaces using a simulated lighting model.

In[10]:= **Plot3D[Sin[x y], {x, 0, 3}, {y, 0, 3}]**

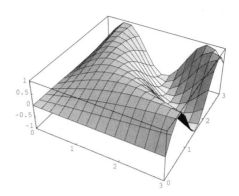

Lighting -> False switches off the simulated lighting, and instead shades surfaces with gray levels determined by height.

In[11]:= **Show[%, Lighting -> False]**

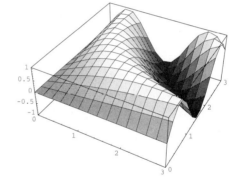

This shows the surface with shading determined by GrayLevel[x/3].

In[12]:= **Plot3D[{Sin[x y], GrayLevel[x/3]},**
                       {x, 0, 3}, {y, 0, 3}]

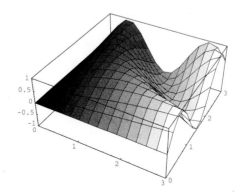

The inclusion of shading and a mesh are usually great assets in understanding the form of a surface. On some vector graphics output devices, however, you may not be able to get shading. You should also realize that when shading is included, it may take a long time to render the surface on your output device.

To add an extra element of realism to three-dimensional graphics, *Mathematica* by default colors three-dimensional surfaces using a simulated lighting model. In the default case, *Mathematica* assumes that there are three light sources shining on the object from the upper right of the picture. Section 34.2 describes how you can set up other light sources, and how you can specify the reflection properties of an object.

While in most cases, particularly with color output devices, simulated lighting is an asset, it can sometimes be confusing. If you set the option `Lighting -> False`, then *Mathematica* will not use simulated lighting, but will instead shade all surfaces with gray levels determined by their height.

With `Lighting -> False`, *Mathematica* shades surfaces according to height. You can also tell *Mathematica* explicitly how to shade each element of a surface. This allows you effectively to use shading to display an extra coordinate at each point on your surface.

`Plot3D[{f, GrayLevel[s]}, {x, xmin, xmax}, {y, ymin, ymax}]`
  plot a surface corresponding to *f*, shaded in gray according to the function *s*

`Plot3D[{f, Hue[s]}, {x, xmin, xmax}, {y, ymin, ymax}]`
  shade by varying color hue rather than gray level

Specifying shading functions for surfaces.

■ 20.2 Parametric Plots

`ParametricPlot3D[{f_x, f_y, f_z}, {t, tmin, tmax}]`
  make a parametric plot of a three-dimensional curve

`ParametricPlot3D[{f_x, f_y, f_z}, {t, tmin, tmax}, {u, umin, umax}]`
  make a parametric plot of a three-dimensional surface

`ParametricPlot3D[{f_x, f_y, f_z, s}, ... ]`
  shade the parts of the parametric plot according to the function *s*

`ParametricPlot3D[{{f_x, f_y, f_z}, {g_x, g_y, g_z}, ... }, ... ]`
  plot several objects together

Three-dimensional parametric plots.

`ParametricPlot3D[{`f_x`, `f_y`, `f_z`}, {`t`, `$tmin$`, `$tmax$`}]` is the direct analog in three dimensions of `ParametricPlot[{`f_x`, `f_y`}, {`t`, `$tmin$`, `$tmax$`}]` in two dimensions. In both cases, *Mathematica* effectively generates a sequence of points by varying the parameter t, then forms a curve by joining these points. With `ParametricPlot`, the curve is in two dimensions; with `ParametricPlot3D`, it is in three dimensions. `ParametricPlot` was discussed in Section 8.2.

This makes a parametric plot of a helical curve. Varying t produces circular motion in the *x, y* plane, and linear motion in the *z* direction.	*In[1]:=* **ParametricPlot3D[{Sin[t], Cos[t], t/3}, {t, 0, 15}]**

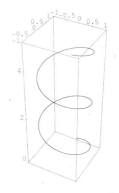

This produces a helicoid surface by taking the helical curve shown above, and at each section of the curve drawing a quadrilateral.	*In[2]:=* **ParametricPlot3D[{u Sin[t], u Cos[t], t/3},** 　　　　　　　　　**{t, 0, 15}, {u, -1, 1}]**

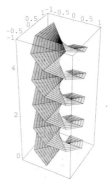

`ParametricPlot3D[{`f_x`, `f_y`, `f_z`}, {`t`, `$tmin$`, `$tmax$`}, {`u`, `$umin$`, `$umax$`}]` creates a surface, rather than a curve. The surface is formed from a collection of quadrilaterals. The corners of the quadrilaterals have coordinates corresponding to the values of the f_i when t and u take on values in a regular grid.

Here the *x* and *y* coordinates for the quadrilaterals are given simply by t and u. The result is a surface plot of the kind that can be produced by `Plot3D`.

In[3]:= `ParametricPlot3D[{t, u, Sin[t u]},`
`{t, 0, 3}, {u, 0, 3}]`

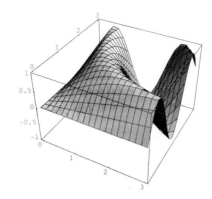

This shows the same surface as before, but with the *y* coordinates distorted by a quadratic transformation.

In[4]:= `ParametricPlot3D[{t, u^2, Sin[t u]},`
`{t, 0, 3}, {u, 0, 3}]`

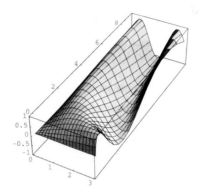

In general, it is possible to construct many complicated surfaces using `ParametricPlot3D`. In each case, you can think of the surfaces as being formed by "distorting" or "rolling up" the *t*, *u* coordinate grid in a certain way.

This produces a cylinder. Varying the t parameter yields a circle in the x, y plane, while varying u moves the circles in the z direction.

```
In[5]:= ParametricPlot3D[{Sin[t], Cos[t], u},
                          {t, 0, 2Pi}, {u, 0, 4}]
```

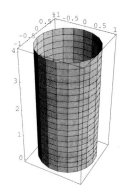

A small change produces a cone.

```
In[6]:= ParametricPlot3D[{u Sin[t], u Cos[t], 2 u},
                          {t, 0, 2Pi}, {u, 0, 4}]
```

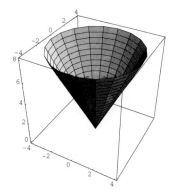

You should realize that when you draw surfaces with ParametricPlot3D, the exact choice of parametrization is often crucial. You should be careful, for example, to avoid parametrizations in which all or part of your surface is covered more than once. Such multiple coverings often lead to discontinuities in the mesh drawn on the surface, and may make ParametricPlot3D take much longer to render the surface.

This produces a torus. Varying t yields a circle, while varying u rotates the circle around the z axis to form the torus.

In[7]:= **ParametricPlot3D[**
   {Cos[t] (3 + Cos[u]), Sin[t] (3 + Cos[u]), Sin[u]},
   {t, 0, 2Pi}, {u, 0, 2Pi}]

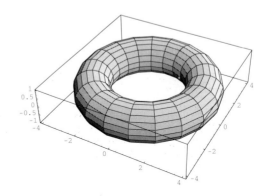

This produces a sphere.

In[8]:= **ParametricPlot3D[**
   {Cos[t] Cos[u], Sin[t] Cos[u], Sin[u]},
   {t, 0, 2Pi}, {u, -Pi/2, Pi/2}]

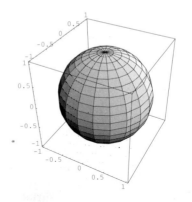

21. Other Plots

■ 21.1 Contour Plots

> ContourPlot[*f*, {*x*, *xmin*, *xmax*}, {*y*, *ymin*, *ymax*}]
>
> $\qquad$ make a contour plot of *f* as a function of *x* and *y*

Contour plots.

This gives a contour plot of the function $\sin(x)\sin(y)$.

In[1]:= **ContourPlot[Sin[x] Sin[y], {x, -2, 2}, {y, -2, 2}]**

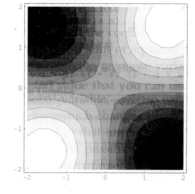

Particularly if you use a display or printer that does not handle gray levels well, you may find it better to switch off shading in contour plots.

In[2]:= **Show[%, ContourShading -> False]**

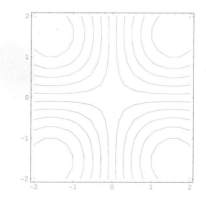

A contour plot gives you essentially a "topographic map" of a function. The contours join points on the surface that have the same height. The default is to have contours corresponding to a sequence of equally spaced *z* values. Contour plots produced by *Mathematica* are by default shaded, in such a way that regions with higher *z* values are lighter.

option name	default value	
PlotRange	Automatic	the range of values to be included; you can specify {*zmin*, *zmax*}, All or Automatic
Contours	10	what contours to use
ContourLines	True	whether to draw contour lines
ContourStyle	Automatic	style to use for contour lines
ContourShading	True	whether to shade regions in the plot
ColorFunction	Automatic	colors to use for shading; Hue uses a sequence of hues
PlotPoints	15	number of evaluation points in each direction

Some options for `ContourPlot`. All but the last one can be used in `Show`.

In constructing a contour plot, the first issue is what contours to use. With the default setting `Contours -> 10`, *Mathematica* uses a sequence of 10 contour levels equally spaced between the minimum and maximum values defined by the `PlotRange` option.

This creates a contour plot with two contours.

`In[3]:= Show[%, ContourShading -> True, Contours -> {-.5, .5}]`

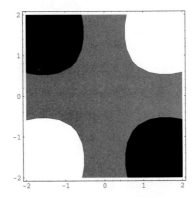

To find the contour associated with a particular z value, *Mathematica* effectively has to solve an implicit equation. Given the value of the contour, the goal is to find those values of x and y for which $f(x,y) = z$, where f is the function you are plotting.

Contours -> n	use a sequence of n equally spaced contours
Contours -> $\{z_1, z_2, \ldots\}$	use contours with values $z_1, z_2, \ldots$

Specifying contours.

This increases the density of contours, and tells *Mathematica* to use a finer grid.

```
In[4]:= ContourPlot[Sin[x] Sin[y], {x, -2, 2}, {y, -2, 2},
        ContourShading -> False, Contours -> 20, PlotPoints ->
        35];
```

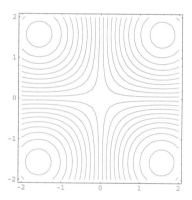

You should realize that if you do not evaluate your function on a fine enough grid, there may be inaccuracies in your contour plot. One point to notice is that whereas a curve generated by Plot may be inaccurate if your function varies too quickly in a particular region, the shape of contours can be inaccurate if your function varies too slowly. A rapidly varying function gives a regular pattern of contours, but a function that is almost flat can give irregular contours. In most cases the best way to improve upon a severely jagged contour plot is to increase the setting of the PlotPoints option to ContourPlot.

■ 21.2 Density Plots

DensityPlot[f, {x, *xmin*, *xmax*}, {y, *ymin*, *ymax*}]
make a density plot of f

Density plots.

Most of the options for density and contour plots are the same as those for ordinary two-dimensional plots. There are, however, a few additional options.

Density plots show the values of your function at a regular array of points. Lighter regions are higher.

$In[1]:=$ **DensityPlot[Sin[x] Sin[y], {x, -2, 2}, {y, -2, 2}]**

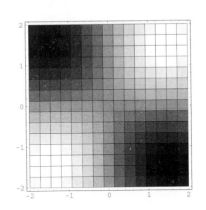

You can get rid of the mesh like this. But unless you have a very large number of regions, plots usually look better when you include the mesh.

$In[2]:=$ **Show[%, Mesh -> False]**

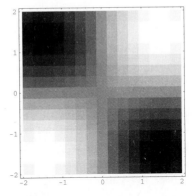

In a density plot, the color of each cell represents its value. By default, each cell is assigned a gray level, running from black to white as the value of the cell increases. In general, however, you can specify other "color maps" for the relation between the value of a cell and its color. The option ColorFunction allows you to specify a function which is applied to each cell value to find the color of the cell. The cell values are scaled so as to run between 0 and 1 in a particular density plot. The function you give as the setting for ColorFunction may return any *Mathematica* color directive, such as GrayLevel, Hue or RGBColor. A common setting to use is ColorFunction -> Hue.

option name	default value	
Mesh	True	whether to draw a mesh
MeshStyle	Automatic	a style for the mesh
ColorFunction	Automatic	how to assign colors to each cell
PlotPoints	15	number of evaluation points in each direction

Some options for `DensityPlot`. All but the last one can be used in `Show`.

Here is a density plot with the default ColorFunction.

In[3]:= **DensityPlot[Sin[x y], {x, -1, 1}, {y, -1, 1}]**

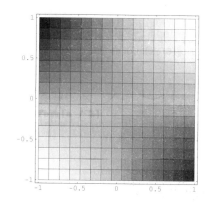

This defines a different "color map".

In[4]:= **newcolor[x_] := GrayLevel[x^3]**

This gives a density plot with the different "color map".

In[5]:= **Show[%%, ColorFunction -> newcolor]**

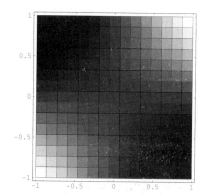

There are some slight subtleties associated with labeling density and contour plots. Both the Axes and Frame options from ordinary two-dimensional graphics can be used. But setting AxesOrigin -> Automatic keeps the axes outside the plot in both cases.

■ 21.3 Plotting Lists of Data

Just as you can plot points and curves using ListPlot, you can also plot surfaces, contours, and density from lists of data, instead of functions. These *Mathematica* commands for plotting lists of data are direct analogs of Plot3D, ContourPlot, and DensityPlot. ListPlot was discussed in Section 8.3.

ListPlot3D[{{z_{11}, z_{12}, ... }, {z_{21}, z_{22}, ... }, ... }]	
	make a three-dimensional plot of the array of heights z_{yx}
ListContourPlot[*array*]	make a contour plot from an array of heights
ListDensityPlot[*array*]	make a density plot

Functions for plotting lists of data.

This gives a rectangular array of values. The array is quite large, so we end the input with a semicolon to stop the result from being printed out.

In[1]:= **t3 = Table[Mod[y, x], {x, 20}, {y, 20}] ;**

This makes a three-dimensional plot of the array of values.

In[2]:= **ListPlot3D[t3]**

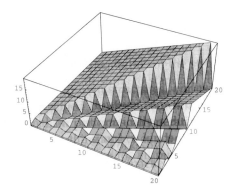

You can redraw the plot using Show, as usual.

In[3]:= **Show[%, ViewPoint -> {1.5, -0.5, 0}]**

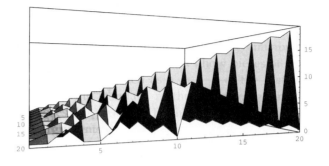

This gives a density plot of the array of values.

In[4]:= **ListDensityPlot[t3]**

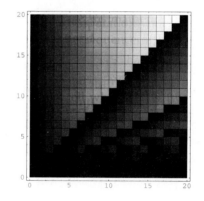

■ 21.4 Some Special Plots

Mathematica includes a full graphics programming language, as will be discussed in detail in Part 4. In this language, you can set up many different kinds of plots. A few of the common ones are included in standard *Mathematica* packages.

`<<Graphics`Graphics``	load a package with additional graphics functions
`LogPlot[f, {x, xmin, xmax}]`	generate a log-linear plot
`LogLogPlot[f, {x, xmin, xmax}]`	generate a log-log plot
`LogListPlot[list]`	generate a log-linear plot from a list of data
`LogLogListPlot[list]`	generate a log-log plot from a list of data
`PolarPlot[r, {t, tmin, tmax}]`	generate a polar plot of the radius r as a function of angle t
`ErrorListPlot[{{x_1, y_1, dy_1}, ... }]`	generate a plot of data with error bars
`TextListPlot[{{x_1, y_1, "s_1"}, ... }]`	plot a list of data with each point given by the text string s_i
`BarChart[list]`	plot a list of data as a bar chart
`PieChart[list]`	plot a list of data as a pie chart
`PlotVectorField[{f_x, f_y}, {x, xmin, xmax}, {y, ymin, ymax}]`	plot the vector field corresponding to the vector function f
`ListPlotVectorField[list]`	plot the vector field corresponding the two-dimensional array of vectors in *list*
`SphericalPlot3D[r, {theta, min, max}, {phi, min, max}]`	generate a three-dimensional spherical plot

Some special plotting functions defined in standard *Mathematica* packages.

This loads the standard *Mathematica* package of additional graphics functions.

`In[1]:= <<Graphics`Graphics``

This generates a log-linear plot.

In[2]:= `LogPlot[ Exp[-x] + 4 Exp[-2x], {x, 0, 6} ]`

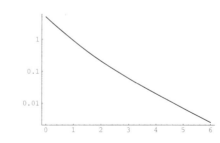

This plots the first ten primes using the integers 1, 2, 3, … as plotting symbols.

In[3]:= `TextListPlot[p = Table[Prime[n], {n, 10}]]`

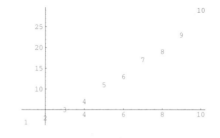

Here is a bar chart of the primes.

In[4]:= `BarChart[p]`

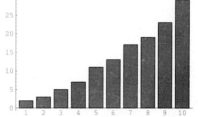

This gives a pie chart.

In[5]:= `PieChart[p]`

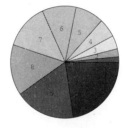

Interlude 2.   **Packages and Statistics**

22. Packages

■ 22.1 *Mathematica* Packages

One of the most important features of *Mathematica* is that it is an extensible system. There is a certain amount of mathematical and other functionality that is built into *Mathematica*. But by using the *Mathematica* language, it is always possible to add more functionality.

For many kinds of calculations, what is built into the standard version of *Mathematica* will be quite sufficient. However, if you work in a particular specialized area, you may find that you often need to use certain functions that are not built into *Mathematica*.

In such cases, you may well be able to find a *Mathematica* package that contains the functions you need. *Mathematica* packages are files written in the *Mathematica* language. They consist of collections of *Mathematica* definitions which "teach" *Mathematica* about particular application areas.

Get["*name*"] or <<*name*	read in the package
Needs["*name*"]	read in the package not more than once

Reading in *Mathematica* packages.

If you want to use functions from a particular package, you must first read the package into *Mathematica*. The details of how to do this are discussed in Section 29.1.

```
Geometry`Polytopes`              Miscellaneous`CityData`
Graphics`Animation`              Miscellaneous`Music`
Graphics`Arrow`                  Miscellaneous`Units`
Graphics`Colors`                 Miscellaneous`WorldPlot`
Graphics`Filled Plot`            Examples`CellularAutomata`
Graphics`Graphics`               Examples`Collatz`
Graphics`Graphics3D`             Examples`Life`
Graphics`ImplicitPlot`           ProgrammingExamples`Collatz`
Graphics`Legend`                 ProgrammingExamples`Fibonacci1`
Graphics`MultipleListPlot`       ProgrammingExamples`MakeFunctions`
Graphics`Polyhedra`              ProgrammingExamples`PrintTime`
Graphics`Shapes`                 ProgrammingExamples`RandomWalk`
Miscellaneous`Audio`             ProgrammingExamples`Transcript`
Miscellaneous`ChemicalElements`  ProgrammingExamples`TrigSimplification`
```

Elementary standard packages.

```
Algebra`ReIm`                       LinearAlgebra`Orthogonalization`
Algebra`SymbolicSum`                Miscellaneous`PhysicalConstants`
Algebra`Trigonometry`               ProgrammingExamples`Newton`
Calculus`Limit`                     ProgrammingExamples`TrigDefine`
Graphics`SurfaceOfRevolution`       NumericalMath`ComputerArithmetic`
LinearAlgebra`MatrixManipulation`   NumericalMath`Microscope`
LinearAlgebra`CrossProduct`
```

Some intermediate standard packages.

Mathematica uses the notion of "contexts" to specify packages in a way that is independent of the computer system being used. Contexts in *Mathematica* work somewhat like file directories in many operating systems. The name of a context ends with `, the backquote or grave accent character (ASCII decimal code 96), which is called a "context mark" in *Mathematica*.

Like directories in many operating systems, contexts in *Mathematica* can be hierarchical. Thus, for example, $name_1$`$name_2$`$name_3$` can be a context name.

There are a number of subtleties associated with such issues as conflicts between names of functions in different packages. An important point to note is that you must not refer to a function that you will read from a package before actually reading in the package. If you do this by mistake, you will have to execute the command Remove["*function-name*"] to get rid of the function before you read in the package which defines it. If you do not call Remove, *Mathematica* will use "your" version of the function, rather than the one from the package.

Just mentioning Red before loading in the package where it is defined will block its real definition.

```
In[1]:= Red
Out[1]= Red
```

This command reads in the *Mathematica* package. The error message warns us about the problem.

```
In[2]:= <<Graphics`Colors`
Red::shdw: Warning: Symbol Red appears in multiple contexts
    {Graphics`Colors`, Global`}; definitions in context
    Graphics`Colors` may shadow or be shadowed by other
    definitions.
```

We don't get the value of Red as defined in the package.

```
In[3]:= Red
Out[3]= Red
```

This removes the shadowing Red. Note the need for double quotes.

```
In[4]:= Remove["Red"]
```

Now we get the definition of Red as given in the package.

```
In[5]:= Red
Out[5]= RGBColor[1., 0., 0.]
```

You can explicitly tell *Mathematica* to read in a package at any point using the command <<*context*`. Often, however, you want to set it up so that a particular package is read in only if it is needed. The command `Needs["`*context*`'"]` tells *Mathematica* to read in a package if it has not been read in before. This is the preferred way to load the standard packages.

This command reads in a particular *Mathematica* package only if it wasn't read before.	*In[6]:=* **Needs["Graphics`Shapes`"]**

These are the objects defined in the package.

In[7]:= **?Graphics`Shapes`***

AffineShape	DoubleHelix	RotateShape	TranslateShape
Cone	Helix	Sphere	WireFrame
Cylinder	MoebiusStrip	Torus	

One of them is a Moebius strip.

In[7]:= **Show[Graphics3D[MoebiusStrip[]]]**

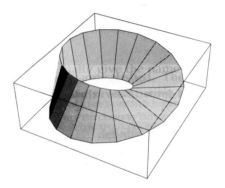

The fact that *Mathematica* can be extended using packages means that the boundary of exactly what is "part of *Mathematica*" is quite blurred. As far as usage is concerned, there is actually no difference between functions defined in packages and functions that are fundamentally built into *Mathematica*.

In fact, a fair number of the functions described in this book are actually implemented as *Mathematica* packages. However, on most *Mathematica* systems, the necessary packages have been preloaded, so that the functions they define are always present. (On some systems with severe memory limitations, even these packages may be loaded only on request.)

As a practical matter, the functions that should be considered "part of *Mathematica*" are probably those that are present in all *Mathematica* systems. It is these functions that are primarily discussed in this book.

Nevertheless, most versions of *Mathematica* come with a standard set of *Mathematica* packages, which contain definitions for many more functions. Some of these functions are mentioned in this book. But to get them, you must usually read in the necessary packages explicitly.

Of course, it is possible to set your *Mathematica* system up so that particular packages are preloaded, or are automatically loaded when needed. If you do this, then there may be many functions that appear as standard in your version of *Mathematica*, but which are not documented in this book.

One point that should be mentioned is the relationship between packages and notebooks. Both are stored as files on your computer system, and both can be read into *Mathematica*. However, a notebook is intended to be displayed, typically with a notebook interface, while a package is intended only to be used as *Mathematica* input. Many notebooks in fact contain sections that can be considered as packages, and which contain sequences of definitions intended for input to *Mathematica*.

There are more than a hundred *Mathematica* packages besides the ones listed in this section. For more complete information, see the Wolfram Research technical report, *Guide to Standard Mathematica Packages*.

BeginPackage ▪ EndPackage ▪ Begin ▪ End ▪ Remove ▪ $Context ▪ $ContextPath ▪ $Packages ▪ DeclarePackage ▪ Names ▪ Context ▪ Contexts

Other *Mathematica* functions related to packages and contexts. (See page xvi.)

23. Statistics

■ 23.1 Pseudorandom Numbers

Random[ ]	a pseudorandom real between 0 and 1
Random[Real, *xmax*]	a pseudorandom real between 0 and *xmax*
Random[Real, {*xmin*, *xmax*}]	a pseudorandom real between *xmin* and *xmax*
Random[Integer]	0 or 1 with probability $\frac{1}{2}$
Random[Integer, {*imin*, *imax*}]	a pseudorandom integer between *imin* and *imax*, inclusive
SeedRandom[ ]	reseed the pseudorandom generator, with the time of day
SeedRandom[s]	reseed with the integer *s*

Pseudorandom number generation.

This gives a list of three pseudorandom numbers.

```
In[1]:= Table[Random[ ], {3}]
Out[1]= {0.0560708, 0.6303, 0.359894}
```

Here is a 30-digit pseudorandom real number in the range 0 to 1.

```
In[2]:= Random[Real, {0, 1}, 30]
Out[2]= 0.748823044099679773836330229338
```

This gives a list of eight pseudorandom integers between 100 and 200 (inclusive).

```
In[3]:= Table[Random[Integer, {100, 200}], {8}]
Out[3]= {120, 108, 109, 147, 146, 189, 188, 187}
```

If you call Random[ ] repeatedly, you should get a "typical" sequence of numbers, with no particular pattern. There are many ways to use such numbers.

One common way to use pseudorandom numbers is in making numerical tests of hypotheses. For example, if you believe that two symbolic expressions are mathematically equal, you can test this by plugging in "typical" numerical values for symbolic parameters, and then comparing the numerical results. (If you do this, you should be careful about numerical accuracy problems and about functions of complex variables that may not have unique values.)

Here is a symbolic equation.

```
In[4]:= Sin[Cos[x]] == Cos[Sin[x]]
Out[4]= Sin[Cos[x]] == Cos[Sin[x]]
```

Substituting in a random numerical value shows that the equation is not always True.

```
In[5]:= % /. x -> Random[ ]
Out[5]= False
```

Other common uses of pseudorandom numbers include simulating probabilistic processes, and sampling large spaces of possibilities. The pseudorandom numbers that *Mathematica* generates are always uniformly distributed over the range you specify.

Random is unlike almost any other *Mathematica* function in that every time you call it, you potentially get a different result. If you use Random in a calculation, therefore, you may get different answers on different occasions.

The sequences that you get from Random[ ] are not in most senses "truly random", although they should be "random enough" for practical purposes. The sequences are in fact produced by applying a definite mathematical algorithm, starting from a particular "seed". If you give the same seed, then you get the same sequence.

When *Mathematica* starts up, it takes the time of day (measured in small fractions of a second) as the seed for the pseudorandom number generator. Two different *Mathematica* sessions will therefore almost always give different sequences of pseudorandom numbers.

If you want to make sure that you always get the same sequence of pseudorandom numbers, you can explicitly give a seed for the pseudorandom generator, using SeedRandom.

This reseeds the pseudorandom generator.	In[6]:= **SeedRandom[143]**
Here are three pseudorandom numbers.	In[7]:= **Table[Random[ ], {3}]** Out[7]= {0.952312, 0.93591, 0.813754}
If you reseed the pseudorandom generator with the same seed, you get the same sequence of pseudorandom numbers.	In[8]:= **SeedRandom[143]; Table[Random[ ], {3}]** Out[8]= {0.952312, 0.93591, 0.813754}

If you want to extract only the first sequence of elements for which a predicate
is True, you can use TakeWhile.

```
In[5]:= TakeWhile[col2, NumberQ]

Out[5]= {3, 6, 4}
```

Here is the length of the sequence.

```
In[6]:= LengthWhile[col2, NumberQ]

Out[6]= 3
```

Frequencies [*list*]	give the distinct elements in *list* paired with their frequencies
QuantileForm [*list*]	give the sorted elements in *list* paired with their quantile positions
CumulativeSums [*list*]	give the cumulative sums of *list*

Functions that summarize data.

Once you have your data in the correct list format, you can use Frequencies to observe the distribution of the data. The output of this function, as well as that of QuantileForm, is a list in the correct format for use in various plotting functions. This provides a simple way to observe your sample.

This gives a list of the elements of
newdata along with their frequency of
occurrence.

```
In[7]:= freq = Frequencies[newdata]

Out[7]= {{1, 3}, {2, 4}, {1, 5}, {1, 6}}
```

This loads another package, which
contains assorted graphics functions.

```
In[8]:= <<Graphics`Graphics`
```

Here is a histogram of our data.

```
In[9]:= BarChart[freq]
```

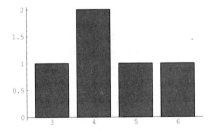

If your sample size is fairly large, it may be difficult to clearly summarize your data using Frequencies. In this case it is better to count the frequency of data points contained in a collection of intervals. BinCounts and RangeCounts do this for the cases of constant and variable length intervals, respectively. You can also use CategoryCounts to count frequencies of particular types of data.

For each of these three functions, there is also a corresponding list function that gives the elements themselves that fall in the specified intervals or match specified types of data.

BinCounts[*data*, {*min*, *max*, *dx*}]

>   list the number of elements in *data* that lie in bins from *min*
>   to *max* in steps of *dx*

RangeCounts[*data*, {c_1, c_2, ...}]

>   list the number of elements in *data* that lie between
>   successive cutoffs c_i

CategoryCounts[*data*, {{e_{11}, e_{12}, ...}, ...}]

>   list the number of elements in *data* that match any element
>   in e_i

BinLists[*data*, {*min*, *max*, *dx*}]

>   list the elements in *data* that lie in bins from *min* to *max* in
>   steps of *dx*

RangeLists[*data*, {c_1, c_2, ...}]

>   list the elements in *data* that lie between successive cutoffs c_i

CategoryLists[*data*, {{e_{11}, e_{12}, ...}, ...}]

>   list the elements in *data* that match any element in e_i

Functions that categorize data.

This gives a list of randomly generated values of the sine function.

```
In[10]:= sindata = N[Table[Sin[Pi Random[]],{100}]];
```

These are the frequencies of data for intervals between 0 and 1 of length 0.2.

```
In[11]:= freq = BinCounts[sindata, {0, 1, 0.2}]
Out[11]= {8, 14, 23, 14, 41}
```

This is a list of the midpoints of the five intervals.

```
In[12]:= midpoints = {0.1, 0.3, 0.5, 0.7, 0.9}
Out[12]= {0.1, 0.3, 0.5, 0.7, 0.9}
```

This is the histogram for our data set using a function from the Graphics`Graphics` package that was previously loaded.

```
In[13]:= BarChart[Transpose[{freq, midpoints}]]
```

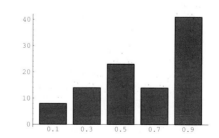

■ 23.4 Statistics`DescriptiveStatistics`

Descriptive statistics refers to properties of distributions, such as location, dispersion and shape. The functions in this package compute descriptive statistics of lists of data. You can calculate some of the standard descriptive statistics for various known distributions by using the Statistics`ContinuousDistributions` and Statistics`DiscreteDistributions` packages.

Note that this package is automatically loaded when most other statistical packages are used. For example, all the functions described below are available for use with the package Statistics`HypothesisTests`.

The statistics are calculated assuming that each value of data x_i has probability equal to $\frac{1}{n}$, where n is the number of elements in the data.

Mean[*data*]	average value $\frac{1}{n}\sum_i x_i$
Median[*data*]	median (central value)
Mode[*data*]	mode
GeometricMean[*data*]	geometric mean $\prod_i x_i^{\frac{1}{n}}$
HarmonicMean[*data*]	harmonic mean $n/\sum_i \frac{1}{x_i}$
RootMeanSquare[*data*]	root mean square $\sqrt{\frac{1}{n}\sum_i x_i^2}$
TrimmedMean[*data*, *f*]	mean of remaining entries, when a fraction f is removed from each end of the sorted list of data
TrimmedMean[*data*, {f_1, f_2}]	mean of remaining entries, when fractions f_1 and f_2 are dropped from each end of the sorted data
Quantile[*data*, *q*]	q^{th} quantile
InterpolatedQuantile[*data*, *q*]	q^{th} quantile of the distribution inferred by linear interpolation of the entries in the list of data
Quartiles[*data*]	list of quartiles
LocationReport[*data*]	list of location statistics including Mean, HarmonicMean and Median

Location statistics.

Location statistics describe where the data are located. The most common functions include measures of central tendency like the mean, median and mode. Quantile[*data*, *q*] gives the location before which ($100q$) percent of the data lie. In other words, Quantile gives a value z such that the probability that $(x_i < z)$ is less than or equal to q and the probability that $(x_i \leq z)$ is greater than or equal to q. The quantile values at $q = 0.25$, 0.5 and 0.75 are called the quartiles, and you can obtain them using `Quartiles`.

This loads the package.	`In[1]:= <<Statistics`DescriptiveStatistics``
Here is a data set.	`In[2]:= data = {6.5, 3.8, 6.6, 5.7, 6.0, 6.4, 5.3}` `Out[2]= {6.5, 3.8, 6.6, 5.7, 6., 6.4, 5.3}`
This gives some general location information about our data.	`In[3]:= LocationReport[data]` `Out[3]= {Mean -> 5.75714, HarmonicMean -> 5.57523, Median -> 6.}`
You can use the replacement operator `/.` to extract a particular statistic from the report.	`In[4]:= m = Mean /. %` `Out[4]= 5.75714`
This is the mean when the smallest entry in the list is excluded. `TrimmedMean` allows you to describe the data with removed outliers.	`In[5]:= TrimmedMean[data, {1/7, 0}]` `Out[5]= 6.08333`

`SampleRange[`*data*`]`	range
`Variance[`*data*`]`	unbiased estimate of variance, $\frac{1}{n-1}\sum_i (x_i - \overline{x})^2$
`VarianceMLE[`*data*`]`	maximum likelihood estimate of variance, $\frac{1}{n}\sum_i (x_i - \overline{x})^2$
`VarianceOfSampleMean[`*data*`]`	unbiased estimate of variance of sample mean, $\frac{1}{n}$`Variance[`*data*`]`
`StandardDeviation[`*data*`]`	standard deviation
`StandardDeviationMLE[`*data*`]`	maximum likelihood estimate of standard deviation
`StandardErrorOfSampleMean[`*data*`]`	standard deviation of the sample mean
`MeanDeviation[`*data*`]`	mean absolute deviation, $\frac{1}{n}\sum_i |x_i - \overline{x}|$
`MedianDeviation[`*data*`]`	median absolute deviation, median of $|x_i - median|$ values
`InterquartileRange[`*data*`]`	interquartile range
`QuartileDeviation[`*data*`]`	quartile deviation
`DispersionReport[`*data*`]`	list of dispersion statistics including `Variance`, `StandardDeviation`, `SampleRange`, `MeanDeviation`, `MedianDeviation` and `QuartileDeviation`

Dispersion statistics.

Dispersion statistics summarize the scatter or spread of the data. Most of these functions describe deviation from a particular location. For instance, variance is a measure of deviation from the mean, and standard deviation is just the square root of the variance.

The range is a value describing the total spread of the data. SampleRange gives the difference between the largest and smallest value in *data*, while InterquartileRange gives the difference between the 0.75[th] and the 0.25[th] quartiles.

This gives an unbiased estimate for the variance of the data with $n - 1$ as the divisor.

```
In[6]:= var1 = Variance[data]

Out[6]= 0.962857
```

Here is the maximum likelihood estimate with division by n.

```
In[7]:= var2 = VarianceMLE[data]

Out[7]= 0.825306
```

We can check the relationship between the two estimators.

```
In[8]:= var1 (Length[data] - 1) == var2 Length[data]

Out[8]= True
```

CentralMoment[*data*, *r*]	r[th] central moment $\frac{1}{n}\sum_i(x_i - \bar{x})^r$
Skewness[*data*]	coefficient of skewness
PearsonSkewness1[*data*]	Pearson's first coefficient of skewness
PearsonSkewness2[*data*]	Pearson's second coefficient of skewness
QuartileSkewness[*data*]	quartile coefficient of skewness
Kurtosis[*data*]	kurtosis coefficient
KurtosisExcess[*data*]	kurtosis excess
ShapeReport[*data*]	list of shape statistics including Skewness, QuartileSkewness and KurtosisExcess

Shape statistics.

You can get some information about the shape of a distribution using shape statistics. Skewness describes the amount of asymmetry. Kurtosis measures the concentration of data around the peak and in the tails versus the concentration in the flanks.

Skewness is calculated by dividing the third central moment by the cube of the standard deviation. Pearson's two coefficients provide two other well-known measures of skewness. PearsonSkewness1 and PearsonSkewness2 are found by multiplying three times the difference between the mean and either the mode or the median, respectively, and dividing this quantity by the standard deviation of the sample. Quartile skewness gives a measure of asymmetry within the first and third quartiles.

Kurtosis is calculated by dividing the fourth central moment by the square of the variance of the data. KurtosisExcess is shifted so that it is zero for the normal distribution, positive for distributions with a prominent peak and heavy tails, and negative for distributions with prominent flanks.

Here is the second central moment, which is the same as the maximum likelihood estimate of variance.	`In[9]:= CentralMoment[data, 2]`
	
	`Out[9]= 0.825306`

A negative value for skewness indicates that the distribution underlying the data has a long left-sided tail.	`In[10]:= Skewness[data]`
	
	`Out[10]= -0.953132`

■ 23.5 Statistics`DiscreteDistributions`

This package gives you access to the most commonly used discrete statistical distributions. You can compute their densities, means, variances and other related properties. The distributions themselves are represented in the symbolic form *name*[*param₁*, *param₂*, ...]. Functions such as Mean, which give properties of statistical distributions, take the symbolic representation of the distribution as an argument.

`BernoulliDistribution[p]`	discrete Bernoulli distribution with mean p
`BinomialDistribution[n, p]`	binomial distribution for n trials with probability p
`DiscreteUniformDistribution[n]`	
	discrete uniform distribution with n states
`GeometricDistribution[p]`	discrete geometric distribution with mean $1/p - 1$
`PoissonDistribution[mu]`	Poisson distribution with mean μ

Some statistical distributions from the package `DiscreteDistributions`.

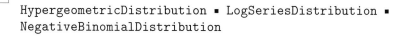

`HypergeometricDistribution` ▪ `LogSeriesDistribution` ▪
`NegativeBinomialDistribution`

Other discrete distributions from the package `DiscreteDistributions`. (See page xvi.)

Most of the common discrete statistical distributions can be understood by considering a sequence of "trials", each with two possible outcomes, say "success" and "failure".

The **Bernoulli distribution** BernoulliDistribution[*p*] is the probability distribution for a single trial in which success, corresponding to value 1, occurs with probability p, and failure, corresponding to value 0, occurs with probability $1 - p$.

The **binomial distribution** BinomialDistribution[n, p] is the distribution of the number of successes that occur in n independent trials when the probability for success in an individual trial is p.

The **geometric distribution** GeometricDistribution[p] is the distribution of the total number of trials before the first success occurs in a sequence of trials where the probability for success in each individual trial is p.

The **discrete uniform distribution** DiscreteUniformDistribution[n] is the distribution of an experiment with n outcomes that occur with equal probabilities.

The **Poisson distribution** PoissonDistribution[mu] is the distribution of the number of points that lie in a unit interval, when the density of points is mu.

PDF[$dist$, x]	probability density function at x
CDF[$dist$, x]	cumulative distribution function at x
Quantile[$dist$, q]	q^{th} quantile
Domain[$dist$]	range of values of the variable (support)
Mean[$dist$]	mean
Variance[$dist$]	variance
StandardDeviation[$dist$]	standard deviation
Skewness[$dist$]	coefficient of skewness
Kurtosis[$dist$]	coefficient of kurtosis
CharacteristicFunction[$dist$, t]	characteristic function $\phi(t)$
Random[$dist$]	pseudorandom number with specified distribution

Functions of statistical distributions.

The **cumulative distribution function** (cdf) at x for a discrete distribution is given by the sum of the **probability density function** (pdf) up to x. In this package the distributions are represented in symbolic form. PDF[$dist$, x] evaluates the density at x if x is a numerical value, and otherwise leaves the function in symbolic form. Similarly, CDF[$dist$, x] gives the cumulative distribution. Domain[$dist$] gives the domain of PDF[$dist$, x] and CDF[$dist$, x].

The quantile Quantile[$dist$, q] is effectively the inverse of the cdf. It gives the value of x at which CDF[$dist$, x] reaches q. The median is given by Quantile[$dist$, $1/2$]; quartiles, deciles and percentiles can also be expressed as quantiles. Quantiles are used in constructing confidence intervals for statistical parameters.

The mean Mean[*dist*] is the expectation of the random variable distributed according to *dist* and is usually denoted by μ. The mean is given by $\sum x f(x)$, where $f(x)$ is the pdf of the distribution. The variance Variance[*dist*] is given by $\sum (x - \mu)^2 f(x)$. The square root of the variance is called the standard deviation, and is usually denoted by σ.

The Skewness[*dist*] and Kurtosis[*dist*] functions give shape statistics summarizing the asymmetry and the peakedness of a distribution, respectively. Skewness is given by $\sigma^{-3} \sum (x - \mu)^3 f(x)$ and kurtosis is given by $\sigma^{-4} \sum (x - \mu)^4 f(x)$.

The function CharacteristicFunction[*dist*, *t*] is given by $\phi(t) = \sum f(x) \exp(itx)$. Each distribution has a unique characteristic function, which is sometimes used instead of the pdf to define a distribution.

Random[*dist*] gives pseudorandom numbers from the specified distribution. It can be used with a seed like other built-in forms of Random, as described in Section 23.1 of this book.

This loads the package.	*In[1]:=* **<<Statistics`DiscreteDistributions`**
Here is a symbolic representation of the binomial distribution for 34 trials, each having probability 0.3 of success.	*In[2]:=* **bdist = BinomialDistribution[34, 0.3]** *Out[2]=* BinomialDistribution[34, 0.3]
This is the mean of the distribution.	*In[3]:=* **Mean[bdist]** *Out[3]=* 10.2
You can get the equation for the mean by using symbolic variables as arguments.	*In[4]:=* **Mean[BinomialDistribution[n, p]]** *Out[4]=* n p
Here is the 0.5th quantile, which is equal to the median.	*In[5]:=* **Quantile[bdist, 0.5]** *Out[5]=* 10
This gives the characteristic function of the geometric distribution.	*In[6]:=* **CharacteristicFunction[GeometricDistribution[p], x]** *Out[6]=* $\dfrac{p}{1 - E^{I x} (1 - p)}$

■ 23.6 Statistics`ContinuousDistributions`

This package gives you access to the most commonly used continuous statistical distributions.

Several distributions are derived from the normal or Gaussian distribution. These distributions can also be found in the Statistics`NormalDistribution` package. You should use Statistics`NormalDistribution` instead of this package when you need only the normal, Student *t*, chi-square, or *F*-ratio distributions.

`ChiSquareDistribution[n]`	chi-square distribution with n degrees of freedom
`FRatioDistribution[n₁, n₂]`	F-ratio distribution with n_1 numerator and n_2 denominator degrees of freedom
`NormalDistribution[mu, sigma]`	
	normal (Gaussian) distribution with mean μ and standard deviation σ
`StudentTDistribution[n]`	Student t distribution with n degrees of freedom

Common distributions derived from the normal distribution.

`NoncentralChiSquareDistribution` ▪ `NoncentralStudentTDistribution` ▪ `NoncentralFRatioDistribution`

Other noncentral distributions, derived from the normal distribution. (See page xvi.)

The **normal distribution** is the approximate distribution of a large sum of independent random variables, each having the same mean and variance. Sums of random fluctuations occur frequently in nature, making the normal distribution and distributions based on them important examples of continuous probability distributions.

If the X_i represent normal random variables with unit variance and mean zero, then $\sum_{i=1}^{r} X_i^2$ has a **chi-square distribution** with r degrees of freedom. If a normal variable is standardized by subtracting its mean and dividing by its standard deviation, then the sum of squares of such quantities follows this distribution. The chi-square distribution is most typically used when describing the variance of normal samples.

A variable that has a **Student t distribution** can also be written as a function of normal random variables. Let X be a normal variable with unit variance and zero mean and Z be a chi-square variable with r degrees of freedom. In this case, $X/\sqrt{Z/r}$ has a t distribution with r degrees of freedom. The Student t distribution is symmetric about the vertical axis, and characterizes the ratio of a normal variable to its standard deviation. When $r = 1$, the t distribution is the same as the Cauchy distribution.

The **F-ratio distribution** is the distribution of the ratio of two chi-square variables divided by their respective degrees of freedom. It is commonly used when comparing the variances of two populations in hypothesis testing.

ExponentialDistribution[*lambda*]

        exponential distribution with scale parameter λ

LaplaceDistribution[*mu*, *beta*]

        Laplace (double exponential) distribution with mean μ and variance parameter β

UniformDistribution[*min*, *max*]

        uniform distribution on the interval {*min*, *max*}

Continuous statistical distributions.

BetaDistribution ▪ CauchyDistribution ▪ ChiDistribution ▪ ExtremeValueDistribution ▪ GammaDistribution ▪ HalfNormalDistribution ▪ LogNormalDistribution ▪ LogisticDistribution ▪ RayleighDistribution ▪ WeibullDistribution

Other continuous statistical distributions. (See page xvi.)

The **exponential distribution** ExponentialDistribution[*lambda*] is often used in describing the waiting time between events. In particular, if the number of events is Poisson distributed, then the waiting time between events is exponentially distributed. ExponentialDistribution is the continuous analog of the discrete distribution GeometricDistribution.

The **Laplace distribution** LaplaceDistribution[*mu*, *beta*] is the distribution of the difference of two independent random variables with identical exponential distributions.

The **uniform distribution** UniformDistribution[*min*, *max*], commonly referred to as the rectangular distribution, characterizes a random variable whose value is everywhere equally likely. An example of a uniformly distributed random variable is the location of a point chosen randomly on a line from *min* to *max*. UniformDistribution is the continuous analog of the discrete distribution DiscreteUniformDistribution.

The **cumulative distribution function** (cdf) at x for a continuous distribution is given by the integral of the **probability density function** (pdf) up to x. In this package distributions are represented in symbolic form. PDF[*dist*, *x*] evaluates the density at x if x is a numerical value, and otherwise leaves the function in symbolic form whenever possible. Similarly, CDF[*dist*, *x*] gives the cumulative distribution and Mean[*dist*] gives the mean of the specified distribution.

The mean is given by $\int x f(x)\,dx$, where $f(x)$ is the pdf of the distribution. The variance Variance[*dist*] is given by $\int (x - \mu)^2 f(x)\,dx$. Skewness is given by $\sigma^{-3} \int (x - \mu)^3 f(x)\,dx$ and kurtosis is given by $\sigma^{-4} \int (x - \mu)^4 f(x)\,dx$. The characteristic function CharacteristicFunction[*dist*, *t*] is given by $\phi(t) = \int f(x) \exp(itx)\,dx$.

For a more complete description of the various functions of a statistical distribution, see the description of their continuous analogs in the section concerning the package `Statistics`DiscreteDistributions``.

This loads the package.	`In[1]:= <<Statistics`ContinuousDistributions``
This gives a symbolic representation of the normal distribution with 3 as the mean and 1 as the standard deviation.	`In[2]:= ndist = NormalDistribution[3, 1]` `Out[2]= NormalDistribution[3, 1]`
Here is the probability density function evaluated at 10.	`In[3]:= PDF[ndist, 10]` `Out[3]= 9.13472 10`$^{-12}$
Here is a plot of the probability density function, demonstrating the bell-shaped curve of the normal distribution.	`In[4]:= Plot[PDF[ndist, x], {x, 0, 10}]`

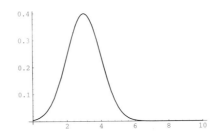

This generates a pseudorandom number from the ndist distribution.	`In[5]:= Random[ndist]` `Out[5]= 1.360060860063131`

■ 23.7 `Statistics`LinearRegression``

The built-in function Fit finds the least-squares fit to a data set as a linear combination of given basis functions. This is precisely what one needs for linear regression. The function Regress provided in this package augments Fit by giving a list of commonly used statistics. You can control the output using option values such as RSquared, EstimatedVariance, and ANOVATable, so that only the information that you need is printed.

Linear regression finds the linear combination of defined basis functions that best approximates the data in terms of least squares. The basis functions, f_j, define the model by specifying the predictors as functions of the independent variables. The resulting model looks like $y_i = \beta_1 f_{1i} + \beta_2 f_{2i} + \ldots + \beta_{pi} f_{pi} + e_i$, where y_i is the ith response, f_{ji} is the jth basis function of the ith case, and e_i is the error of the ith case.

Estimates of the coefficients $\beta_1, \beta_2, \ldots$ are calculated to minimize $\sum_i e_i^2$, the residual sum of squares. For example, you can do simple linear regression by defining your basis functions as $f_1 = 1$ and $f_2 = x$, in which case β_1 and β_2 are found to minimize $\sum_i [y_i - (\beta_1 + \beta_2 x_i)]^2$.

Regress[*data*, {1, x, x^2}, x]   fit a quadratic model

Regress[*data*, {1, x, y, x y}, {x,y}]

fit a model that includes interaction between independent
variables x and y

Regress[*data*, {f_1, f_2, ... }, *vars*]

fit the data using a linear combination of the functions f_i of
the variables *vars*

Using **Regress**.

The arguments of **Regress** are of the same form as those of **Fit**. The data you give can be a list of
pairs consisting of the observed values of the independent variables and the responses. The basis functions f_j must be functions of the symbols you give as variables. These symbols correspond to the independent variables represented in the data.

You can also give a vector of data points. In this case, **Regress** assumes that this vector represents
the values of a response variable with the independent variable having values 1, 2, ...

{y_1, y_2, ... }   *data* is a list of response values where a single independent
variable is assumed to take the values 1, 2, ...

{{x_{11}, x_{12}, ... , y_1}, {x_{21}, x_{22}, ... , y_2}, ... }

data is a matrix where x_{ik} is the value of the ith case of the kth
independent variable, and y_i is the ith response

Ways of specifying data in **Regress**.

This loads the package.

In[1]:= <<Statistics`LinearRegression`

Here is a set of data. The first element
in each pair gives the value of the
independent variable, while the second
gives the observed response.

In[2]:= data={{.211,150},{.248,189},{.351,253},
         {.182,142},{.091,97},{.167,124},
         {.232,172},{.055,90},{.284,209},
         {.138,107}};

Part 3.

The *Mathematica* Language

24. Expressions

■ 24.1 Everything Is an Expression

Mathematica handles many different kinds of things: mathematical formulas, lists and graphics, to name a few. Although they often look very different, *Mathematica* represents all of these things in one uniform way. They are all *expressions*.

A prototypical example of a *Mathematica* expression is f[x, y]. You might use f[x, y] to represent a mathematical function $f(x, y)$. The function is named f, and it has two arguments, x and y.

You do not always have to write expressions in the form f[x, y, ...]. For example, x + y is also an expression. When you type in x + y, *Mathematica* converts it to the standard form Plus[x, y]. Then, when it prints it out again, it gives it as x + y.

The same is true of other "operators", such as ∧ (Power) and / (Divide).

In fact, everything you type into *Mathematica* is treated as an expression.

x + y + z	Plus[x, y, z]
x y z	Times[x, y, z]
x∧n	Power[x, n]
{a, b, c}	List[a, b, c]
a -> b	Rule[a, b]
a = b	Set[a, b]

Some examples of *Mathematica* expressions.

You can see the full form of any expression by using FullForm[*expr*].

Here is an expression.	*In[1]:=* **x + y + z**
	Out[1]= x + y + z
This is the full form of the expression.	*In[2]:=* **FullForm[%]**
	Out[2]//FullForm= Plus[x, y, z]
Here is another expression.	*In[3]:=* **1 + x∧2 + (y + z)∧2**
	Out[3]= $1 + x^2 + (y + z)^2$
Its full form has several nested pieces.	*In[4]:=* **FullForm[%]**
	Out[4]//FullForm= Plus[1, Power[x, 2], Power[Plus[y, z], 2]]

The object *f* in an expression *f*[*x*, *y*, ...] is known as the *head* of the expression. You can extract it using Head[*expr*]. Particularly when you write programs in *Mathematica*, you will often want to test the head of an expression to find out what kind of thing the expression is.

Head gives the "function name" f.	`In[5]:= Head[f[x, y]]`
	
	`Out[5]= f`

Here Head gives the name of the "operator".	`In[6]:= Head[a + b + c]`
	
	`Out[6]= Plus`

Everything has a head.	`In[7]:= Head[{a, b, c}]`
	
	`Out[7]= List`

Numbers also have heads.	`In[8]:= Head[23432]`
	
	`Out[8]= Integer`

You can distinguish different kinds of numbers by their heads.	`In[9]:= Head[2 / 3]`
	
	`Out[9]= Rational`

You might not have expected this result.	`In[10]:= Head[a / b]`
	
	`Out[10]= Times`

FullForm provides the explanation.	`In[11]:= FullForm[a / b]`
	
	`Out[11]//FullForm= Times[a, Power[b, -1]]`

Head[*expr*]	give the head of an expression: the *f* in *f*[*x*, *y*]
FullForm[*expr*]	display an expression in the full form used by *Mathematica*

Functions for manipulating expressions.

You can refer to parts of an expression such as *f*[*g*[*a*], *g*[*b*]] just as you refer to parts of nested lists.

This extracts part {2,1} of the expression 1 + x^2.	`In[12]:= (1 + x^2) [[2, 1]]`
	
	`Out[12]= x`

To see what part is {2,1}, you can look at the full form of the expression.	`In[13]:= FullForm[1 + x^2]`
	
	`Out[13]//FullForm= Plus[1, Power[x, 2]]`

■ 24.2 The Meaning of Expressions

The notion of expressions is a crucial unifying principle in *Mathematica*. It is the fact that every object in *Mathematica* has the same underlying structure that makes it possible for *Mathematica* to cover so many areas with a comparatively small number of basic operations.

Although all expressions have the same basic structure, there are many different ways that expressions can be used. Here are a few of the interpretations you can give to the parts of an expression.

meaning of f	*meaning of x, y, ...*	*examples*
Function	arguments or parameters	`Sin[x]` or `f[x, y]`
Command	arguments or parameters	`Expand[(x + 1)^2]`
Operator	operands	`x + y` or `a = b`
Head	elements	`{a, b, c}`
Object type	contents	`RGBColor[r, g, b]`

Some interpretations of parts of expressions.

Expressions in *Mathematica* are often used to specify operations. So, for example, typing in 2 + 3 causes 2 and 3 to be added together, while `Factor[x^6 - 1]` performs factorization.

Perhaps an even more important use of expressions in *Mathematica*, however, is to maintain a structure, which can then be acted on by other functions. An expression like `{a, b, c}` does not specify an operation. It merely maintains a list structure, which contains a collection of three elements. Other functions, such as `Reverse` or `Dot`, can act on this structure.

The full form of the expression `{a, b, c}` is `List[a, b, c]`. The head `List` performs no operations. Instead, its purpose is to serve as a "tag" to specify the "type" of the structure.

You can use expressions in *Mathematica* to create your own structures. For example, you might want to represent points in three-dimensional space, specified by three coordinates. You could give each point as `point[x, y, z]`. The "function" `point` again performs no operation. It serves merely to collect the three coordinates together, and to label the resulting object as a `point`.

You can think of expressions like `point[x, y, z]` as being "packets of data", tagged with a particular head. Even though all expressions have the same basic structure, you can distinguish different "types" of expressions by giving them different heads. You can then set up transformation rules and programs which treat different types of expressions in different ways.

■ 24.3 Special Ways to Input Expressions

Mathematica allows you to use special notation for many common operators. For example, although internally *Mathematica* represents a sum of two terms as Plus[x, y], you can enter this expression in the much more convenient form x + y.

The *Mathematica* language has a definite grammar which specifies how your input should be converted to internal form. One aspect of the grammar is that it specifies how pieces of your input should be grouped. For example, if you enter an expression such as a + b ∧ c, the *Mathematica* grammar specifies that this should be considered, following standard mathematical notation, as a + (b ∧ c) rather than (a + b) ∧ c. *Mathematica* chooses this grouping because it treats the operator ∧ as having a higher *precedence* than +. In general, the arguments of operators with higher precedence are grouped before those of operators with lower precedence.

You should realize that absolutely every special input form in *Mathematica* is assigned a definite precedence. This includes not only the traditional mathematical operators, but also forms such as ->, := or the semicolons used to separate expressions in a *Mathematica* program.

The table on pages 349–352 gives all the operators of *Mathematica* in order of decreasing precedence. The precedence is arranged, where possible, to follow standard mathematical usage, and to minimize the number of parentheses that are usually needed.

You will find, for example, that relational operators such as < have lower precedence than arithmetic operators such as +. This means that you can write expressions such as x + y > 7 without using parentheses.

There are nevertheless many cases where you do have to use parentheses. For example, since ; has a lower precedence than =, you need to use parentheses to write x = (a ; b). *Mathematica* interprets the expression x = a ; b as (x = a) ; b. In general, it can never hurt to include extra parentheses, but it can cause a great deal of trouble if you leave parentheses out, and *Mathematica* interprets your input in a way you do not expect.

f[x, y]	standard form for f[x, y]
f @ x	prefix form for f[x]
x // f	postfix form for f[x]
x ~ f ~ y	infix form for f[x, y]

Four ways to write expressions in *Mathematica*.

There are several common types of operators in *Mathematica*. The + in x + y is an "infix" operator. The − in −p is a "prefix" operator. Even when you enter an expression such as f[x, y, ...] *Mathematica* allows you to do it in ways that mimic infix, prefix and postfix forms.

■ 25.3 Applying Functions to Lists

In an expression like f[{a, b, c}] you are giving a list as the argument to a function. Often you need instead to apply a function directly to the elements of a list, rather than to the list as a whole. You can do this in *Mathematica* using Apply.

This makes each element of the list an argument of the function f.	In[1]:= **Apply[f, {a, b, c}]** Out[1]= f[a, b, c]
This gives Plus[a, b, c] which yields the sum of the elements in the list.	In[2]:= **Apply[Plus, {a, b, c}]** Out[2]= a + b + c
Similarly this gives Times[a, b, c], the product of the elements in the list.	In[3]:= **Apply[Times, {a, b, c}]** Out[3]= a b c
Here is the definition of the statistical mean, written using Apply.	In[4]:= **mean[list_] := Apply[Plus, list] / Length[list]**

Apply[*f*, {*a*, *b*, ... }]   apply *f* to a list, giving *f*[*a*, *b*, ...]

Applying functions to lists.

■ 25.4 Applying Functions to Parts of Expressions

If you have a list of elements, it is often important to be able to apply a function separately to each of the elements. You can do this in *Mathematica* using Map.

This applies f separately to each element in a list.	In[1]:= **Map[f, {a, b, c}]** Out[1]= {f[a], f[b], f[c]}
You can use Map to find the length of each of the sublists of a list.	In[2]:= **Map[Length, {{1, 3, 4}, {5, 6, 7}, {2, 1, 6, 6}}]** Out[2]= {3, 3, 4}

Map[*f*, {*a*, *b*, ... }]   apply *f* to each element in a list, giving {*f*[*a*], *f*[*b*], ... }

Applying a function to each element in a list.

What Map[*f*, *expr*] effectively does is to "wrap" the function *f* around each element of the expression *expr*. You can use Map on any expression, not just a list.

This applies f to each element in the sum.	In[3]:= **Map[f, a + b + c]** Out[3]= f[a] + f[b] + f[c]

This applies Log to both sides of an equation.

In[4]:= **Map[Log, x == y]**

Out[4]= Log[x] == Log[y]

This applies the function Sqrt to each argument of g.

In[5]:= **Map[Sqrt, g[x^2, x^3]]**

Out[5]= g[Sqrt[x^2], Sqrt[x^3]]

Map[*f*, *expr*] applies *f* to the first level of parts in *expr*. You can use MapAll[*f*, *expr*] to apply *f* to *all* the parts of *expr*.

This defines a 2×2 matrix m.

In[6]:= **m = {{a, b}, {c, d}}**

Out[6]= {{a, b}, {c, d}}

Map applies f to the first level of m, in this case the rows of the matrix.

In[7]:= **Map[f, m]**

Out[7]= {f[{a, b}], f[{c, d}]}

MapAll applies f at *all* levels in m. If you look carefully at this expression, you will see an f wrapped around every part.

In[8]:= **MapAll[f, m]**

Out[8]= f[{f[{f[a], f[b]}], f[{f[c], f[d]}]}]

Map[*f*, *expr*]	apply *f* to the first-level parts of *expr*
MapAll[*f*, *expr*]	apply *f* to all parts of *expr*

Ways to apply a function to different parts of expressions.

■ 25.5 Pure Functions

Function[*x*, *body*]	a pure function in which *x* is replaced by any argument you provide
Function[{*x₁*, *x₂*, ... }, *body*]	a pure function that takes several arguments
body &	a pure function with arguments specified as # or #1, #2, etc.

Pure functions.

When you use functional operations such as Nest and Map, you always have to specify a function to apply. In all the examples above, we have used the "name" of a function to specify the function. Pure functions allow you to give functions which can be applied to arguments, without having to define explicit names for the functions.

This defines a function h.

In[1]:= **h[x_] := x f[x]**

| Having defined h, you can now use its name in Map. | `In[2]:= Map[h, {a, b, c}]` |
| | `Out[2]= {a f[a], b f[b], c f[c]}` |

| Here is a way to get the same result using a pure function. | `In[3]:= Map[ # f[#] &, {a, b, c} ]` |
| | `Out[3]= {a f[a], b f[b], c f[c]}` |

There are several equivalent ways to write pure functions in *Mathematica*. The idea in all cases is to construct an object which, when supplied with appropriate arguments, computes a particular function. Thus, for example, if *fun* is a pure function, then *fun* [*a*] evaluates the function with argument *a*.

| Here is a pure function which represents the operation of squaring. | `In[4]:= Function[x, x^2]` |
| | `Out[4]= Function[x, x^2]` |

| Supplying the argument n to the pure function yields the square of n. | `In[5]:= %[n]` |
| | `Out[5]= n^2` |

You can use a pure function wherever you would usually give the name of a function.

| You can use a pure function in Map. | `In[6]:= Map[ Function[x, x^2], a + b + c ]` |
| | `Out[6]= a^2 + b^2 + c^2` |

| Or in Fold. | `In[7]:= Fold[Function[{x, y}, 1 / (x + y)], 0, {a, b, c}]` |
| | $$Out[7]= \cfrac{1}{\cfrac{1}{\cfrac{1}{a} + b} + c}$$ |

If you are going to use a particular function repeatedly, then you can define the function using $f[x\_] := body$, and refer to the function by its name f. On the other hand, if you only intend to use a function once, you will probably find it better to give the function in pure function form, without ever naming it.

#	the first variable in a pure function
#*n*	the nth variable in a pure function

Short forms for pure functions.

Just as the name of a function is irrelevant if you do not intend to refer to the function again, so also the names of arguments in a pure function are irrelevant. *Mathematica* allows you to avoid using explicit names for the arguments of pure functions, and instead to specify the arguments by giving "slot numbers" #*n*. In a *Mathematica* pure function, #*n* stands for the nth argument you supply. # stands for the first argument.

1/# & is a short form for a pure function that takes the reciprocal of its argument.

```
In[8]:= Map[ 1/# &, a + b + c ]

          1   1   1
Out[8]= - + - + -
          a   b   c
```

This applies a function that takes the first two elements from each list. By using a pure function, you avoid having to define the function separately.

```
In[9]:= Map[Take[#, 2]&, {{2, 1, 7}, {4, 1, 5}, {3, 1, 2}}]

Out[9]= {{2, 1}, {4, 1}, {3, 1}}
```

Using short forms for pure functions, you can simplify the definition of tonumber given on page 233.

```
In[10]:= tonumber[digits_] := Fold[(10 #1 + #2)&, 0, digits]
```

This variation gives a "tower of powers".

```
In[11]:= Fold[#1 ^ #2 &, a, {b, c, d, e}]

                b  c  d  e
Out[11]= (((a ) ) )
```

When you use short forms for pure functions, it is very important that you do not forget the ampersand. If you leave the ampersand out, *Mathematica* will not know that the expression you give is to be used as a pure function.

When you use the ampersand notation for pure functions, you must be careful about the grouping of pieces in your input. As shown in Section A2.2 the ampersand notation has fairly low precedence, which means that you can type expressions like #1 + #2 & without parentheses. On the other hand, if you want, for example, to set an option to be a pure function, you need to use parentheses, as in *option -> (fun &)*.

■ 25.6 Selecting Parts of Expressions with Functions

Section 3.5 showed how you can pick out elements of lists based on their *positions*. Often, however, you will need to select elements based not on *where* they are, but rather on *what* they are.

Select [*list*, *f*] selects elements of *list* using the function *f* as a criterion. Select applies *f* to each element of *list* in turn, and keeps only those for which the result is True.

This finds the primes from 1000 to 1050.

```
In[1]:= Select[Range[1000, 1050], PrimeQ]

Out[1]= {1009, 1013, 1019, 1021, 1031, 1033, 1039, 1049}
```

This selects the elements of the list for which the pure function yields True, *i.e.*, those numerically greater than 4.

```
In[2]:= Select[{2, 15, 1, a, 16, 17}, # > 4 &]

Out[2]= {15, 16, 17}
```

You can use Select to pick out pieces of any expression, not just elements of a list.

This gives a sum of terms involving x, y and z.

```
In[3]:= t = Expand[(x + y + z)^2]

          2            2            2
Out[3]= x + 2 x y + y + 2 x z + 2 y z + z
```

You can use `Select` to pick out only those terms in the sum that do not involve the symbol x.

```
In[4]:= Select[t, FreeQ[#, x]&]
          2           2
Out[4]= y  + 2 y z + z
```

Or those that do.

```
In[5]:= Select[t, Not[FreeQ[#, x]]&]
          2
Out[5]= x  + 2 x y + 2 x z
```

`Select[`*expr, f*`]`	select the elements in *expr* for which the function *f* gives `True`
`Select[`*expr, f, n*`]`	select the first *n* elements in *expr* for which the function *f* gives `True`

Selecting pieces of expressions.

This gives the first element which satisfies the criterion you specify.

```
In[6]:= Select[{-1, 3, 10, 12, 14}, # > 3 &, 1]
Out[6]= {10}
```

SameTest ▪ SlotSequence ▪ MapAt ▪ MapIndexed ▪ MapThread ▪ FlattenAt ▪ Scan ▪ ComposeList ▪ Thread ▪ Inner ▪ Outer ▪ Distribute ▪ Identity ▪ Composition ▪ Operate ▪ Through ▪ Compile ▪ CompiledFunction

Other *Mathematica* functions related to functional programming. (See page xvi.)

26. Patterns

■ 26.1 Classes of Expressions

Patterns are used throughout *Mathematica* to represent classes of expressions. A simple example of a pattern is the expression f[x_]. This pattern represents the class of expressions with the form f[*anything*].

The main power of patterns comes from the fact that many operations in *Mathematica* can be done not only with single expressions, but also with patterns that represent whole classes of expressions.

You can use patterns in transformation rules to specify how classes of expressions should be transformed.

$In[1]:= $ **f[a] + f[b] /. f[x_] -> x^2**

$Out[1]= a^2 + b^2$

You can use patterns to count all the expressions in a particular class.

$In[2]:= $ **Count[{f[a], g[b], f[c]}, f[x_]]**

$Out[2]= 2$

The basic object that appears in almost all *Mathematica* patterns is _ (pronounced "blank"). The fundamental rule is simply that _ *stands for any expression*.

Thus, for example, the pattern f[_] stands for any expression of the form f[*anything*]. The pattern f[x_] also stands for any expression of the form f[*anything*], but gives the name x to the expression *anything*, allowing you to refer to it on the right-hand side of a transformation rule.

You can put blanks anywhere in an expression. What you get is a pattern which matches all expressions that can be made by "filling in the blanks" in any way.

f[n_]	f with any argument, named n
f[n_, m_]	f with two arguments, named n and m
x^n_	x to any power, with the power named n
x_^n_	any expression to any power
a_ + b_	a sum of two expressions
{a_, b_}	a list of two expressions
f[n_, n_]	f with two *identical* arguments

Some examples of patterns.

You can construct patterns for expressions with any structure.

$In[3]:= $ **q[{a, b}] + q[c] /. q[{x_, y_}] -> p[x + y]**

$Out[3]= p[a + b] + q[c]$

One of the most common uses of patterns is for "destructuring" function arguments. If you make a definition for f[list_], then you need to use expressions like list[[1]] explicitly in order to pick out elements of the list. But if you know for example that the list will always have two elements, then it is usually much more convenient to give a definition for f[{x_, y_}] instead. Then you can refer to the elements of the list directly as x and y. In addition, *Mathematica* will not use the definition you have given unless the argument of f really is of the required form of a list of two expressions.

Here is one way to define a function which takes a list of two elements, and evaluates the first element raised to the power of the second element.	`In[4]:= g[list_] := Part[list, 1] ^ Part[list, 2]`

Here is a much more elegant way to make the definition, using a pattern.	`In[5]:= h[{x_, y_}] := x ^ y`

A crucial point to understand is that *Mathematica* patterns represent classes of expressions with a given *structure*. One pattern will match a particular expression if the structure of the pattern is the same as the structure of the expression, in the sense that by filling in blanks in the pattern you can get the expression. Even though two expressions may be *mathematically equal*, they cannot be represented by the same *Mathematica* pattern unless they have the same structure.

Thus, for example, the pattern (1 + x_)^2 can stand for expressions like (1 + a)^2 or (1 + b^3)^2 that have the same *structure*. However, it cannot stand for the expression 1 + 2 a + a^2. Although this expression is *mathematically equal* to (1 + a)^2, it does not have the same *structure* as the pattern (1 + x_)^2.

The fact that patterns in *Mathematica* specify the *structure* of expressions is crucial in making it possible to set up transformation rules which change the *structure* of expressions, while leaving them mathematically equal.

It is worth realizing that in general it would be quite impossible for *Mathematica* to match patterns by mathematical, rather than structural, equivalence. In the case of expressions like (1 + a)^2 and 1 + 2 a + a^2, you can determine equivalence just by using functions like Expand and Factor. But there is no general way to find out whether an arbitrary pair of mathematical expressions are equal.

As another example, the pattern x^_ will match the expression x^2. It will not, however, match the expression 1, even though this could be considered as x^0. You should understand that in all cases pattern matching in *Mathematica* is fundamentally structural.

The x^n_ matches only x^2 and x^3. 1 and x can mathematically be written as x^n, but do not have the same structure.	`In[6]:= {1, x, x^2, x^3} /. x^n_ -> r[n]`
	
	`Out[6]= {1, x, r[2], r[3]}`

Another point to realize is that the structure *Mathematica* uses in pattern matching is the full form of expressions printed by FullForm. Thus, for example, an object such as 1/x, whose full form is Power[x, -1] will be matched by the pattern x_^n_, but not by the pattern x_/y_, whose full form is Times[x_, Power[y_, -1]].

The full form of the expressions in the list contains explicit powers of b, so the transformation rule can be applied.	`In[7]:= {a/b, 1/b^2, 2/b^2} /. b^n_ -> d[n]`
	
	`Out[7]= {a d[-1], d[-2], 2 d[-2]}`

Although *Mathematica* does not use mathematical equivalences such as $x^1 = x$ when matching patterns, it does use certain structural equivalences. Thus, for example, *Mathematica* takes account of properties such as commutativity and associativity in pattern matching.

To apply this transformation rule, *Mathematica* makes use of the commutativity and associativity of addition.

```
In[8]:= f[a + b] + f[a + c] + f[b + d] /.
                f[a + x_] + f[c + y_] -> p[x, y]

Out[8]= f[b + d] + p[b, a]
```

The discussion so far has considered only pattern objects such as x_ which can stand for any single expression. In later subsections, we discuss the constructs that *Mathematica* uses to extend and restrict the classes of expressions represented by patterns.

■ 26.2 Finding Expressions That Match a Pattern

Cases [*list*, *form*]	give the elements of *list* that match *form*
Count [*list*, *form*]	give the number of elements in *list* that match *form*
Position [*list*, *form*]	give the positions of elements in *list* that match *form*
DeleteCases [*expr*, *form*]	delete elements of *expr* that match *form*

Picking out or deleting elements that match a pattern.

This gives the elements of the list which match the pattern x^_.

```
In[1]:= Cases[ {3, a^2, x, x^2, x^3}, x^_ ]

Out[1]= {x , x }
            2   3
```

Here is the total number of elements which match the pattern.

```
In[2]:= Count[ {3, a^2, x, x^2, x^3}, x^_ ]

Out[2]= 2
```

You can apply functions like Cases not only to lists, but to expressions of any kind.

```
In[3]:= Cases[ 3 + a^2 + x + x^2 + x^3, x^_ ]

Out[3]= {x , x }
            2   3
```

This gives the positions of the elements which match the pattern.

```
In[4]:= Position[ {3, a^2, x, x^2, x^3}, x^_ ]

Out[4]= {{4}, {5}}
```

This deletes the elements which match x^n_.

```
In[5]:= DeleteCases[ {3, a^2, x, x^2, x^3}, x^n_ ]

Out[5]= {3, a , x}
              2
```

■ 26.3 Naming Pieces of Patterns

Particularly when you use transformation rules, you often need to name pieces of patterns. An object like *x_* stands for any expression, but gives the expression the name *x*. You can then, for example, use this name on the right-hand side of a transformation rule.

An important point is that when you use *x_*, *Mathematica* requires that all occurrences of blanks with the same name *x* in a particular expression must stand for the same expression.

Thus f[x_, x_] can only stand for expressions in which the two arguments of f are exactly the same. f[_, _], on the other hand, can stand for any expression of the form f[*x*, *y*], where *x* and *y* need not be the same.

The transformation rule applies only to cases where the two arguments of f are identical.	*In[1]:=* {f[a, a], f[a, b]} /. f[x_, x_] -> p[x] *Out[1]=* {p[a], f[a, b]}

Mathematica allows you to give names not just to single blanks, but to any piece of a pattern. The object *x*:*pattern* in general represents a pattern which is assigned the name *x*. In transformation rules, you can use this mechanism to name exactly those pieces of a pattern that you need to refer to on the right-hand side of the rule.

_	any expression
*x_*	any expression, to be named *x*
x:*pattern*	an expression to be named *x*, matching *pattern*

Patterns with names.

This gives a name to the complete form _^_ so you can refer to it as a whole on the right-hand side of the transformation rule.	*In[2]:=* f[a^b] /. f[x:_^_] -> p[x] *Out[2]=* p[a^b]
Here the exponent is named n, while the whole object is x.	*In[3]:=* f[a^b] /. f[x:_^n_] -> p[x, n] *Out[3]=* p[a^b, b]

When you give the same name to two pieces of a pattern, you constrain the pattern to match only those expressions in which the corresponding pieces are identical.

Here the pattern matches both cases.	*In[4]:=* {f[h[4], h[4]], f[h[4], h[5]]} /. f[h[_], h[_]] -> q *Out[4]=* {q, q}
Now both arguments of f are constrained to be the same, and only the first case matches.	*In[5]:=* {f[h[4], h[4]], f[h[4], h[5]]} /. f[x:h[_], x_] -> r[x] *Out[5]=* {r[h[4]], f[h[4], h[5]]}

■ 26.4 Specifying Types of Expression in Patterns

You can tell a lot about what "type" of expression something is by looking at its head. Thus, for example, an integer has head `Integer`, while a list has head `List`.

In a pattern, `_h` and `x_h` represent expressions that are constrained to have head `h`. Thus, for example, `_Integer` represents any integer, while `_List` represents any list.

x_h	an expression with head h
$x\_Integer$	an integer
x_Real	an approximate real number
$x\_Complex$	a complex number
x_List	a list
x_Symbol	a symbol

Patterns for objects with specified heads.

This replaces just those elements that are integers.

```
In[1]:= {a, 4, 5, b} /. x_Integer -> p[x]
Out[1]= {a, p[4], p[5], b}
```

You can think of making an assignment for `f[x_Integer]` as like defining a function `f` that must take an argument of "type" `Integer`.

This defines a value for the function `gamma` when its argument is an integer.

```
In[2]:= gamma[n_Integer] := (n - 1)!
```

The definition applies only when the argument of `gamma` is an integer.

```
In[3]:= gamma[4] + gamma[x]
Out[3]= 6 + gamma[x]
```

The object `4.` has head `Real`, so the definition does not apply.

```
In[4]:= gamma[4.]
Out[4]= gamma[4.]
```

This defines values for expressions with integer exponents.

```
In[5]:= d[x_^n_Integer] := n x^(n-1)
```

The definition is used only when the exponent is an integer.

```
In[6]:= d[(a+b)^3] + d[x^4] + d[x^(1/2)]
                     2        3
Out[6]= 3 (a + b)  + 4 x  + d[Sqrt[x]]
```

■ 26.5 Putting Constraints on Patterns

Mathematica provides a general mechanism for specifying constraints on patterns. All you need do is to put /; *condition* at the end of a pattern to signify that it applies only when the specified condition is True. You can read the operator /; as "slash-semi", "whenever" or "provided that".

pattern /; *condition*	a pattern that matches only when a condition is satisfied
lhs :> *rhs* /; *condition*	a rule that applies only when a condition is satisfied
lhs := *rhs* /; *condition*	a definition that applies only when a condition is satisfied

Putting conditions on patterns and transformation rules.

This gives a definition for fac that applies only when its argument n is positive.	`In[1]:= fac[n_ /; n > 0] := n!`
The definition for fac is used only when the argument is positive.	`In[2]:= fac[4] + fac[-4]` `Out[2]= 24 + fac[-4]`
This counts the negative elements in the list.	`In[3]:= Count[{-1, 3, -4, 5, -2}, x_ /; x < 0]` `Out[3]= 3`

You can use /; on whole definitions and transformation rules, as well as on individual patterns. In general, you can put /; *condition* at the end of any := definition or :> rule to tell *Mathematica* that the definition or rule applies only when the specified condition holds. Note that /; conditions should not usually be put at the end of = definitions or -> rules, since they will then be evaluated immediately, as discussed in Section 27.5.

Here is another way to give a definition for fac which applies only when its argument n is positive.	`In[4]:= fac2[n_] := n! /; n > 0`
Once again, fac2 evaluates only when its argument is positive.	`In[5]:= fac2[4] + fac2[-4]` `Out[5]= 24 + fac2[-4]`

■ 26.6 Patterns Involving Alternatives

patt₁ | *patt₂* | ...	a pattern that can have one of several forms

Specifying patterns that involve alternatives.

This defines h to give p when its argument is either a or b.	`In[1]:= h[a | b] := p`

The first two cases give p.	*In[2]:=* **{h[a], h[b], h[c], h[d]}**
	Out[2]= **{p, p, h[c], h[d]}**
You can also use alternatives in transformation rules.	*In[3]:=* **{a, b, c, d} /. (a | b) -> p**
	Out[3]= **{p, p, c, d}**
Here is another example, in which one of the alternatives is itself a pattern.	*In[4]:=* **{1, x, x^2, x^3, y^2} /. (x | x^_) -> q**
	Out[4]= **{1, q, q, q, y^2}**

When you use alternatives in patterns, you should make sure that the same set of names appear in each alternative. When a pattern like (a[x_] | b[x_]) matches an expression, there will always be a definite expression that corresponds to the object x. On the other hand, if you try to match a pattern like (a[x_] | b[y_]), then there will be a definite expression corresponding either to x, or to y, but not to both. As a result, you cannot use x and y to refer to definite expressions, for example on the right-hand side of a transformation rule.

Here f is used to name the head, which can be either a or b.	*In[5]:=* **{a[2], b[3], c[4], a[5]} /. (f:(a|b))[x_] -> r[f, x]**
	Out[5]= **{r[a, 2], r[b, 3], c[4], r[a, 5]}**

■ 26.7 Functions with Variable Numbers of Arguments

A pattern like $f[x_, y_]$ stands only for instances of the function with exactly two arguments. Sometimes you need to set up patterns that can allow any number of arguments.

You can do this using *multiple blanks*. While a single blank such as x_ stands for a single *Mathematica* expression, a double blank such as x__ stands for a sequence of one or more expressions.

Here x__ stands for the sequence of expressions (a, b, c).	*In[1]:=* **f[a, b, c] /. f[x__] -> p[x, x, x]**
	Out[1]= **p[a, b, c, a, b, c, a, b, c]**
Here is a more complicated definition, which picks out pairs of duplicated elements in h.	*In[2]:=* **h[a___, x_, b___, x_, c___] := hh[x] h[a, b, c]**
The definition is applied twice, picking out the two paired elements.	*In[3]:=* **h[2, 3, 2, 4, 5, 3]**
	Out[3]= **h[4, 5] hh[2] hh[3]**

"Double blanks" __ stand for sequences of one or more expressions. "Triple blanks" ___ stand for sequences of zero or more expressions. You should be very careful whenever you use triple blank patterns. It is easy to make a mistake that can lead to an infinite loop. For example, if you define p[x_, y___] := p[x] q[y], then typing in p[a] will lead to an infinite loop, with y repeatedly matching a sequence with zero elements. Unless you are sure you want to include the case of zero elements, you should always use double blanks rather than triple blanks.

_	any single expression
$x\_$	any single expression, to be named x
__	any sequence of one or more expressions
$x\_\_$	sequence named x
$x\_\_h$	sequence of expressions, all of whose heads are h
$x\_\_\_$	sequence of zero or more expressions
$x\_\_\_h$	sequence of zero or more expressions, all of whose heads are h

More kinds of pattern objects.

When you use multiple blanks, there are often several matches that are possible for a particular expression. In general, *Mathematica* tries first those matches that assign the shortest sequences of arguments to the first multiple blanks that appear in the pattern.

Using the trick of adding a condition which prints but always fails, you can see the sequence of matches that *Mathematica* tries.

```
In[4]:= f[a, b, c, d, e] /. f[x__, y__] :> q /; Print[{x}, {y}]

{a}{b, c, d, e}
{a, b}{c, d, e}
{a, b, c}{d, e}
{a, b, c, d}{e}

Out[4]= f[a, b, c, d, e]
```

NumberQ ▪ IntegerQ ▪ Positive ▪ Negative ▪ NonNegative ▪ VectorQ ▪ MatrixQ ▪ PolynomialQ ▪ TrueQ ▪ AtomQ ▪ ValueQ

Other *Mathematica* functions, related to tests. (See page xvi).

Pattern ▪ Optional ▪ Repeated ▪ RepeatedNull ▪ PatternTest ▪ Literal ▪ Orderless ▪ Flat ▪ OneIdentity

Other *Mathematica* functions related to patterns. (See page xvi).

27. Transformation Rules and Definitions

■ 27.1 Applying Transformation Rules

expr /. *lhs* -> *rhs*	apply a transformation rule to *expr*
expr /. {*lhs₁* -> *rhs₁*, *lhs₂* -> *rhs₂*, ... }	
	try a sequence of rules on each part of *expr*

$$expr\ /.\ lhs\ \text{->}\ rhs \qquad \text{apply a transformation rule to } expr$$
$$expr\ /.\ \{lhs_1\ \text{->}\ rhs_1,\ lhs_2\ \text{->}\ rhs_2,\ \dots\}$$

Applying transformation rules.

The replacement operator /. (pronounced "slash-dot") applies rules to expressions.

```
In[1]:= x + y /. x -> 3
Out[1]= 3 + y
```

You can give a list of rules to apply. Each rule will be tried once on each part of the expression.

```
In[2]:= x + y /. {x -> a, y -> b}
Out[2]= a + b
```

expr /. {*rules₁*, *rules₂*, ... }	give a list of the results from applying each of the *rulesᵢ* to *expr*

Applying lists of transformation rules.

If you give a list of lists of rules, you get a list of results.

```
In[3]:= x + y /. {{x -> 1, y -> 2}, {x -> 4, y -> 2}}
Out[3]= {3, 6}
```

Functions such as Solve and NSolve return lists whose elements are lists of rules, each representing a solution.

```
In[4]:= Solve[x^3 - 5x^2 +2x + 8 == 0, x]
Out[4]= {{x -> -1}, {x -> 2}, {x -> 4}}
```

When you apply these rules, you get a list of results, one corresponding to each solution.

```
In[5]:= x^2 + 6 /. %
Out[5]= {7, 10, 22}
```

When you use *expr* /. *rules*, each rule is tried in turn on each part of *expr*. As soon as a rule applies, the appropriate transformation is made, and the resulting part is returned.

The rule for x^3 is tried first; if it does not apply, the rule for x^n_ is used.

```
In[6]:= {x^2, x^3, x^4} /. {x^3 -> u, x^n_ -> p[n]}
Out[6]= {p[2], u, p[4]}
```

A result is returned as soon as the rule has been applied, so the inner instance of h is not replaced.

```
In[7]:= h[x + h[y]] /. h[u_] -> u^2
Out[7]= (x + h[y])^2
```

The replacement *expr* /. *rules* tries each rule just once on each part of *expr*.

Here is the result when x is taken to be 1 + a.

```
In[7]:= dlog[1 + a]
Out[7]= 2 Cot[1 + a] Log[Sin[1 + a]]
```

An important point to notice in the example above is that there is nothing special about the name x that appears in the x_ pattern. It is just a symbol, indistinguishable from an x that appears in any other expression.

$f[x\_]$ = *expr*	define a function which gives the value *expr* for any particular value of x

Defining functions for evaluating expressions.

You can use = and := not only to define functions, but also to assign values to variables. If you type x = *value*, then *value* is immediately evaluated, and the result is assigned to x. On the other hand, if you type x := *value*, then *value* is not immediately evaluated. Instead, it is maintained in an unevaluated form, and is evaluated afresh each time x is used.

This evaluates Random[ ] to find a pseudorandom number, then assigns this number to r1.

```
In[8]:= r1 = Random[ ]
Out[8]= 0.0560708
```

Here Random[ ] is maintained in an unevaluated form, to be evaluated afresh each time r2 is used.

```
In[9]:= r2 := Random[ ]
```

Here are values for r1 and r2.

```
In[10]:= {r1, r2}
Out[10]= {0.0560708, 0.6303}
```

The value of r1 never changes. Every time r2 is used, however, a new pseudorandom number is generated.

```
In[11]:= {r1, r2}
Out[11]= {0.0560708, 0.359894}
```

The distinction between immediate and delayed assignments is particularly important when you set up chains of assignments.

This defines a to be 1.

```
In[12]:= a = 1
Out[12]= 1
```

Here a + 2 is evaluated to give 3, and the result is assigned to be the value of ri.

```
In[13]:= ri = a + 2
Out[13]= 3
```

Here a + 2 is maintained in an unevaluated form, to be evaluated every time the value of rd is requested.

```
In[14]:= rd := a + 2
```

In this case, ri and rd give the same values.

```
In[15]:= {ri, rd}
Out[15]= {3, 3}
```

Now the value of a is changed.

$In[16]:= \mathbf{a = 2}$

$Out[16]= 2$

Now rd uses the new value for a, while ri keeps its original value.

$In[17]:= \mathbf{\{ri, rd\}}$

$Out[17]= \{3, 4\}$

You can use delayed assignments such as $t := rhs$ to set up variables whose values you can find in a variety of different "environments". Every time you ask for t, the expression rhs is evaluated using the current values of the objects on which it depends.

The right-hand side of the delayed assignment is maintained in an unevaluated form.

$In[18]:= \mathbf{t := \{a, Factor[x^a - 1]\}}$

This sets a to 4, then finds the value of t.

$In[19]:= \mathbf{a = 4; t}$

$Out[19]= \{4, (-1 + x) (1 + x) (1 + x^2)\}$

Here a is 6.

$In[20]:= \mathbf{a = 6; t}$

$Out[20]= \{6, (-1 + x) (1 + x) (1 - x + x^2) (1 + x + x^2)\}$

In the example above, the symbol a acts as a "global variable", whose value affects the value of t. When you have a large number of parameters, many of which change only occasionally, you may find this kind of setup convenient. However, you should realize that implicit or hidden dependence of one variable on others can often become quite confusing. When possible, you should make all dependencies explicit, by defining functions which take all necessary parameters as arguments.

lhs -> *rhs*	*rhs* is evaluated when the rule is given
lhs :> *rhs*	*rhs* is evaluated when the rule is used

Two types of transformation rules in *Mathematica*.

Just as you can make immediate and delayed assignments in *Mathematica*, so you can also set up immediate and delayed transformation rules.

The right-hand side of this rule is evaluated when you give the rule.

$In[21]:= \mathbf{f[x\_] \rightarrow Expand[(1 + x)^2]}$

$Out[21]= f[x\_] \rightarrow 1 + 2 x + x^2$

A rule like this is probably not particularly useful.

$In[22]:= \mathbf{f[x\_] \rightarrow Expand[x]}$

$Out[22]= f[x\_] \rightarrow x$

Here the right-hand side of the rule is maintained in an unevaluated form, to be evaluated every time the rule is used.

$In[23]:= \mathbf{f[x\_] :> Expand[x]}$

$Out[23]= f[x\_] :> Expand[x]$

Applying the rule causes the expansion $In[24]:= f[(1 + p)^2] /. f[x_] :> Expand[x]$
to be done.

$$Out[24]= 1 + 2 p + p^2$$

In analogy with assignments, you should typically use -> when you want to replace an expression with a definite value, and you should use :> when you want to give a command for finding the value.

■ 27.6 Functions That Remember Values They Have Found

When you make a function definition using :=, the value of the function is recomputed every time you ask for it. In some kinds of calculations, you may end up asking for the same function value many times. You can save time in these cases by having *Mathematica* remember all the function values it finds. Here is an "idiom" for defining a function that does this.

$f[x_] := f[x] = rhs$	define a function which remembers values that it finds

Defining a function that remembers values it finds.

This defines a function f which stores $In[1]:= f[x_] := f[x] = f[x - 1] + f[x - 2]$
all values that it finds.

Here are the end conditions for the $In[2]:= f[0] = f[1] = 1$
recursive function f.

$Out[2]= 1$

Here is the original definition of f. $In[3]:= ?f$

Global`f

f[0] = 1

f[1] = 1

f[x_] := f[x] = f[x - 1] + f[x - 2]

This computes f[5]. The computation $In[3]:= f[5]$
involves finding the sequence of values
f[5], f[4], ... f[2].

$Out[3]= 8$

All the values of f found so far are $In[4]:= ?f$
explicitly stored.

Global`f

f[0] = 1

f[1] = 1

f[2] = 2

f[3] = 3

f[4] = 5

f[5] = 8

f[x_] := f[x] = f[x - 1] + f[x - 2]

Expanded a
one you decid
automatically
and Factor th

Here is a list of t
are mathematica

You can write bc
form just by app
form, the equalit
obvious.

You can also see
are equal by wri
factored form.

Although it
may wonder v

There is a k
not always pc
two arbitrarily

In a sense,
sions to a stan
The fact that
equality of ex;

■ **28.3 The 5**

This section de
dure is the on
such as those
non-standard

In the stand
evaluates each
which the san

The three Print
in turn, each prii
returning the val

If you ask for f[5] again, *Mathematica* can just look up the value immediately; it does not have to recompute it.

```
In[4]:= f[5]
Out[4]= 8
```

You can see how a definition like f[x_] := f[x] = f[x-1] + f[x-2] works. The function f[x_] is defined to be the "program" f[x] = f[x-1] + f[x-2]. When you ask for a value of the function f, the "program" is executed. The program first calculates the value of f[x-1] + f[x-2], then saves the result as f[x].

It is often a good idea to use functions that remember values when you implement mathematical *recursion relations* in *Mathematica*. In a typical case, a recursion relation gives the value of a function f with an integer argument x in terms of values of the same function with arguments $x-1$, $x-2$, etc. The Fibonacci function definition $f(x) = f(x-1)+f(x-2)$ used above is an example of this kind of recursion relation. The point is that if you calculate say $f(10)$ by just applying the recursion relation over and over again, you end up having to recalculate quantities like $f(5)$ many times. In a case like this, it is therefore better just to *remember* the value of $f(5)$, and look it up when you need it, rather than having to recalculate it.

There is of course a trade-off involved in remembering values. It is faster to find a particular value, but it takes more memory space to store all of them. You should usually define functions to remember values only if the total number of different values that will be produced is comparatively small, or the expense of recomputing them is very great.

Increment ▪ AddTo ▪ Decrement ▪ SubtractFrom ▪ PreIncrement ▪ PreDecrement ▪ TimesBy ▪ DivideBy ▪ AppendTo ▪ PrependTo ▪ TagSet ▪ TagSetDelayed ▪ TagUnset ▪ UpSet ▪ UpSetDelayed ▪ Protect ▪ Unprotect ▪ Definition ▪ FullDefinition ▪ DownValues ▪ UpValues ▪ ReplaceAll ▪ ReplaceRepeated

Other *Mathematica* functions related to assignments and rules. (See page xvi.)

for all these
Plus are set

Through the b
this expressior
unparenthesiz

Whenever
invocations

A functic

like a + c
to put all si
all the term

Mathematica s
into a standar

Two important pr

There ar
if two expr

When the tw
standard ord
seen to be eq
leaving the r

You cou
orderings (
ficient proc

One mi;
sions to a s
quite easy

For poly
purposes.
Mathematic
add and s

There is
Factor, y(
ful if you

This assigns the symbol ps to be Plus.

```
In[2]:= ps = Plus
Out[2]= Plus
```

The head ps is evaluated first, so this expression behaves just like a sum of terms.

```
In[3]:= ps[ps[a, b], c]
Out[3]= a + b + c
```

As soon as *Mathematica* has evaluated the head of an expression, it sees whether the head is a symbol that has the attributes of being flat, orderless or listable. If this is the case, then immediately after evaluating the elements of the expression *Mathematica* performs the transformations associated with these attributes.

The next step in the standard evaluation procedure is to use definitions that *Mathematica* knows for the expression it is evaluating. *Mathematica* first tries to use definitions that you have made, and if there are none that apply, it tries built-in definitions.

If *Mathematica* finds a definition that applies, it performs the corresponding transformation on the expression. The result is another expression, which must then in turn be evaluated according to the standard evaluation procedure.

- Evaluate the head of the expression.

- Evaluate each element in turn.

- Apply transformations associated with the attributes flat, orderless and listable.

- Apply any definitions that you have given.

- Apply any built-in definitions.

- Evaluate the result.

The standard evaluation procedure.

As discussed in Section 28.1, *Mathematica* follows the principle that each expression is evaluated until no further definitions apply. This means that *Mathematica* must continue re-evaluating results until it gets an expression which remains unchanged through the evaluation procedure.

Here is an example that shows how the standard evaluation procedure works on a simple expression. We assume that a = 7.

```
        2 a x + a^2 + 1    here is the original expression
Plus[Times[2, a, x], Power[a, 2], 1]
                         this is the internal form
```

```
        Times[2, a, x]    this is evaluated first
        Times[2, 7, x]    a is evaluated to give 7
        Times[14, x]      built-in definitions for Times give this result
```

```
        Power[a, 2]       this is evaluated next
        Power[7, 2]       here is the result after evaluating a
              49          built-in definitions for Power give this result
```

```
Plus[Times[14, x], 49, 1]    here is the result after the arguments of Plus have been
                             evaluated
    Plus[50, Times[14, x]]   built-in definitions for Plus give this result
```

```
        50 + 14 x         the result is printed like this
```

A simple example of evaluation in *Mathematica*.

■ 28.4 Relational and Logical Operators

$x == y$	equal
$x != y$	unequal
$x > y$	greater than
$x >= y$	greater than or equal to
$x < y$	less than
$x <= y$	less than or equal to
$x == y == z$	all equal
$x != y != z$	all unequal (distinct)
$x > y > z$, etc.	strictly decreasing, etc.

Relational operators.

This tests whether 10 is less than 7. The result is False.

```
In[1]:= 10 < 7
Out[1]= False
```

Not all of these numbers are unequal, so this gives False.

```
In[2]:= 3 != 2 != 3
Out[2]= False
```

You can mix < and <=.

```
In[3]:= 3 < 5 <= 6
Out[3]= True
```

Mathematica does not know whether this is true or false.

```
In[4]:= x > y
Out[4]= x > y
```

$!p$	not
p && q && ...	and
p || q || ...	or
Xor[p, q, ...]	exclusive or
If[p, *then*, *else*]	give *then* if p is True, and *else* if p is False
LogicalExpand[*expr*]	expand out logical expressions

Logical operations.

Both tests give True, so the result is True.

```
In[5]:= 7 > 4 && 2 != 3
Out[5]= True
```

You should remember that the logical operations ==, && and || are all *double characters* in *Mathematica*. (If you have used the C programming language, you will recognize this notation as being the same as in C.)

Mathematica does not know whether this is true or false.

```
In[6]:= p && q
Out[6]= p && q
```

Mathematica leaves this expression unchanged.

```
In[7]:= (p || q) && !(r || s)
Out[7]= (p || q) && !(r || s)
```

You can use LogicalExpand to expand out the terms.

```
In[8]:= LogicalExpand[ % ]
Out[8]= p && !r && !s || q && !r && !s
```

■ 28.5 Conditionals

Mathematica provides various ways to set up *conditionals*, which specify that particular expressions should be evaluated only if certain conditions hold.

lhs := *rhs* /; *test*	use the definition only if *test* evaluates to True
If[*test*, *then*, *else*]	evaluate *then* if *test* is True, and *else* if it is False
Which[*test₁*, *value₁*, *test₂*, ...]	evaluate the *testᵢ* in turn, giving the value associated with the first one that is True
Switch[*expr*, *form₁*, *value₁*, *form₂*, ...]	compare *expr* with each of the *formᵢ*, giving the value associated with the first form it matches
Switch[*expr*, *form₁*, *value₁*, *form₂*, ... , _, *def*]	use *def* as a default value

Conditional constructs.

The test gives False, so the *"else"* expression y is returned.

```
In[1]:= If[7 > 8, x, y]
Out[1]= y
```

Only the *"else"* expression is evaluated here. The *"then"* expression is ignored.

```
In[2]:= If[7 > 8, Print[x], Print[y]]
y
```

When you write programs in *Mathematica*, you will often have a choice between making a single definition whose right-hand side involves several branches controlled by If functions, or making several

$expr_1$ && $expr_2$ && $expr_3$	evaluate until one of the $expr_i$ is found to be False
$expr_1$ || $expr_2$ || $expr_3$	evaluate until one of the $expr_i$ is found to be True

Evaluation of logical expressions.

This function involves a combination of two tests.	`In[19]:= t[x_] := (x != 0 && 1/x < 3)`
Here both tests are evaluated.	`In[20]:= t[2]`
	`Out[20]= True`
Here the first test yields False, so the second test is not tried. The second test would involve 1/0, and would generate an error.	`In[21]:= t[0]`
	`Out[21]= False`

The way that *Mathematica* evaluates logical expressions allows you to combine sequences of tests where later tests may make sense only if the earlier ones are satisfied. The behavior, which is analogous to that found in languages such as C, is convenient in constructing many kinds of *Mathematica* programs.

■ 28.6 Loops and Control Structures

The execution of a *Mathematica* program involves the evaluation of a sequence of *Mathematica* expressions. In simple programs, the expressions to be evaluated may be separated by semicolons, and evaluated one after another. Often, however, you need to evaluate expressions several times, in some kind of "loop".

Do[*expr*, {*i*, *imax*}]	evaluate *expr* repetitively, with *i* varying from 1 to *imax* in steps of 1
Do[*expr*, {*i*, *imin*, *imax*, *di*}]	evaluate *expr* with *i* varying from *imin* to *imax* in steps of *di*
Do[*expr*, {*n*}]	evaluate *expr* *n* times

Simple looping constructs.

This evaluates Print[i^2], with i running from 1 to 4.	`In[1]:= Do[Print[i^2], {i, 4}]`
	`1`
	`4`
	`9`
	`16`

This executes an assignment for t in a loop with k running from 2 to 6 in steps of 2.

$In[2]:=$ `t = x; Do[t = 1/(1 + k t), {k, 2, 6, 2}]; t`

$$Out[2]= \cfrac{1}{1 + \cfrac{6}{1 + \cfrac{4}{1 + 2 x}}}$$

The way iteration is specified in Do is exactly the same as in functions like Table and Sum. Just as in those functions, you can set up several nested loops by giving a sequence of iteration specifications to Do.

This loops over values of i from 1 to 4, and for each value of i, loops over j from 1 to i-1.

$In[3]:=$ `Do[Print[{i,j}], {i, 4}, {j, i-1}]`

```
{2, 1}
{3, 1}
{3, 2}
{4, 1}
{4, 2}
{4, 3}
```

Sometimes you may want to repeat a particular operation a certain number of times, without changing the value of an iteration variable. You can specify this kind of repetition in Do just as you can in Table and other iteration functions.

This repeats the assignment t = 1 + t^2 three times.

$In[4]:=$ `t = x; Do[t = 1 + t^2, {3}]; t`

$$Out[4]= 1 + (1 + (1 + x^2)^2)^2$$

You can put a procedure inside Do.

$In[5]:=$ `t = 67; Do[Print[t]; t = Floor[t/2], {3}]`

```
67
33
16
```

Nest[*f*, *expr*, *n*]	apply *f* to *expr* *n* times
FixedPoint[*f*, *expr*]	start with *expr*, and apply *f* repeatedly until the result no longer changes

Applying functions repetitively.

Do allows you to repeat operations by evaluating a particular expression many times with different values for iteration variables. Often, however, you can make more elegant and efficient programs using the functional programming constructs discussed in Section 25.2. Nest[*f*, *x*, *n*], for example, allows you to apply a function repeatedly to an expression.

This nests f three times.

$In[6]:=$ `Nest[f, x, 3]`

$Out[6]=$ `f[f[f[x]]]`

By nesting a pure function, you can get the same result as in the example with Do above.

In[7]:= **Nest[Function[t, 1 + t^2], x, 3]**

$$Out[7]= 1 + (1 + (1 + x^2)^2)^2$$

Nest allows you to apply a function a specified number of times. Sometimes, however, you may simply want to go on applying a function until the results you get no longer change. You can do this using FixedPoint[*f*, *x*].

FixedPoint goes on applying a function until the result no longer changes.

In[8]:= **FixedPoint[Function[t, Print[t]; Floor[t/2]], 67]**

```
67
33
16
8
4
2
1
0
```

Out[8]= 0

You can use FixedPoint to imitate the evaluation process in *Mathematica*. In general, FixedPoint goes on until two successive results it gets are the same.

While[*test*, *body*]	evaluate *body* repetitively, so long as *test* is True
For[*start*, *test*, *incr*, *body*]	evaluate *start*, then repetitively evaluate *expr* and *incr*, until *test* fails

General loop constructs.

Functions like Do, Nest and FixedPoint provide rather structured ways to make loops in *Mathematica* programs. Sometimes, however, you need to create loops with less structure. In such cases, you may find it convenient to use the functions While and For, which perform operations repeatedly, stopping when a specified condition fails to be true.

The While loop continues until the condition fails.

In[9]:= **n = 17; While[(n = Floor[n/2]) != 0, Print[n]]**

```
8
4
2
1
```

The functions While and For in *Mathematica* are similar to the control structures while and for in languages such as C. Notice, however, that there are a number of important differences. For example, the roles of comma and semicolon are reversed in *Mathematica* For loops relative to those in C.

This is a very common form for a For loop.

In[10]:= **For[i=1, i < 4, i = i + 1, Print[i]]**

```
1
2
3
```

Here is a more complicated For loop. Notice that the loop terminates as soon as the test i^2 < 10 fails.

$In[11]:=$ **For[i=1; t=x, i^2 < 10, i = i + 1, t = t^2 + i;**
                                 Print[t]]

$$1 + x^2$$

$$2 + (1 + x^2)^2$$

$$3 + (2 + (1 + x^2)^2)^2$$

In *Mathematica*, both While and For always evaluate the loop test before evaluating the body of the loop. As soon as the loop test fails to be True, While and For terminate. The body of the loop is thus only evaluated in situations where the loop test is True.

The loop test fails immediately, so the body of the loop is never evaluated. ·

$In[12]:=$ **While[False, Print[x]]**

In a While or For loop, or in general in any *Mathematica* procedure, the *Mathematica* expressions you give are evaluated in a definite sequence. You can think of this sequence as defining the "flow of control" in the execution of a *Mathematica* program.

In most cases, you should try to keep the flow of control in your *Mathematica* programs as simple as possible. The more the flow of control depends for example on specific values generated during the execution of the program, the more difficult you will typically find it to understand the structure and operation of the program.

Functional programming constructs typically involve very simple flow of control. While and For loops are always more complicated, since they are set up to make the flow of control depend on the values of the expressions given as tests. Nevertheless, even in such loops, the flow of control does not usually depend on the values of expressions given in the body of the loop.

■ 28.7 Modules and Local Variables

Mathematica normally assumes that all your variables are *global*. This means that every time you use a name like x, *Mathematica* normally assumes that you are referring to the *same* object.

Particularly when you write programs, however, you may not want all your variables to be global. You may, for example, want to use the name x to refer to two quite different variables in two different programs. In this case, you need the x in each program to be treated as a *local* variable.

You can set up local variables in *Mathematica* using *modules*. Within each module, you can give a list of variables which are to be treated as local to the module.

Module[{x, y, ... }, *body*]	a module with local variables x, y, ...

Creating modules in *Mathematica*.

This defines the global variable t to have value 17.

In[1]:= **t = 17**

Out[1]= 17

The t inside the module is local, so it can be treated independently of the global t.

In[2]:= **Module[{t}, t=8; Print[t]]**

8

The global t still has value 17.

In[3]:= **t**

Out[3]= 17

The most common way that modules are used is to set up temporary or intermediate variables inside functions you define. It is important to make sure that such variables are kept local. If they are not, then you will run into trouble whenever their names happen to coincide with the names of other variables.

The intermediate variable t is specified to be local to the module.

In[4]:= **f[v_] := Module[{t}, t = (1 + v)^2; t = Expand[t]]**

This runs the function f.

In[5]:= **f[a + b]**

Out[5]= $1 + 2\,a + a^2 + 2\,b + 2\,a\,b + b^2$

The global t still has value 17.

In[6]:= **t**

Out[6]= 17

When you set up a local variable in a module, *Mathematica* initially assigns no value to the variable. This means that you can use the variable in a purely symbolic way, even if there was a global value defined for the variable outside the module.

This uses the global value of t defined above, and so yields a number.

In[7]:= **Expand[(1 + t)^3]**

Out[7]= 5832

Here Length simply receives a number as its argument.

In[8]:= **Length[Expand[(1 + t)^3]]**

Out[8]= 0

The local variable t has no value, so it acts as a symbol, and Expand produces the anticipated algebraic result.

In[9]:= **Module[{t}, Length[Expand[(1 + t)^3]]]**

Out[9]= 4

Module [{$x = x_0$, $y = y_0$, ... }, *body*]
          a module with initial values for local variables

Assigning initial values to local variables.

This specifies t to be a local variable, with initial value u.

In[10]:= **g[u_] := Module[{ t = u }, t = t + t/(1 + u)]**

This uses the definition of **g**.

$In[11]:=$ **g[a]**

$$Out[11]= a + \frac{a}{1 + a}$$

You can define initial values for any of the local variables in a module. The initial values are always evaluated before the module is executed. As a result, even if a variable x is defined as local to the module, the global x will be used if it appears in an expression for an initial value.

The initial value of u is taken to be the global value of t.

$In[12]:=$ **Module[{t = 6, u = t}, {t, u}]**

$Out[12]=$ {6, 17}

---

lhs := Module[*vars*, *rhs* /; *cond*]   share local variables between *rhs* and *cond*

Using local variables in definitions with conditions.

When you set up /; conditions for definitions, you often need to introduce temporary variables. In many cases, you may want to share these temporary variables with the body of the right-hand side of the definition. *Mathematica* allows you to enclose the whole right-hand side of your definition in a module, including the condition.

This defines a function with a condition attached.

$In[13]:=$ **h[x_] := Module[{t}, t^2 - 1 /; (t = x - 4) > 1]**

Mathematica shares the value of the local variable t between the condition and the body of the right-hand side.

$In[14]:=$ **h[10]**

$Out[14]=$ 35

■ 28.8 Generating Output

In the most common way of using *Mathematica* you never in fact explicitly have to issue a command to generate output. Usually, *Mathematica* automatically prints out the final result that it gets from processing input you gave. Sometimes, however, you may want to get *Mathematica* to print out expressions at intermediate stages in its operation. You can do this using the function Print.

Print[*expr*$_1$, *expr*$_2$, ...]   print the *expr*$_i$, with no spaces in between, but with a newline (line feed) at the end

---

Printing expressions.

Each Print generates a newline.

$In[1]:=$ **Print[a, b]; Print[c]**

ab
c

This prints a table of the first five integers and their squares.

```
In[2]:= Do[Print[i, "  ", i^2], {i, 5}]
1  1
2  4
3  9
4  16
5  25
```

Print simply takes the arguments you give, and prints them out one after the other, with no spaces in between. In many cases, you will need to print output in a more complicated format. You can do this by giving an output form as an argument to Print.

This prints the matrix in the form of a table.

```
In[3]:= Print[TableForm[{{1, 2}, {3, 4}}]]
1    2

3    4
```

The output generated by Print is usually given in the standard *Mathematica* output format. You can however explicitly specify that some other output format should be used.

This prints output in *Mathematica* input form.

```
In[4]:= Print[InputForm[a^2 + b^2]]
a^2 + b^2
```

With ▪ Unique ▪ Block ▪ $ModuleNumber ▪ $SessionID

Other *Mathematica* functions related to scoping. (See page xvi.)

SameTest ▪ Break ▪ Continue ▪ Goto ▪ Label ▪ Return ▪ Throw ▪ Catch ▪ Check ▪
CheckAbort ▪ Interrupt ▪ Abort ▪ TimeConstrained ▪ MemoryConstrained ▪
AbortProtect ▪ Input ▪ Pause

Other *Mathematica* functions related to flow control. (See page xvi.)

Unevaluated ▪ Literal ▪ Hold ▪ HoldForm ▪ ReleaseHold ▪ HeldPart ▪
ReplaceHeldPart ▪ ToString ▪ ToExpression ▪ Update ▪ $IterationLimit ▪
$RecursionLimit ▪ $MaxPrecision

Other *Mathematica* functions, related to evaluation control. (See page xvi.)

Trace ▪ TraceDialog ▪ TracePrint ▪ TraceScan ▪ Dialog ▪ Stack ▪ StackBegin ▪ StackInhibit ▪ StackComplete ▪ TraceDepth ▪ TraceForward ▪ TraceBackward ▪ TraceAbove ▪ TraceOriginal ▪ TraceInternal ▪ MatchLocalNames

Other *Mathematica* functions, related to debugging. (See page xvi.)

Attributes ▪ SetAttributes ▪ ClearAttributes ▪ ClearAll ▪ Orderless ▪ Flat ▪ OneIdentity ▪ Listable ▪ Constant ▪ Protected ▪ Locked ▪ ReadProtected ▪ HoldFirst ▪ HoldRest ▪ HoldAll ▪ Temporary ▪ Stub

Other *Mathematica* functions, related to attributes. (See page xvi.)

Interlude 3. **Other Capabilities**

29. Other Capabilities

■ 29.1 Reading and Writing *Mathematica* Files

On systems with notebook-based interfaces, you will usually find it easier to save whole notebooks, rather than saving specific *Mathematica* expressions and definitions. The standard notebook interface for *Mathematica* allows you to specify certain cells of *Mathematica* input as being "initialization cells". These cells can contain definitions and results that are automatically set up again whenever you open the notebook.

You can also use files on your computer system to store definitions and results from *Mathematica*. The most general approach is to store everything as plain text that is appropriate for input to *Mathematica*. With this approach, a version of *Mathematica* running on one computer system produces files that can be read by a version running on any computer system. In addition, such files can be manipulated by other standard programs, such as text editors.

<<*name*	read in a plain text file of *Mathematica* input
expr >> *name*	output *expr* to a file as plain text
expr >>> *name*	append *expr* to a file
!!*name*	display the contents of a plain text file

Reading and writing files.

This expands $(x + y)^3$, and outputs the result to a file called `tmp`.	`In[1]:= Expand[ (x + y)^3 ]  >> tmp`

Here are the contents of `tmp`. They can be used directly as input for *Mathematica*.	`In[2]:= !!tmp`
	
	`x^3 + 3*x^2*y + 3*x*y^2 + y^3`

This reads in `tmp`, evaluating the *Mathematica* input it contains.	`In[2]:= <<tmp` $Out[2]= x^3 + 3 x^2 y + 3 x y^2 + y^3$

The redirection operators >> and >>> are convenient for storing results you get from *Mathematica*. The function Save["*name*", f, g, ...] allows you to save definitions for variables and functions.

Save["*name*", f, g, ...]	save definitions for variables or functions in a file

Saving definitions in plain text files.

Here is a definition for a function f.	`In[3]:= f[x_] := x^2 + c`

This gives c the value 17.

```
In[4]:= c = 17

Out[4]= 17
```

This saves the definition of f in the file ftmp.

```
In[5]:= Save["ftmp", f]
```

Mathematica automatically saves both the actual definition of f, and the definition of c on which it depends.

```
In[6]:= !!ftmp

f[x_] := x^2 + c

c = 17
```

This clears the definitions of f and c.

```
In[6]:= Clear[f, c]
```

You can reinstate the definitions you saved simply by reading in the file ftmp.

```
In[7]:= <<ftmp

Out[7]= 17
```

```
Directory ▪ SetDirectory ▪ ResetDirectory ▪ DirectoryStack ▪ ParentDirectory ▪
HomeDirectory ▪ $Path ▪ FileNames ▪ ContextToFilename ▪ CopyFile ▪ RenameFile ▪
DeleteFile ▪ FileByteCount ▪ FileDate ▪ SetFileDate ▪ FileType ▪
CreateDirectory ▪ DeleteDirectory ▪ RenameDirectory ▪ CopyDirectory ▪
OpenTemporary ▪ Run ▪ RunThrough ▪ $TemporaryPrefix ▪ $Version ▪
$VersionNumber ▪ $ReleaseNumber ▪ $CreationDate ▪ $DumpDates ▪ Environment ▪
$System ▪ $OperatingSystem ▪ $MachineType ▪ $MachineName ▪ $MachineID ▪
$DumpSupported ▪ $LinkSupported ▪ $PipeSupported
```

Mathematica options related to the file system. (See page xvi.)

■ 29.2 Reading Data

With <<, you can read files which contain *Mathematica* expressions given in input form. Sometimes, however, you may instead need to read files of *data* in other formats. For example, you may have data generated by an external program which consists of a sequence of numbers separated by spaces. This data cannot be read directly as *Mathematica* input. However, the function ReadList can take such data from a file and convert it to a *Mathematica* list.

ReadList["*file*", Number]	read a sequence of numbers from a file, and put them in a *Mathematica* list

Reading numbers from a file.

Here is a file of numbers.   *In[1]:=* `!!numbers`

                                                     ```
                                                     56.5    -23    14
                                                     23       78    12.78
                                                     ```

This reads all the numbers in the file, and   *In[1]:=* `ReadList["numbers", Number]`
returns a list of them.
                                                     Out[1]= `{56.5, -23, 14, 23, 78, 12.78}`

`ReadList["`*file*`", {Number, Number}]`

> read numbers from a file, putting each successive pair into a separate list

`ReadList["`*file*`", Table[Number, {`*n*`}]]`

> put each successive block of *n* numbers in a separate list

`ReadList["`*file*`", Number, RecordLists -> True]`

> put all the numbers on each line of the file into a separate list

---

Reading blocks of numbers.

This puts each successive pair of   *In[2]:=* `ReadList["numbers", {Number, Number}]`
numbers from the file into a separate list.
                                                     Out[2]= `{{56.5, -23}, {14, 23}, {78, 12.78}}`

This makes each line in the file into a   *In[3]:=* `ReadList["numbers", Number, RecordLists -> True]`
separate list.
                                                     Out[3]= `{{56.5, -23, 14}, {23, 78, 12.78}}`

`ReadList` can handle numbers which are given in Fortran-like "E" notation. Thus, for example, `ReadList` will read `2.5E+5` as 2.5×10^5. Note that `ReadList` can handle numbers with any number of digits of precision.

Here is a file containing numbers in   *In[4]:=* `!!bignum`
Fortran-like "E" notation.
                                                     ```
                                                     4.5E-5     7.8E4
                                                     2.5E2      -8.9
                                                     ```

`ReadList` can handle numbers given in   *In[4]:=* `ReadList["bignum", Number]`
this form.
                                                     Out[4]= `{0.000045, 78000., 250., -8.9}`

`RecordLists` ▪ `RecordSeparators` ▪ `WordSeparators` ▪ `NullRecords` ▪ `NullWords` ▪
`TokenWords` ▪ `Byte` ▪ `Character` ▪ `Expression` ▪ `Record` ▪ `String` ▪ `Word` ▪
`WordSearch` ▪ `AnchoredSearch` ▪ `IgnoreCase` ▪ `InputStream`

Mathematica options related to input. (See page xvi.)

Read ▪ FindList ▪ Find ▪ Skip ▪ EndOfFile ▪ OpenRead ▪ Close ▪ Streams ▪ StreamPosition

Other *Mathematica* functions related to file input. (See page xvi.)

Splice ▪ Display ▪ Write ▪ WriteString ▪ OpenWrite ▪ Encode ▪ OpenAppend ▪ Close

Other *Mathematica* functions related to file output. (See page xvi.)

Install ▪ Uninstall ▪ $Linked ▪ $LinkSupported

Other *Mathematica* functions, related to communicating with other programs. (See page xvi.)

■ 29.3 Strings

While much of what *Mathematica* does involves the structure and meaning of expressions, you can also use *Mathematica* to handle pure strings of text. You can give any string of text in the form "*text*".

"*text*"	a string containing arbitrary text

Text strings.

In the standard output format, *Mathematica* does not explicitly show the quotation marks around text strings. These are included, however, if you ask for the input form.

In the standard *Mathematica* output form, the quotation marks are not included.

```
In[1]:= "Here is some text."
Out[1]= Here is some text.
```

The quotation marks are included in input form.

```
In[2]:= InputForm[%]
Out[2]//InputForm= "Here is some text."
```

The fact that quotation marks around strings are not shown in the standard *Mathematica* output format is important in being able to use strings to create output forms. However, it does have the consequence that a symbol x and a string "x" look the same in the standard output format. You can always see the difference by asking for the input form.

The symbol x and the string "x" are quite different objects, even though they look the same in the standard output format.

```
In[3]:= x != "x"
Out[3]= x != x
```

Here is another family of functions that are similar to `ColumnForm`, `TableForm` and `MatrixForm`.

```
InputForm ▪ OutputForm ▪ CForm ▪ FortranForm ▪ TeXForm ▪ TreeForm ▪ Short ▪
Shallow ▪ Format ▪ StringForm ▪ SequenceForm ▪ HoldForm ▪ Subscripted ▪
Subscript ▪ Superscript ▪ PrecedenceForm ▪ LineBreak ▪ StringBreak ▪
Continuation ▪ Indent ▪ Skeleton ▪ StringSkeleton
```

Other *Mathematica* functions, related to formatting output. (See page xvi.)

```
PageWidth ▪ TotalWidth ▪ FormatType ▪ $PrePrint ▪ StringConversion ▪
$StringConversion ▪ OutputStream ▪ Options ▪ SetOptions ▪ $Output ▪ $Echo ▪
$Messages ▪ $Urgent ▪ $Display ▪ $DisplayFunction ▪ $DefaultFont
```

Mathematica options related to output. (See page xvi.)

Part 4.　**Graphics and Sound**

30. Manipulating Plots

■ 30.1 Redrawing Plots

Mathematica saves information about every plot you produce, so that you can later redraw it. When you redraw plots, you can change some of the options you use.

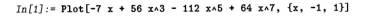

Show[*plot*]	redraw a plot
Show[*plot*, *option* -> *value*]	redraw with options changed

Redrawing plots.

Here is a simple plot. -Graphics- is usually printed on the output line to stand for the information that *Mathematica* saves about the plot.

In[1]:= **Plot[-7 x + 56 x^3 - 112 x^5 + 64 x^7, {x, -1, 1}]**

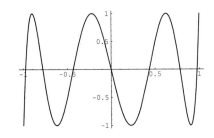

You can redraw the plot from the previous line without having to recalculate it.

In[2]:= **Show[%]**

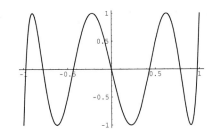

When you redraw the plot, you can change some of the options. This changes the choice of y scale.

In[3]:= **Show[%, PlotRange -> {-1, 2}]**

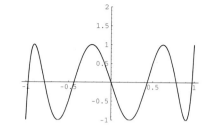

This takes the plot from the previous line, and changes another option in it.

In[4]:= **Show[%, PlotLabel -> "A Chebyshev Polynomial"]**

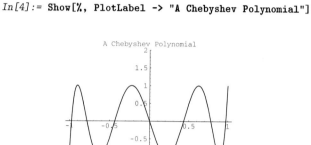

By using Show with a sequence of different options, you can look at the same plot in many different ways. You may want to do this, for example, if you are trying to find the best possible setting of options.

When you make a plot, *Mathematica* saves the list of points it used, together with some other information. Using what is saved, you can redraw plots in many different ways with Show. However, you should realize that no matter what options you specify, Show still has the same basic set of points to work with. So, for example, if you set the options so that *Mathematica* displays a small portion of your original plot magnified, you will probably be able to see the individual sample points that Plot used. Options like PlotPoints can only be set in the original Plot command itself. (*Mathematica* always plots the actual points it has; it avoids using smoothed or splined curves, which can give misleading results in mathematical graphics.)

Here is a simple plot.

In[5]:= `Plot[Cos[x], {x, -Pi, Pi}]`

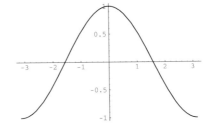

This shows a small region of the plot in a magnified form. At this resolution, you can see the individual line segments that were produced by the original `Plot` command.

In[6]:= `Show[%, PlotRange -> {{0, .3}, {.92, 1}}]`

■ 30.2 Multiple Plots

You can also use `Show` to combine plots. It does not matter whether the plots have the same scales: *Mathematica* will always choose new scales to include the points you want.

`Show[plot_1, plot_2, ... ]`	combine several plots

Combining plots.

This sets gj0 to be a plot of $J_0(x)$ from $x = 0$ to 10.

In[1]:= `gj0 = Plot[BesselJ[0, x], {x, 0, 10}]`

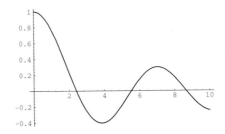

Here is a plot of $Y_1(x)$ from $x = 1$ to 10.   *In[2]:=* **gy1 = Plot[BesselY[1, x], {x, 1, 10}]**

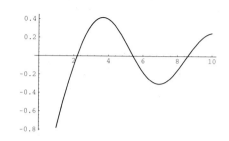

This shows the previous two plots combined into one. Notice that the scale is adjusted appropriately.   *In[3]:=* **gjy = Show[gj0, gy1]**

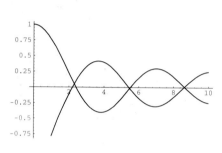

Using Show[*plot₁*, *plot₂*, ...] you can combine several plots into one. GraphicsArray allows you to draw several plots in an array.

Show[GraphicsArray[{*plot₁*, *plot₂*, ... }]]
                          draw several plots side by side

Show[GraphicsArray[{{*plot₁*}, {*plot₂*}, ... }]]
                          draw a column of plots

Show[GraphicsArray[{{*plot₁₁*, *plot₁₂*, ... }, ... }]]
                          draw a rectangular array of plots

Show[GraphicsArray[*plots*, GraphicsSpacing -> {*h*, *v*}]]
                          put the specified horizontal and vertical spacing between
                          the plots

Drawing arrays of plots.

This shows the plots given above in an array.

`In[4]:= Show[GraphicsArray[{{gj0, gjy}, {gy1, gjy}}]]`

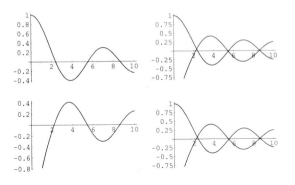

If you redisplay an array of plots using Show, any options you specify will be used by the whole array, rather than for individual plots.

`In[5]:= Show[%, Frame -> True, FrameTicks -> None]`

Here is a way to change options for all the plots in the array.

`In[6]:= Show[ % /. (Ticks -> Automatic) -> (Ticks -> None) ]`

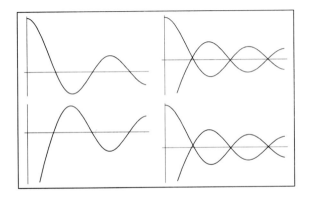

GraphicsArray by default puts a narrow border around each of the plots in the array it gives. You can change the size of this border by setting the option GraphicsSpacing -> {*h*, *v*}. The parameters *h* and *v* give the horizontal and vertical spacings to be used, as fractions of the width and height of the plots.

This increases the horizontal spacing, but decreases the vertical spacing between the plots in the array.

In[7]:= **Show[%, GraphicsSpacing -> {0.3, 0}]**

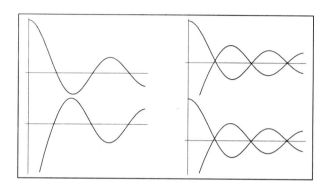

■ 30.3 Making Plots within Plots

Section 30.2 described how you can make regular arrays of plots using GraphicsArray. Using the Rectangle graphics primitive, however, you can combine and superimpose plots in any way.

Rectangle[{*xmin*, *ymin*}, {*xmax*, *ymax*}, *graphics*]
                      render a graphics object within the specified rectangle

Creating a subplot.

Here is a three-dimensional plot.   *In[1]:=* **p3 = Plot3D[Sin[x] Exp[y], {x, -5, 5}, {y, -2, 2}]**

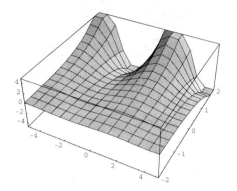

This creates a two-dimensional graphics   *In[2]:=* **Show[Graphics[{Rectangle[{0, 0}, {1, 1}, p3],**
object which contains two copies of the   **Rectangle[{0.8, 0.8}, {1.2, 1.4}, p3]}]]**
three-dimensional plot.

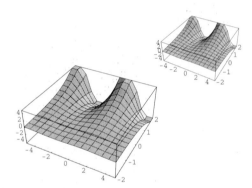

Mathematica can render any graphics object within a `Rectangle`. In all cases, what it puts in the rectangle is a scaled down version of what would be obtained if you displayed the graphics object on its own. Notice that in general the display area for the graphics object will be sized so as to touch at least one pair of edges of the rectangle.

31. Animation and Sound

■ 31.1 Animated Graphics

On many computer systems, *Mathematica* can produce not only static images, but also animated graphics or "movies".

The basic idea in all cases is to generate a sequence of "frames" which can be displayed in rapid succession. You can use the standard *Mathematica* graphics functions described above to produce each frame. The mechanism for displaying the frames as a movie depends on the *Mathematica* interface you are using. With a notebook-based interface, you typically put the frames in a sequence of cells, then select the cells and choose a command to animate them.

When you produce a sequence of frames for a movie, it is important that different frames be consistent. Thus, for example, you should typically give an explicit setting for the PlotRange option, rather than using the default Automatic setting, in order to ensure that the scales used in different frames are the same. If you have three-dimensional graphics with different view points, you should similarly set SphericalRegion -> True in order to ensure that the scaling of different plots is the same.

This generates a list of graphics objects. Setting DisplayFunction -> Identity stops Plot3D from rendering the graphics it produces. Explicitly setting PlotRange ensures that the scale is the same in each piece of graphics.

```
In[1]:= Table[ Plot3D[ BesselJ[0, Sqrt[x^2 + y^2] + t],
                {x, -10, 10}, {y, -10, 10}, Axes -> False,
                PlotRange -> {-0.5, 1.0},
                DisplayFunction -> Identity ],
            {t, 0, 8} ]

Out[1]= {-SurfaceGraphics-, -SurfaceGraphics-,
   -SurfaceGraphics-, -SurfaceGraphics-, -SurfaceGraphics-,
   -SurfaceGraphics-, -SurfaceGraphics-, -SurfaceGraphics-,
   -SurfaceGraphics-}
```

On an appropriate computer system, ShowAnimation[%] would animate the graphics. This partitions the graphics into three rows, and shows the resulting array of images.

```
In[2]:= Show[ GraphicsArray[ Partition[%, 3] ] ]
```

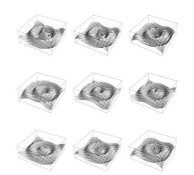

■ 31.2 Sound

On some computer systems, *Mathematica* can produce not only graphics but also sound. *Mathematica* treats graphics and sound in a closely analogous way.

For example, just as you can use Plot[*f*, {*x*, *xmin*, *xmax*}] to plot a function, so also you can use Play[*f*, {*t*, 0, *tmax*}] to "play" a function. Play takes the function to define the waveform for a sound: the values of the function give the amplitude of the sound as a function of time.

Play[*f*, {*t*, 0, *tmax*}]	play a sound with amplitude *f* as a function of time *t* in seconds

Playing a function.

On a suitable computer system, this plays a pure tone with a frequency of 440 hertz for one second.

```
In[1]:= Play[Sin[2Pi 440 t], {t, 0, 1}]

Out[1]= -Sound-
```

Sounds produced by Play can have any waveform. They do not, for example, have to consist of a collection of harmonic pieces. In general, the amplitude function you give to Play specifies the instantaneous signal associated with the sound. This signal is typically converted to a voltage, and ultimately to a displacement. Note that *amplitude* is sometimes defined to be the *peak* signal associated with a sound; in *Mathematica*, it is always the *instantaneous* signal as a function of time.

This plays a more complex sound.

```
In[2]:= Play[ Sin[700 t + 25 t Sin[350 t]], {t, 0, 4} ]

Out[2]= -Sound-
```

Play is set up so that the time variable that appears in it is always measured in absolute seconds. When a sound is actually played, its amplitude is sampled a certain number of times every second. You can specify the sample rate by setting the option SampleRate.

Play[*f*, {*t*, 0, *tmax*}, SampleRate -> *r*]	play a sound, sampling it *r* times a second

Specifying the sample rate for a sound.

In general, the higher the sample rate, the better high-frequency components in the sound will be rendered. A sample rate of *r* typically allows frequencies up to *r*/2 hertz. The human auditory system can typically perceive sounds in the frequency range 20 to 22000 hertz (depending somewhat on age and sex). The fundamental frequencies for the 88 notes on a piano range from 27.5 to 4096 hertz.

The standard sample rate used for compact disk players is 44100. The effective sample rate in a typical telephone system is around 8000. On most computer systems, the default sample rate used by *Mathematica* is around 8000.

You can use Play[{f_1, f_2}, ...] to produce stereo sound. In general, *Mathematica* supports any number of sound channels.

ListPlay[{a_1, a_2, ... }, SampleRate -> r]

        play a sound with a sequence of amplitude levels

Playing sampled sounds.

The function ListPlay allows you simply to give a list of values which are taken to be sound amplitudes sampled at a certain rate.

When sounds are actually rendered by *Mathematica*, only a certain range of amplitudes is allowed. The option PlayRange in Play and ListPlay specifies how the amplitudes you give should be scaled to fit in the allowed range. The settings for this option are analogous to those for the PlotRange graphics option discussed on page 86.

PlayRange -> Automatic (default)

        use an internal procedure to scale amplitudes

    PlayRange -> All   scale so that all amplitudes fit in the allowed range

PlayRange -> {*amin*, *amax*}   make amplitudes between *amin* and *amax* fit in the allowed range, and clip others

---

Specifying the scaling of sound amplitudes.

While it is often convenient to use the default setting PlayRange -> Automatic, you should realize that Play may run significantly faster if you give an explicit PlayRange specification, so it does not have to derive one.

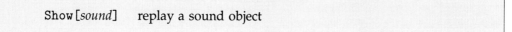

        Show[*sound*]   replay a sound object

Replaying a sound object.

Both Play and ListPlay return Sound objects which contain procedures for synthesizing sounds. You can replay a particular Sound object using the function Show that is also used for redisplaying graphics.

32. The Structure of Graphics

■ 32.1 How Graphics Are Represented

Chapter 8 discussed how to use functions like Plot and ListPlot to plot graphs of functions and data. In this chapter, we discuss how *Mathematica* represents such graphics, and how you can program *Mathematica* to create more complicated images.

Graphics Objects

The basic idea is that *Mathematica* represents all graphics in terms of a collection of *graphics primitives*. The primitives are objects like Point, Line and Polygon, that represent elements of a graphical image, as well as directives such as RGBColor, Thickness and SurfaceColor.

This generates a plot of a list of points.   *In[1]:=* **ListPlot[Table[Prime[n], {n, 20}]]**

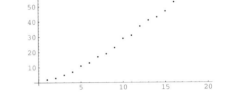

InputForm shows how *Mathematica* represents the graphics. Each point is represented as a Point graphics primitive. All the various graphics options used in this case are also given.

In[2]:= **InputForm[%]**

Out[2]//InputForm=
```
  Graphics[{Point[{1, 2}], Point[{2, 3}], Point[{3, 5}],
    Point[{4, 7}], Point[{5, 11}], Point[{6, 13}],
    Point[{7, 17}], Point[{8, 19}], Point[{9, 23}],
    Point[{10, 29}], Point[{11, 31}], Point[{12, 37}],
    Point[{13, 41}], Point[{14, 43}], Point[{15, 47}],
    Point[{16, 53}], Point[{17, 59}], Point[{18, 61}],
    Point[{19, 67}], Point[{20, 71}]},
   {PlotRange -> Automatic, AspectRatio -> GoldenRatio^(-1),
    DisplayFunction :> $DisplayFunction,
    ColorOutput -> Automatic, Axes -> Automatic,
    AxesOrigin -> Automatic, PlotLabel -> None,
    AxesLabel -> None, Ticks -> Automatic, GridLines -> None,
    Prolog -> {}, Epilog -> {}, AxesStyle -> Automatic,
    Background -> Automatic, DefaultColor -> Automatic,
    DefaultFont :> $DefaultFont, RotateLabel -> True,
    Frame -> False, FrameStyle -> Automatic,
    FrameTicks -> Automatic, FrameLabel -> None,
    PlotRegion -> Automatic}]
```

Each complete piece of graphics in *Mathematica* is represented as a *graphics object*. There are several different kinds of graphics objects, corresponding to different types of graphics. Each kind of graphics object has a definite head which identifies its type.

Graphics[*list*]	general two-dimensional graphics
DensityGraphics[*list*]	density plot
ContourGraphics[*list*]	contour plot
SurfaceGraphics[*list*]	three-dimensional surface
Graphics3D[*list*]	general three-dimensional graphics
GraphicsArray[*list*]	array of other graphics objects

Graphics objects in *Mathematica*.

The functions like Plot and ListPlot discussed in Chapter 8 all work by building up *Mathematica* graphics objects, and then displaying them.

You can create other kinds of graphical images in *Mathematica* by building up your own graphics objects. Since graphics objects in *Mathematica* are just symbolic expressions, you can use all the standard *Mathematica* functions to manipulate them.

Displaying Graphics

Once you have created a graphics object, you must then display it. The function Show allows you to display any *Mathematica* graphics object.

Show[*g*]	display a graphics object
Show[*g₁*, *g₂*, ...]	display several graphics objects combined
Show[GraphicsArray[{{*g₁₁*, *g₁₂*, ... }, ... }]]	
	display an array of graphics objects

Displaying graphics objects.

This uses Table to generate a polygon graphics primitive.

```
In[3]:= poly = Polygon[
            Table[N[{Cos[n Pi/5], Sin[n Pi/5]}], {n, 0, 5}] ]
Out[3]= Polygon[{{1., 0}, {0.809017, 0.587785},
        {0.309017, 0.951057}, {-0.309017, 0.951057},
        {-0.809017, 0.587785}, {-1., 0}}]
```

This creates a two-dimensional graphics object that contains the polygon graphics primitive. In standard output format, the graphics object is given simply as -Graphics-.

```
In[4]:= Graphics[ poly ]
Out[4]= -Graphics-
```

InputForm shows the complete graphics object.

```
In[5]:= InputForm[%]

Out[5]//InputForm=
   Graphics[Polygon[{{1., 0},
       {0.809016994374947, 0.5877852522924732},
       {0.3090169943749474, 0.951056516295153},
       {-0.3090169943749474, 0.951056516295154},
       {-0.809016994374947, 0.5877852522924733}, {-1., 0}}]]
```

This displays the graphics object you have created.

```
In[6]:= Show[%]
```

Graphics Directives

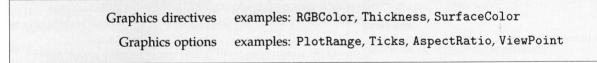

Graphics directives	examples: RGBColor, Thickness, SurfaceColor
Graphics options	examples: PlotRange, Ticks, AspectRatio, ViewPoint

Local and global ways to modify graphics.

Given a particular list of graphics primitives, *Mathematica* provides two basic mechanisms for modifying the final form of graphics you get. First, you can insert into the list of graphics primitives certain *graphics directives*, such as RGBColor, which modify the subsequent graphical elements in the list. In this way, you can specify how a particular set of graphical elements should be rendered.

This takes the list of graphics primitives created above, and adds the graphics directive GrayLevel[0.3].

```
In[7]:= Graphics[ {GrayLevel[0.3], poly} ]

Out[7]= -Graphics-
```

Now the polygon is rendered in gray.   *In[8]:=* **Show[%]**

By inserting graphics directives, you can specify how particular graphical elements should be rendered. Often, however, you want to make global modifications to the way a whole graphics object is rendered. You can do this using *graphics options*.

Graphics Options

By adding the graphics option Frame you can modify the overall appearance of the graphics.

In[9]:= **Show[%, Frame -> True]**

Show returns a graphics object with the options in it.

In[10]:= **InputForm[%]**

Out[10]//InputForm=
```
Graphics[{GrayLevel[0.3],
  Polygon[{{1., 0}, {0.809016994374947, 0.5877852522924732},
    {0.3090169943749474, 0.951056516295153},
    {-0.3090169943749474, 0.951056516295154},
    {-0.809016994374947, 0.5877852522924733}, {-1., 0}}]},
  {Frame -> True}]
```

You can specify graphics options in Show. As a result, it is straightforward to take a single graphics object, and show it with many different choices of graphics options.

Notice however that Show always returns the graphics objects it has displayed. If you specify graphics options in Show, then these options are automatically inserted into the graphics objects that Show returns. As a result, if you call Show again on the same objects, the same graphics options will be used,

With PlotRange -> All, the outlying point is included, and the coordinate system is correspondingly modified.

In[5]:= **Show[%, PlotRange -> All]**

The option PlotRange allows you to specify a rectangular region in the original coordinate system, and to drop any graphical elements that lie outside this region. In order to render the remaining elements, however, *Mathematica* then has to determine how to position this rectangular region with respect to the final display area.

The option PlotRegion allows you to specify where the corners of the rectangular region lie within the final display area. The positions of the corners are specified in scaled coordinates, which are defined to run from 0 to 1 across the display area. The default is PlotRegion -> {{0, 1}, {0, 1}}, which specifies that the rectangular region should fill the whole display area.

By specifying PlotRegion, you can effectively add "margins" around your plot.

In[6]:= **Plot[ArcTan[x], {x, 0, 10},**
                        PlotRegion -> {{0.2, 0.8}, {0.3, 0.7}}]

AspectRatio -> *r*	make the ratio of height to width for the display area equal to *r*
AspectRatio -> Automatic	determine the shape of the display area from the original coordinate system

Specifying the shape of the display area.

What we have discussed so far is how *Mathematica* translates the original coordinates you specify into positions in the final display area. What remains to discuss, however, is what the final display area is like.

On most computer systems, there is a certain fixed region of screen or paper into which the *Mathematica* display area must fit. How it fits into this region is determined by its "shape" or aspect ratio. In general, the option AspectRatio specifies the ratio of height to width for the final display area.

It is important to note that the setting of AspectRatio does not affect the meaning of the scaled or display coordinates. These coordinates always run from 0 to 1 across the display area. What AspectRatio does is to change the shape of this display area.

This generates a graphic object corresponding to a hexagon.

```
In[7]:= hex = Graphics[Polygon[
            Table[{Sin[n Pi/3], Cos[n Pi/3]}, {n, 6}] ]] ;
```

This renders the hexagon in a display area whose height is three times its width.

```
In[8]:= Show[hex, AspectRatio -> 3]
```

For two-dimensional graphics, AspectRatio is set by default to the fixed value of 1/GoldenRatio. Sometimes, however, you may want to determine the aspect ratio for a plot from the original coordinate system used in the plot. Typically what you want is for one unit in the *x* direction in the original coordinate system to correspond to the same distance in the final display as one unit in the *y* direction. In this way, objects that you define in the original coordinate system are displayed with their "natural shape". You can make this happen by setting the option AspectRatio -> Automatic.

With AspectRatio -> Automatic, the aspect ratio of the final display area is determined from the original coordinate system, and the hexagon is shown with its "natural shape".

```
In[9]:= Show[hex, AspectRatio -> Automatic]
```

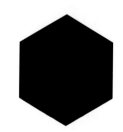

Using scaled coordinates, you can specify the sizes of graphical elements as fractions of the size of the display area. You cannot, however, tell *Mathematica* the actual physical size at which a particular graphical element should be rendered. Of course, this size ultimately depends on the details of your graphics output device, and cannot be determined for certain within *Mathematica*. Nevertheless, graphics directives such as `AbsoluteThickness` discussed on page 97 do allow you to indicate "absolute sizes" to use for particular graphical elements. The sizes you request in this way will be respected by most, but not all, output devices. (For example, if you optically project an image, it is neither possible nor desirable to maintain the same absolute size for a graphical element within it.)

■ 33.2 Coordinate Systems for Three-Dimensional Graphics

Whenever *Mathematica* draws a three-dimensional object, it always effectively puts a cuboidal box around the object. With the default option setting `Boxed -> True`, *Mathematica* in fact draws the edges of this box explicitly. But in general, *Mathematica* automatically "clips" any parts of your object that extend outside of the cuboidal box.

The option `PlotRange` specifies the range of *x*, *y* and *z* coordinates that *Mathematica* should include in the box. As in two dimensions the default setting is `PlotRange -> Automatic`, which makes *Mathematica* use an internal algorithm to try and include the "interesting parts" of a plot, but drop outlying parts. With `PlotRange -> All`, *Mathematica* will include all parts.

This loads a package defining various polyhedra.	`In[1]:= <<Graphics`Polyhedra` ;`
This creates a stellated icosahedron.	`In[2]:= stel = Stellate[Icosahedron[ ]] ;`
Here is the stellated icosahedron, drawn in a box.	`In[3]:= Show[Graphics3D[stel], Axes -> True]`

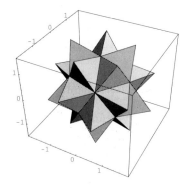

With this setting for PlotRange, many parts of the stellated icosahedron lie outside the box, and are clipped.

In[4]:= **Show[%, PlotRange -> {-1, 1}]**

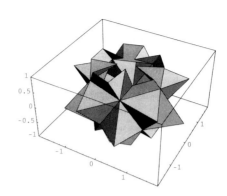

Much as in two dimensions, you can use either "original" or "scaled" coordinates to specify the positions of elements in three-dimensional objects. Scaled coordinates, specified as Scaled[{sx, sy, sz}] are taken to run from 0 to 1 in each dimension. The coordinates are set up to define a right-handed coordinate system on the box.

{x, y, z}	original coordinates
Scaled[{sx, sy, sz}]	scaled coordinates, running from 0 to 1 in each dimension

Coordinate systems for three-dimensional objects.

This puts a cuboid in one corner of the box.

In[5]:= **Show[Graphics3D[{stel,**
Cuboid[Scaled[{0, 0, 0}],
Scaled[{0.2, 0.2, 0.2}]]}]]

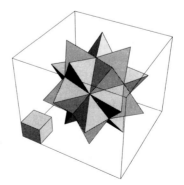

This defines a function which maps alternating ranges of values into black and white.

```
In[2]:= stripes[f_] :=
            If[Mod[f, 1] > 0.5, GrayLevel[1], GrayLevel[0]]
```

This shows the surface colored with black and white stripes.

```
In[3]:= Show[exp, ColorFunction :> (stripes[5 #]&)]
```

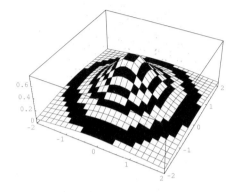

The second way to change the default coloring of surfaces is to supply an explicit second array along with the array of heights. ColorFunction is then applied to the elements of this second array, rather than the array of heights, to find the color directives to use. In the second array, you can effectively specify the value of another coordinate for each point on the surface. This coordinate will be plotted using color, rather than position.

You can generate an array of color values automatically using Plot3D[{*f*, *s*}, ...]. If you give the array explicitly in ListPlot3D or SurfaceGraphics, you should realize that with an $n \times n$ array of heights, you need an $(n - 1) \times (n - 1)$ array to specify colors. The reason is that the heights are specified for *points* on a grid, whereas the colors are specified for *squares* on the grid.

When you supply a second function or array to Plot3D, ListPlot3D, and so on, the default setting for the ColorFunction option is Automatic. This means that the function or array should contain explicit *Mathematica* color directives, such as GrayLevel or RGBColor. However, if you give another setting, such as ColorFunction -> Hue, then the function or array can yield pure numbers or other data which are converted to color directives when the function specified by ColorFunction is applied.

Plot3D[{*f*, *s*}, {*x*, *xmin*, *xmax*}, {*y*, *ymin*, *ymax*}]

        plot a surface whose height is determined by *f* and whose color is determined by *s*

ListPlot3D[*height*, *color*]   generate a colored surface plot from an array of heights and colors

SurfaceGraphics[*height*, *color*]   a graphics object representing a surface with a specified array of heights and colors

Specifying arrays of colors for surfaces.

This plots a surface with gray level determined by the *y* coordinate.

In[4]:= **Plot3D[{Sin[x] Sin[y]^2, GrayLevel[y/3]},**
                    {x, 0, 3}, {y, 0, 3}]

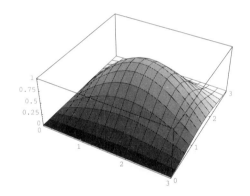

This puts a random gray level in each grid square. Notice that the array of grid squares is 9×9, whereas the array of grid points is 10×10.

In[5]:= **ListPlot3D[Table[i/j, {i, 10}, {j, 10}],**
              Table[GrayLevel[Random[ ]], {i, 9}, {j, 9}]]

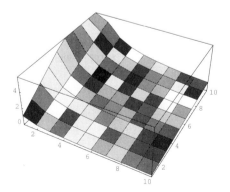

35. Labeling Graphics

■ 35.1 Labeling Two-Dimensional Graphics

`Axes -> True`	give a pair of axes
`GridLines -> Automatic`	draw grid lines on the plot
`Frame -> True`	put axes on a frame around the plot
`PlotLabel -> "text"`	give an overall label for the plot

Ways to label two-dimensional plots.

Here is a plot, using the default
`Axes -> True`.

`In[1]:= bp = Plot[BesselJ[2, x], {x, 0, 10}]`

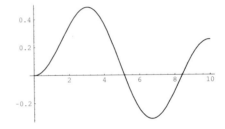

Setting `Frame -> True` generates a frame
with axes, and removes tick marks from
the ordinary axes.

`In[2]:= Show[bp, Frame -> True]`

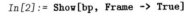
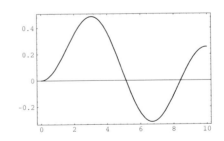

This includes grid lines, which are shown in light blue on color displays.

In[3]:= **Show[%, GridLines -> Automatic]**

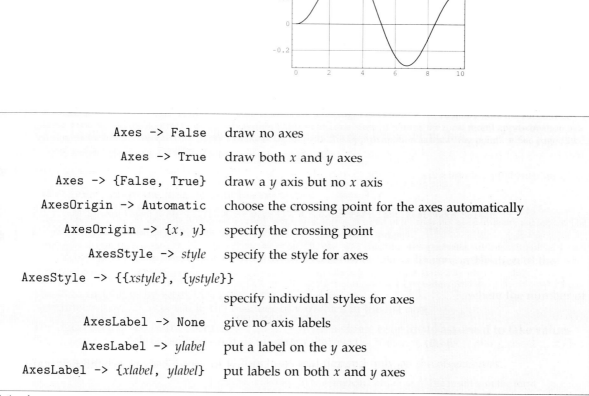

Axes -> False	draw no axes
Axes -> True	draw both x and y axes
Axes -> {False, True}	draw a y axis but no x axis
AxesOrigin -> Automatic	choose the crossing point for the axes automatically
AxesOrigin -> {x, y}	specify the crossing point
AxesStyle -> *style*	specify the style for axes
AxesStyle -> {{*xstyle*}, {*ystyle*}}	specify individual styles for axes
AxesLabel -> None	give no axis labels
AxesLabel -> *ylabel*	put a label on the y axes
AxesLabel -> {*xlabel*, *ylabel*}	put labels on both x and y axes

Options for axes.

This makes the axes cross at the point {5, 0}, and puts a label on each axis.

In[4]:= **Show[bp, AxesOrigin -> {5, 0}, AxesLabel -> {"x", "y"}]**

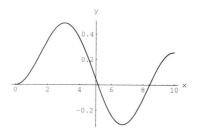

`Frame -> False`	draw no frame
`Frame -> True`	draw a frame around the plot
`FrameStyle -> `*style*	specify a style for the frame
`FrameStyle -> {{`*xmstyle*`}, {`*ymstyle*`}, ... }`	
	specify styles for each edge of the frame
`FrameLabel -> None`	give no frame labels
`FrameLabel -> {`*xmlabel, ymlabel,* `... }`	
	put labels on edges of the frame
`RotateLabel -> False`	do not rotate text in labels
`FrameTicks -> None`	draw no tick marks on frame edges
`FrameTicks -> Automatic`	position tick marks automatically
`FrameTicks -> {{`*xmticks, ymticks,* `... }}`	
	specify tick marks for frame edges

Options for frame axes.

The `Axes` option allows you to draw a single pair of axes in a plot. Sometimes, however, you may instead want to show the scales for a plot on a frame, typically drawn around the whole plot. The option `Frame` allows you effectively to draw four axes, corresponding to the four edges of the frame around a plot. These four axes are ordered clockwise, starting from the one at the bottom.

This draws frame axes, and labels each of them.

```
In[9]:= Show[bp, Frame -> True,
            FrameLabel -> {"label 1", "label 2",
                          "label 3", "label 4"}]
```

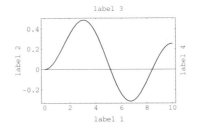

GridLines -> None	draw no grid lines
GridLines -> Automatic	position grid lines automatically
GridLines -> {xgrid, ygrid}	specify grid lines in analogy with tick marks

Options for grid lines.

Grid lines in *Mathematica* work very much like tick marks. As with tick marks, you can specify explicit positions for grid lines. There is no label or length to specify for grid lines. However, you can specify a style.

This generates *x* but not *y* grid lines.   *In[10]:=* **Show[bp, GridLines -> {Automatic, None}]**

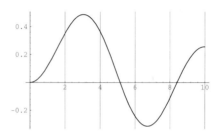

■ 35.2 Labeling Three-Dimensional Graphics

Mathematica provides various options for labeling three-dimensional graphics. Some of these options are directly analogous to those for two-dimensional graphics, discussed in Section 35.1. Others are different.

Boxed -> True	draw a cuboidal bounding box around the graphics (default)
Axes -> True	draw *x*, *y* and *z* axes on the edges of the box (default for SurfaceGraphics)
Axes -> {False, False, True}	draw the *z* axis only
FaceGrids -> All	draw grid lines on the faces of the box
PlotLabel -> *text*	give an overall label for the plot

Some options for labeling three-dimensional graphics.

This loads a package containing various polyhedra.   *In[1]:=* **<<Graphics`Polyhedra` ;**

The default for Graphics3D is to include a box, but no other forms of labeling.

In[2]:= **Show[Graphics3D[Dodecahedron[ ]]]**

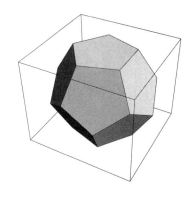

Setting the option Axes -> True adds *x*, *y* and *z* axes.

In[3]:= **Show[%, Axes -> True]**

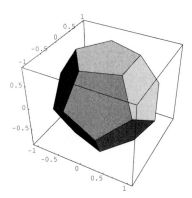

This adds grid lines to each face of the box.

In[4]:= **Show[%, FaceGrids -> All]**

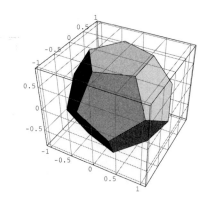

BoxStyle -> *style*	specify the style for the box
AxesStyle -> *style*	specify the style for axes
AxesStyle -> {{*xstyle*}, {*ystyle*}, {*zstyle*}}	
	specify separate styles for each axis

Style options.

This makes the box dashed, and draws axes which are thicker than normal.

```
In[5]:= Show[Graphics3D[Dodecahedron[ ]],
            BoxStyle -> Dashing[{0.02, 0.02}],
            Axes -> True, AxesStyle -> Thickness[0.01]]
```

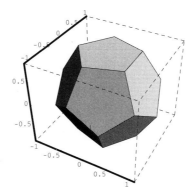

By setting the option `Axes -> True`, you tell *Mathematica* to draw axes on the edges of the three-dimensional box. However, for each axis, there are in principle four possible edges on which it can be drawn. The option `AxesEdge` allows you to specify on which edge to draw each of the axes.

AxesEdge -> Automatic	use an internal algorithm to choose where to draw all axes
AxesEdge -> {*xspec*, *yspec*, *zspec*}	
	give separate specifications for each of the *x*, *y* and *z* axes
None	do not draw this axis
Automatic	decide automatically where to draw this axis
{*dir$_i$*, *dir$_j$*}	specify on which of the four possible edges to draw this axis

Specifying where to draw three-dimensional axes.

This draws the *x* on the edge with larger *y* and *z* coordinates, draws no *y* axis, and chooses automatically where to draw the *z* axis.

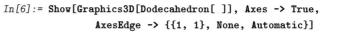

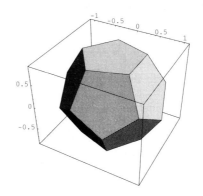

When you draw the *x* axis on a three-dimensional box, there are four possible edges on which the axis can be drawn. These edges are distinguished by having larger or smaller *y* and *z* coordinates. When you use the specification {*dir_y*, *dir_z*} for where to draw the *x* axis, you can set the *dir_i* to be +1 or −1 to represent larger or smaller values for the *y* and *z* coordinates.

AxesLabel -> None	give no axis labels
AxesLabel -> *zlabel*	put a label on the *z* axis
AxesLabel -> {*xlabel*, *ylabel*, *zlabel*}	
	put labels on all three axes

Axis labels in three-dimensional graphics.

You can use AxesLabel to label edges of the box, without necessarily drawing scales on them.

In[7]:= **Show[Graphics3D[Dodecahedron[ ]], Axes -> True, AxesLabel -> {"x", "y", "z"}, Ticks -> None]**

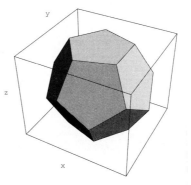

`Ticks -> None`	draw no tick marks
`Ticks -> Automatic`	place tick marks automatically
`Ticks -> {`*xticks*`, `*yticks*`, `*zticks*`}`	tick mark specifications for each axis

Settings for the `Ticks` option.

You can give the same kind of tick mark specifications in three dimensions as were described for two-dimensional graphics in Section 35.1 above.

`FaceGrids -> None`	draw no grid lines on faces
`FaceGrids -> All`	draw grid lines on all faces
`FaceGrids -> {`*face₁*`, `*face₂*`, ... }`	draw grid lines on the faces specified by the *face*ᵢ
`FaceGrids -> {{`*face₁*`, {`*xgrid₁*`, `*ygrid₁*`}}, ... }`	use *xgrid*ᵢ, *ygrid*ᵢ to determine where and how to draw grid lines on each face

Drawing grid lines in three dimensions.

Mathematica allows you to draw grid lines on the faces of the box that surrounds a three-dimensional object. If you set `FaceGrids -> All`, grid lines are drawn in gray on every face. By setting `FaceGrids -> {`*face₁*`, `*face₂*`, ... }` you can tell *Mathematica* to draw grid lines only on specific faces. Each face is specified by a list $\{dir_x,\ dir_y,\ dir_z\}$, where two of the dir_i must be 0, and the third one is +1 or −1. For each face, you can also explicitly tell *Mathematica* where and how to draw the grid lines, using the same kind of specifications as you give for the `GridLines` option in two-dimensional graphics.

This draws grid lines only on the top and bottom faces of the box.

```
In[8]:= Show[Graphics3D[Dodecahedron[ ]],
            FaceGrids -> {{0, 0, 1}, {0, 0, -1}}]
```

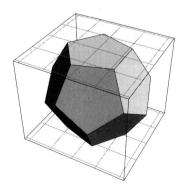

36. Text in Graphics

■ 36.1 Fonts for Text in Graphics

$DefaultFont	the default font to use in graphics
{"*name*", *size*}	a font with specified name and size

Font specifications in *Mathematica*.

All text that is included in *Mathematica* graphics must be in a definite *font*. The default font to use is typically specified by the value of the global variable $DefaultFont.

Every font in *Mathematica* has a *name*, and a *size*. The size gives the basic height of characters in the font. It is specified in absolute units of printer's points, with one point being 1/72 inches. (The main text of this book, for example, is set in 10-point type.)

Since font sizes are specified in absolute units, the size of pieces of text in *Mathematica* plots always remain fixed whatever size the whole plots are. The only way to change the size of the text is explicitly to change the font size.

Here is the default font used in producing graphics in this book.

```
In[1]:= $DefaultFont
Out[1]= {Courier, 5.5}
```

This changes the default font to use in graphics.

```
In[2]:= $DefaultFont = {"Courier-Oblique", 7}
Out[2]= {Courier-Oblique, 7}
```

Now all text in the plot is slightly larger than normal, and italic.

```
In[3]:= Plot[Sin[Sin[x]], {x, 0, Pi}]
```

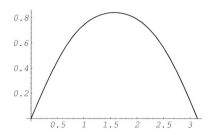

If you reset the global variable $DefaultFont, you change the default font to use in all graphics. Often you may want to specify a different default font only for a particular *Mathematica* plot. You can do this using the DefaultFont option that exists for Show, Plot and other *Mathematica* graphics functions.

In other cases, you may want to specify a font only for a specific piece of text. In such cases, you can wrap the text with a FontForm directive.

DefaultFont -> *font*	an option to change the default font in a particular plot
FontForm["*text*", *font*]	a piece of text in a specific font

More local ways to specify fonts.

This uses an italic font for labeling the axes, and a larger bold font for the overall plot label.

```
In[4]:= Show[%, DefaultFont -> {"Times-Italic", 6},
           PlotLabel ->
               FontForm["The label", {"Helvetica-Bold", 12}]]
```

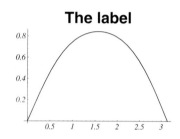

The most complicated aspect of using fonts in *Mathematica* graphics is their naming. When you tell *Mathematica* to use a font with a particular name, all that *Mathematica* actually does is to pass that request through to your final rendering device. It is then up to this device to find the appropriate font, and render it.

The problem is that not all devices support the same set of fonts. In all cases, *Mathematica* specifies fonts by inserting their names in the PostScript code it sends to your rendering device. Rendering devices that have built-in PostScript interpreters typically support at least some minimal set of standard fonts. Usually these fonts include "Courier", "Helvetica" and "Times", and their "*Name*-Bold", "*Name*-Oblique" and "*Name*-BoldOblique" variants. ("Times" has Italic in place of Oblique.) If you ask for a font that your rendering device does not have, it will typically substitute another font.

Although *Mathematica* can in principle produce text in any font that your rendering device supports, you should realize that with some fonts, the text you get may not be properly aligned when it occurs on several lines. Only with fonts such as Courier that are monospaced so that every character is given the same horizontal space can you be sure that text will always be aligned correctly.

■ 36.2 Graphics Primitives for Text

With the Text graphics primitive, you can insert text at any position in two- or three-dimensional *Mathematica* graphics. Unless you explicitly specify a font using FontForm, the text will be given in your current default font.

Text[*expr*, {*x*, *y*}]	text centered at the point {*x*, *y*}
Text[*expr*, {*x*, *y*}, {-1, 0}]	text with its left-hand end at {*x*, *y*}
Text[*expr*, {*x*, *y*}, {1, 0}]	right-hand end at {*x*, *y*}
Text[*expr*, {*x*, *y*}, {0, -1}]	centered above {*x*, *y*}
Text[*expr*, {*x*, *y*}, {0, 1}]	centered below {*x*, *y*}
Text[*expr*, {*x*, *y*}, {*dx*, *dy*}]	text positioned so that {*x*, *y*} is at relative coordinates {*dx*, *dy*} within the box that bounds the text
Text[*expr*, {*x*, *y*}, {*dx*, *dy*}, {0, 1}]	
	text oriented vertically to read from bottom to top
Text[*expr*, {*x*, *y*}, {*dx*, *dy*}, {0, -1}]	
	text that reads from top to bottom
Text[*expr*, {*x*, *y*}, {*dx*, *dy*}, {-1, 0}]	
	text that is upside-down

Two-dimensional text.

This generates five pieces of text, and displays them in a plot.

```
In[1]:= Show[Graphics[
            Table[ Text[Expand[(1 + x)^n], {n, n}], {n, 5} ] ],
          PlotRange -> All]
```

$$1 + 5 x + 10 x^2 + 10 x^3 + 5 x^4 + x^5$$

$$1 + 4 x + 6 x^2 + 4 x^3 + x^4$$

$$1 + 3 x + 3 x^2 + x^3$$

$$1 + 2 x + x^2$$

$$1 + x$$

When you specify an offset for text, the relative coordinates that are used are taken to run from -1 to 1 in each direction across the box that bounds the text. The point {0, 0} in this coordinate system is defined to be center of the text. Note that the offsets you specify need not lie in the range -1 to 1.

Note that you can specify the color of a piece of text by preceding the Text graphics primitive with an appropriate RGBColor or other graphics directive.

Here is some vertically oriented text with its left-hand side at the point {2, 2}.

```
In[2]:= Show[Graphics[
            Text[FontForm["Some text", {"Courier-Bold", 14}],
                {2, 2}, {-1, 0}, {0, 1}]], Frame -> True]
```

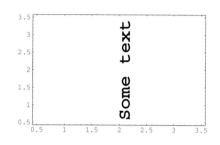

Text[*expr*, {*x*, *y*, *z*}]	text centered at the point {*x*, *y*, *z*}
Text[*expr*, {*x*, *y*, *z*}, {*sdx*, *sdy*}]	
	text with a two-dimensional offset

Three-dimensional text.

This loads a package containing definitions of polyhedra.

```
In[3]:= <<Graphics`Polyhedra` ;
```

This puts text at the specified position in three dimensions.

```
In[4]:= Show[Graphics3D[{Dodecahedron[ ],
            Text["a point", {2, 2, 2}, {1, 1}]}]]
```

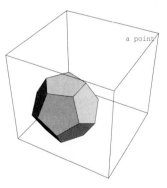

Note that when you use text in three-dimensional graphics, *Mathematica* assumes that the text is never hidden by any polygons or other objects.

Appendix.

Summary of *Mathematica*

expr and *expr$_i$*	any expression
symb	any symbol
n	a non-negative integer
string and *string$_i$*	"cccc" or a sequence of letters, digits and special characters
filename	like *string*, but can include more characters described below
digits	a sequence of digits (including letters when *base* is above 10)

Objects used in the tables of special input forms.

Precedence and the Ordering of Input Forms

The tables of input forms are arranged in decreasing order of precedence. Input forms in the same box have the same precedence. As discussed in Section 24.3, precedence determines how *Mathematica* groups terms in input expressions. The general rule is that if ⊗ has higher precedence than ⊕, then $a \oplus b \otimes c$ is interpreted as $a \oplus (b \otimes c)$, and $a \otimes b \oplus c$ is interpreted as $(a \otimes b) \oplus c$.

Grouping of Input Forms

The third columns in the tables show how multiple occurrences of a single input form, or of several input forms with the same precedence, are grouped. For example, a/b/c is grouped as (a/b)/c ("left associative"), while a^b^c is grouped as a^(b^c) ("right associative"). No grouping is needed in an expression like a + b + c, since Plus can take any number of arguments. Where the third column of the table is left blank, the input forms cannot be grouped: you always have to insert explicit parentheses.

special input form	full form
#	Slot[1]
#*n*	Slot[*n*]
##	SlotSequence[1]
##*n*	SlotSequence[*n*]
%	Out[ ]
%%	Out[-2]
%%... % (*n* times)	Out[-*n*]
%*n*	Out[*n*]

Additional special input forms, part one.

special input form	full form
_	Blank[ ]
_*expr*	Blank[*expr*]
__	BlankSequence[ ]
__*expr*	BlankSequence[*expr*]
___	BlankNullSequence[ ]
___*expr*	BlankNullSequence[*expr*]
_.	Optional[Blank[ ]]
*symb*_	Pattern[*symb*,Blank[ ]]
*symb*_*expr*	Pattern[*symb*,Blank[*expr*]]
*symb*__	Pattern[*symb*,BlankSequence[ ]]
*symb*__*expr*	Pattern[*symb*,BlankSequence[*expr*]]
*symb*___	Pattern[*symb*,BlankNullSequence[ ]]
*symb*___*expr*	Pattern[*symb*,BlankNullSequence[*expr*]]
*symb*_.	Optional[Pattern[*symb*,Blank[ ]]]

Additional special input forms, part two.

Spaces and Multiplication

Spaces in *Mathematica* denote multiplication, just as they do in standard mathematical notation. In addition, *Mathematica* takes complete expressions that are adjacent, not necessarily separated by spaces, to be multiplied together.

- x y z ⟶ x*y*z
- 2x ⟶ 2*x
- 2(x+1) ⟶ 2*(x+1)
- c(x+1) ⟶ c*(x+1)
- (x+1)(y+2) ⟶ (x+1)*(y+2)
- x! y ⟶ x!*y
- x!y ⟶ x!*y

Alternative forms for multiplication.

An expression like x!y could potentially mean either (x!)*y or x*(!y). The first interpretation is chosen because Factorial has higher precedence than Not.

A4. Patterns and Transformation Rules

■ A4.1 Patterns

Patterns stand for classes of expressions. They contain *pattern objects* which represent sets of possible expressions.

_	any expression
*x*_	any expression, given the name *x*
x : *pattern*	a pattern, given the name *x*
pattern ? *test*	a pattern that yields True when *test* is applied to its value
_*h*	any expression with head *h*
*x*_*h*	any expression with head *h*, given the name *x*
__	any sequence of one or more expressions
___	any sequence of zero or more expressions
*x*__ and *x*___	sequences of expressions, given the name *x*
__*h* and ___*h*	sequences of expressions, each with head *h*
*x*__*h* and *x*___*h*	sequences of expressions with head *h*, given the name *x*
pattern /; *cond*	a pattern for which *cond* evaluates to True

Pattern objects.

When several pattern objects with the same name occur in a single pattern, all the objects must stand for the same expression. Thus f[x_, x_] can stand for f[2, 2] but not f[2, 3].

In a pattern object such as _h, the head *h* can be any expression, but cannot itself be a pattern.

A pattern object such as x__ stands for a *sequence* of expressions. So, for example, f[x__] can stand for f[a, b, c], with x being the *sequence* (a, b, c). If you use x, say in the result of a transformation rule, the sequence will be spliced into the function in which x appears. Thus g[u, x, u] would become g[u, a, b, c, u].

A pattern like f[x__, y__, z__] can match an expression like f[a, b, c, d, e] with several different choices of x, y and z. The choices with x and y of minimum length are tried first. In general, when there are multiple __ or ___ in a single function, the case that is tried first takes all the __ and ___ to stand for sequences of minimum length, except the last one, which stands for "the rest" of the arguments.

■ A4.2 Assignments

lhs = *rhs*	immediate assignment: *rhs* is evaluated at the time of assignment
lhs := *rhs*	delayed assignment: *rhs* is evaluated when the value of *lhs* is requested

The two basic types of assignment in *Mathematica*.

Assignments in *Mathematica* specify transformation rules for expressions.

In the case of an assignment like *f*[*args*] = *rhs*, *Mathematica* looks at *f*, then the head of *f*, then the head of that, and so on, until it finds a symbol with which to associate the assignment.

The transformation rules associated with a particular symbol *s* are always stored in a definite order, and are tested in that order when they are used. Each time you make an assignment, the corresponding transformation rule is inserted at the end of the list of transformation rules associated with *s*, except in the following cases:

- The left-hand side of the transformation rule is identical to a transformation rule that has already been stored, and any /; conditions on the right-hand side are also identical. In this case, the new transformation rule is inserted in place of the old one.

- *Mathematica* determines that the new transformation rule is more specific than a rule already present, and would never be used if it were placed after this rule. In this case, the new rule is placed before the old one. Note that in many cases it is not possible to determine whether one rule is more specific than another; in such cases, the new rule is always inserted at the end.

■ A4.3 Clearing and Removing Objects

expr =.	clear a value defined for *expr*
f /: *expr* =.	clear a value associated with *f* defined for *expr*
Clear[*s₁*, *s₂*, ...]	clear all values for the symbols *sᵢ*
Remove[*s₁*, *s₂*, ...]	clear all values, and then remove the names of the *sᵢ*

Ways to clear and remove objects.

Clear and Remove can take string patterns as arguments, to specify action on all symbols whose names match the string pattern.

■ A4.4 Transformation Rules

lhs -> *rhs*	immediate rule: *rhs* is evaluated when the rule is first given
lhs :> *rhs*	delayed rule: *rhs* is evaluated when the rule is used

The two basic types of transformation rules in *Mathematica*.

Replacements for pattern variables that appear in transformation rules are effectively done using `ReplaceAll` (the `/.` operator).

A5. Listing of Built-in *Mathematica* Objects

■ A5.1 Introduction

This section gives an alphabetical list of all the built-in objects described or mentioned in this book. Greater detail can usually be found in the book *Mathematica: A System for Doing Mathematics by Computer*, Second Edition (referred to here as "The *Mathematica* Book").

The list does not include objects that are defined in *Mathematica* packages, even those distributed as a standard part of the *Mathematica* system. Note also that options which appear only in a single built-in *Mathematica* function are sometimes not given as separate entries in the list.

Objects that are part of *Mathematica* but that are not described in this book are indicated by □.

Note that in a typical version of *Mathematica*, there are some additional objects present, which are not included in this list. You should avoid using such objects. Some may be provided for compatibility with older *Mathematica* systems; others may be preliminary or experimental. In general, however, the specifications of such objects can be expected to change.

In many versions of *Mathematica*, you can access the text given in this section directly. Typing ?*F*, for example, will typically give you the main description of the object *F* from this section.

■ A5.2 Conventions in This Listing

`text in this style`	literal *Mathematica* input that you type in as it is printed (*e.g.*, function names)
text in this style	expressions that you fill in (*e.g.*, function arguments)
object₁, *object₂*, ...	a sequence of any number of expressions

Conventions used in the list of built-in objects.

□ Abort

(Mentioned on page 274.) Use on-line help or see pages 311 and 750 of The *Mathematica* Book.

□ AbortProtect

(Mentioned on page 274.) Use on-line help or see pages 311 and 750 of The *Mathematica* Book.

■ Abs

Abs[z] gives the absolute value of the real or complex number z.

For complex numbers z, Abs[z] gives the modulus |z|. ■ Abs[z] is left unevaluated if *expr* is not a number. ■ See pages 41 and 43. ■ See also: Re, Im, Arg, Mod, ComplexExpand.

■ AbsoluteDashing

AbsoluteDashing[{d_1, d_2, ... }] is a graphics directive which specifies that lines which follow are to be drawn dashed, with successive segments having absolute lengths $d_1, d_2, ...$ (repeated cyclically).

The absolute lengths are measured in units of printer's points, approximately equal to $\frac{1}{72}$ of an inch. ■ AbsoluteDashing[{ }] specifies that lines should be solid. ■ AbsoluteDashing can be used in both two- and three-dimensional graphics. ■ See page 97. ■ See also: AbsoluteThickness, Thickness, GrayLevel, Hue, RGBColor.

■ AbsolutePointSize

AbsolutePointSize[d] is a graphics directive which specifies that points which follow are to be shown if possible as circular regions with absolute diameter d.

The absolute diameter is measured in units of printer's points, approximately equal to $\frac{1}{72}$ of an inch. ■ AbsolutePointSize can be used in both two- and three-dimensional graphics. ■ See page 96. ■ See also: PointSize, Thickness.

■ AbsoluteThickness

AbsoluteThickness[d] is a graphics directive which specifies that lines which follow are to be drawn with absolute thickness d.

The absolute thickness is measured in units of printer's points, approximately equal to $\frac{1}{72}$ of an inch. ■ AbsoluteThickness can be used in both two- and three-dimensional graphics. ■ See page 97. ■ See also: AbsoluteDashing, PointSize, Dashing.

□ AbsoluteTime

(Mentioned on page 283.) Use on-line help or see pages 524 and 751 of The *Mathematica* Book.

□ AccountingForm

(Mentioned on page 53.) Use on-line help or see pages 350 and 751 of The *Mathematica* Book.

■ **Accuracy**

Accuracy[x] gives the number of digits to the right of the decimal point in the number x.

If x is not a number, Accuracy[x] gives the minimum value of Accuracy for all the numbers that appear in x. ■ Accuracy gives Infinity when applied to exact numbers, such as integers. ■ Accuracy assumes a precision of $MachinePrecision when applied to machine precision numbers. ■ Accuracy can yield a negative result when applied to zero precision numbers. ■ See page 47. ■ See also: Precision, N, Chop, SetAccuracy.

□ **AccuracyGoal**

(Mentioned on page 140.) Use on-line help or see pages 687 and 751 of The *Mathematica* Book.

□ **AddTo**

(Mentioned on page 257.) Use on-line help or see pages 248 and 751 of The *Mathematica* Book.

□ **AiryAi**

(Mentioned on page 51.) Use on-line help or see pages 570 and 751 of The *Mathematica* Book.

□ **AiryAiPrime**

(Mentioned on page 51.) Use on-line help or see pages 570 and 752 of The *Mathematica* Book.

□ **AiryBi**

(Mentioned on page 51.) Use on-line help or see pages 570 and 752 of The *Mathematica* Book.

□ **AiryBiPrime**

(Mentioned on page 51.) Use on-line help or see pages 570 and 752 of The *Mathematica* Book.

□ **AlgebraicRules**

(Mentioned on pages 69 and 78.) Use on-line help or see pages 622 and 752 of The *Mathematica* Book.

■ **All**

All is a setting used for certain options.

For example, PlotRange -> All specifies that all points are to be included in a plot. ■ See page 85.

■ **Alternatives**

p_1 | p_2 | ... is a pattern object which represents any of the patterns p_i.

Example: _Integer | _Real represents an object with head either Integer or Real. ■ Unless the same set of pattern names appears in all of the p_i, you cannot use these pattern names on the right-hand side of transformation rules for the pattern. Thus, for example, you can use x in a[x_] | b[x_], but you can use neither x nor y in a[x_] | b[y_]. ■ See page 244. ■ See also: Optional.

■ **AmbientLight**

AmbientLight is an option to Graphics3D and related functions that gives the level of simulated ambient illumination in a three-dimensional picture.

The setting for AmbientLight must be a GrayLevel, Hue or RGBColor directive. ■ See page 328. ■ See also: Lighting, LightSources, SurfaceColor.

□ AnchoredSearch

(Mentioned on page 280.) Use on-line help or see pages 501 and 752 of The *Mathematica* Book.

■ And

e_1 && e_2 && ... is the logical AND function. It evaluates its arguments in order, giving False immediately if any of them are False, and True if they are all True.

And gives symbolic results when necessary. It applies no simplification rules, except removing initial arguments that are True. ■ See page 264. ■ See also: LogicalExpand.

■ Apart

Apart[*expr*] rewrites a rational expression as a sum of terms with minimal denominators.

Apart[*expr*, *var*] treats all variables other than *var* as constants.

Example: Apart[(x^2+1)/(x-1)] $\longrightarrow$ $1 + \dfrac{2}{-1 + x} + x$. ■ Apart gives the partial fraction decomposition of a rational expression. ■ Apart[*expr*, *var*] writes *expr* as a polynomial in *var* together with a sum of ratios of polynomials, where the degree in *var* of each numerator polynomial is less than that of the corresponding denominator polynomial.
■ Apart[(x + y)/(x - y), x] $\longrightarrow$ $1 - \dfrac{2 y}{-x + y}$. ■ Apart[(x + y)/(x - y), y] $\longrightarrow$ $-1 + \dfrac{2 x}{x - y}$.
■ Apart[*expr*, Trig -> True] treats trigonometric functions as rational functions of exponentials, and manipulates them accordingly. ■ See page 67. ■ See also: Together, Cancel, PolynomialQuotient.

■ Append

Append[*expr*, *elem*] gives *expr* with *elem* appended.

Examples: Append[{a,b}, c] $\longrightarrow$ {a, b, c}; Append[f[a], b+c] $\longrightarrow$ f[a, b + c]. ■ See page 116. ■ See also: Prepend, Insert, AppendTo.

□ AppendTo

(Mentioned on page 257.) Use on-line help or see pages 249 and 753 of The *Mathematica* Book.

■ Apply

Apply[*f*, *expr*] or *f* @@ *expr* replaces the head of *expr* by *f*.

Examples: Apply[f, {a, b, c}] $\longrightarrow$ f[a, b, c]; Apply[Plus, g[a, b]] $\longrightarrow$ a + b. ■ The default value for *levelspec* in Apply is {0}. ■ Example: Apply[f, {{a,b},{c,d}}] $\longrightarrow$ f[{a, b}, {c, d}]. ■ See page 234. ■ See also: Map, Scan, MapThread.

■ ArcCos

ArcCos[z] gives the arc cosine $\cos^{-1}(z)$ of the complex number z.

Mathematical function (see Section A3.7). ■ All results are given in radians. ■ For real z between -1 and 1, the results are always in the range 0 to π. ■ See page 42.

■ ArcCosh

ArcCosh[z] gives the inverse hyperbolic cosine $\cosh^{-1}(z)$ of the complex number z.

Mathematical function (see Section A3.7). ■ See page 42. ■ See also: ArcSech.

■ ArcCot

ArcCot[z] gives the arc cotangent $\cot^{-1}(z)$ of the complex number z.

Mathematical function (see Section A3.7). ■ All results are given in radians. ■ For real z, the results are always in the range $-\pi/2$ to $\pi/2$, excluding 0. ■ See page 42.

■ ArcCoth

ArcCoth[z] gives the inverse hyperbolic cotangent $\coth^{-1}(z)$ of the complex number z.

Mathematical function (see Section A3.7). ■ See page 42.

■ ArcCsc

ArcCsc[z] gives the arc cosecant $\csc^{-1}(z)$ of the complex number z.

Mathematical function (see Section A3.7). ■ All results are given in radians. ■ For real z outside the interval -1 to 1, the results are always in the range $-\pi/2$ to $\pi/2$, excluding 0. ■ See page 42.

■ ArcCsch

ArcCsch[z] gives the inverse hyperbolic cosecant $\operatorname{csch}^{-1}(z)$ of the complex number z.

Mathematical function (see Section A3.7). ■ See page 42.

■ ArcSec

ArcSec[z] gives the arc secant $\sec^{-1}(z)$ of the complex number z.

Mathematical function (see Section A3.7). ■ All results are given in radians. ■ For real z outside the interval -1 to 1, the results are always in the range 0 to π, excluding $\pi/2$. ■ See page 42.

■ ArcSech

ArcSech[z] gives the inverse hyperbolic secant $\operatorname{sech}^{-1}(z)$ of the complex number z.

Mathematical function (see Section A3.7). ■ See page 42.

■ ArcSin

ArcSin[z] gives the arc sine $\sin^{-1}(z)$ of the complex number z.

Mathematical function (see Section A3.7). ■ All results are given in radians. ■ For real z between -1 and 1, the results are always in the range $-\pi/2$ to $\pi/2$. ■ See page 42.

■ ArcSinh

ArcSinh[z] gives the inverse hyperbolic sine $\sinh^{-1}(z)$ of the complex number z.

Mathematical function (see Section A3.7). ■ See page 42. ■ See also: ArcCsch.

■ ArcTan

ArcTan[z] gives the arc tangent $\tan^{-1}(z)$ of the complex number z.

ArcTan[x, y] gives the arc tangent of $\frac{y}{x}$, taking into account which quadrant the point (x, y) is in.

Mathematical function (see Section A3.7). ■ All results are given in radians. ■ For real z, the results are always in the range $-\pi/2$ to $\pi/2$. ■ If x or y is complex, then ArcTan[x, y] gives $-i \log\left(\frac{x+i\,y}{\sqrt{x^2+y^2}}\right)$. When $x^2+y^2 = 1$, ArcTan[x, y] gives the number ϕ such that $x = \cos\phi$ and $y = \sin\phi$. ■ See page 42. ■ See also: Arg.

■ **ArcTanh**

ArcTanh[z] gives the hyperbolic arc tangent $\tanh^{-1}(z)$ of the complex number z.

Mathematical function (see Section A3.7). ■ See page 42. ■ See also: ArcCoth.

■ **Arg**

Arg[z] gives the argument of the complex number z.

Mathematical function (see Section A3.7). ■ Arg[z] gives the phase angle of z in radians. ■ The result from Arg[z] is always between $-\pi$ and $+\pi$. ■ See page 43. ■ See also: ArcTan, Sign.

□ **ArithmeticGeometricMean**

(Mentioned on page 57.) Use on-line help or see pages 580 and 755 of The *Mathematica* Book.

■ **Array**

Array[f, n] generates a list of length n, with elements $f[i]$.

Array[f, {n_1, n_2, ... }] generates an $n_1 \times n_2 \times ...$ array of nested lists, with elements $f[i_1, i_2, ...]$.

Array[f, *dims*, *origin*] generates a list using the specified index origin (default 1).

Array[f, *dims*, *origin*, h] uses head h, rather than List, for each level of the array.

Example: Array[f, 3] ⟶ {f[1], f[2], f[3]}.
■ Array[f, {2, 3}] ⟶ {{f[1, 1], f[1, 2], f[1, 3]}, {f[2, 1], f[2, 2], f[2, 3]}} generates a 2×3 matrix. ■ Array[#1^#2 &, {2, 2}] ⟶ {{1, 1}, {2, 4}}. ■ Array[f, 3, 0] ⟶ {f[0], f[1], f[2]} generates an array with index origin 0. ■ Array[f, 3, 1, Plus] ⟶ f[1] + f[2] + f[3]. ■ Note that the dimensions given to Array are *not* in standard *Mathematica* iterator notation. ■ See pages 150 and 151. ■ See also: Table.

■ **AspectRatio**

AspectRatio is an option for Show and related functions which specifies the ratio of height to width for a plot.

AspectRatio determines the scaling for the final image shape. ■ AspectRatio -> Automatic determines the ratio of height to width from the actual coordinate values in the plot. ■ The default value AspectRatio -> 1/GoldenRatio is used for two-dimensional plots. AspectRatio -> Automatic is used for three-dimensional plots. ■ See page 316. ■ See also: BoxRatios, PlotRegion.

□ **AtomQ**

(Mentioned on page 246.) Use on-line help or see pages 228 and 756 of The *Mathematica* Book.

□ **Attributes**

(Mentioned on page 275.) Use on-line help or see pages 271 and 756 of The *Mathematica* Book.

■ **Automatic**

Automatic represents an option value that is to be chosen automatically by a built-in function.

See page 85.

■ Axes

Axes is an option for graphics functions that specifies whether axes should be drawn.

Axes -> True draws all axes. ■ Axes -> False draws no axes. ■ Axes -> {False, True} draws a y axis but no x axis in two dimensions. ■ Axes -> Automatic omits an axis in certain cases where an axis is probably not wanted. For example, if the option Frame -> True is also being used in two dimensions, axes that would otherwise appear at the edge of the plot are omitted. ■ The default value Axes -> Automatic is used for two-dimensional plots. Axes -> True is used for three-dimensional plots. ■ In two dimensions, axes are drawn to cross at the position specified by the option AxesOrigin. ■ In three dimensions, axes are drawn on the edges of the bounding box specified by the option AxesEdge. ■ See pages 330 and 335. ■ See also: AxesLabel, Frame, GridLines, Boxed.

■ AxesEdge

AxesEdge is an option for 3D graphics functions that specifies on which edges of the bounding box axes should be drawn.

AxesEdge -> {{dir_y, dir_z}, {dir_x, dir_z}, {dir_x, dir_y}} specifies on which three edges of the bounding box axes are drawn. The dir_i must be either +1 or -1, and specify whether axes are drawn on the edge of the box with a larger or smaller value of coordinate i, respectively. ■ The default setting AxesEdge -> Automatic chooses automatically on which exposed box edges axes should be drawn. ■ Any pair {dir_i, dir_j} in the setting for AxesEdge can be replaced by Automatic to specify that the position of the corresponding axis is to be chosen automatically. ■ Any pair {dir_i, dir_j} can be replaced by None, in which case the corresponding axis will not be drawn. ■ If you explicitly specify on which edge to draw an axis, the axis will be drawn on that edge, whether or not the edge is exposed with the view point you have chosen. ■ See page 337.

■ AxesLabel

AxesLabel is an option for graphics functions that specifies labels for axes.

AxesLabel -> None specifies that no labels should be given. ■ AxesLabel -> *label* specifies a label for the y axis of a two-dimensional plot, and the z axis of a three-dimensional plot. ■ AxesLabel -> {*xlabel*, *ylabel*, ... } specifies labels for different axes. ■ By default, axes labels in two-dimensional graphics are placed at the ends of the axes. In three-dimensional graphics, they are aligned with the middles of the axes. ■ Any expression can be specified as a label. It will be given in OutputForm. Arbitrary strings of text can be given as "*text*". ■ See pages 331 and 338. ■ See also: PlotLabel, FrameLabel.

■ AxesOrigin

AxesOrigin is an option for two-dimensional graphics functions which specifies where any axes drawn should cross.

AxesOrigin -> {x, y} specifies that the axes should cross at the point {x, y}. ■ AxesOrigin -> Automatic uses an internal algorithm to determine where the axes should cross. If the point {0, 0} is within, or close to, the plotting region, then it is usually chosen as the axis origin. ■ In contour and density plots, AxesOrigin -> Automatic puts axes outside the plotting area. ■ See page 331.

■ AxesStyle

AxesStyle is an option for graphics functions which specifies how axes should be rendered.

AxesStyle can be used in both two- and three-dimensional graphics. ■ AxesStyle -> *style* specifies that all axes are to be generated with the specified graphics directive, or list of graphics directives. ■ AxesStyle -> {{*xstyle*}, {*ystyle*}, ... } specifies that axes should use graphics directives *xstyle*, ... The styles must be enclosed in lists, perhaps of length one. ■ Styles can be specified using graphics directives such as Dashing, Hue and Thickness. ■ The default color of axes is specified by the option DefaultColor. ■ See pages 331 and 337. ■ See also: Prolog, Epilog, PlotStyle, FrameStyle.

☐ Composition

(Mentioned on page 238.) Use on-line help or see pages 213 and 768 of The *Mathematica* Book.

■ CompoundExpression

$expr_1$; $expr_2$; ... evaluates the $expr_i$ in turn, giving the last one as the result.

CompoundExpression evaluates its arguments in a sequence corresponding to the control flow. ■ The returned value can be the result of Return[*expr*]. ■ $expr_1$; $expr_2$; returns value Null. If it is given as input, the resulting output will not be printed. Out[*n*] will nevertheless be assigned to be the value of $expr_2$. ■ See pages 36 and 351. ■ See also: Block.

■ Condition

patt /; *test* is a pattern which matches only if the evaluation of *test* yields True.

lhs :> *rhs* /; *test* represents a rule which applies only if the evaluation of *test* yields True.

lhs := *rhs* /; *test* is a definition to be used only if *test* yields True.

Example: The pattern x_ /; x > 0 represents an expression which must be positive. ■ All pattern variables used in *test* must also appear in *patt*. ■ Example: f[x_] := fp[x] /; x > 1 defines a function in the case when $x > 1$. ■ *lhs* := Module[{*vars*}, *rhs* /; *test*] allows local variables to be shared between *test* and *rhs*. You can use the same construction with Block and With. ■ See pages 244 and 265. ■ See also: If, Switch, Which, PatternTest.

■ Conjugate

Conjugate[z] gives the complex conjugate z^* of the complex number z.

Mathematical function (see Section A3.7). ■ See page 43.

☐ Constant

(Mentioned on page 275.) Use on-line help or see pages 272, 625 and 768 of The *Mathematica* Book.

☐ Constants

Use on-line help or see pages 625 and 768 of The *Mathematica* Book.

■ ConstrainedMax

ConstrainedMax[*f*, {*inequalities*}, {x, y, ... }] finds the global maximum of *f* in the domain specified by the inequalities. The variables $x, y, ...$ are all assumed to be non-negative.

ConstrainedMax returns a list of the form {f_{max}, {x -> x_{max}, y -> y_{max}, ... }}, where f_{max} is the maximum value of *f* in the specified domain, and $x_{max}, y_{max}, ...$ give the point at which the maximum is attained. ■ ConstrainedMax implements linear programming. It can always get a result so long as *f* and the inequalities you specify depend only linearly on the variables $x, y, ...$. The inequalities can contain no parameters other than the explicit variables you specify. The inequalities cannot involve complex numbers. ■ ConstrainedMax returns unevaluated if the inequalities are inconsistent.
■ ConstrainedMax returns an infinite result if the value of *f* is unbounded in the domain specified by the inequalities.
■ ConstrainedMax yields exact rational number results if *f* and the inequalities are specified exactly. ■ ConstrainedMax accepts both strict inequalities of the form *lhs* < *rhs*, and non-strict ones of the form *lhs* <= *rhs*. It also accepts equalities of the form *lhs* == *rhs*. ■ When ConstrainedMax returns rational number results, it assumes that all inequalities are not strict. Thus, for example, ConstrainedMax may return x -> 1/2, even though strict inequalities allow only $\frac{1}{2} - \epsilon$.
■ ConstrainedMax finds approximate numerical results if its input contains approximate numbers. The option Tolerance specifies the tolerance to be used for internal comparisons. The default is Tolerance -> Automatic, which does exact comparisons for exact numbers, and uses tolerance 10^{-6} for approximate numbers. ■ See page 134. ■ See also: LinearProgramming, FindMinimum.

■ **ConstrainedMin**

ConstrainedMin[f, {*inequalities*}, {x, y, ... }] finds the global minimum of f in the domain specified by the inequalities. The variables $x, y, ...$ are all assumed to be non-negative.

See notes for ConstrainedMax. ■ See page 134.

□ **Context**

(Mentioned on page 205.) Use on-line help or see pages 334 and 769 of The *Mathematica* Book.

□ **Contexts**

(Mentioned on page 205.) Use on-line help or see pages 334, 385 and 769 of The *Mathematica* Book.

□ **ContextToFilename**

(Mentioned on page 279.) Use on-line help or see pages 492 and 769 of The *Mathematica* Book.

□ **Continuation**

(Mentioned on page 284.) Use on-line help or see pages 517 and 769 of The *Mathematica* Book.

□ **Continue**

(Mentioned on page 274.) Use on-line help or see pages 293 and 770 of The *Mathematica* Book.

■ ContourGraphics

ContourGraphics[*array*] is a representation of a contour plot.

array must be a rectangular array of real numbers, representing *z* values. ■ The following options can be given:

AspectRatio	1	ratio of height to width
Axes	False	whether to draw axes
AxesLabel	None	axes labels
AxesOrigin	Automatic	where axes should cross
AxesStyle	{}	graphics directives to specify the style for axes
Background	Automatic	background color for the plot
ColorFunction	Automatic	function specifying the color of regions between contour lines
ContourLines	True	whether to draw explicit contour lines
Contours	10	what contours to use
ContourShading	True	whether to shade the regions between contours
ContourStyle	Automatic	the style for contour lines
DefaultColor	Automatic	the default color for plot elements
DefaultFont	$DefaultFont	the default font for text
DisplayFunction	$DisplayFunction	function for generating output
Epilog	{}	graphics primitives to be rendered after the main plot
Frame	True	whether to put a frame around the plot
FrameLabel	None	frame labels
FrameStyle	Automatic	graphics directives giving the style for the frame
FrameTicks	Automatic	frame tick marks
MeshRange	Automatic	ranges of *x* and *y* coordinates
PlotLabel	None	a label for the plot
PlotRange	Automatic	range of *z* values to include
PlotRegion	Automatic	the final display region to be filled
Prolog	{}	graphics primitives to be rendered before the main plot
RotateLabel	True	whether to rotate *y* labels on the frame
Ticks	Automatic	tick marks

■ ContourGraphics[*g*] converts DensityGraphics and SurfaceGraphics objects to ContourGraphics. The resulting graphics can be rendered using Show. ■ ContourGraphics is generated by ContourPlot and ListContourPlot. ■ See page 299. ■ See also: ListContourPlot, DensityGraphics.

■ ContourLines

ContourLines is an option for contour plots which specifies whether to draw explicit contour lines.

ContourLines -> True draws contour lines. ContourLines -> False does not. ■ See page 192. ■ See also: ContourStyle, Contours, ContourSmoothing.

■ ContourPlot

ContourPlot[f, {x, $xmin$, $xmax$}, {y, $ymin$, $ymax$}] generates a contour plot of f as a function of x and y.

You should use Evaluate to evaluate the function to be plotted if this can safely be done before specific numerical values are supplied. ■ ContourPlot has the same options as ContourGraphics, with the following additions:

| Compiled | True | whether to compile the function to plot |
| PlotPoints | 15 | the number of points in each direction at which to sample the function |

■ ContourPlot has the default option setting Frame -> True. ■ ContourPlot returns a ContourGraphics object, with the MeshRange option set. ■ See page 191. ■ See also: DensityPlot.

■ Contours

Contours is an option for ContourGraphics specifying the contours to use.

Contours -> n chooses n equally spaced contours between the minimum and maximum z values. ■ Contours -> {z_1, z_2, ... } specifies the explicit z values of contours to use. ■ See page 192.

■ ContourShading

ContourShading is an option for contour plots which specifies whether the regions between contour lines should be shaded.

With ContourShading -> False, regions between contour lines are left blank. ■ With ContourShading -> True, regions are colored based on the setting for the option ColorFunction. The default is to color the regions with gray levels running from black to white with increasing height. ■ The value given as the argument for the ColorFunction function is the average of the values of the contour lines bounding a particular region, scaled so that it lies between 0 and 1. ■ See page 192.

□ ContourSmoothing

Use on-line help or see pages 427, 429 and 771 of The *Mathematica* Book.

■ ContourStyle

ContourStyle is an option for contour plots that specifies the style in which contour lines should be drawn.

ContourStyle -> *style* specifies that all contour lines are to be generated with the specified graphics directive, or list of graphics directives. ■ ContourStyle -> {{$style_1$}, {$style_2$}, ... } specifies that successive contour lines should use graphics directives $style_1$, ... The styles must be enclosed in lists, perhaps of length one. ■ The $style_i$ are used cyclically. ■ Styles can be specified using graphics directives such as Dashing, Hue and Thickness. ■ See page 192. ■ See also: PlotStyle.

□ CopyDirectory

(Mentioned on page 279.) Use on-line help or see pages 493 and 772 of The *Mathematica* Book.

□ CopyFile

(Mentioned on page 279.) Use on-line help or see pages 492 and 772 of The *Mathematica* Book.

■ Cos

Cos[z] gives the cosine of z.

Mathematical function (see Section A3.7). ■ The argument of Cos is assumed to be in radians. (Multiply by Degree to convert from degrees.) ■ See page 42. ■ See also: ArcCos, Sec.

■ Cosh

Cosh[*z*] gives the hyperbolic cosine of *z*.

Mathematical function (see Section A3.7). ■ $\cosh(z) = \frac{1}{2}(e^z + e^{-z})$. ■ See page 42. ■ See also: ArcCosh, Sech.

□ CosIntegral

(Mentioned on page 51.) Use on-line help or see pages 570 and 772 of The *Mathematica* Book.

■ Cot

Cot[*z*] gives the cotangent of *z*.

Mathematical function (see Section A3.7). ■ The argument of Cot is assumed to be in radians. (Multiply by Degree to convert from degrees.) ■ $\cot(z) = 1/\tan(z)$. ■ See page 42. ■ See also: ArcCot.

■ Coth

Coth[*z*] gives the hyperbolic cotangent of *z*.

Mathematical function (see Section A3.7). ■ See page 42. ■ See also: ArcCoth.

■ Count

Count[*list*, *pattern*] gives the number of elements in *list* that match *pattern*.

See pages 115 and 241. ■ See also: FreeQ, MemberQ, Cases, Select, Position.

□ CreateDirectory

(Mentioned on page 279.) Use on-line help or see pages 493 and 773 of The *Mathematica* Book.

■ Csc

Csc[*z*] gives the cosecant of *z*.

Mathematical function (see Section A3.7). ■ The argument of Csc is assumed to be in radians. (Multiply by Degree to convert from degrees.) ■ $\csc(z) = 1/\sin(z)$. ■ See page 42. ■ See also: ArcCsc.

■ Csch

Csch[*z*] gives the hyperbolic cosecant of *z*.

Mathematical function (see Section A3.7). ■ $\operatorname{csch}(z) = 1/\sinh(z)$. ■ See page 42. ■ See also: ArcCsch.

□ Cubics

Use on-line help or see page 773 of The *Mathematica* Book.

■ Cuboid

Cuboid[{*xmin*, *ymin*, *zmin*}] is a three-dimensional graphics primitive that represents a unit cuboid, oriented parallel to the axes.

Cuboid[{*xmin*, *ymin*, *zmin*}, {*xmax*, *ymax*, *zmax*}] specifies a cuboid by giving the coordinates of opposite corners.

Each face of the cuboid (rectangular parallelepiped) is effectively a Polygon object. ■ You can specify how the faces and edges of the cuboid should be rendered using the same graphics directives as for polygons. ■ The coordinates of the corners of the cuboid can be given using Scaled. ■ See page 99. ■ See also: Polygon, Rectangle.

☐ Cyclotomic

> (Mentioned on page 69.) Use on-line help or see pages 601 and 773 of The *Mathematica* Book.

■ D

> D[f, x] gives the partial derivative $\frac{\partial}{\partial x} f$.
>
> D[f, {x, n}] gives the multiple derivative $\frac{\partial^n}{\partial x^n} f$.
>
> D[f, x_1, x_2, ...] gives $\frac{\partial}{\partial x_1} \frac{\partial}{\partial x_2} ... f$.
>
> All quantities that do not explicitly depend on the x_i are taken to have zero partial derivative.
> ■ D[f, x_1, ... , NonConstants -> {v_1, ... }] specifies that the v_i implicitly depend on the x_i, so that they do not have zero partial derivative. ■ The derivatives of built-in mathematical functions are evaluated when possible in terms of other built-in mathematical functions. ■ D uses the chain rule to simplify derivatives of unknown functions. ■ See page 122.
> ■ See also: Dt, Derivative.

■ Dashing

> Dashing[{r_1, r_2, ... }] is a two-dimensional graphics directive which specifies that lines which follow are to be drawn dashed, with successive segments of lengths $r_1, r_2, ...$ (repeated cyclically). The r_i is given as a fraction of the total width of the graph.
>
> Dashing can be used in both two- and three-dimensional graphics. ■ Dashing[{ }] specifies that lines should be solid.
> ■ See page 97. ■ See also: AbsoluteDashing, Thickness, GrayLevel, Hue, RGBColor.

☐ Date

> (Mentioned on page 283.) Use on-line help or see pages 523 and 774 of The *Mathematica* Book.

☐ DeclarePackage

> (Mentioned on page 205.) Use on-line help or see pages 342 and 774 of The *Mathematica* Book.

☐ Decompose

> (Mentioned on page 69.) Use on-line help or see pages 601 and 774 of The *Mathematica* Book.

☐ Decrement

> (Mentioned on page 257.) Use on-line help or see pages 248 and 774 of The *Mathematica* Book.

☐ Default

> Use on-line help or see pages 734 and 775 of The *Mathematica* Book.

■ DefaultColor

> DefaultColor is an option for graphics functions which specifies the default color to use for lines, points, etc.
>
> The setting for DefaultColor must be a CMYKColor, GrayLevel, Hue or RGBColor directive. ■ The default setting is DefaultColor -> Automatic, which gives a default color complementary to the background specified. ■ See page 304.
> ■ See also: Prolog, Background.

■ **DefaultFont**

> **DefaultFont** is an option for graphics functions which specifies the default font to use for text.
>
> DefaultFont -> {"*font*", *size*} specifies the name and size of the font to use. ■ The font is used by default for all text, including labels and tick marks. ■ See notes for FontForm. ■ The default setting is DefaultFont :> $DefaultFont. ■ See page 340.

□ **Definition**

> (Mentioned on page 257.) Use on-line help or see pages 479 and 775 of The *Mathematica* Book.

■ **Degree**

> **Degree** gives the number of radians in one degree. It has a numerical value of $\frac{\pi}{180}$.
>
> You can multiply by Degree to convert from degrees to radians. ■ Example: 30 Degree represents 30°. ■ See page 30.

■ **Delete**

> Delete[*expr*, *n*] deletes the element at position *n* in *expr*. If *n* is negative, the position is counted from the end.
>
> Delete[*expr*, {*i*, *j*, ... }] deletes the part at position {*i*, *j*, ... }.
>
> Delete[*expr*, {{i_1, j_1, ... }, {i_2, j_2, ... }, ... }] deletes parts at several positions.
>
> Example: Delete[{a, b, c, d}, 3] ⟶ {a, b, d}. ■ Delete[{a, b, c, d}, {{1}, {3}}] ⟶ {b, d}. ■ Deleting the head of a particular element in an expression is equivalent to applying FlattenAt to the expression at that point. ■ Example: Delete[{a, {b}, c}, {2, 0}] ⟶ {a, b, c}. ■ See page 116. ■ See also: Insert, MapAt, ReplacePart, FlattenAt, DeleteCases.

■ **DeleteCases**

> DeleteCases[*expr*, *pattern*] removes all elements of *expr* which match *pattern*.
>
> DeleteCases[*expr*, *pattern*, *levspec*] removes all parts of *expr* on levels specified by *levspec* which match *pattern*.
>
> Example: DeleteCases[{1, a, 2, b}, _Integer] ⟶ {a, b}. ■ With the option Heads -> True, you can delete heads with DeleteCases. Deleting the head of a particular element in an expression is equivalent to applying FlattenAt to the expression at that point. ■ Example:
> DeleteCases[{1, f[2, 3], 4}, f, {2}, Heads -> True] ⟶ {1, 2, 3, 4}. ■ See page 241. ■ See also: Cases, ReplaceAll, Delete.

□ **DeleteDirectory**

> (Mentioned on page 279.) Use on-line help or see pages 493 and 776 of The *Mathematica* Book.

□ **DeleteFile**

> (Mentioned on page 279.) Use on-line help or see pages 492 and 776 of The *Mathematica* Book.

□ **Denominator**

> (Mentioned on pages 53 and 65.) Use on-line help or see pages 82 and 776 of The *Mathematica* Book.

■ **DensityGraphics**

DensityGraphics [*array*] is a representation of a density plot.

array must be a rectangular array of real numbers, representing z values. ■ The following options can be given:

AspectRatio	1	ratio of height to width
Axes	False	whether to draw axes
AxesLabel	None	axes labels
AxesOrigin	Automatic	where axes should cross
AxesStyle	Automatic	graphics directives to specify the style for axes
Background	Automatic	background color for the plot
ColorFunction	Automatic	function specifying the color for each cell
DefaultColor	Automatic	the default color for plot elements
DefaultFont	$DefaultFont	the default font for text
DisplayFunction	$DisplayFunction	function for generating output
Epilog	{}	graphics primitives to be rendered after the main plot
Frame	True	whether to put a frame around the plot
FrameLabel	None	frame labels
FrameStyle	Automatic	graphics directives giving the style for the frame
FrameTicks	Automatic	frame tick marks
Mesh	True	whether to draw a mesh
MeshRange	Automatic	ranges of x and y coordinates
MeshStyle	Automatic	graphics directives to specify the style for mesh lines
PlotLabel	None	a label for the plot
PlotRange	Automatic	range of z values to include
PlotRegion	Automatic	the final display region to be filled
Prolog	{}	graphics primitives to be rendered before the main plot
RotateLabel	True	whether to rotate y labels on the frame
Ticks	Automatic	tick marks

■ DensityGraphics can be displayed using Show. ■ DensityGraphics is generated by DensityPlot and ListDensityPlot. ■ DensityGraphics [*g*] converts ContourGraphics and SurfaceGraphics objects to DensityGraphics. The resulting graphics can be rendered using Show. ■ See page 299. ■ See also: ListDensityPlot, ContourGraphics, Raster, RasterArray.

■ **DensityPlot**

DensityPlot [*f*, {*x*, *xmin*, *xmax*}, {*y*, *ymin*, *ymax*}] makes a density plot of *f* as a function of *x* and *y*.

You should use Evaluate to evaluate the function to be plotted if this can safely be done before specific numerical values are supplied. ■ DensityPlot has the same options as DensityGraphics, with the following addition:

PlotPoints   15   the number of points in each direction at which to sample the function

■ DensityPlot has the default option setting Frame -> True. ■ DensityPlot returns a DensityGraphics object, with the MeshRange option set. ■ See page 193. ■ See also: ContourPlot.

□ **Depth**

(Mentioned on page 119.) Use on-line help or see pages 199 and 778 of The *Mathematica* Book.

■ Derivative

f' represents the derivative of a function *f* of one argument.

Derivative[*n₁*, *n₂*, ...] [*f*] is the general form, representing a function obtained from *f* by differentiating *n₁* times with respect to the first argument, *n₂* times with respect to the second argument, and so on.

f' is equivalent to Derivative[1][*f*]. ■ *f''* evaluates to Derivative[2][*f*]. ■ You can think of Derivative as a *functional operator* which acts on functions to give derivative functions. ■ Derivative is generated when you apply D to functions whose derivatives *Mathematica* does not know. ■ *Mathematica* attempts to convert Derivative[*n*][*f*] and so on to pure functions. Whenever Derivative[*n*][*f*] is generated, *Mathematica* rewrites it as D[*f*[#]&, {#, *n*}]. If *Mathematica* finds an explicit value for this derivative, it returns this value. Otherwise, it returns the original Derivative form. ■ Example: Cos' ⟶ -Sin[#1] &. ■ See page 124. ■ See also: D, Dt.

■ Det

Det[*m*] gives the determinant of the square matrix *m*.

Det[*m*, Modulus -> *p*] computes the determinant modulo *p*. ■ See page 157. ■ See also: Minors, RowReduce, NullSpace.

■ DiagonalMatrix

DiagonalMatrix[*list*] gives a matrix with the elements of *list* on the leading diagonal, and 0 elsewhere.

See page 151. ■ See also: IdentityMatrix.

□ Dialog

(Mentioned on pages 275 and 283.) Use on-line help or see pages 520 and 778 of The *Mathematica* Book.

□ DialogIndent

Use on-line help or see pages 517 and 779 of The *Mathematica* Book.

□ DialogProlog

Use on-line help or see pages 522 and 779 of The *Mathematica* Book.

□ DialogSymbols

Use on-line help or see pages 522 and 779 of The *Mathematica* Book.

□ DigitBlock

(Mentioned on page 53.) Use on-line help or see pages 351 and 779 of The *Mathematica* Book.

□ DigitQ

(Mentioned on page 283.) Use on-line help or see pages 378 and 779 of The *Mathematica* Book.

■ Dimensions

Dimensions[*expr*] gives a list of the dimensions of *expr*.

Dimensions[*expr*, *n*] gives a list of the dimensions of *expr* down to level *n*.

expr must be a *full array*, with all the pieces of *expr* at a particular level having the same length. (The elements of *expr* can then be thought of as filling up a hyper-rectangular region.) ■ Each successive level in *expr* sampled by Dimensions must have the same head. ■ Example: Dimensions[{{a,b,c},{d,e,f}}] ⟶ {2, 3}. ■ See page 151. ■ See also: TensorRank, VectorQ, MatrixQ.

■ DirectedInfinity

DirectedInfinity[ ] represents an infinite numerical quantity whose direction in the complex plane is unknown.

DirectedInfinity[*z*] represents an infinite numerical quantity that is a positive real multiple of the complex number *z*.

You can think of DirectedInfinity[*z*] as representing a point in the complex plane reached by starting at the origin and going an infinite distance in the direction of the point *z*. ■ The following conversions are made:

Infinity	DirectedInfinity[1]
-Infinity	DirectedInfinity[-1]
ComplexInfinity	DirectedInfinity[ ]

■ Certain arithmetic operations are performed on DirectedInfinity quantities. ■ In OutputForm, DirectedInfinity[*z*] is printed in terms of Infinity, and DirectedInfinity[ ] is printed as ComplexInfinity. ■ See page 125. ■ See also: Indeterminate.

□ Directory

(Mentioned on page 279.) Use on-line help or see pages 489 and 780 of The *Mathematica* Book.

□ DirectoryStack

(Mentioned on page 279.) Use on-line help or see pages 489 and 780 of The *Mathematica* Book.

■ Disk

Disk[{*x*, *y*}, *r*] is a two-dimensional graphics primitive that represents a filled disk of radius *r* centered at the point *x*, *y*.

Disk[{*x*, *y*}, {r_x, r_y}] yields an elliptical disk with semi-axes r_x and r_y.

Disk[{*x*, *y*}, *r*, {*theta$_1$*, *theta$_2$*}] represents a segment of a disk.

Angles are measured in radians counter-clockwise from the positive *x* direction.
■ Disk[{*x*, *y*}, {r_x, r_y}, {*theta$_1$*, *theta$_2$*}] yields an elliptical disk segment obtained by transforming a circular disk segment with the specified starting and ending angles. ■ Scaled can be used in the radius specification (see notes for Circle). ■ See page 92. ■ See also: Circle, Polygon.

□ Dispatch

Use on-line help or see pages 246 and 780 of The *Mathematica* Book.

□ Display

(Mentioned on page 281.) Use on-line help or see pages 465 and 781 of The *Mathematica* Book.

■ **DisplayFunction**

> `DisplayFunction` is an option for graphics and sound functions that specifies the function to apply to graphics and sound objects in order to display them.
>
> The default setting for `DisplayFunction` in graphics functions is `$DisplayFunction`, and in sound functions is `$SoundDisplayFunction`. ■ Setting `DisplayFunction -> Identity` will cause the objects to be returned, but no display to be generated. ■ See page 83. ■ See also: `Show`.

□ **Distribute**

> (Mentioned on page 238.) Use on-line help or see pages 216 and 781 of The *Mathematica* Book.

■ **Divide**

> x/y or `Divide[x, y]` is equivalent to $x\ y^{\wedge}-1$.
>
> x/y is converted to $x\ y^{\wedge}-1$ on input. ■ See page 27.

□ **DivideBy**

> (Mentioned on page 257.) Use on-line help or see pages 248 and 781 of The *Mathematica* Book.

■ **Divisors**

> `Divisors[n]` gives a list of the integers that divide n.
>
> Example: `Divisors[12]` ⟶ `{1, 2, 3, 4, 6, 12}`. ■ `Divisors[n, GaussianIntegers -> True]` includes divisors that are Gaussian integers. ■ See page 55. ■ See also: `FactorInteger`.

□ **DivisorSigma**

> (Mentioned on page 57.) Use on-line help or see pages 556 and 782 of The *Mathematica* Book.

■ **Do**

> `Do[expr, {imax}]` evaluates *expr imax* times.
>
> `Do[expr, {i, imax}]` evaluates *expr* with the variable i successively taking on the values 1 through *imax* (in steps of 1).
>
> `Do[expr, {i, imin, imax}]` starts with $i = imin$. `Do[expr, {i, imin, imax, di}]` uses steps *di*.
>
> `Do[expr, {i, imin, imax}, {j, jmin, jmax}, ... ]` evaluates *expr* looping over different values of j, etc. for each i.
>
> Do uses the standard *Mathematica* iteration specification. ■ You can use `Return` inside Do. ■ Unless an explicit `Return` is used, the value returned by Do is `Null`. ■ See page 268. ■ See also: `For`, `While`, `Table`, `Nest`, `Fold`.

■ Dot

$a.b.c$ or Dot[a, b, c] gives products of vectors, matrices and tensors.

$a.b$ gives an explicit result when a and b are lists with appropriate dimensions. It contracts the last direction in a with the first direction in b. ■ Various applications of Dot:

$\{a_1,\ a_2\}\ .\ \{b_1,\ b_2\}$	scalar product of vectors
$\{a_1,\ a_2\}\ .\ \{\{m_{11},\ m_{12}\},\ \{m_{21},\ m_{22}\}\}$	product of a vector and a matrix
$\{\{m_{11},\ m_{12}\},\ \{m_{21},\ m_{22}\}\}\ .\ \{a_1,\ a_2\}$	product of a matrix and a vector
$\{\{m_{11},\ m_{12}\},\ \{m_{21},\ m_{22}\}\}\ .\ \{\{n_{11},\ n_{12}\},\ \{n_{21},\ n_{22}\}\}$	product of two matrices

Examples: {a, b} . {c, d} $\longrightarrow$ a c + b d. ■ {{a, b}, {c, d}} . {x, y} $\longrightarrow$ {a x + b y, c x + d y}.
■ The result of applying Dot to two tensors $T_{i_1 i_2 \cdots i_n}$ and $U_{j_1 j_2 \cdots j_m}$ is the tensor $\sum_k T_{i_1 i_2 \cdots i_{n-1} k} U_{k j_2 \cdots j_m}$. Dot effectively contracts the last index of the first tensor with the first index of the second tensor. Applying Dot to a rank n tensor and a rank m tensor gives a rank $n + m - 2$ tensor. ■ When its arguments are not lists, Dot remains unevaluated. It has the attribute Flat. ■ See pages 149 and 154. ■ See also: Inner, Outer, NonCommutativeMultiply.

□ DownValues

(Mentioned on page 257.) Use on-line help or see pages 266 and 782 of The *Mathematica* Book.

■ Drop

Drop[*list*, *n*] gives *list* with its first *n* elements dropped.

Drop[*list*, *-n*] gives *list* with its last *n* elements dropped.

Drop[*list*, {*n*}] gives *list* with its nth element dropped.

Drop[*list*, {*m*, *n*}] gives *list* with elements *m* through *n* dropped.

Drop uses the standard *sequence specification* (see page 357). ■ Example: Drop[{a,b,c,d,e}, 2] $\longrightarrow$ {c, d, e}.
■ Drop[{a,b,c,d,e}, -3] $\longrightarrow$ {a, b}. ■ Drop can be used on an object with any head, not necessarily List. ■ See page 113. ■ See also: Rest, StringDrop, Take, Cases.

■ DSolve

DSolve[*eqn*, *y*, *x*] solves a differential equation for the function *y*, with independent variable *x*.

DSolve[{eqn_1, eqn_2, ... }, {y_1, y_2, ... }, *x*] solves a list of differential equations.

DSolve[*eqn*, *y*[*x*], *x*] gives solutions for *y*[*x*] rather than for the function *y* itself. ■ Example:

DSolve[y'[x] == 2 a x, y[x], x] $\longrightarrow$ {{y[x] -> a x^2 + C[1]}}. ■ Differential equations must be stated in terms of derivatives such as y'[x], obtained with D, not total derivatives obtained with Dt. ■ DSolve generates constants of integration indexed by successive integers. The option DSolveConstants specifies the function to apply to each index. The default is DSolveConstants -> C, which yields constants of integration C[1], C[2], ...
■ DSolveConstants -> (Module[{C}, C]&) guarantees that the constants of integration are unique, even across different invocations of DSolve. ■ Boundary conditions can be specified by giving equations such as y'[0] == b. ■ See page 173. ■ See also: NDSolve, Solve.

■ Dt

Dt[f, x] gives the total derivative $\frac{d}{dx} f$.

Dt[f] gives the total differential df.

Dt[f, $\{x, n\}$] gives the multiple derivative $\frac{d^n}{dx^n} f$.

Dt[f, x_1, x_2, ...] gives $\frac{d}{dx_1} \frac{d}{dx_2} ... f$.

Dt[f, x_1, ... , Constants -> $\{c_1,$ ... $\}$] specifies that the c_i are constants, which have zero total derivative. ■ Symbols with attribute Constant are taken to be constants, with zero total derivative. ■ If an object is specified to be a constant, then all functions with that object as a head are also taken to be constants. ■ All quantities not explicitly specified as constants are assumed to depend on the x_i. ■ Example: Dt[x y] ⟶ y Dt[x] + x Dt[y]. ■ Dt[x y, Constants -> {x}] ⟶ x Dt[y, Constants -> {x}]. ■ You can specify total derivatives by assigning values to Dt[f], etc. ■ See page 123. ■ See also: D, Derivative.

□ Dump

(Mentioned on page 283.) Use on-line help or see pages 531 and 783 of The *Mathematica* Book.

■ E

E is the exponential constant e (base of natural logarithms), with numerical value ≃ 2.71828.

Mathematical constant (see Section A3.8). ■ See page 30. ■ See also: Exp.

■ EdgeForm

EdgeForm[g] is a three-dimensional graphics directive which specifies that edges of polygons are to be drawn using the graphics directive or list of graphics directives g.

EdgeForm[ ] draws no edges of polygons. ■ The directives RGBColor, CMYKColor, GrayLevel, Hue and Thickness can be used in EdgeForm. ■ EdgeForm does not affect the rendering of Line objects. ■ See page 106. ■ See also: FaceForm, Line.

■ Eigensystem

Eigensystem[m] gives a list $\{values, vectors\}$ of the eigenvalues and eigenvectors of the square matrix m.

Eigensystem finds numerical eigenvalues and eigenvectors if m contains approximate real numbers. ■ The elements of m can be complex. ■ All the nonzero eigenvectors given are independent. If the number of eigenvectors is equal to the number of non-zero eigenvalues, then corresponding eigenvalues and eigenvectors are given in corresponding positions in their respective lists. ■ If there are more eigenvalues than independent eigenvectors, then each extra eigenvalue is paired with a vector of zeros. ■ The eigenvalues and eigenvectors satisfy the matrix equation m.Transpose[$vectors$] == Transpose[$vectors$].DiagonalMatrix[$values$]. ■ See page 162. ■ See also: NullSpace.

■ Eigenvalues

Eigenvalues[m] gives a list of the eigenvalues of the square matrix m.

Eigenvalues finds numerical eigenvalues if m contains approximate real numbers. ■ Repeated eigenvalues appear with their appropriate multiplicity. ■ An $n \times n$ matrix gives a list of exactly n eigenvalues, not necessarily distinct. ■ See page 162. ■ See also: Det.

■ Eigenvectors

Eigenvectors [*m*] gives a list of the eigenvectors of the square matrix *m*.

Eigenvectors finds numerical eigenvectors if *m* contains approximate real numbers. ■ Eigenvectors corresponding to degenerate eigenvalues are chosen to be linearly independent. ■ Eigenvectors are not normalized. ■ For an $n \times n$ matrix, Eigenvectors always returns a list of length *n*. The list contains each of the independent eigenvectors of the matrix, followed if necessary by an appropriate number of vectors of zeros. ■ Eigenvectors [*m*, ZeroTest -> *test*] applies *test* to determine whether expressions should be assumed to be zero. ■ See page 162. ■ See also: NullSpace.

■ Eliminate

Eliminate [*eqns*, *vars*] eliminates variables between a set of simultaneous equations.

Equations are given in the form *lhs* == *rhs*. ■ Simultaneous equations can be combined either in a list or with &&. ■ A single variable or a list of variables can be specified. ■ Example: Eliminate [{x == 2 + y, y == z}, y] ⟶ x == 2 + z. ■ Variables can be any expressions. ■ Eliminate works primarily with linear and polynomial equations. ■ See page 77. ■ See also: Reduce, SolveAlways, Solve, MainSolve, AlgebraicRules.

□ EllipticE

(Mentioned on page 51.) Use on-line help or see pages 580 and 784 of The *Mathematica* Book.

□ EllipticExp

(Mentioned on page 51.) Use on-line help or see pages 580 and 785 of The *Mathematica* Book.

□ EllipticF

(Mentioned on page 51.) Use on-line help or see pages 580 and 785 of The *Mathematica* Book.

□ EllipticK

(Mentioned on page 51.) Use on-line help or see pages 580 and 785 of The *Mathematica* Book.

□ EllipticLog

(Mentioned on page 51.) Use on-line help or see pages 580 and 785 of The *Mathematica* Book.

□ EllipticPi

(Mentioned on page 51.) Use on-line help or see pages 580 and 785 of The *Mathematica* Book.

□ EllipticTheta

(Mentioned on page 51.) Use on-line help or see pages 580 and 785 of The *Mathematica* Book.

□ Encode

(Mentioned on page 281.) Use on-line help or see pages 480 and 786 of The *Mathematica* Book.

□ End

(Mentioned on page 205.) Use on-line help or see pages 339 and 786 of The *Mathematica* Book.

□ EndOfFile

(Mentioned on page 281.) Use on-line help or see pages 498 and 786 of The *Mathematica* Book.

☐ **EndPackage**

(Mentioned on page 205.) Use on-line help or see pages 339 and 786 of The *Mathematica* Book.

☐ **EngineeringForm**

(Mentioned on page 53.) Use on-line help or see pages 350 and 786 of The *Mathematica* Book.

☐ **Environment**

(Mentioned on page 279.) Use on-line help or see pages 743 and 786 of The *Mathematica* Book.

■ **Epilog**

Epilog is an option for graphics functions which gives a list of graphics primitives to be rendered after the main part of the graphics is rendered.

In three-dimensional graphics, two-dimensional graphics primitives can be specified by the Epilog option. The graphics primitives are rendered in a 0,1 coordinate system. ▪ See page 304. ▪ See also: Prolog, AxesStyle, PlotStyle, DisplayFunction.

■ **Equal**

lhs == *rhs* returns True if *lhs* and *rhs* are identical.

lhs == *rhs* is used to represent a symbolic equation, to be manipulated using functions like Solve. ▪ *lhs* == *rhs* returns True if *lhs* and *rhs* are identical expressions. ▪ *lhs* == *rhs* returns False if *lhs* and *rhs* are determined to be unequal by comparisons between numbers or other raw data, such as strings. ▪ Approximate numbers are considered equal if they differ in at most their last two decimal digits. ▪ 2 == 2. gives True. ▪ e_1 == e_2 == e_3 gives True if all the e_i are equal. ▪ Equal[e] gives True. ▪ See page 264. ▪ See also: SameQ, Unequal, Order.

■ **Erf**

Erf[z] gives the error function erf(z).

Erf[z_0, z_1] gives the generalized error function erf(z_1) − erf(z_0).

Mathematical function (see Section A3.7). ▪ Erf[z] is the integral of the Gaussian distribution, given by erf(z) = $\frac{2}{\sqrt{\pi}} \int_0^z e^{-t^2} dt$. ▪ Erf[$z_0$, z_1] is given by $\frac{2}{\sqrt{\pi}} \int_{z_0}^{z_1} e^{-t^2} dt$. ▪ See pages 48 and 51. ▪ See also: ExpIntegralE, ExpIntegralEi.

■ **Erfc**

Erfc[z] gives the complementary error function erfc(z).

Erfc[z] is given by erfc(z) = 1 − erf(z). ▪ See notes for Erf. ▪ See pages 48 and 51.

☐ **EulerE**

(Mentioned on page 57.) Use on-line help or see pages 558 and 787 of The *Mathematica* Book.

☐ **EulerGamma**

Use on-line help or see pages 566 and 787 of The *Mathematica* Book.

☐ **EulerPhi**

(Mentioned on page 57.) Use on-line help or see pages 556 and 787 of The *Mathematica* Book.

- ## Evaluate

    Evaluate[*expr*] causes *expr* to be evaluated, even if it appears as the argument of a function whose attributes specify that it should be held unevaluated.

    See page 88. ▪ See also: ReleaseHold.

- ## EvenQ

    EvenQ[*expr*] gives True if *expr* is an even integer, and False otherwise.

    EvenQ[*expr*] returns False unless *expr* is manifestly an even integer (*i.e.*, has head Integer, and is even). ▪ You can use EvenQ[*x*] = True to override the normal operation of EvenQ, and effectively define *x* to be an even integer. ▪ See page 54. ▪ See also: IntegerQ, OddQ, TrueQ.

- ## □ Exit

    (Mentioned on page 283.) Use on-line help or see pages 519, 747 and 788 of The *Mathematica* Book.

- ## Exp

    Exp[*z*] is the exponential function.

    Mathematical function (see Section A3.7). ▪ Exp[*z*] is converted to E∧*z*. ▪ See page 42. ▪ See also: Power, E.

- ## Expand

    Expand[*expr*] expands out products and positive integer powers in *expr*.

    Expand[*expr*, *patt*] avoids expanding elements of *expr* which do not contain terms matching the pattern *patt*.

    Expand works only on positive integer powers. ▪ Expand applies only to the top level in *expr*.
    ▪ Expand[*expr*, Trig -> True] treats trigonometric functions as rational functions of exponentials, and expands them accordingly. ▪ Example: Expand[2 Sin[x]∧2, Trig -> True] ⟶ 1 - Cos[2 x]. ▪ See page 63. ▪ See also: Distribute, Apart, Series, Factor, LogicalExpand, PowerExpand.

- ## ExpandAll

    ExpandAll[*expr*] expands out all products and integer powers in any part of *expr*.

    ExpandAll[*expr*, *patt*] avoids expanding parts of *expr* which do not contain terms matching the pattern *patt*.

    ExpandAll[*expr*] effectively maps Expand and ExpandDenominator onto every part of *expr*. ·
    ▪ ExpandAll[*expr*, Trig -> True] treats trigonometric functions as rational functions of exponentials, and expands them accordingly. ▪ See page 67.

- ## ExpandDenominator

    ExpandDenominator[*expr*] expands out products and powers that appear as denominators in *expr*.

    ExpandDenominator works only on negative integer powers. ▪ ExpandDenominator applies only to the top level in *expr*.
    ▪ See page 67. ▪ See also: Together.

- ## ExpandNumerator

    ExpandNumerator[*expr*] expands out products and powers that appear in the numerator of *expr*.

    ExpandNumerator works on terms that have positive integer exponents. ▪ ExpandNumerator applies only to the top level in *expr*. ▪ See page 67.

■ **FrameStyle**

> **FrameStyle** is an option for two-dimensional graphics functions that specifies how the edges of a frame should be rendered.
>
> **FrameStyle** -> *style* specifies that all edges of the frame are to be generated with the specified graphics directive, or list of graphics directives. ■ **FrameStyle** -> {{*xmstyle*}, {*ymstyle*}, ... } specifies that different edges of the frame should be generated with different styles. The edges are ordered clockwise starting from the bottom edge. All styles must be enclosed in lists, perhaps of length one. ■ Styles can be specified using graphics directives such as **Dashing**, **Hue** and **Thickness**. ■ The default color of frame edges is specified by the option **DefaultColor**. ■ See page 334. ■ See also: **Prolog**, **Epilog**, **AxesStyle**.

■ **FrameTicks**

> **FrameTicks** is an option for two-dimensional graphics functions that specifies tick marks for the edges of a frame.
>
> The following settings can be given for **FrameTicks**:

None	no tick marks drawn
Automatic	tick marks placed automatically
{*xmticks*, *ymticks*, ... }	tick mark options specified separately for each edge

> When tick mark specifications are given separately for each edge, the edges are ordered clockwise starting from the bottom of the frame. ■ With the **Automatic** setting, tick marks are usually placed at points whose coordinates have the minimum number of digits in their decimal representation. ■ For each edge, tick marks can be specified as described in the notes for **Ticks**. ■ See page 334. ■ See also: **Ticks**, **GridLines**, **FaceGrids**.

□ **FreeQ**

> (Mentioned on page 115.) Use on-line help or see pages 228 and 798 of The *Mathematica* Book.

□ **FromCharacterCode**

> (Mentioned on page 283.) Use on-line help or see pages 366 and 799 of The *Mathematica* Book.

□ **FromDate**

> (Mentioned on page 283.) Use on-line help or see pages 524 and 799 of The *Mathematica* Book.

□ **FullDefinition**

> (Mentioned on page 257.) Use on-line help or see pages 479 and 799 of The *Mathematica* Book.

■ **FullForm**

> **FullForm**[*expr*] prints as the full form of *expr*, with no special syntax.
>
> Example: **FullForm**[a + b^2] ⟶ **Plus**[a, **Power**[b, 2]]. ■ **FullForm** acts as a "wrapper", which affects printing, but not evaluation. ■ See page 226. ■ See also: **InputForm**, **TreeForm**.

□ **FullGraphics**

> (Mentioned on page 302.) Use on-line help or see pages 398 and 799 of The *Mathematica* Book.

■ **FullOptions**

FullOptions [*expr*] gives the full settings of options explicitly specified in an expression such as a graphics object.

FullOptions [*expr*, *name*] gives the full setting for the option *name*.

FullOptions [*expr*, {*name₁*, *name₂*, ... }] gives a list of the full settings for the options *nameᵢ*.

FullOptions gives the actual settings for options used internally by *Mathematica* when the setting given is Automatic or All. ■ You can use FullOptions on graphics options such as PlotRange and Ticks. ■ See pages 302 and 306. ■ See also: Options, FullGraphics.

■ **Function**

Function [*body*] or *body*& is a pure function. The formal parameters are # (or #1), #2, etc.

Function [*x*, *body*] is a pure function with a single formal parameter *x*.

Function [{*x₁*, *x₂*, ... }, *body*] is a pure function with a list of formal parameters.

Example: (# + 1)&[x] ⟶ 1 + x. ■ Map[(# + 1)&, {x, y, z}] ⟶ {1 + x, 1 + y, 1 + z}. ■ When Function [*body*] or *body*& is applied to a set of arguments, # (or #1) is replaced by the first argument, #2 by the second, and so on. #0 is replaced by the function itself. ■ If there are more arguments supplied than #*i* in the function, the remaining arguments are ignored. ■ ## stands for the sequence of all arguments supplied. ■ ##*n* stands for arguments from number *n* on. ■ f[##, ##2]& [x, y, z] ⟶ f[x, y, z, y, z]. ■ Function is analogous to λ in LISP or formal logic. ■ Function has attribute HoldAll. The function body is evaluated only after the formal parameters have been replaced by arguments. ■ The named formal parameters x_i in Function[{*x₁*, ... }, *body*] are treated as local, and are renamed $x_i$$ when necessary to avoid confusion with actual arguments supplied to the function. ■ Function [*params*, *body*, {*attr₁*, *attr₂*, ... }] represents a pure function that is to be treated as having attributes *attrᵢ* for the purpose of evaluation. ■ See page 235. ■ See also: Apply, CompiledFunction.

■ **Gamma**

Gamma [*z*] is the Euler gamma function $\Gamma(z)$.

Mathematical function (see Section A3.7). The gamma function satisfies $\Gamma(z) = \int_0^\infty t^{z-1} e^{-t} dt$. ■ See pages 48 and 51. ■ See also: Factorial, LogGamma, PolyGamma, RiemannSiegelTheta.

□ **GammaRegularized**

(Mentioned on page 51.) Use on-line help or see pages 573 and 800 of The *Mathematica* Book.

□ **GaussianIntegers**

(Mentioned on pages 57 and 69.) Use on-line help or see pages 556 and 800 of The *Mathematica* Book.

■ **GCD**

GCD [*n₁*, *n₂*, ...] gives the greatest common divisor of the integers *nᵢ*.

Integer mathematical function (see Section A3.7). ■ GCD [*n₁*, ...] gives the integer factors common to all the *nᵢ*. ■ See page 55. ■ See also: PolynomialGCD, Rational, LCM, ExtendedGCD.

□ **GegenbauerC**

(Mentioned on page 51.) Use on-line help or see pages 567 and 801 of The *Mathematica* Book.

☐ **Hypergeometric1F1**

> (Mentioned on page 51.) Use on-line help or see pages 570 and 807 of The *Mathematica* Book.

☐ **Hypergeometric2F1**

> (Mentioned on page 51.) Use on-line help or see pages 570 and 807 of The *Mathematica* Book.

☐ **HypergeometricU**

> (Mentioned on page 51.) Use on-line help or see pages 570 and 807 of The *Mathematica* Book.

■ **I**

> I represents the imaginary unit $\sqrt{-1}$.
>
> Numbers containing I are converted to the type Complex. ■ See pages 30, 40 and 43. ■ See also: Re, Im, ComplexExpand, GaussianIntegers.

■ **Identity**

> Identity[*expr*] gives *expr* (the identity operation).
>
> See pages 238 and 302. ■ See also: Composition, Through, InverseFunction.

■ **IdentityMatrix**

> IdentityMatrix[*n*] gives the $n \times n$ identity matrix.
>
> See page 151. ■ See also: DiagonalMatrix, Table.

■ **If**

> If[*condition*, *t*, *f*] gives *t* if *condition* evaluates to True, and *f* if it evaluates to False.
>
> If[*condition*, *t*, *f*, *u*] gives *u* if *condition* evaluates to neither True nor False.
>
> If evaluates only the argument determined by the value of the condition. ■ If[*condition*, *t*, *f*] is left unevaluated if *condition* evaluates to neither True nor False. ■ If[*condition*, *t*] gives Null if *condition* evaluates to False. ■ See page 265. ■ See also: Switch, Which, Condition.

☐ **IgnoreCase**

> (Mentioned on page 280.) Use on-line help or see pages 379 and 808 of The *Mathematica* Book.

■ **Im**

> Im[*z*] gives the imaginary part of the complex number *z*.
>
> Im[*expr*] is left unevaluated if *expr* is not a number. ■ See page 43. ■ See also: Re, Abs, Arg, ComplexExpand.

☐ **Implies**

> Use on-line help or see pages 619 and 808 of The *Mathematica* Book.

■ **In**

> In[*n*] is a global object that is assigned to have a delayed value of the nth input line.
>
> Typing In[*n*] causes the nth input line to be re-evaluated. ■ In[ ] gives the last input line. ■ In[-k] gives the input k lines back. ■ See page 35. ■ See also: InString, Out, $Line.

□ Increment

(Mentioned on page 257.) Use on-line help or see pages 248 and 808 of The *Mathematica* Book.

□ Indent

(Mentioned on page 284.) Use on-line help or see pages 517 and 809 of The *Mathematica* Book.

■ Indeterminate

Indeterminate is a symbol that represents a numerical quantity whose magnitude cannot be determined.

Computations like 0/0 generate Indeterminate. ■ A message is produced whenever an operation first yields Indeterminate as a result. ■ See page 125. ■ See also: DirectedInfinity, Check.

■ Infinity

Infinity is a symbol that represents a positive infinite quantity.

Infinity is converted to DirectedInfinity[1]. ■ Certain arithmetic operations work with Infinity. ■ Example: 1/Infinity $\longrightarrow$ 0. ■ See pages 30 and 125. ■ See also: ComplexInfinity, Indeterminate.

□ Infix

Use on-line help or see pages 362 and 809 of The *Mathematica* Book.

□ Information

(Mentioned on pages 24 and 355.) Use on-line help or see pages 69, 722 and 809 of The *Mathematica* Book.

□ Inner

(Mentioned on pages 119 and 238.) Use on-line help or see pages 669 and 810 of The *Mathematica* Book.

□ Input

(Mentioned on page 274.) Use on-line help or see pages 522 and 810 of The *Mathematica* Book.

■ InputForm

InputForm[*expr*] prints as a version of *expr* suitable for input to *Mathematica*.

Example: InputForm[x^2 + 1/a] $\longrightarrow$ a^(-1) + x^2. ■ InputForm always produces one-dimensional output, suitable to be typed as lines of *Mathematica* input. ■ InputForm acts as a "wrapper", which affects printing, but not evaluation. ■ Put (>>) produces InputForm by default. ■ See pages 284, 298 and 300. ■ See also: OutputForm, FullForm.

□ InputStream

(Mentioned on page 280.) Use on-line help or see pages 484 and 810 of The *Mathematica* Book.

□ InputString

Use on-line help or see pages 522 and 810 of The *Mathematica* Book.

■ **MeshRange**

MeshRange is an option for ListPlot3D, SurfaceGraphics, ListContourPlot, ListDensityPlot and related functions which specifies the range of x and y coordinates that correspond to the array of z values given.

MeshRange -> {{*xmin*, *xmax*}, {*ymin*, *ymax*}} specifies ranges in x and y. Mesh lines are taken to be equally spaced. ■ MeshRange -> Automatic takes x and y to be a grid of integers determined by indices in the array. ■ Settings for MeshRange are produced automatically by Plot3D, etc. for insertion into SurfaceGraphics etc. ■ MeshRange is used to determine tick values for surface, contour and density plots. ■ See page 311. ■ See also: PlotRange, PlotPoints.

■ **MeshStyle**

MeshStyle is an option for Plot3D, ContourPlot, DensityPlot and related functions which specifies how mesh lines should be rendered.

MeshStyle can be set to a list of graphics directives including Dashing, Thickness, GrayLevel, Hue and RGBColor. ■ See pages 195 and 311. ■ See also: Mesh, AxesStyle, Prolog, Epilog, DisplayFunction.

■ **Message**

Message[*symbol*::*tag*] prints the message *symbol*::*tag* unless it has been switched off.

Message[*symbol*::*tag*, e_1, e_2, ...] prints a message, inserting the values of the e_i as needed.

You can switch off a message using Off[*symbol*::*tag*]. You can switch on a message using On[*symbol*::*tag*]. ■ Between any two successive input lines, *Mathematica* prints a message with a particular name at most three times. On the last occurrence, it prints the message General::stop. ■ See page 26. ■ See also: Print, Write, On, Off, Check, MessageList.

□ **MessageList**

(Mentioned on pages 26 and 283.) Use on-line help or see pages 389, 513 and 826 of The *Mathematica* Book.

□ **MessageName**

(Mentioned on page 26.) Use on-line help or see pages 387 and 826 of The *Mathematica* Book.

□ **Messages**

(Mentioned on page 26.) Use on-line help or see pages 387 and 826 of The *Mathematica* Book.

■ **Min**

Min[x_1, x_2, ...] yields the numerically smallest of the x_i.

Min[{x_1, x_2, ... }, {y_1, ... }, ...] yields the smallest element of any of the lists.

Min yields a definite result if all its arguments are real numbers. ■ In other cases, Min carries out some simplifications. ■ Min[ ] gives Infinity. ■ See page 41. ■ See also: Max, Order.

■ **Minors**

Minors[*m*, *k*] gives a matrix consisting of the determinants of all $k \times k$ submatrices of m.

The results for different submatrices are given in lexicographic order. ■ See page 157. ■ See also: Det.

■ **Minus**

$-x$ is the arithmetic negation of x.

$-x$ is converted to Times[-1, x] on input. ■ See page 27. ■ See also: Subtract.

■ Mod

Mod[*m*, *n*] gives the remainder on division of *m* by *n*.

The sign of Mod[*m*, *n*] is always the same as the sign of *n*. ■ Mod[*m*, *n*] is equivalent to *m* - *n* Quotient[*m*, *n*]. ■ Mod[*x*, *y*] can have Rational and Real as well as Integer arguments. ■ See page 54. ■ See also: Quotient, PolynomialMod, PolynomialRemainder.

□ Modular

(Mentioned on page 78.) Use on-line help or see pages 620 and 827 of The *Mathematica* Book.

■ Module

Module[{*x*, *y*, ... }, *expr*] specifies that occurrences of the symbols *x*, *y*, ... in *expr* should be treated as local.

Module[{*x* = x_0, ... }, *expr*] defines initial values for *x*, ...

Module allows you to set up local variables with names that are local to the module. ■ Module creates new symbols to represent each of its local variables every time it is called. ■ Module creates a symbol with name *xxx*$*nnn* to represent a local variable with name *xxx*. The number *nnn* is the current value of $ModuleNumber. ■ The value of $ModuleNumber is incremented every time any module is used. ■ Before evaluating *expr*, Module substitutes new symbols for each of the local variables that appear anywhere in *expr* except as local variables in scoping constructs. ■ Symbols created by Module carry the attribute Temporary. ■ Symbols created by Module can be returned from modules. ■ You can use Module[{*vars*}, *body* /; *cond*] as the right-hand side of a transformation rule with a condition attached. ■ Module has attribute HoldAll. ■ Module constructs can be nested in any way. ■ Module implements lexical scoping. ■ See page 271. ■ See also: With, Block, Unique.

□ Modulus

(Mentioned on pages 69, 78 and 163.) Use on-line help or see pages 602, 620 and 827 of The *Mathematica* Book.

□ MoebiusMu

(Mentioned on page 57.) Use on-line help or see pages 556 and 828 of The *Mathematica* Book.

□ Multinomial

(Mentioned on page 50.) Use on-line help or see pages 558 and 828 of The *Mathematica* Book.

■ N

N[*expr*] gives the numerical value of *expr*.

N[*expr*, *n*] does computations to *n*-digit precision.

N[*expr*, *n*] performs computations with *n*-digit precision numbers. Often the results will have fewer than *n* digits of precision. ■ N[*expr*] does computations with machine precision numbers. ■ N converts integers, rational numbers and the components of complex numbers to Real form. ■ You can define numerical values of functions using *f*/: N[*f*[*args*]] := *value* and N[*f*[*args*], *n*] := *value*. ■ See page 31. ■ See also: Chop, CompiledFunction, Rationalize, $MachinePrecision.

□ NameQ

(Mentioned on page 283.) Use on-line help or see pages 385 and 828 of The *Mathematica* Book.

□ Names

(Mentioned on pages 205 and 283.) Use on-line help or see pages 385 and 828 of The *Mathematica* Book.

■ **On**

On [*symbol* : : *tag*] switches on a message, so that it can be printed.

On [*s*] switches on tracing for the symbol *s*.

On [*m₁*, *m₂*, ...] switches on several messages.

On [ ] switches on tracing for all symbols.

When tracing is switched on, each evaluation of a symbol, on its own, or as a function, is printed, together with the result. ■ Note that the tracing information is printed when a function *returns*. As a result, traces of recursive functions appear in the opposite order from their calls. ■ On [*s*] is equivalent to On [*s* : : trace]. ■ On [ ] is equivalent to On [*s* : : trace] for all symbols. ■ See page 26.

□ **OneIdentity**

(Mentioned on pages 246 and 275.) Use on-line help or see pages 230, 272 and 835 of The *Mathematica* Book.

□ **OpenAppend**

(Mentioned on page 281.) Use on-line help or see pages 485 and 835 of The *Mathematica* Book.

□ **OpenRead**

(Mentioned on page 281.) Use on-line help or see pages 499 and 836 of The *Mathematica* Book.

□ **OpenTemporary**

(Mentioned on page 279.) Use on-line help or see pages 482 and 836 of The *Mathematica* Book.

□ **OpenWrite**

(Mentioned on page 281.) Use on-line help or see pages 485 and 836 of The *Mathematica* Book.

□ **Operate**

(Mentioned on page 238.) Use on-line help or see pages 214 and 836 of The *Mathematica* Book.

□ **Optional**

(Mentioned on pages 246 and 353.) Use on-line help or see pages 234, 719 and 836 of The *Mathematica* Book.

- ## Options

  `Options[`*symbol*`]` gives the list of default options assigned to a symbol.

  `Options[`*expr*`]` gives the options explicitly specified in a particular expression such as a graphics object.

  `Options[`*stream*`]` or `Options["`*sname*`"]` gives options associated with a particular stream.

  `Options[`*expr, name*`]` gives the setting for the option *name* in an expression.

  `Options[`*expr, {name₁, name₂, ... }*`]` gives a list of the settings for the options *nameᵢ*.

  Many built-in functions allow you to give additional arguments that specify options with rules of the form *name* -> *value*. ▪ `Options[`*f*`]` gives the list of rules to be used for the options associated with a function *f* if no explicit rules are given when the function is called. ▪ `Options` always returns a list of transformation rules for option names. ▪ You can assign a value to `Options[`*symbol*`]` to redefine all the default option settings for a function. ▪ `SetOptions[`*symbol, name* -> *value*`]` can be used to specify individual default options. ▪ You can use `Options` on `InputStream` and `OutputStream` objects. If there is only one stream with a particular name, you can give the name as a string as the argument of `Options`. ▪ See pages 284, 302, 306 and 357. ▪ See also: `FullOptions`.

- ## Or

  e_1 `||` e_2 `||` ... is the logical OR function. It evaluates its arguments in order, giving `True` immediately if any of them are `True`, and `False` if they are all `False`.

  `Or` gives symbolic results when necessary. It applies no simplification rules, except removing initial arguments that are `False`. ▪ See page 264. ▪ See also: `Xor`, `LogicalExpand`.

- ## Order

  Use on-line help or see pages 215 and 837 of The *Mathematica* Book.

- ## OrderedQ

  (Mentioned on page 119.) Use on-line help or see pages 133, 228 and 837 of The *Mathematica* Book.

- ## Orderless

  (Mentioned on pages 246 and 275.) Use on-line help or see pages 272 and 837 of The *Mathematica* Book.

- ## Out

  `%`*n* or `Out[`*n*`]` is a global object that is assigned to be the value produced on the nth output line.

  `%` gives the last result generated.

  `%%` gives the result before last. `%%...%` (*k* times) gives the kth previous result.

  `Out[ ]` is equivalent to `%`. ▪ `Out[`-*k*`]` is equivalent to `%%...%` (*k* times). ▪ See page 35. ▪ See also: `In`, `$Line`, `MessageList`.

- ## Outer

  (Mentioned on pages 119, 163 and 238.) Use on-line help or see pages 669 and 838 of The *Mathematica* Book.

- ## OutputForm

  (Mentioned on page 284.) Use on-line help or see pages 343 and 838 of The *Mathematica* Book.

- ## OutputStream

  (Mentioned on page 284.) Use on-line help or see pages 484 and 838 of The *Mathematica* Book.

■ Permutations

Permutations[*list*] generates a list of all possible permutations of the elements in *list*.

Example:
Permutations[{a,b,c}] ⟶ {{a, b, c}, {a, c, b}, {b, a, c}, {b, c, a}, {c, a, b}, {c, b, a}}.
■ There are $n!$ permutations of a list of n distinct elements. ■ The object *list* need not have head List. ■ See page 117.
■ See also: Sort, Signature, Reverse, RotateLeft.

■ Pi

Pi is π, with numerical value ≃ 3.14159.

Mathematical constant (see Section A3.8). ■ See page 30. ■ See also: Degree.

■ Play

Play[*f*, {*t*, *tmin*, *tmax*}] plays a sound whose amplitude is given by *f* as a function of time *t* in seconds between *tmin* and *tmax*.

Play[{f_1, f_2}, {*t*, *tmin*, *tmax*}] produces stereo sound. The left-hand channel is given first.
■ Play[{f_1, f_2, ... }, ...] generates sound output on any number of channels. ■ The following options can be given:

DisplayFunction	$SoundDisplayFunction	function for generating output
Epilog	{}	sound or graphics to be used as an epilog
PlayRange	Automatic	the range of amplitude levels to include
Prolog	{}	sound or graphics to be used as a prolog
SampleDepth	8	how many bits to use to represent each amplitude level
SampleRate	8192	how many times per second amplitude samples should be generated

■ Play returns a Sound object. ■ See page 296. ■ See also: ListPlay, SampledSoundFunction, Show.

■ PlayRange

PlayRange is an option for Play and related functions which specifies what range of sound amplitude levels should be included.

All amplitudes are scaled so that the amplitude levels to be included lie within the range that can be output. ■ Amplitude levels outside the range specified are clipped. ■ The possible settings for PlayRange are:

All	include all amplitude levels
Automatic	outlying levels are dropped
{*amin*, *amax*}	explicit amplitude limits

■ See page 297. ■ See also: SampleDepth.

■ Plot

Plot[*f*, {*x*, *xmin*, *xmax*}] generates a plot of *f* as a function of *x* from *xmin* to *xmax*.

Plot[{*f₁*, *f₂*, ... }, {*x*, *xmin*, *xmax*}] plots several functions *f*ᵢ.

You should use Evaluate to evaluate the function to be plotted if this can safely be done before specific numerical values are supplied. ■ Plot has the same options as Graphics, with the following additions:

MaxBend	10.	maximum bend between segments
PlotDivision	20.	maximum subdivision factor in sampling
PlotPoints	25	initial number of sample points
PlotStyle	Automatic	graphics directives to specify the style for each curve

■ Plot uses the default setting Axes -> Automatic. ■ Plot initially evaluates *f* at a number of equally spaced sample points specified by PlotPoints. Then it uses an adaptive algorithm to choose additional sample points, attempting to produce a curve in which the bend between successive segments is less than MaxBend. It subdivides a given interval by a factor of at most PlotDivision. ■ You should realize that with the finite number of sample points used, it is possible for Plot to miss features in your function. To check your results, you should increase the setting for PlotPoints. ■ Plot returns a Graphics object. ■ See pages 79 and 87. ■ See also: ListPlot, Graphics.

■ Plot3D

Plot3D[*f*, {*x*, *xmin*, *xmax*}, {*y*, *ymin*, *ymax*}] generates a three-dimensional plot of *f* as a function of *x* and *y*.

Plot3D[{*f*, *s*}, {*x*, *xmin*, *xmax*}, {*y*, *ymin*, *ymax*}] generates a three-dimensional plot in which the height of the surface is specified by *f*, and the shading is specified by *s*.

You should use Evaluate to evaluate the function to be plotted if this can safely be done before specific numerical values are supplied. ■ Plot3D has the same options as SurfaceGraphics, with the following addition:

PlotPoints	15	the number of sample points in each direction

■ Plot3D has the default option setting Axes -> True. ■ Plot3D returns a SurfaceGraphics object. ■ The function *f* should give a real number for all values of *x* and *y* at which it is evaluated. There will be holes in the final surface at any values of *x* and *y* for which *f* does not yield a real number value. ■ If Lighting -> False and no shading function *s* is specified, the surface is shaded according to height. The shading is determined by the option ColorFunction; the default is gray levels. ■ The shading function *s* must yield GrayLevel, Hue or RGBColor directives, or SurfaceColor objects. ■ Plot3D includes a setting for the MeshRange option in the SurfaceGraphics object it returns. ■ See page 180. ■ See also: ListPlot3D, ContourPlot, DensityPlot, Graphics3D.

■ PlotDivision

PlotDivision is an option for Plot which specifies the maximum amount of subdivision to be used in attempting to generate a smooth curve.

Plot initially uses PlotPoints equally spaced sample points. In attempting to generate curves with no bends larger than MaxBend, Plot subdivides by at most a factor of PlotDivision. ■ The finest resolution in Plot is of order 1/(PlotPoints PlotDivision). ■ See page 87. ■ See also: MaxBend.

■ PlotJoined

PlotJoined is an option for ListPlot that specifies whether the points plotted should be joined by a line.

The style of the line can be specified using the option PlotStyle. ■ See page 81. ■ See also: Line.

■ PlotLabel

PlotLabel is an option for graphics functions that specifies an overall label for a plot.

PlotLabel -> None specifies that no label should be given. ■ **PlotLabel ->** *label* specifies a label to give. ■ Any expression can be used as a label. It will be given in **OutputForm**. Arbitrary strings of text can be given as *"text"*. ■ See page 330. ■ See also: **AxesLabel**.

■ PlotPoints

PlotPoints is an option for plotting functions that specifies how many sample points to use.

The sample points are equally spaced. ■ In **Plot**, an adaptive procedure is used to choose more sample points. ■ With a single variable, **PlotPoints ->** *n* specifies the total number of sample points to use. ■ With two variables, **PlotPoints ->** *n* specifies that *n* points should be used in both *x* and *y* directions. ■ **PlotPoints ->** $\{n_x, n_y\}$ specifies different numbers of sample points for the *x* and *y* directions. ■ See page 87. ■ See also: **PlotDivision**.

■ PlotRange

PlotRange is an option for graphics functions that specifies what points to include in a plot.

PlotRange can be used for both two- and three-dimensional graphics. ■ The following settings can be used:

All	all points are included
Automatic	outlying points are dropped
{min, max}	explicit limits for *y* (2D) or *z* (3D)
{{xmin, xmax}, ... }	explicit limits

■ When no explicit limits are given for a particular coordinate, a setting of **Automatic** is assumed. ■ With the **Automatic** setting, the distribution of coordinate values is found, and any points sufficiently far out in the distribution are dropped. Such points are often produced as a result of singularities in functions being plotted. ■ A setting of the form *{min,* **Automatic***}* specifies a particular minimum value for a coordinate, and a maximum value to be determined automatically. ■ **FullOptions** gives the explicit form of **PlotRange** specifications when **Automatic** settings are given. ■ See page 86. ■ See also: **PlotRegion, AspectRatio, FullOptions**.

■ PlotRegion

PlotRegion is an option for graphics functions that specifies what region of the final display area a plot should fill.

PlotRegion -> *{{sxmin, sxmax}, {symin, symax}}* specifies the region in scaled coordinates that the plot should fill in the final display area. ■ The scaled coordinates run from 0 to 1 in each direction. ■ The default setting **PlotRegion ->** *{{0, 1}, {0, 1}}* specifies that the plot should fill the whole display area. ■ When the plot does not fill the whole display area, the remainder of the area is rendered according to the setting for the option **Background**. ■ See page 315. ■ See also: **PlotRange, AspectRatio, Scaled, SphericalRegion**.

■ PlotStyle

PlotStyle is an option for **Plot** and **ListPlot** that specifies the style of lines or points to be plotted.

PlotStyle -> *style* specifies that all lines or points are to be generated with the specified graphics directive, or list of graphics directives. ■ **PlotStyle ->** $\{\{style_1\}, \{style_2\}, ... \}$ specifies that successive lines generated should use graphics directives $style_1, ...$. The styles must be enclosed in lists, perhaps of length one. ■ The $style_i$ are used cyclically. ■ Styles can be specified using graphics directives such as **Dashing, Hue** and **Thickness**. ■ See pages 87 and 303. ■ See also: **Graphics**.

■ Plus

$x + y + z$ represents a sum of terms.

Plus has attributes Flat, Orderless and OneIdentity. ■ The default value for arguments of Plus, as used in x_. patterns, is 0. ■ Plus[ ] is taken to be 0. ■ Plus[x] is x. ■ $x + 0$ evaluates to x, but $x + 0.0$ is left unchanged. ■ See page 27. ■ See also: Minus, Subtract, AddTo, Increment.

□ Pochhammer

(Mentioned on page 50.) Use on-line help or see pages 571 and 844 of The *Mathematica* Book.

■ Point

Point[*coords*] is a graphics primitive that represents a point.

The coordinates can be given either in the absolute form {x, y} or {x, y, z} or in scaled form Scaled[{x, y}] or Scaled[{x, y, z}]. ■ Points are rendered if possible as circular regions. Their diameters can be specified using the graphics primitive PointSize. ■ Point diameters are not accounted for in hidden surface elimination for three-dimensional graphics. ■ Shading and coloring of points can be specified using CMYKColor, GrayLevel, Hue or RGBColor. ■ See pages 89 and 99. ■ See also: Text.

■ PointSize

PointSize[*d*] is a graphics directive which specifies that points which follow are to be shown if possible as circular regions with diameter d. The diameter d is given as a fraction of the total width of the graph.

PointSize can be used in both two- and three-dimensional graphics. ■ The initial default is PointSize[0.008] for two-dimensional graphics, and PointSize[0.01] for three-dimensional graphics. ■ See page 96. ■ See also: AbsolutePointSize, Thickness.

□ PolyGamma

(Mentioned on page 50.) Use on-line help or see pages 571 and 844 of The *Mathematica* Book.

■ Polygon

Polygon[{pt_1, pt_2, ... }] is a graphics primitive that represents a filled polygon.

Polygon can be used in both Graphics and Graphics3D (two- and three-dimensional graphics). ■ The positions of points can be specified either in absolute coordinates as {x, y} or {x, y, z}, or in scaled coordinates as Scaled[{x, y}] or Scaled[{x, y, z}]. ■ The boundary of the polygon is formed by joining the last point you specify to the first one. ■ In two dimensions, self-intersecting polygons are allowed. ■ In three dimensions, planar polygons that do not intersect themselves will be drawn exactly as you specify them. Other polygons will be broken into triangles. ■ You can use graphics directives such as GrayLevel and RGBColor to specify how polygons should be filled. ■ In three dimensions, the shading can be produced from simulated illumination. ■ In three-dimensional graphics, polygons are considered to have both a front and a back face. The sense of a polygon is defined in terms of its first three vertices. When taken in order, these vertices go in a *counter-clockwise* direction when viewed from the *front*. (The frontward normal is thus obtained from a *right-hand* rule.) ■ You can use FaceForm to specify colors for the front and back faces of polygons. ■ In three-dimensional graphics, edges of polygons are shown as lines, with forms specified by the graphics directive EdgeForm. ■ See pages 89 and 99. ■ See also: Raster, Rectangle, Cuboid, SurfaceColor.

□ PolygonIntersections

Use on-line help or see pages 467 and 845 of The *Mathematica* Book.

□ PolyLog

(Mentioned on page 50.) Use on-line help or see pages 571 and 845 of The *Mathematica* Book.

☐ **PolynomialGCD**

(Mentioned on page 69.) Use on-line help or see pages 598 and 845 of The *Mathematica* Book.

☐ **PolynomialLCM**

(Mentioned on page 69.) Use on-line help or see pages 598 and 845 of The *Mathematica* Book.

☐ **PolynomialMod**

(Mentioned on page 69.) Use on-line help or see pages 598 and 846 of The *Mathematica* Book.

☐ **PolynomialQ**

(Mentioned on pages 69 and 246.) Use on-line help or see pages 593 and 846 of The *Mathematica* Book.

☐ **PolynomialQuotient**

(Mentioned on page 69.) Use on-line help or see pages 598 and 846 of The *Mathematica* Book.

☐ **PolynomialRemainder**

(Mentioned on page 69.) Use on-line help or see pages 598 and 846 of The *Mathematica* Book.

■ **Position**

Position[*expr*, *pattern*] gives a list of the positions at which objects matching *pattern* appear in *expr*.

Position[*expr*, *pattern*, *levspec*] finds only objects that appear on levels specified by *levspec*.

Example: Position[{1+x^2, 5, x^4}, x^_] ⟶ {{1, 2}, {3}}. ■ Position[*expr*, *pattern*] tests all the subparts of *expr* in turn to try and find ones that match *pattern*. ■ Position returns a list of positions in a form suitable for use in MapAt. ■ The default level specification for Position is Infinity, with Heads -> True.
■ Position[*list*, *pattern*, {1}, Heads -> False] finds positions only of objects that appear as complete elements of *list*. ■ Position[*expr*, *pattern*, *levspec*, *n*] gives the positions of the first *n* parts of *expr* which match the pattern.
■ See pages 115 and 241. ■ See also: Cases, Count, StringPosition, Insert, Delete.

☐ **Positive**

(Mentioned on page 246.) Use on-line help or see page 846 of The *Mathematica* Book.

☐ **Postfix**

Use on-line help or see pages 362 and 847 of The *Mathematica* Book.

☐ **PostScript**

Use on-line help or see pages 465 and 847 of The *Mathematica* Book.

■ **Power**

x^*y* gives *x* to the power *y*.

Mathematical function (see Section A3.7). ■ Exact rational number results are given when possible for roots of the form $n^{\frac{1}{m}}$. ■ For complex numbers x and y, Power gives the principal value of $e^{y \log(x)}$. ■ $(a\ b)$^c is automatically converted to a^$c\ b$^c only if c is an integer. ■ $(a$^$b)$^c is automatically converted to a^$(b\ c)$ only if c is an integer. ■ See page 27.
■ See also: Sqrt, Exp, PowerExpand, PowerMod, Log.

■ **PowerExpand**

PowerExpand[*expr*] expands all powers of products and powers.

Example: PowerExpand[Sqrt[x y]] ⟶ Sqrt[x] Sqrt[y]. ■ PowerExpand converts $(a\ b) \wedge c$ to $a \wedge c\ b \wedge c$, whatever the form of c is. ■ PowerExpand also converts $(a \wedge b) \wedge c$ to $a \wedge (b\ c)$, whatever the form of c is. ■ The transformations made by PowerExpand are correct in general only if c is an integer or a and b are positive real numbers. ■ See page 65. ■ See also: Expand, Distribute.

□ **PowerMod**

(Mentioned on page 57.) Use on-line help or see pages 556 and 847 of The *Mathematica* Book.

□ **PrecedenceForm**

(Mentioned on page 284.) Use on-line help or see pages 362 and 847 of The *Mathematica* Book.

■ **Precision**

Precision[*x*] gives the number of digits of precision in the number x.

If x is not a number, Precision[*x*] gives the minimum value of Precision for all the numbers that appear in x. ■ Precision gives Infinity when applied to exact numbers, such as integers. ■ Precision gives $MachinePrecision for machine-precision numbers. ■ See page 47. ■ See also: Accuracy, N, Chop, SetPrecision, MachineNumberQ.

□ **PrecisionGoal**

(Mentioned on page 140.) Use on-line help or see pages 688 and 848 of The *Mathematica* Book.

□ **PreDecrement**

(Mentioned on page 257.) Use on-line help or see pages 248 and 848 of The *Mathematica* Book.

□ **Prefix**

Use on-line help or see pages 362 and 848 of The *Mathematica* Book.

□ **PreIncrement**

(Mentioned on page 257.) Use on-line help or see pages 248 and 848 of The *Mathematica* Book.

■ **Prepend**

Prepend[*expr*, *elem*] gives *expr* with *elem* prepended.

Examples: Prepend[{a, b}, x] ⟶ {x, a, b}; Prepend[f[a], x + y] ⟶ f[x + y, a]. ■ See page 116. ■ See also: Append, Insert.

□ **PrependTo**

(Mentioned on page 257.) Use on-line help or see pages 249 and 848 of The *Mathematica* Book.

■ **Prime**

Prime[*n*] gives the nth prime number.

Prime[1] is 2. ■ On most computer systems, Prime[*n*] for n up to 10^8 can be obtained quite quickly. ■ See page 55. ■ See also: FactorInteger, PrimeQ, PrimePi.

■ Range

Range[*imax*] generates the list {1, 2, ... , *imax*}.

Range[*imin*, *imax*] generates the list {*imin*, ... , *imax*}. Range[*imin*, *imax*, *di*] uses step *di*.

Example: Range[4] ⟶ {1, 2, 3, 4}. ■ The arguments to Range need not be integers. ■ Range starts from *imin*, and successively adds increments of *di* until the result is greater than *imax*. ■ Range[0, 1, .3] ⟶ {0, 0.3, 0.6, 0.9}. ■ Range[x, x+2] ⟶ {x, 1 + x, 2 + x}. ■ Range uses the standard *Mathematica* iteration specification, as applied to a single variable. ■ See page 150. ■ See also: Table.

■ Raster

Raster[{{a_{11}, a_{12}, ... }, ... }] is a two-dimensional graphics primitive which represents a rectangular array of gray cells.

Raster[*array*, ColorFunction -> *f*] specifies that each cell should be rendered using the graphics directives obtained by applying the function *f* to the cell value a_{ij}, which must be between 0 and 1. ■ Raster[*array*, ColorFunction -> Hue] generates an array in which cell values are specified by hues. ■ If *array* has dimensions {*m*, *n*}, then Raster[*array*] is assumed to occupy the rectangle Rectangle[{0, 0}, {*m*, *n*}]. ■ Raster[*array*, {{*xmin*, *ymin*}, {*xmax*, *ymax*}}] specifies that the raster should be taken instead to fill the rectangle Rectangle[{*xmin*, *ymin*}, {*xmax*, *ymax*}]. ■ Scaled coordinates can be used to specify the rectangle. ■ Raster[*array*, *rect*, {*zmin*, *zmax*}] specifies that cell values should be scaled so that *zmin* corresponds to 0 and *zmax* corresponds to 1. Cell values outside this range are clipped. ■ See page 93. ■ See also: RasterArray, DensityGraphics, GraphicsArray.

■ RasterArray

RasterArray[{{g_{11}, g_{12}, ... }, ... }] is a two-dimensional graphics primitive which represents a rectangular array of cells colored according to the graphics directives g_{ij}.

Each of the g_{ij} must be GrayLevel, RGBColor or Hue. ■ If *array* has dimensions {*m*, *n*}, then RasterArray[*array*] is assumed to occupy the rectangle Rectangle[{0, 0}, {*m*, *n*}]. ■ RasterArray[*array*, {{*xmin*, *ymin*}, {*xmax*, *ymax*}}] specifies that the raster should be taken instead to fill the rectangle Rectangle[{*xmin*, *ymin*}, {*xmax*, *ymax*}]. ■ Scaled coordinates can be used to specify the rectangle. ■ See page 93. ■ See also: Raster, GraphicsArray.

■ Rational

Rational is the head used for rational numbers.

You can enter a rational number in the form *n/m*. ■ The pattern object _Rational can be used to stand for a rational number. It cannot stand for a single integer. ■ You have to use Numerator and Denominator to extract parts of Rational numbers. ■ See page 40. ■ See also: Integer, Numerator, Denominator.

□ Rationalize

(Mentioned on page 53.) Use on-line help or see pages 536 and 852 of The *Mathematica* Book.

□ Raw

(Mentioned on page 230.) Use on-line help or see pages 712 and 852 of The *Mathematica* Book.

■ Re

Re[*z*] gives the real part of the complex number *z*.

Re[*expr*] is left unevaluated if *expr* is not a number. ■ See page 43. ■ See also: Im, Abs, Arg, ComplexExpand.

□ Read

(Mentioned on page 281.) Use on-line help or see pages 499 and 853 of The *Mathematica* Book.

■ ReadList

ReadList ["*file*"] reads all the remaining expressions in a file, and returns a list of them.

ReadList ["*file*", *type*] reads objects of the specified type from a file, until the end of the file is reached. The list of objects read is returned.

ReadList ["*file*", {*type₁*, *type₂*, ... }] reads objects with a sequence of types, until the end of the file is reached.

ReadList ["*file*", *types*, *n*] reads only the first *n* objects of the specified types.

The option setting RecordLists -> True makes ReadList create separate sublists for objects that appear in separate records. ▪ With the default setting RecordSeparators -> {"\n"}, RecordLists -> True puts objects on separate lines into separate sublists. ▪ The option RecordSeparators gives a list of strings which are taken to delimit records. ▪ ReadList prints a message if any of the objects remaining in the file are not of the specified types. ▪ ReadList ["*file*", {*type₁*, ... }] looks for the sequence of *typeᵢ* in order. If the end of file is reached while part way through the sequence of *typeᵢ*, EndOfFile is returned in place of the elements in the sequence that have not yet been read. ▪ See page 279. ▪ See also: FindList.

□ ReadProtected

(Mentioned on page 275.) Use on-line help or see pages 272 and 854 of The *Mathematica* Book.

■ Real

Real is the head used for real (floating-point) numbers.

_Real can be used to stand for a real number in a pattern. ▪ You can enter a floating-point number of any length. ▪ You can enter a number in scientific notation by explicitly giving the form *mantissa* 10^*exponent*. ▪ You can enter a floating-point number in base *b* using *b*^^*digits*. The base must be less than 36. The letters a–z or A–Z are used in sequence to stand for digits 10 through 35. ▪ Real is also used to indicate an approximate real number in ReadList. ▪ See page 40. ▪ See also: RealDigits, BaseForm, Number.

■ RealDigits

RealDigits [*x*] gives a list of the digits in the approximate real number *x*, together with the number of digits that are to the left of the decimal point in ordinary (not scientific) notation.

RealDigits [*x*, *b*] gives a list of base-*b* digits in *x*.

RealDigits [*x*] returns a list of digits whose length is equal to Precision[*x*]. ▪ The base *b* in RealDigits [*x*, *b*] need not be an integer. For any real *b* such that *b* > 1, RealDigits [*x*, *b*] successively finds the largest integer multiples of powers of *b* that can be removed while leaving a non-negative remainder. ▪ See page 53. ▪ See also: MantissaExponent, IntegerDigits, BaseForm.

□ Record

(Mentioned on page 280.) Use on-line help or see pages 495 and 854 of The *Mathematica* Book.

□ RecordLists

(Mentioned on page 280.) Use on-line help or see pages 494 and 855 of The *Mathematica* Book.

□ RecordSeparators

(Mentioned on page 280.) Use on-line help or see pages 496 and 855 of The *Mathematica* Book.

■ **Rectangle**

Rectangle[{*xmin*, *ymin*}, {*xmax*, *ymax*}] is a two-dimensional graphics primitive that represents a filled rectangle, oriented parallel to the axes.

Rectangle[{*xmin*, *ymin*}, {*xmax*, *ymax*}, *graphics*] gives a rectangle filled with the specified graphics.

Rectangle[Scaled[{*xmin*, *ymin*}], Scaled[{*xmax*, *ymax*}]] can also be used.
■ Rectangle[{*xmin*, *ymin*}, {*xmax*, *ymax*}] is equivalent to a suitable Polygon with four corners. ■ You can use graphics directives such as GrayLevel and RGBColor to specify how Rectangle[{*xmin*, *ymin*}, {*xmax*, *ymax*}] should be filled. ■ In Rectangle[{*xmin*, *ymin*}, {*xmax*, *ymax*}, *graphics*], *graphics* can be any graphics object. ■ The rectangle is taken as the complete display area in which the graphics object is rendered. ■ When rectangles overlap, their backgrounds are effectively taken to be transparent. ■ Fonts and absolute size specifications are not affected by the size of the rectangle in which the graphics are rendered. ■ The options DisplayFunction and ColorOutput are ignored for graphics objects given inside Rectangle. ■ See page 89. ■ See also: Polygon, Raster, RasterArray, Cuboid, GraphicsArray.

□ **Reduce**

(Mentioned on page 78.) Use on-line help or see pages 614 and 855 of The *Mathematica* Book.

□ **ReleaseHold**

(Mentioned on page 274.) Use on-line help or see pages 282 and 856 of The *Mathematica* Book.

■ **Remove**

Remove[*symbol₁*, ...] removes symbols completely, so that their names are no longer recognized by *Mathematica*.

Remove["*form₁*", "*form₂*", ...] removes all symbols whose names match any of the string patterns *formᵢ*.

You can use Remove to get rid of symbols that you do not need, and which may shadow symbols in contexts later on your context path. ■ Remove["*context*`*"] removes all symbols in a particular context. ■ Remove does not affect symbols with the attribute Protected. ■ Once you have removed a symbol, you will never be able to refer to it again, unless you recreate it. ■ If you have an expression that contains a symbol which you remove, the removed symbol will be printed as Removed["*name*"], where its name is given in a string. ■ See pages 205 and 361. ■ See also: Clear.

□ **RenameDirectory**

(Mentioned on page 279.) Use on-line help or see pages 493 and 856 of The *Mathematica* Book.

□ **RenameFile**

(Mentioned on page 279.) Use on-line help or see pages 492 and 856 of The *Mathematica* Book.

□ **RenderAll**

Use on-line help or see pages 466 and 856 of The *Mathematica* Book.

□ **Repeated**

(Mentioned on pages 246 and 351.) Use on-line help or see pages 237, 717 and 856 of The *Mathematica* Book.

□ **RepeatedNull**

(Mentioned on pages 246 and 351.) Use on-line help or see pages 237, 717 and 857 of The *Mathematica* Book.

☐ Replace

Use on-line help or see pages 245 and 857 of The *Mathematica* Book.

■ ReplaceAll

expr /. *rules* applies a rule or list of rules in an attempt to transform each subpart of an expression *expr*.

Example: x + 2 /. x -> a ⟶ 2 + a. ■ ReplaceAll looks at each part of *expr*, tries all the *rules* on it, and then goes on to the next part of *expr*. The first rule that applies to a particular part is used; no further rules are tried on that part, or on any of its subparts. ■ ReplaceAll applies a particular rule only once to an expression. ■ Example: x /. x -> x + 1 ⟶ 1 + x. ■ See the notes on Replace for a description of how rules are applied to each part of *expr*. ■ *expr* /. *rules* returns *expr* if none of the rules apply. ■ See pages 247 and 257. ■ See also: Rule, Set.

☐ ReplaceHeldPart

(Mentioned on page 274.) Use on-line help or see pages 282 and 857 of The *Mathematica* Book.

☐ ReplacePart

(Mentioned on page 119.) Use on-line help or see pages 128, 195 and 857 of The *Mathematica* Book.

☐ ReplaceRepeated

(Mentioned on page 257.) Use on-line help or see pages 244 and 858 of The *Mathematica* Book.

☐ ResetDirectory

(Mentioned on page 279.) Use on-line help or see pages 489, 490 and 858 of The *Mathematica* Book.

☐ Residue

(Mentioned on page 148.) Use on-line help or see pages 648 and 858 of The *Mathematica* Book.

■ Rest

Rest[*expr*] gives *expr* with the first element removed.

Example: Rest[{a, b, c}] ⟶ {b, c}. ■ Rest[*expr*] is equivalent to Drop[*expr*, 1]. ■ See page 113. ■ See also: Drop, First, Part, Take.

☐ Resultant

(Mentioned on page 69.) Use on-line help or see pages 598 and 858 of The *Mathematica* Book.

■ Return

Return[*expr*] returns the value *expr* from a function.

Return[ ] returns the value Null.

Return[*expr*] exits control structures within the definition of a function, and gives the value *expr* for the whole function. ■ Return is effective only if it is generated as the value of a segment in a compound expression, or as the body of a control structure. Return also works in Scan. ■ See page 274. ■ See also: Break, Throw.

■ **Simplify**

Simplify[*expr*] performs a sequence of algebraic transformations on *expr*, and returns the simplest form it finds.

Simplify[*expr*] returns the form of *expr* that it finds which has the smallest LeafCount. ■ Simplify tries expanding and factoring parts of expressions, keeping track of which transformations make the parts simplest. ■ Simplify[*expr*, Trig -> False] does not use trigonometric identities. ■ See page 64. ■ See also: Factor, Expand.

■ **Sin**

Sin[z] gives the sine of *z*.

Mathematical function (see Section A3.7). ■ The argument of Sin is assumed to be in radians. (Multiply by Degree to convert from degrees.) ■ See page 42. ■ See also: ArcSin, Csc.

□ **SingularValues**

(Mentioned on page 163.) Use on-line help or see pages 665 and 868 of The *Mathematica* Book.

■ **Sinh**

Sinh[z] gives the hyperbolic sine of *z*.

Mathematical function (see Section A3.7). ■ See page 42. ■ See also: ArcSinh, Csch.

□ **SinIntegral**

(Mentioned on page 51.) Use on-line help or see pages 571 and 868 of The *Mathematica* Book.

□ **SixJSymbol**

(Mentioned on page 57.) Use on-line help or see pages 561 and 868 of The *Mathematica* Book.

□ **Skeleton**

(Mentioned on page 284.) Use on-line help or see pages 517 and 868 of The *Mathematica* Book.

□ **Skip**

(Mentioned on page 281.) Use on-line help or see pages 499 and 869 of The *Mathematica* Book.

■ **Slot**

represents the first argument supplied to a pure function.

#*n* represents the nth argument.

is used to represent arguments or formal parameters in pure functions of the form *body*& or Function[*body*]. ■ # is equivalent to Slot[ ] or Slot[1]. ■ #*n* is equivalent to Slot[*n*]. *n* must be a non-negative integer. ■ #0 gives the head of the function, *i.e.*, the pure function itself. ■ See page 236.

□ **SlotSequence**

(Mentioned on page 238.) Use on-line help or see pages 208 and 869 of The *Mathematica* Book.

■ Solve

Solve[*eqns*, *vars*] attempts to solve an equation or set of equations for the variables *vars*.

Solve[*eqns*, *vars*, *elims*] attempts to solve the equations for *vars*, eliminating the variables *elims*.

Equations are given in the form *lhs* == *rhs*. ■ Simultaneous equations can be combined either in a list or with &&. ■ A single variable or a list of variables can be specified. ■ Solve[*eqns*] tries to solve for all variables in *eqns*. ■ Example: Solve[3 x + 9 == 0, x]. ■ Solve gives explicit solutions as rules of the form *x* -> *sol*. ■ When there are several variables, the solution is given as a list of rules: {*x* -> s_x, *y* -> s_y, ... }. ■ When there are several solutions, Solve gives a list of them. ■ When a particular root has multiplicity greater than one, Solve gives several copies of the corresponding solution. ■ Solve deals primarily with linear and polynomial equations. ■ The option InverseFunctions specifies whether Solve should use inverse functions to try and find solutions to more general equations. The default is InverseFunctions -> Automatic. In this case, Solve can use inverse functions, but prints a warning message. See notes on InverseFunctions. ■ Solve gives generic solutions only. It discards solutions that are valid only when the parameters satisfy special conditions. Reduce gives the complete set of solutions. ■ Solve will not always be able to get explicit solutions to equations. It will give the explicit solutions it can, then give a symbolic representation of the remaining solutions, in terms of the function Roots. If there are sufficiently few symbolic parameters, you can then use N to get numerical approximations to the solutions. ■ Solve gives {} if there are no possible solutions to the equations. ■ Solve[*eqns*, ... , Mode -> Modular] solves equations with equality required only modulo an integer. You can specify a particular modulus to use by including the equation Modulus == *p*. If you do not include such an equation, Solve will attempt to solve for the possible moduli. ■ See pages 72, 75 and 77. ■ See also: Reduce, Eliminate, Roots, NSolve, FindRoot, LinearSolve, DSolve.

□ SolveAlways

(Mentioned on page 78.) Use on-line help or see pages 620 and 870 of The *Mathematica* Book.

■ Sort

Sort[*list*] sorts the elements of *list* into canonical order.

Sort[*list*, *p*] sorts using the ordering function *p*.

Example: Sort[{b, c, a}] ⟶ {a, b, c}. ■ The canonical order for strings is determined by the character ordering in $StringOrder. ■ Symbols are ordered according to their textual names. ■ Integers, rational and approximate real numbers are ordered by their numerical values. ■ Expressions are ordered by comparing their parts in a depth-first manner. Shorter expressions come first. ■ Sort[*list*, *p*] applies the function *p* to pairs of elements in *list* to determine whether they are in order. The default function *p* is OrderedQ[{#1, #2}]&. ■ Example: Sort[{4, 1, 3}, Greater] ⟶ {4, 3, 1}. ■ Sort can be used on expressions with any head, not only List. ■ See page 117. ■ See also: Order, OrderedQ, Orderless, $StringOrder.

□ Sound

Use on-line help or see pages 474 and 870 of The *Mathematica* Book.

□ SpellingCorrection

Use on-line help or see pages 384 and 870 of The *Mathematica* Book.

□ SphericalHarmonicY

(Mentioned on page 51.) Use on-line help or see pages 567 and 870 of The *Mathematica* Book.

■ **SphericalRegion**

SphericalRegion is an option for three-dimensional graphics functions which specifies whether the final image should be scaled so that a sphere drawn around the three-dimensional bounding box would fit in the display area specified.

SphericalRegion -> False scales three-dimensional images to be as large as possible, given the display area specified. ▪ SphericalRegion -> True scales three-dimensional images so that a sphere drawn around the three-dimensional bounding box always fits in the display area specified. ▪ The center of the sphere is taken to be at the center of the bounding box. The radius of the sphere is chosen so that the bounding box just fits within the sphere. ▪ With SphericalRegion -> True, the image of a particular object remains consistent in size, regardless of the orientation of the object. ▪ SphericalRegion -> True overrides any setting given for ViewCenter. ▪ See page 324. ▪ See also: PlotRegion, ViewPoint.

□ **Splice**

(Mentioned on page 281.) Use on-line help or see pages 184 and 871 of The *Mathematica* Book.

■ **Sqrt**

Sqrt[z] gives the square root of z.

Mathematical function (see Section A3.7). ▪ Sqrt[z] is converted to z^(1/2). ▪ Sqrt[z^2] is not automatically converted to z. ▪ Sqrt[a b] is not automatically converted to Sqrt[a] Sqrt[b]. ▪ These conversions can be done using PowerExpand. ▪ See page 29. ▪ See also: Power, PowerExpand.

□ **Stack**

(Mentioned on page 275.) Use on-line help or see pages 306 and 871 of The *Mathematica* Book.

□ **StackBegin**

(Mentioned on page 275.) Use on-line help or see pages 308 and 872 of The *Mathematica* Book.

□ **StackComplete**

(Mentioned on page 275.) Use on-line help or see pages 308 and 872 of The *Mathematica* Book.

□ **StackInhibit**

(Mentioned on page 275.) Use on-line help or see pages 307 and 872 of The *Mathematica* Book.

□ **StirlingS1**

(Mentioned on page 57.) Use on-line help or see pages 558 and 872 of The *Mathematica* Book.

□ **StirlingS2**

(Mentioned on page 57.) Use on-line help or see pages 558 and 872 of The *Mathematica* Book.

□ **StreamPosition**

(Mentioned on page 281.) Use on-line help or see pages 503 and 872 of The *Mathematica* Book.

□ **Streams**

(Mentioned on page 281.) Use on-line help or see pages 519 and 872 of The *Mathematica* Book.

■ String

> String is the head of a character string "*text*".
>
> Strings can contain any sequence of 8- or 16-bit characters. ■ *x*_String can be used as a pattern that represents a string. ■ String is used as a tag to indicate strings in ReadList, terminated by RecordSeparators characters. ■ See pages 280 and 282. ■ See also: ToExpression, ToString, SyntaxQ, Characters.

□ StringBreak

> (Mentioned on page 284.) Use on-line help or see pages 517 and 873 of The *Mathematica* Book.

□ StringByteCount

> (Mentioned on page 283.) Use on-line help or see pages 374 and 873 of The *Mathematica* Book.

□ StringConversion

> (Mentioned on page 284.) Use on-line help or see pages 469, 487 and 873 of The *Mathematica* Book.

□ StringDrop

> (Mentioned on page 283.) Use on-line help or see pages 376 and 873 of The *Mathematica* Book.

□ StringForm

> (Mentioned on page 284.) Use on-line help or see pages 348 and 874 of The *Mathematica* Book.

□ StringInsert

> (Mentioned on page 283.) Use on-line help or see pages 376 and 874 of The *Mathematica* Book.

■ StringJoin

> "s_1" <> "s_2" <> ... , StringJoin["s_1", "s_2", ...] or StringJoin[{"s_1", "s_2", ... }] yields a string consisting of a concatenation of the s_i.
>
> Example: "the" <> " " <> "cat" ⟶ the cat. ■ StringJoin has attribute Flat. ■ When arguments are not strings, StringJoin is left in symbolic form. ■ See page 282. ■ See also: Join, Characters.

□ StringLength

> (Mentioned on page 283.) Use on-line help or see pages 376 and 874 of The *Mathematica* Book.

□ StringMatchQ

> (Mentioned on page 283.) Use on-line help or see pages 383 and 874 of The *Mathematica* Book.

□ StringPosition

> (Mentioned on page 283.) Use on-line help or see pages 376 and 875 of The *Mathematica* Book.

□ StringReplace

> (Mentioned on page 283.) Use on-line help or see pages 376 and 875 of The *Mathematica* Book.

□ StringReverse

> (Mentioned on page 283.) Use on-line help or see pages 376 and 875 of The *Mathematica* Book.

■ Text

Text [*expr*, *coords*] is a graphics primitive that represents text corresponding to the printed form of *expr*, centered at the point specified by *coords*.

The *text* is printed by default in OutputForm. ■ Text can be used in both two- and three-dimensional graphics. ■ The coordinates can be specified either as {*x*, *y*, ... } or as Scaled[{*x*, *y*, ... }]. ■ Text [*expr*, *coords*, *offset*] specifies an offset for the block of text relative to the coordinates given. Giving an offset {*sdx*, *sdy*} specifies that the point {*x*, *y*} should lie at relative coordinates {*sdx*, *sdy*} within the bounding rectangle that encloses the text. Each relative coordinate runs from −1 to +1 across the bounding rectangle. ■ The offsets specified need not be in the range -1 to +1. ■ Here are sample offsets to use in two-dimensional graphics:

{0, 0}	text centered at {*x*, *y*}
{-1, 0}	left-hand end at {*x*, *y*}
{1, 0}	right-hand end at {*x*, *y*}
{0, -1}	centered above {*x*, *y*}
{0, 1}	centered below {*x*, *y*}

■ Text [*expr*, *coords*, *offset*, *dir*] specifies the orientation of the text is given by the direction vector *dir*. Possible values of *dir* are:

{1, 0}	ordinary horizontal text
{0, 1}	vertical text reading from bottom to top
{0, -1}	vertical text reading from top to bottom
{-1, 0}	horizontal upside-down text

■ Text in three-dimensional graphics is placed at a position that corresponds to the projection of the point {*x*, *y*, *z*} specified. Text is drawn in front of all other objects. ■ The font for text can be specified using FontForm. If no FontForm specification is given, the font is determined from the option DefaultFont, which is by default set to the global variable $DefaultFont. ■ You can specify the color of text using CMYKColor, GrayLevel, Hue and RGBColor directives. ■ The option StringConversion for Display can be used to specify a function to be applied to strings generated from Text which contain special characters. ■ See pages 89 and 342. ■ See also: PlotLabel, AxesLabel.

□ TextForm

Use on-line help or see pages 739 and 882 of The *Mathematica* Book.

■ Thickness

Thickness [*r*] is a graphics directive which specifies that lines which follow are to be drawn with a thickness *r*. The thickness *r* is given as a fraction of the total width of the graph.

Thickness can be used in both two- and three-dimensional graphics. ■ The initial default is Thickness [0.004] for two-dimensional graphics, and Thickness [0.001] for three-dimensional graphics ■ See page 97. ■ See also: AbsoluteThickness, PointSize, Dashing.

□ Thread

(Mentioned on pages 119 and 238.) Use on-line help or see pages 216 and 883 of The *Mathematica* Book.

□ ThreeJSymbol

(Mentioned on page 57.) Use on-line help or see pages 561 and 883 of The *Mathematica* Book.

□ Through

(Mentioned on page 238.) Use on-line help or see pages 214 and 883 of The *Mathematica* Book.

☐ **Throw**

> (Mentioned on page 274.) Use on-line help or see pages 293 and 883 of The *Mathematica* Book.

■ **Ticks**

> **Ticks** is an option for graphics functions that specifies tick marks for axes.
>
> The following settings can be given for **Ticks**:
>
> | | |
> |---|---|
> | None | no tick marks drawn |
> | Automatic | tick marks placed automatically |
> | {*xticks*, *yticks*, ... } | tick mark options specified separately for each axis |
>
> With the **Automatic** setting, tick marks are usually placed at points whose coordinates have the minimum number of digits in their decimal representation. ■ For each axis, the following tick mark options can be given:
>
> | | |
> |---|---|
> | None | no tick marks drawn |
> | Automatic | tick mark positions and labels chosen automatically |
> | {x_1, x_2, ... } | tick marks drawn at the specified positions |
> | {{x_1, $label_1$}, {x_2, $label_2$}, ... } | tick marks drawn with the specified labels |
> | {{x_1, $label_1$, len_1},... } | tick marks with specified scaled length |
> | {{x_1, $label_1$, {$plen_1$, $mlen_1$}}, ... } | ticks marks with specified lengths in the positive and negative directions |
> | {{x_1, $label_1$, len_1, $style_1$}, ... } | ticks marks with specified styles |
> | *func* | a function to be applied to *xmin*, *xmax* to get the tick mark option |
>
> If no explicit labels are given, the tick mark labels are given as the numerical values of the tick mark positions. ■ Any expression can be given as a tick mark label. The expressions are formatted in **OutputForm**. ■ Tick mark lengths are given as a fraction of the distance across the whole plot. ■ Tick mark styles can involve graphics directives such as **RGBColor** and **Thickness**. ■ The tick mark function *func*[*xmin*, *xmax*] may return any other tick mark option. ■ **Ticks** can be used in both two- and three-dimensional graphics. ■ **FullOptions** gives the explicit form of **Ticks** specifications when **Automatic** settings are given. ■ See pages 332 and 339. ■ See also: **Axes**, **AxesLabel**, **FrameTicks**, **GridLines**, **MeshRange**.

☐ **TimeConstrained**

> (Mentioned on pages 274 and 283.) Use on-line help or see pages 525 and 884 of The *Mathematica* Book.

■ **Times**

> *x**y*z or *x* *y* *z* represents a product of terms.
>
> The default value for arguments of **Times**, as used in x_. patterns, is 1. ■ **Times[ ]** is taken to be 1. ■ **Times**[*x*] is *x*. ■ 0 *x* evaluates to 0, but 0.0 *x* is left unchanged. ■ See page 27. ■ See also: **Divide**, **NonCommutativeMultiply**, **Dot**.

☐ **TimesBy**

> (Mentioned on page 257.) Use on-line help or see pages 248 and 884 of The *Mathematica* Book.

☐ **TimeUsed**

> (Mentioned on page 283.) Use on-line help or see pages 524 and 885 of The *Mathematica* Book.

☐ **TimeZone**

> (Mentioned on page 283.) Use on-line help or see pages 523 and 885 of The *Mathematica* Book.

☐ **Timing**

> (Mentioned on page 283.) Use on-line help or see pages 525 and 885 of The *Mathematica* Book.

□ **ToCharacterCode**

(Mentioned on page 283.) Use on-line help or see pages 366 and 885 of The *Mathematica* Book.

□ **ToDate**

(Mentioned on page 283.) Use on-line help or see pages 524 and 885 of The *Mathematica* Book.

□ **ToExpression**

(Mentioned on pages 274 and 283.) Use on-line help or see pages 380 and 885 of The *Mathematica* Book.

■ **Together**

Together[*expr*] puts terms in a sum over a common denominator, and cancels factors in the result.

Example: Together[1/x + 1/(1-x)] $\longrightarrow$ $-(\dfrac{1}{(-1 + x)\ x})$. ■ Together makes a sum of terms into a single rational function. ■ The denominator of the result of Together is the lowest common multiple of the denominators of each of the terms in the sum. ■ Together avoids expanding out denominators unless it is necessary. ■ Together is effectively the inverse of Apart. ■ Together[*expr*, Trig -> True] treats trigonometric functions as rational functions of exponentials, and manipulates them accordingly. ■ See page 67. ■ See also: Collect, Cancel, Factor.

□ **ToHeldExpression**

(Mentioned on page 283.) Use on-line help or see pages 381 and 886 of The *Mathematica* Book.

□ **TokenWords**

(Mentioned on page 280.) Use on-line help or see pages 496 and 886 of The *Mathematica* Book.

□ **ToLowerCase**

(Mentioned on page 283.) Use on-line help or see pages 378 and 886 of The *Mathematica* Book.

□ **ToRules**

Use on-line help or see pages 607 and 886 of The *Mathematica* Book.

□ **ToString**

(Mentioned on pages 274 and 283.) Use on-line help or see pages 380 and 886 of The *Mathematica* Book.

□ **TotalHeight**

Use on-line help or see page 886 of The *Mathematica* Book.

□ **TotalWidth**

(Mentioned on page 284.) Use on-line help or see pages 517 and 887 of The *Mathematica* Book.

□ **ToUpperCase**

(Mentioned on page 283.) Use on-line help or see pages 378 and 887 of The *Mathematica* Book.

□ **Trace**

(Mentioned on page 275.) Use on-line help or see pages 295 and 887 of The *Mathematica* Book.

☐ **TraceAbove**

> (Mentioned on page 275.) Use on-line help or see pages 302 and 887 of The *Mathematica* Book.

☐ **TraceBackward**

> (Mentioned on page 275.) Use on-line help or see pages 302 and 888 of The *Mathematica* Book.

☐ **TraceDepth**

> (Mentioned on page 275.) Use on-line help or see pages 301 and 888 of The *Mathematica* Book.

☐ **TraceDialog**

> (Mentioned on page 275.) Use on-line help or see pages 305 and 888 of The *Mathematica* Book.

☐ **TraceForward**

> (Mentioned on page 275.) Use on-line help or see pages 302 and 888 of The *Mathematica* Book.

☐ **TraceOff**

> Use on-line help or see pages 300 and 888 of The *Mathematica* Book.

☐ **TraceOn**

> Use on-line help or see pages 300 and 889 of The *Mathematica* Book.

☐ **TraceOriginal**

> (Mentioned on page 275.) Use on-line help or see pages 303 and 889 of The *Mathematica* Book.

☐ **TracePrint**

> (Mentioned on page 275.) Use on-line help or see pages 305 and 889 of The *Mathematica* Book.

☐ **TraceScan**

> (Mentioned on page 275.) Use on-line help or see pages 305 and 889 of The *Mathematica* Book.

■ **Transpose**

> Transpose [*list*] transposes the first two levels in *list*.
>
> Transpose [*list*, $\{n_1, n_2, \ldots\}$] transposes *list* so that the kth level in *list* is the n_k^{th} level in the result.
>
> Example: Transpose[{{a,b},{c,d}}] ⟶ {{a, c}, {b, d}}. ■ Transpose gives the usual transpose of a matrix. ■ See page 151. ■ See also: Flatten.

☐ **TreeForm**

> (Mentioned on page 284.) Use on-line help or see pages 197, 344 and 890 of The *Mathematica* Book.

■ ViewPoint

ViewPoint is an option for Graphics3D and SurfaceGraphics which gives the point in space from which the objects plotted are to be viewed.

ViewPoint -> {x, y, z} gives the position of the view point relative to the center of the three-dimensional box that contains the object being plotted. ■ The view point is given in a special scaled coordinate system in which the longest side of the bounding box has length 1. The center of the bounding box is taken to have coordinates {0, 0, 0}. ■ Common settings for ViewPoint are:

{1.3, -2.4, 2}	default setting
{0, -2, 0}	directly in front
{0, -2, 2}	in front and up
{0, -2, -2}	in front and down
{-2, -2, 0}	left-hand corner
{2, -2, 0}	right-hand corner
{0, 0, 2}	directly above

■ Choosing ViewPoint further away from the object reduces the distortion associated with perspective. ■ The view point must lie outside the bounding box. ■ The coordinates of the corners of the bounding box in the special coordinate system used for ViewPoint are determined by the setting for the BoxRatios option. ■ See page 320. ■ See also: ViewCenter, ViewVertical, SphericalRegion.

■ ViewVertical

ViewVertical is an option for Graphics3D and SurfaceGraphics which specifies what direction in scaled coordinates should be vertical in the final image.

The default setting is ViewVertical -> {0, 0, 1}, which specifies that the z axis in your original coordinate system should end up vertical in the final image. ■ The setting for ViewVertical is given in scaled coordinates, which run from 0 to 1 across each dimension of the bounding box. ■ Only the direction of the vector specified by ViewVertical is important; its magnitude is irrelevant. ■ See page 322.

□ WeierstrassP

(Mentioned on page 51.) Use on-line help or see pages 584 and 894 of The *Mathematica* Book.

□ WeierstrassPPrime

(Mentioned on page 51.) Use on-line help or see pages 584 and 894 of The *Mathematica* Book.

■ Which

Which[$test_1$, $value_1$, $test_2$, $value_2$, ...] evaluates each of the $test_i$ in turn, returning the value of the $value_i$ corresponding to the first one that yields True.

Example: Which[1==2, x, 1==1, y] ⟶ y. ■ If any of the $test_i$ evaluated by Which give neither True nor False, then the whole Which object is returned unevaluated. ■ You can make Which return a "default value" by taking the last $test_i$ to be True. ■ If all the $test_i$ evaluate to False, Which returns Null. ■ See page 265. ■ See also: Switch.

■ While

While[*test*, *body*] evaluates *test*, then *body*, repetitively, until *test* first fails to give True.

While[*test*] does the loop with a null body. ■ Unless Return[ ] is generated, the final value returned by While is Null. ■ Example: i=0; While[i < 0, tot += f[i]; i++]. Note that the roles of ; and , are *reversed* relative to the C programming language. ■ See page 270. ■ See also: Do, For, Nest, Fold, Select.

□ `With`

(Mentioned on page 274.) Use on-line help or see pages 320 and 894 of The *Mathematica* Book.

□ `Word`

(Mentioned on page 280.) Use on-line help or see pages 495 and 894 of The *Mathematica* Book.

□ `WordSearch`

(Mentioned on page 280.) Use on-line help or see pages 501 and 894 of The *Mathematica* Book.

□ `WordSeparators`

Use on-line help or see pages 495 and 895 of The *Mathematica* Book.

□ `WorkingPrecision`

(Mentioned on page 140.) Use on-line help or see pages 687 and 895 of The *Mathematica* Book.

□ `Write`

(Mentioned on page 281.) Use on-line help or see pages 485 and 895 of The *Mathematica* Book.

□ `WriteString`

(Mentioned on page 281.) Use on-line help or see pages 485 and 895 of The *Mathematica* Book.

■ `Xor`

`Xor[`e_1`, ` e_2`, ... ]` is the logical XOR (exclusive OR) function.

It gives `True` if an odd number of the e_i are `True`, and the rest are `False`. It gives `False` if an even number of the e_i are `True`, and the rest are `False`.

`Xor` gives symbolic results when necessary, and applies various simplification rules to them. ■ See page 264. ■ See also: `LogicalExpand`.

□ `ZeroTest`

(Mentioned on page 163.) Use on-line help or see pages 662 and 896 of The *Mathematica* Book.

■ `Zeta`

`Zeta[`s`]` gives the Riemann zeta function $\zeta(s)$.

`Zeta[`s`, ` a`]` gives the generalized Riemann zeta function $\zeta(s,a)$.

Mathematical function (see Section A3.7). ■ $\zeta(s) = \sum_{k=1}^{\infty} k^{-s}$. ■ $\zeta(s,a) = \sum_{k=0}^{\infty} (k+a)^{-s}$, where any term with $k+a=0$ is excluded. ■ See page 48. ■ See also: `PolyLog`, `LerchPhi`, `RiemannSiegelZ`, `PrimePi`.

□ `$Aborted`

Use on-line help or see pages 311 and 896 of The *Mathematica* Book.

□ `$BatchInput`

Use on-line help or see pages 529 and 896 of The *Mathematica* Book.

☐ **$BatchOutput**

Use on-line help or see pages 529 and 896 of The *Mathematica* Book.

☐ **$CommandLine**

Use on-line help or see pages 529 and 896 of The *Mathematica* Book.

☐ **$Context**

(Mentioned on page 205.) Use on-line help or see pages 333 and 896 of The *Mathematica* Book.

☐ **$ContextPath**

(Mentioned on page 205.) Use on-line help or see pages 334 and 897 of The *Mathematica* Book.

☐ **$CreationDate**

(Mentioned on page 279.) Use on-line help or see pages 529 and 897 of The *Mathematica* Book.

■ **$DefaultFont**

$DefaultFont gives the default font to use for text in graphics.

The value of $DefaultFont must be of the form {"*font*", *size*}, where *font* gives the name of the font to use, and *size* gives its size in printer's points. ■ $DefaultFont is the default setting for the option DefaultFont. ■ The initial value for $DefaultFont is typically {"Courier", 10}. ■ See pages 284 and 340.

☐ **$Display**

(Mentioned on pages 283 and 284.) Use on-line help or see pages 518, 742 and 897 of The *Mathematica* Book.

■ **$DisplayFunction**

$DisplayFunction gives the default setting for the option DisplayFunction in graphics functions.

See pages 284 and 303. ■ See also: Display, Put, Run, $SoundDisplayFunction.

☐ **$DumpDates**

(Mentioned on page 279.) Use on-line help or see pages 529 and 897 of The *Mathematica* Book.

☐ **$DumpSupported**

(Mentioned on page 279.) Use on-line help or see pages 530 and 897 of The *Mathematica* Book.

☐ **$Echo**

(Mentioned on page 284.) Use on-line help or see pages 518, 742 and 898 of The *Mathematica* Book.

☐ **$Epilog**

(Mentioned on page 283.) Use on-line help or see pages 519 and 898 of The *Mathematica* Book.

☐ **$Failed**

Use on-line help or see pages 477 and 898 of The *Mathematica* Book.

□ **$IgnoreEOF**

Use on-line help or see pages 520, 748 and 898 of The *Mathematica* Book.

□ **$Input**

(Mentioned on page 283.) Use on-line help or see pages 519 and 898 of The *Mathematica* Book.

□ **$Inspector**

Use on-line help or see pages 744 and 898 of The *Mathematica* Book.

□ **$IterationLimit**

(Mentioned on page 274.) Use on-line help or see pages 309 and 898 of The *Mathematica* Book.

□ **$Language**

(Mentioned on page 26.) Use on-line help or see pages 391, 519 and 899 of The *Mathematica* Book.

□ **$Letters**

(Mentioned on page 283.) Use on-line help or see pages 379 and 899 of The *Mathematica* Book.

■ **$Line**

$Line is a global variable that specifies the number of the current input line.

You can reset $Line. ■ See page 283. ■ See also: In, Out.

□ **$Linked**

(Mentioned on page 281.) Use on-line help or see pages 529 and 899 of The *Mathematica* Book.

□ **$LinkSupported**

(Mentioned on pages 279 and 281.) Use on-line help or see pages 530 and 899 of The *Mathematica* Book.

□ **$MachineEpsilon**

(Mentioned on page 48.) Use on-line help or see pages 546 and 899 of The *Mathematica* Book.

□ **$MachineID**

(Mentioned on page 279.) Use on-line help or see pages 530 and 899 of The *Mathematica* Book.

□ **$MachineName**

(Mentioned on page 279.) Use on-line help or see pages 530 and 900 of The *Mathematica* Book.

□ **$MachinePrecision**

(Mentioned on page 48.) Use on-line help or see pages 540, 546 and 900 of The *Mathematica* Book.

□ **$MachineType**

(Mentioned on page 279.) Use on-line help or see pages 530 and 900 of The *Mathematica* Book.

□ **$MaxMachineNumber**

(Mentioned on page 48.) Use on-line help or see pages 546 and 900 of The *Mathematica* Book.

☐ **$MessageList**

(Mentioned on page 26.) Use on-line help or see pages 389 and 900 of The *Mathematica* Book.

☐ **$MessagePrePrint**

Use on-line help or see pages 388, 519 and 900 of The *Mathematica* Book.

☐ **$Messages**

(Mentioned on page 284.) Use on-line help or see pages 518, 742 and 900 of The *Mathematica* Book.

☐ **$MinMachineNumber**

(Mentioned on page 48.) Use on-line help or see pages 546 and 901 of The *Mathematica* Book.

☐ **$ModuleNumber**

(Mentioned on page 274.) Use on-line help or see pages 322 and 901 of The *Mathematica* Book.

☐ **$NewMessage**

(Mentioned on page 26.) Use on-line help or see pages 390 and 901 of The *Mathematica* Book.

☐ **$NewSymbol**

(Mentioned on page 26.) Use on-line help or see pages 386 and 901 of The *Mathematica* Book.

☐ **$Notebooks**

Use on-line help or see pages 529 and 901 of The *Mathematica* Book.

☐ **$OperatingSystem**

(Mentioned on page 279.) Use on-line help or see pages 530 and 901 of The *Mathematica* Book.

☐ **$Output**

(Mentioned on pages 283 and 284.) Use on-line help or see pages 518, 742 and 901 of The *Mathematica* Book.

☐ **$Packages**

(Mentioned on page 205.) Use on-line help or see pages 338 and 902 of The *Mathematica* Book.

☐ **$Path**

(Mentioned on page 279.) Use on-line help or see pages 490 and 902 of The *Mathematica* Book.

☐ **$PipeSupported**

(Mentioned on page 279.) Use on-line help or see pages 530 and 902 of The *Mathematica* Book.

☐ **$Post**

(Mentioned on page 283.) Use on-line help or see pages 514 and 902 of The *Mathematica* Book.

☐ **$Pre**

(Mentioned on page 283.) Use on-line help or see pages 514 and 902 of The *Mathematica* Book.

☐ **\$PrePrint**

(Mentioned on pages 283 and 284.) Use on-line help or see pages 514 and 902 of The *Mathematica* Book.

☐ **\$PreRead**

(Mentioned on page 283.) Use on-line help or see pages 514 and 903 of The *Mathematica* Book.

☐ **\$RecursionLimit**

(Mentioned on page 274.) Use on-line help or see pages 308, 309 and 903 of The *Mathematica* Book.

☐ **\$ReleaseNumber**

(Mentioned on page 279.) Use on-line help or see pages 529 and 903 of The *Mathematica* Book.

☐ **\$SessionID**

(Mentioned on page 274.) Use on-line help or see pages 324, 530 and 903 of The *Mathematica* Book.

☐ **\$SoundDisplayFunction**

Use on-line help or see pages 476 and 903 of The *Mathematica* Book.

☐ **\$StringConversion**

(Mentioned on page 284.) Use on-line help or see pages 371 and 903 of The *Mathematica* Book.

☐ **\$StringOrder**

Use on-line help or see pages 379 and 904 of The *Mathematica* Book.

☐ **\$SyntaxHandler**

(Mentioned on page 283.) Use on-line help or see pages 514 and 904 of The *Mathematica* Book.

☐ **\$System**

(Mentioned on page 279.) Use on-line help or see pages 530 and 904 of The *Mathematica* Book.

☐ **\$TimeUnit**

(Mentioned on page 283.) Use on-line help or see pages 524 and 904 of The *Mathematica* Book.

☐ **\$Urgent**

(Mentioned on page 284.) Use on-line help or see pages 518, 742 and 904 of The *Mathematica* Book.

☐ **\$Version**

(Mentioned on page 279.) Use on-line help or see pages 529 and 904 of The *Mathematica* Book.

☐ **\$VersionNumber**

(Mentioned on page 279.) Use on-line help or see pages 529 and 905 of The *Mathematica* Book.

Index